T0345012

AI

Delving into the deeply enigmatic nature of artificial intelligence (AI), *AI: Unexplainable, Unpredictable, Uncontrollable* explores the various reasons why the field is so challenging. Written by one of the founders of the field of AI safety, this book addresses some of the most fascinating questions facing humanity, including the nature of intelligence, consciousness, values, and knowledge.

Moving from a broad introduction to the core problems, such as the unpredictability of AI outcomes or the difficulty in explaining AI decisions, this book arrives at more complex questions of ownership and control, conducting an in-depth analysis of potential hazards and unintentional consequences. The book then concludes with philosophical and existential considerations, probing into questions of AI personhood, consciousness, and the distinction between human intelligence and artificial general intelligence (AGI).

Bridging the gap between technical intricacies and philosophical musings, *AI: Unexplainable, Unpredictable, Uncontrollable* appeals to both AI experts and enthusiasts looking for a comprehensive understanding of the field, while also being written for a general audience with minimal technical jargon.

Chapman & Hall/CRC Artificial Intelligence and Robotics Series

Series Editor: Roman Yampolskiy

For more information about this series please visit: https://www.routledge.com/Chapman–HallCRC-Artificial-Intelligence-and-Robotics-Series/book-series/ARTILRO

AI
Unexplainable, Unpredictable, Uncontrollable

Roman V. Yampolskiy, PhD

CRC Press
Taylor & Francis Group
Boca Raton London New York

CRC Press is an imprint of the
Taylor & Francis Group, an **informa** business

A CHAPMAN & HALL BOOK

Cover image: CC-BY SA 3.0 by Anna Husfeldt

First edition published 2024
by CRC Press
2385 NW Executive Center Drive, Suite 320, Boca Raton FL 33431
and by CRC Press

4 Park Square, Milton Park, Abingdon, Oxon, OX14 4RN

CRC Press is an imprint of Taylor & Francis Group, LLC

ISBN: 978-1-032-57627-5 (hbk)
ISBN: 978-1-032-57626-8 (pbk)
ISBN: 978-1-003-44026-0 (ebk)

DOI: 10.1201/9781003440260

Typeset in Palatino
by KnowledgeWorks Global Ltd.

To my friend, Jaan Tallinn, the man who did

more for the world than you will ever know.

Contents

Acknowledgments

I would like to thank a great number of people for helping me, sharing their ideas, commenting on my work, supporting my research, or simply inspiring my thinking in many ways. Some of them I had the pleasure of meeting in person, and others are virtual presences on my computer, but ideas are substrate independent, so they are all equally amazing. I am confident that I forgot many important people simply because I am not superintelligent and my memory is terrible. I apologize in advance for any such omissions. I acknowledge contributions of many great scientists by simply citing their work as that is the greatest recognition of scientific contribution anyone can wish for. A huge thank you goes to Max Tegmark, Ian Goodfellow, Kenneth Regan, Edward Frenkel, Sebastien Zany, Søren Elverlin, Melissa Helton, Anna Husfeldt, Thore Husfeldt, David Kelley, David Jilk, Scott Aaronson, Rob Bensinger, Seth Baum, Tony Barrett, and Alexey Turchin. Last but certainly not least I would like to thank Jaan Tallinn and Survival and Flourishing Fund, and Elon Musk and the Future of Life Institute for partially funding my work on AI Safety.

Author

Dr. Roman V. Yampolskiy is a tenured associate professor in the Department of Computer Science and Engineering at the Speed School of Engineering, University of Louisville. He is the founding and current director of the Cyber Security Lab and an author of many books including *Artificial Superintelligence: A Futuristic Approach*, Editor of *AI Safety and Security* and *The Technological Singularity*. During his tenure at UofL, Dr. Yampolskiy has been recognized as: Distinguished Teaching Professor, Professor of the Year, Faculty Favorite, Top 4 Faculty, Leader in Engineering Education, Top 10 of Online College Professor of the Year, and Outstanding Early Career in Education award winner among many other honors and distinctions. Yampolskiy was promoted to a senior member of IEEE and AGI; and member of the Kentucky Academy of Science, and he is a former research advisor for MIRI and associate of GCRI.

Roman Yampolskiy holds a PhD degree from the Department of Computer Science and Engineering at the University at Buffalo. He was a recipient of a four-year NSF (National Science Foundation) IGERT (Integrative Graduate Education and Research Traineeship) fellowship. Before beginning his doctoral studies, Dr. Yampolskiy received a BS/MS (High Honors) combined degree in Computer Science from Rochester Institute of Technology, NY, USA. After completing his PhD dissertation, Dr. Yampolskiy held a position of an Affiliate Academic at the Center for Advanced Spatial Analysis, University of London, College of London. He had previously conducted research at the Laboratory for Applied Computing at the Rochester Institute of Technology and at the Center for Unified Biometrics and Sensors at the University at Buffalo. Dr. Yampolskiy is an alumnus of Singularity University (GSP2012) and a visiting fellow of the Singularity Institute (Machine Intelligence Research Institute).

Dr. Yampolskiy's main area of interest is AI Safety. Dr. Yampolskiy is an author of over 200 publications including multiple journal articles and books. His research has been cited by 1000s of scientists and profiled in popular magazines both American and foreign. Dr. Yampolskiy's research has been featured 10,000+ times in numerous media reports in 40+ languages. Twitter: @romanyam

1

Introduction*

1.1 Introduction

Rapid advances in artificial intelligence (AI) over the past decade have been accompanied by several high-profile failures [1], highlighting the importance of ensuring that intelligent machines are beneficial to humanity. This realization has given rise to the new subfield of research known as AI Safety and Security [2], which encompasses a wide range of research areas and has seen steady growth in publications in recent years [3–10].

However, the underlying assumption in this research is that the problem of controlling highly capable intelligent machines is solvable, though no rigorous mathematical proof or argumentation has been presented to demonstrate that the AI control problem is solvable in principle, let alone in practice. In computer science, it is standard practice to first determine whether a problem belongs to a class of unsolvable problems before investing resources in trying to solve it.

Despite the recognition that the problem of AI control may be one of the most important problems facing humanity, it remains poorly understood, poorly defined, and poorly researched. A computer science problem could be solvable, unsolvable, undecidable, or partially solvable; we don't know the actual status of the AI control problem. It is possible that some forms of control may be possible in certain situations, but it is also possible that partial control may be insufficient in many cases. Without a better understanding of the nature and feasibility of the AI control problem, it is difficult to determine an appropriate course of action [11].

Potential control methodologies for artificial general intelligence (AGI) have been broadly classified into two categories: Methods based on capability control and motivational control [12]. Capability control methods aim to limit the damage that AGI systems can cause by placing them in constrained environments, adding shutdown mechanisms or trip wires. Motivational control methods attempt to design AGI systems to have an innate desire not to cause harm, even in the absence of capacity control

---

* Parts of this chapter have been previously published as On Governability of AI by Roman Yampolskiy. AI Governance in 2020 a Year in Review. June, 2021 and On Defining Differences Between Intelligence and Artificial Intelligence by Roman V. Yampolskiy. Journal of Artificial General Intelligence 11(2), 68-70. 2020.

DOI: 10.1201/9781003440260-1

measures. It is widely recognized that capacity control methods are, at best, temporary safety measures and do not represent a long-term solution to the AGI control problem [12]. Furthermore, it is likely that motivational control measures should be integrated at the design and training phase, rather than after deployment.

1.2 The AI Control Problem

We define the problem of AI control as: *How can humanity remain safely in control while benefiting from a superior form of intelligence?* This is the fundamental problem in the field of AI Safety and Security, which aims to make intelligent systems safe from tampering and secure for all stakeholders involved. Value alignment is currently the most studied approach to achieve security in AI. However, concepts such as safety and security are notoriously difficult to test or measure accurately, even for non-AI software, despite years of research [13]. At best, we can probably distinguish between perfectly safe and as safe as an average person performing a similar task. However, society is unlikely to tolerate machine errors, even if they occur with a frequency typical of human performance or even less frequently. We expect machines to perform better and will not accept partial safety when dealing with such highly capable systems. The impact of AI (both positive and negative [3]) is strongly related to its capability. With respect to possible existential impacts, there is no such thing as partial safety.

An initial understanding of the control problem may suggest designing a machine that accurately follows human commands. However, because of possible conflicting or paradoxical commands, ambiguity of human languages [14], and perverse instance creation problems, this is not a desirable form of control, although some ability to integrate human feedback may be desirable. The solution is thought to require AI to act in the capacity of an ideal advisor, avoiding the problems of misinterpretation of direct commands and the possibility of malevolent commands.

It has been argued that the consequences of an uncontrolled AI could be so severe that even if there is a very small chance of a hostile AI emerging, it is still worthwhile to conduct AI Safety research because the negative utility of such an AI would be astronomical. The common logic is that an extremely high (negative) utility multiplied by a small chance of the event still results in a large disutility and should be taken very seriously. However, the reality is that the chances of a misaligned AI are not small. In fact, in the absence of an effective safety program, that is the only outcome we will get. So the statistics look very compelling in support of a major AI Safety effort. We are looking at an almost guaranteed event with the potential to cause an existential catastrophe. This is not a low-risk, high-reward scenario, but a high-risk, negative-reward situation. No wonder many consider this to be the most important problem humanity has ever faced. The outcome could be prosperity or extinction, and the fate of the universe hangs in the balance. A proof of the solvability or non-solvability of the AI control problem would be the most important proof ever.

1.3 Obstacles to Controlling AI

Controlling an AGI is likely to require a toolbox with certain capabilities, such as explainability, predictability, and model verifiability [15]. However, it is likely that many of the desired tools are not available to us.

- The concept of Unexplainability in AI refers to the impossibility of providing an explanation for certain decisions made by an intelligent system that is 100% accurate and understandable. A complementary concept to Unexplainability, Incomprehensibility of AI addresses the inability of people to fully understand an explanation provided by an AI. We define Incomprehensibility as the impossibility to fully comprehend any 100% accurate explanation for certain decisions of intelligent systems, by any human being [16].

- Unpredictability of AI, one of the many impossibility outcomes in AI Safety, also known as Unknowability, is defined as our inability to accurately and consistently predict what specific actions an intelligent system will take to achieve its goals, even if we know the ultimate goals of the system [17]. It is related to but not the same as the Unexplainability and Incomprehensibility of AI. Unpredictability does not imply that better-than-random statistical analysis is impossible; it simply points to a general limitation on how well such efforts can work, particularly pronounced with advanced generally intelligent systems in novel domains.

- Non-verifiability is a fundamental limitation in the verification of mathematical proofs, computer software, intelligent agent behavior, and all formal systems [18]. It is becoming increasingly obvious that just as we can only have probabilistic confidence in the correctness of mathematical proofs and software implementations, our ability to verify intelligent agents is at best limited.

Many researchers assume that the problem of AI control can be solved despite the absence of any evidence or proof. Before embarking on a quest to build controlled AI, it is important to demonstrate that the problem can be solved so as not to waste valuable resources. The burden of proof is on those who claim that the problem is solvable, and the current absence of such proof speaks loudly about the inherent dangers of the proposal to develop AGI. In fact, Uncontrollability of AI is very likely to be the case, as can be demonstrated by reduction to the problem of human control. There are many open questions to consider regarding the issue of controllability, such as: Can the control problem be solved? Can it be done in principle? Can it be done in practice? Can it be done with a sufficient level of accuracy? How long would it take to do it? Can it be done in time? What are the energy and computational requirements to do it? What would a solution look like? What is the minimum viable solution? How would we know if we solved it? Does the solution scale as the system continues to improve? We argue that unconstrained intelligence cannot be controlled and constrained intelligence cannot innovate. If AGI is not properly controlled, no matter who programmed it, the consequences will be disastrous for everyone, probably its programmers in the first place. No one benefits from uncontrolled AGI.

There seems to be a lack of published evidence to conclude that a less intelligent agent can indefinitely maintain control over a more intelligent agent. As we develop intelligent systems that are less intelligent than we are, we can maintain control, but once such systems become more intelligent than we are, we lose that ability. In fact, as we try to maintain control while designing advanced intelligent agents, we find ourselves in a Catch-22, since the control mechanism needed to maintain control must be smarter or at least as smart as the agent over which we want to maintain control. A whole hierarchy of intelligent systems would need to be built to control increasingly capable systems, leading to infinite regress. Moreover, the problem of controlling such more capable intelligence only becomes more challenging and more obviously impossible for agents with only a static level of intelligence. Whoever is more intelligent will be in control, and those in control will be the ones with the power to make the final decisions. As far as we know, as of this moment, no one in the world has a working AI control mechanism capable of scaling to human-level AI and eventually beyond, or even an idea for a prototype that might work. No one has made verifiable claims to have such a technology. In general, for anyone claiming that the problem of AI control is solvable, the burden of proof is on them. Currently, it appears that our ability to produce intelligent software far outstrips our ability to control or even verify it.

1.4 Defining Safe AI

In "On Defining Artificial Intelligence" Pei Wang presents the following definition [19]: "Intelligence is the capacity of an information-processing system to adapt to its environment while operating with insufficient knowledge and resources" [20]. Wang's definition is perfectly adequate, and he also reviews definitions of intelligence suggested by others, which have by now become standard in the field [21]. However, there is a fundamental difference between defining intelligence in general or human intelligence in particular and defining AI as the title of Wang's paper claims he does. In this chapter, I would like to bring attention to the fundamental differences between designed and natural intelligences [22].

AI is typically designed for the explicit purpose of providing some benefit to its designers and users and it is important to include that distinction in the definition of AI. Wang only once, briefly, mentions the concept of AI Safety [12, 23–26] in his article and doesn't bring it or other related concepts into play. In my opinion, definition of AI which doesn't explicitly mention safety or at least its necessary subcomponents, such as controllability, explainability [27], comprehensibility, predictability [28], and corrigibility [29], is dangerously incomplete.

Development of AGI is predicted to cause a shift in the·trajectory of human civilization [30]. In order to reap the benefits and avoid pitfalls of such powerful technology, it is important to be able to control it. Full control of intelligent system [31] implies capability to limit its performance [32], for example, setting it to a particular level of IQ equivalence. Additional controls may make it possible to turn the system off [33], and turn on/off consciousness [34, 35], free will, autonomous goal selection, and specify moral code [36] the system will apply in its decisions. It should also be possible to modify the system after it is deployed to correct any problems [1, 37] discovered during use. An AI system should be able, to the extent theoretically possible, explain its decisions in a human-comprehensible language. Its designers and end users should be able to predict its general behavior. If needed, the system should be confinable to a restricted environment [38–40], or operate with reduced computational resources. AI should be operating with minimum bias and maximum transparency; it has to be friendly [41], safe, and secure [2].

Consequently, we propose the following definition of AI which compliments Wang's definition: "Artificial Intelligence is a fully controlled agent with a capacity of an information-processing system to adapt to its environment while operating with insufficient knowledge and resources".

1.5 On Governability of AI

In order to make future AIs beneficial for all of humanity, AI governance initiatives attempt to make AI governable by the world's governments, international organizations, and multinational corporations collaborating on establishing a regulatory framework and industry standards. However, direct governance of AI is not meaningful, and what is implied by the term is governance of AI researchers and creators in terms of what products and services they are permitted to develop and how. Whatever it is possible to govern scientists and engineers working on AI depends on the difficulty of creating AGI.

If computational resources and data collection efforts necessary to create AGI are comparable in cost and human capital to the Manhattan Project conducted by the US to develop nuclear bomb technology, governments have a number of "carrots" and "sticks" they can use to guide researchers and to mold the future AI to their specifications. On the other hand, if it turns out that there is a much more efficient way to create the first AGI or a "seed" AI which can grow into a full-blown superintelligence, for example, by a teenager on a $1000 laptop in their garage (an admittedly less likely, but nevertheless possible scenario), governments' attempts at regulation may be futile. We note that historical attempts at software governance (e.g., spam, computer viruses, and deep fakes) had only a very limited amount of success. With AGI as an independent agent, it may be ungovernable because traditional methods of assigning responsibility and punishment-based enforcement are not applicable to software.

Even presuming a, resource-heavy, favorable case for governance, we are still left with a number of established technical limits to AI predictability [17], explainability [16], and controllability [42]. It follows that AI governability, which requires, at least, those three capabilities for successful regulation is likewise only partially achievable, meaning smarter than human AI would be ungovernable by us in some important ways. Finally, even where AI governance is achievable, those in charge may be unwilling to take personal responsibility for AI's failures [43], or deliberate actions even if performed in the context of instituted governance framework. Consequently, a highly capable, creative, and uncontrolled AGI may end up implicitly or even explicitly controlling some of the institutions and individuals, which we entrusted to govern such intelligent software.

1.6 Conclusions

Narrow AI (NAI) systems can be made secure because they represent a finite space of options and therefore, theoretically, all possible bad decisions and errors can be countered. However, for AGI, the space of possible decisions and failures is infinite, which means that there will always remain an infinite number of potential problems, regardless of the number of security patches applied to the system. Such an infinite space of possibilities is impossible to fully debug or even adequately test for security. This is also true for the security of intelligent systems. An NAI presents a finite attack surface, while an AGI gives malicious users and hackers an infinite set of options to work with [44]. From a security perspective, this means that while defenders must protect an infinite space, attackers need to only find one penetration point to succeed. Furthermore, every security patch/mechanism introduced creates new vulnerabilities, ad infinitum. AI Safety research to date can be viewed as discovering new failure modes and creating patches for them, essentially a fixed set of rules for an infinite set of problems. There is a fractal nature to the problem, regardless of how much we "zoom in" on it, we continue to discover many challenges at every level. The AI control problem exhibits a fractal impossibility, meaning that it contains unsolvable subproblems at all levels of abstraction, and is consequently unsolvable as a whole [45].

It is important to keep in mind that the lack of control of AI also means that malevolent actors will not be able to fully exploit AI to their advantage. It is crucial that any path taken in AI development and deployment includes a mechanism to undo any decisions made, should they prove to be undesirable. However, current approaches to AI development do not include this security feature.

1.7 About the Book

In this introductory chapter, we lay the foundation for the central themes that underpin this book's structure, namely the "three U's" of AI: Unpredictability, Unexplainability, and Uncontrollability. The fundamental idea is that as AI becomes more advanced and intelligent, it becomes less predictable, more difficult to explain, and increasingly challenging to control. Each chapter of the book further dissects these premises, adding layers of understanding and bringing forth critical areas of AI which require our attention. Chapters are independent and can be read in any order or skipped.

In the chapters that follow, we probe into some of the inherent impossibility results such as Unpredictability, Unexplainability, and Incomprehensibility, suggesting that not only is it complex to forecast an AI's decisions, but the rationale behind them may remain shrouded, even to their creators. Unverifiability, another intricate concept explored, highlights the challenges surrounding proof verification within AI, casting a shadow on its infallibility.

The essence of AI ownership, as discussed in the chapter "Unownability", challenges traditional notions of accountability, emphasizing the obstacles to claiming ownership over advanced intelligent systems. Simultaneously, the concept of Uncontrollability questions our capacity to manage the rising force of AI, particularly AGI.

The following chapters outline potential threats posed by AI and how they could occur. "Pathways to Danger" delves into the possible routes leading to malevolent AI. The "Accidents" chapter extrapolates the potential risks and unprecedented impacts of AI failures. Each chapter further underscores the notion that AI, in its progression, has the potential to dramatically reshape society, not always to our advantage.

As we shift toward the latter half of the book, we delve into the profound and controversial discussions surrounding AI personhood and consciousness. We evaluate the consequences of granting legal rights to AI, scrutinize the concept of consciousness within machines, and explore the potential emergence of selfish memes and legal system hacking.

The chapter "Personal Universes" deals with the concept of value alignment in AI, an area fraught with difficulties, while proposing a pathway that might allow AI to optimally align with individual human values.

In "Human ≠ AGI", we differentiate between the capabilities of AGI and human-level artificial intelligence (HLAI), asserting that humans, in essence, are not general intelligence. Finally, the last chapter, "Skepticism", scrutinizes the denial or dismissal of AI risk, drawing parallels with other forms of scientific skepticism.

Through this journey, you will explore the fascinating, and at times unnerving, world of AI. By understanding these fundamental concepts and their implications, we can better prepare ourselves for an AI-influenced future. By the end of the book, we hope to have instilled in you an appreciation for the complexities and challenges of AI, and the realization that the path to AI is not just about building intelligent machines but about understanding their intricate relationship with our society and us. Let's embark on this journey together.

References

1. Yampolskiy, R.V., *Predicting future AI failures from historic examples.* Foresight, 2019. **21**(1): p. 138–152.
2. Yampolskiy, R.V., *Artificial Intelligence Safety and Security.* 2018: Chapman and Hall/CRC Press.
3. Cave, S., and K. Dihal, *Hopes and fears for intelligent machines in fiction and reality.* Nature Machine Intelligence, 2019. **1**(2): p. 74–78.
4. Avin, S., et al., *Filling gaps in trustworthy development of AI.* Science, 2021. **374**(6573): p. 1327–1329.
5. Beridze, I., and J. Butcher, *When seeing is no longer believing.* Nature Machine Intelligence, 2019. **1**(8): p. 332–334.
6. Tzachor, A., et al., *Artificial intelligence in a crisis needs ethics with urgency.* Nature Machine Intelligence, 2020. **2**(7): p. 365–366.
7. Cave, S., and S.S. ÓhÉigeartaigh, *Bridging near-and long-term concerns about AI.* Nature Machine Intelligence, 2019. **1**(1): p. 5–6.
8. Theodorou, A., and V. Dignum, *Towards ethical and socio-legal governance in AI.* Nature Machine Intelligence, 2020. **2**(1): p. 10–12.

9. Nature Machine Intelligence, *How to be responsible in AI publication*. Nature Machine Intelligence, 2021. **3**. https://www.nature.com/articles/s42256-021-00355-6

10. Crawford, K., *Time to regulate AI that interprets human emotions*. Nature, 2021. **592**(7853): p. 167–167.

11. Yampolskiy, R., *On controllability of artificial intelligence*, in *IJCAI-21 Workshop on Artificial Intelligence Safety (AI Safety 2021)*. 2020.

12. Bostrom, N., *Superintelligence: Paths, Dangers, Strategies*. 2014: Oxford University Press.

13. Pfleeger, S., and R. Cunningham, *Why measuring security is hard*. IEEE Security & Privacy, 2010. **8**(4): p. 46–54.

14. Howe, W., and R. Yampolskiy, *Impossibility of unambiguous communication as a source of failure in AI systems*, in *AISafety@ IJCAI*. 2021.

15. Yampolskiy, R.V., *AGI control theory*, in *Artificial General Intelligence: 14th International Conference, AGI 2021, Palo Alto, CA, USA, October 15–18, 2021, Proceedings 14*. 2022. Springer.

16. Yampolskiy, R.V., *Unexplainability and incomprehensibility of AI*. Journal of Artificial Intelligence and Consciousness, 2020. **7(2)**: p. 277–291.

17. Yampolskiy, R.V., *Unpredictability of AI: On the impossibility of accurately predicting all actions of a smarter agent*. Journal of Artificial Intelligence and Consciousness, 2020. **7**(1): p. 109–118.

18. Yampolskiy, R.V., *What are the ultimate limits to computational techniques: Verifier theory and unverifiability*. Physica Scripta, 2017. **92**(9): p. 093001.

19. Wang, P., *On defining artificial intelligence*. Journal of Artificial General Intelligence, 2019. **10**(2): p. 1–37.

20. Wang, P., *Non-Axiomatic Reasoning System: Exploring the Essence of Intelligence*. 1995: Citeseer.

21. Legg, S., and M. Hutter, *Universal intelligence: A definition of machine intelligence*. Minds and Machines, 2007. **17**(4): p. 391–444.

22. Yampolskiy, R.V., *On the origin of synthetic life: Attribution of output to a particular algorithm*. Physica Scripta, 2016. **92**(1): p. 013002.

23. Yampolskiy, R.V., *Artificial intelligence safety engineering: Why machine ethics is a wrong approach*, in Philosophy and Theory of Artificial Intelligence, V.C. Müller, Editor. 2013, Springer. p. 389–396.

24. Yampolskiy, R.V., and J. Fox, *Safety Engineering for Artificial General Intelligence*. Topoi. Special Issue on Machine Ethics & the Ethics of Building Intelligent Machines, 2012.

25. Yudkowsky, E., *Complex value systems in friendly AI*, in Artificial General Intelligence, J. Schmidhuber, K. Thórisson, and M. Looks, Editors. 2011, Springer. p. 388–393.

26. Yampolskiy, R.V., *Artificial Superintelligence: A Futuristic Approach*. 2015: Chapman and Hall/CRC.

27. Yampolskiy, R.V., *Unexplainability and Incomprehensibility of Artificial Intelligence*. 2019: https://arxiv.org/abs/1907.03869.

28. Yampolskiy, R.V., *Unpredictability of AI*. arXiv preprint arXiv:1905.13053, 2019.

29. Soares, N., et al., *Corrigibility*, in *Workshops at the Twenty-Ninth AAAI Conference on Artificial Intelligence*. 2015.

30. Baum, S.D., et al., *Long-term trajectories of human civilization*. Foresight, 2019. **21**(1): p. 53–83.

31. Yampolskiy, R.V., *The space of possible mind designs*, in International Conference on Artificial General Intelligence. 2015. Springer.
32. Trazzi, M., and R.V. Yampolskiy, *Building safer AGI by introducing artificial stupidity*. arXiv preprint arXiv:1808.03644, 2018.
33. Hadfield-Menell, D., et al., *The off-switch game*, in Workshops at the Thirty-First AAAI Conference on Artificial Intelligence. 2017.
34. Elamrani, A., and R.V. Yampolskiy, *Reviewing tests for machine consciousness*. Journal of Consciousness Studies, 2019. **26**(5–6): p. 35–64.
35. Yampolskiy, R.V., *Artificial consciousness: An illusionary solution to the hard problem*. Reti, Saperi, Linguaggi, 2018. (2): p. 287–318: https://www.rivisteweb.it/doi/10.12832/92302
36. Majot, A.M., and R.V. Yampolskiy, *AI safety engineering through introduction of self-reference into felicific calculus via artificial pain and pleasure*, in 2014 IEEE International Symposium on Ethics in Science, Technology and Engineering. 2014, IEEE.
37. Scott, P.J., and R.V. Yampolskiy, *Classification schemas for artificial intelligence failures*. arXiv preprint arXiv:1907.07771, 2019.
38. Yampolskiy, R.V., *Leakproofing singularity-artificial intelligence confinement problem*. Journal of Consciousness Studies JCS, 2012. **19**(1–2): p. 194–214. https://www.ingentaconnect.com/contentone/imp/jcs/2012/00000019/f0020001/art00014
39. Armstrong, S., A. Sandberg, and N. Bostrom, *Thinking inside the box: controlling and using an oracle AI*. Minds and Machines, 2012. **22**(4): p. 299–324.
40. Babcock, J., J. Kramár, and R. Yampolskiy, *The AGI containment problem*, in International Conference on Artificial General Intelligence. 2016. Springer.
41. Muehlhauser, L., and N. Bostrom, *Why we need friendly AI*. Think, 2014. **13**(36): p. 41–47.
42. Yampolskiy, R.V., *On controllability of AI*. arXiv preprint arXiv:2008.04071, 2020.
43. Yampolskiy, R.V., *Predicting future AI failures from historic examples*. Foresight, 2019. **21**(1). https://www.emerald.com/insight/content/doi/10.1108/FS-04-2018-0034/full/html
44. Buckner, C., *Understanding adversarial examples requires a theory of artefacts for deep learning*. Nature Machine Intelligence, 2020. **2**(12): p. 731–736.
45. Yampolskiy, R.V., *On the controllability of artificial intelligence: An analysis of limitations*. Journal of Cyber Security and Mobility, 2022: p. 321–404. https://doi.org/10.13052/jcsm2245-1439.1132

2

Unpredictability*

"As machines learn they may develop unforeseen strategies at rates that baffle their programmers"

Norbert Wiener, 1960

"It's a problem writers face every time we consider the creation of intelligences greater than our own"

Vernor Vinge, 2001

"The creative unpredictability of intelligence is not like the noisy unpredictability of a random number generator"

Eliezer Yudkowsky, 2008

2.1 Introduction to Unpredictability

With the increase in capabilities of artificial intelligence (AI), over the last decade, a significant number of researchers have realized the importance of creating not only capable intelligent systems but also making them safe and secure [1–6]. Unfortunately, the field of AI Safety is very young, and researchers are still working to identify its main challenges and limitations. Impossibility results are well known in many fields of inquiry [7–13], and some have now been identified in AI Safety [14–16]. In this chapter, we concentrate on a poorly understood concept of unpredictability of intelligent systems [17], which limits our ability to understand the impact of intelligent systems we are developing and is a challenge for software verification and intelligent system control, as well as AI Safety in general.

In theoretical computer science and in software development in general, many well-known impossibility results are well established, and some of

---

* Reprinted with permission from Unpredictability of AI: On the Impossibility of Accurately Predicting All Actions of a Smarter Agent, Roman V. Yampolskiy, Journal of Artificial Intelligence and Consciousness, Vol 7, Issue No 1., Copyright © 2020 by World Scientific.

them are strongly related to the subject of this chapter, for example, Rice's Theorem states that no computationally effective method can decide if a program will exhibit a particular non-trivial behavior, such as producing a specific output [18]. Similarly, Wolfram's Computational Irreducibility states that complex behaviors of programs can't be predicted without actually running those programs [19]. Any physical system which could be mapped onto a Turing Machine will similarly, exhibit unpredictability [20, 21].

Unpredictability of AI, one of many impossibility results in AI Safety also known as Unknowability [22] or Cognitive Uncontainability [23], is defined as our inability to precisely and consistently predict what specific actions an intelligent system will take to achieve its objectives, even if we know terminal goals of the system. It is related but is not the same as unexplainability and incomprehensibility of AI. Unpredictability does not imply that better-than-random statistical analysis is impossible; it simply points out a general limitation on how well such efforts can perform and is particularly pronounced with advanced generally intelligent systems (superintelligence) in novel domains. In fact, we can present a proof of unpredictability for such, superintelligent, systems.

Proof: This is a proof by contradiction. Suppose not, suppose that unpredictability is wrong and it is possible for a person to accurately predict decisions of superintelligence. That means they can make the same decisions as the superintelligence, which makes them as smart as superintelligence but that is a contradiction as superintelligence is defined as a system smarter than any person is. That means that our initial assumption was false and unpredictability is not wrong.

The amount of unpredictability can be formally measured via the theory of Bayesian surprise, which measures the difference between posterior and prior beliefs of the predicting agent [24–27]. "The unpredictability of intelligence is a very special and unusual kind of surprise, which is not at all like noise or randomness. There is a weird balance between the unpredictability of actions and the predictability of outcomes" [28]. A simple heuristic is to estimate the amount of surprise as proportional to the difference in intelligence between the predictor and the predicted agent. See Yudkowsky [29, 30] for an easy-to-follow discussion on this topic.

Unpredictability is practically observable in current narrow domain systems with superhuman performance. Developers of famous intelligent systems such as Deep Blue (Chess) [31, 32], IBM Watson (Jeopardy) [33], and AlphaZero (Go) [34, 35] did not know what specific decisions their AI was going to make for every turn. All they could predict was that it would try to win using any actions available to it, and win it did. Artificial general intelligence (AGI) developers are in exactly the same situation, they may know the ultimate goals of their system but do not know the actual step-by-step plan it will execute, which of course has serious consequences for AI Safety [36–39]. A reader interested in concrete examples of unanticipated actions of intelligent agents is advised to read two surveys on the subject, one in the domain of evolutionary algorithms [40] and another on narrow AI agents [41].

There are infinitely many paths to every desirable state of the world. Great majority of them are completely undesirable and unsafe, most with negative side effects. In harder and most real-world cases, even the overall goal of the system may not be precisely known or may be known only in abstract terms, aka "make the world better". While in some cases the terminal goal(s) could be learned, even if you can learn to predict an overall outcome with some statistical certainty, you cannot learn to predict all the steps to the goal a system of superior intelligence would take. Lower intelligence can't accurately predict all decisions of higher intelligence, a concept known as *Vinge's Principle* [42]. "Vinge's Principle implies that when an agent is designing another agent (or modifying its own code), it needs to approve the other agent's design without knowing the other agent's exact future actions" [43].

2.2 Predictability: What We Can Predict – A Literature Review

Early realization that superintelligent machines will produce unpredictable futures can be found in the seminal paper by Vernor Vinge [22] on Technological Singularity, in which he talks about unknowable prediction horizon (see also Event Horizon Thesis [44]) beyond which we can predict nothing: "Perhaps it was the science-fiction writers who felt the first concrete impact. After all, the hard science-fiction writers are the ones who try to write specific stories about all that technology may do for us. More and more, these writers felt an opaque wall across the future. Once, they could put such fantasies millions of years in the future. Now they saw that their most diligent extrapolations resulted in the unknowable ..." [22]. However, not everyone agreed [45]. In this section, we provide examples from literature discussing what properties of intelligent systems may in fact be predictable.

Nick Bostrom in his comment, *Singularity and Predictability*, on Vinge's work says [46]: "I am not at all sure that unpredictability would hold. ... I think there are some things that we can predict with a reasonable degree of confidence beyond the singularity. For example, that the superintelligent entity resulting from the singularity would start a spherical colonization wave that would propagate into space at a substantial fraction of the speed of light. ... Another example is that if there are multiple independent competing agents (which I suspect there might not be) then we would expect some aspects of their behaviour to be predictable from considerations of economic rationality. ... It might also be possible to predict things in much greater detail. Since the superintelligences or posthumans that will govern the post-singularity world will be created by us, or might even *be* us, it seems that we should be in a position to influence what values they will have. What their values are will then determine what the world will look like, since due to their advanced technology they will have a great ability to make the world conform to their values and desires. So one could argue that all we have to do in order to predict what will happen after the singularity is to figure out what values the people will have who will create the superintelligence. ... So maybe we can define a fairly small number of hypothesis about what the post-singularity world will be like. Each of these hypotheses would correspond to a plausible value. The plausible values are those that it seems fairly probable that many of the most influential people will have at about the time when the first superintelligence is created. Each of these values defines an attractor, i.e. a state of the world which contains the maximal amount of positive utility according to the value in question. We can then make the prediction that the world is likely to settle into one of these attractors. More specifically, we would expect that within the volume of space that has been colonized, matter would gradually (but perhaps very quickly) be arranged into value-maximal structures – structures that contain as much of the chosen value as possible" [46].

Similarly, Michael Nielsen argues [47]: "What does 'unknowable' mean? It seems to me that the sense in which Vinge uses the term unknowable is equivalent to 'unpredictable', so let's ask the question 'Will the future after the advent of dominant AI necessarily be unpredictable?' instead. ... It seems to me to be ridiculous to claim that we can't make useful predictions about a post-Dominant AI world. Yes, things will change enormously. Our predictions may be much less reliable than before. However, I believe that we can still make some reasonable predictions about such a future. At the very least, we can work on excluding some possibilities. One avenue for doing this is to look at exclusions based upon the laws of physics. An often-made assertion related to the "unpredictability" of a post-Dominant-AI future is that anything allowed by the Laws of Physics will become possible at that point" [47].

Arbital contributors in their discussion of Vingean Uncertainty write: "Furthermore, our ability to think about agents smarter than ourselves is not limited to knowing a particular goal and predicting its achievement. If we found a giant alien machine that seemed very well-designed, we might be able to infer the aliens were superhumanly intelligent even if we didn't know the aliens' ultimate goals. If we saw metal pipes, we could guess that the pipes represented some stable, optimal mechanical solution which was made out of hard metal so as to retain its shape. If we saw superconducting cables, we could guess that this was a way of efficiently transporting electrical work from one place to another, even if we didn't know what final purpose the electricity was being used for. This is the idea behind Instrumental convergence:

if we can recognize that an alien machine is efficiently harvesting and distributing energy, we might recognize it as an intelligently designed artifact in the service of *some* goal even if we don't know the goal" [31].

"'Vingean uncertainty' is the peculiar epistemic state we enter when we're considering sufficiently intelligent programs; in particular, we become less confident that we can predict their exact actions and more confident of the final outcome of those actions. (Note that this rejects the claim that we are epistemically helpless and can know nothing about beings smarter than ourselves.)" [31]. Yudkowsky and Herreshoff reiterate: "Hence although we cannot predict the exact actions of a smarter agent, we may be able to predict the consequences of running that agent by inspecting its design, or select among possible consequences by selecting among possible designs" [48].

Arguments against unpredictability are usually of two general types: "The apparent knownness of a particular domain. (E.g., since we have observed the rules of chemistry with great precision and know their origin in the underlying molecular dynamics, we can believe that even an arbitrarily smart agent should not be able to turn lead into gold using non-radioactive chemical reagents.) ... Backward reasoning from the Fermi Paradox, which gives us weak evidence bounding the capabilities of the most powerful agents possible in our universe. (E.g., even though there might be surprises remaining in the question of how to standardly model physics, any surprise yielding Faster-Than-Light travel to a previously un-traveled point makes the Fermi Paradox harder to explain.)" [49].

In a more practical demonstration of predictability, Israeli and Goldenfeld "... find that computationally irreducible physical processes can be predictable and even computationally reducible at a coarse-grained level of description. The resulting coarse-grained [cellular automata] which we construct emulate the large-scale behavior of the original systems without accounting for small-scale details" [50]. Much of the future work on AI Safety will have to deal with figuring out what is in fact predictable and knowable about intelligent machines, even if most of their future states will forever be unpredictable to us. Next section looks at the early progress in that effort.

2.3 Cognitive Uncontainability

Machine Intelligence Research Institute (MIRI), a leading AI Safety research organization, in the context of their work on safe self-improvement in artificially intelligent agents has investigated unpredictability under the designation of *Cognitive Uncontainability*. The term is meant to infer that the human mind does not and could not conceive of all possible decisions/strategies such advanced intelligent systems could make. "Strong cognitive uncontainability is when the agent knows some facts we don't, that it can use to formulate strategies that we wouldn't be able to recognize in advance as successful. ... When an agent can win using options that we didn't imagine, couldn't invent, and wouldn't understand even if we caught a glimpse of them in advance, it is strongly cognitively uncontainable ..." [23]. "[I]f extremely high confidence must be placed on the ability of self-modifying systems to reason about agents which are smarter than the reasoner, then it seems prudent to develop a theoretical understanding of satisfactory reasoning about smarter agents" [51].

Even subhuman AIs may be unpredictable to human researchers.

"Although Vingean unpredictability is the classic way in which cognitive uncontainability can arise, other possibilities are imaginable. For instance, the AI could be operating in a rich domain and searching a different part of the search space that humans have difficulty handling, while still being dumber or less competent overall than a human. In this case the AI's strategies might still be unpredictable to us, even while it was less effective or competent overall" [23].

"Arguments in favor of strong uncontainability tend to revolve around either:

- The richness and partial unknownness of a particular domain. (E.g. human psychology seems very complicated; has a lot of unknown pathways; and previously discovered exploits often seemed very surprising; therefore we should expect strong uncontainability on the domain of human psychology.)

- Outside-view induction on previous ability advantages derived from cognitive advantages. (The 10th century couldn't contain the 20th century even though all parties involved were biological Homo sapiens; what makes us think we're the first generation to have the real true laws of the universe in our minds?)" [49].

2.4 Conclusions

Unpredictability is an intuitively familiar concept, we can usually predict the outcome of common physical processes without knowing specific behavior of particular atoms, just like we can typically predict overall behavior of the intelligent system without knowing specific intermediate steps. Rahwan and Cebrian observe that "... complex AI agents often exhibit inherent unpredictability: they demonstrate emergent behaviors that are impossible to predict with precision—even by their own programmers. These behaviors manifest themselves only through interaction with the world and with other agents in the environment. ... In fact, Alan Turing and Alonzo Church showed the fundamental impossibility of ensuring an algorithm fulfills certain properties without actually running said algorithm. There are fundamental theoretical limits to our ability to verify that a particular piece of code will always satisfy desirable properties, unless we execute the code, and observe its behavior" [52]. See Rahwan et al. [53] for additional discussion on unpredictability and related issues with machine behavior.

Others have arrived at similar conclusions. "Given the inherent unpredictability of AI, it may not always be feasible to implement specific controls for every activity in which a bot engages" [54]. "As computer programs become more intelligent and less transparent, not only are the harmful effects less predictable, but their decision-making process may also be unpredictable" [55]. "The AI could become so complex that it results in errors and unpredictability, as the AI will be not able to predict its own behavior" [56]. "… the behavior of [artificial intellects] will be so complex as to be unpredictable, and therefore potentially threatening to human beings" [57].

In the context of AI Safety [58–61] and AI governance [62], unpredictability implies that certain standard tools and safety mechanisms would not work to make advanced intelligent systems safe to use. For example, Bathaee writes about legislative control: "… unpredictability makes it very unlikely that the law can appropriately encourage or deter certain effects, and more problematically, the failure of our legal structures will allow people using the algorithms to externalize costs to others without having the ability to pay for the injuries they inflict" [55].

We can conclude that unpredictability of AI will forever make 100% safe AI an impossibility, but we can still strive for Safer AI because we are able to make some predictions about AIs we design. Terminal goals of agents can be completely arbitrary [63], but instrumental goals [64] are universal and all sufficiently intelligent agents will converge on them. Additional analysis indicated that all instrumental goals could be reduced to just one single drive, to become the most intelligent agent possible, a meta-goal for all agents, which as a side-effect may produce superconsciousness [65] impact of which on agent's behavior make may make them even less predictable to us.

References

1. Yampolskiy, R.V., *Artificial Intelligence Safety and Security*. 2018: Chapman and Hall/CRC Press.
2. Callaghan, V., et al., *Technological Singularity*. 2017: Springer.
3. Baum, S.D., et al., *Long-term trajectories of human civilization*. Foresight, 2019. **21**(1): p. 53–83.
4. Duettmann, A., et al., *Artificial General Intelligence: Coordination & Great Powers*.

5. Charisi, V., et al., *Towards moral autonomous systems*. arXiv preprint arXiv: 1703.04741, 2017.

6. Brundage, M., et al., *The malicious use of artificial intelligence: Forecasting, prevention, and mitigation*. arXiv preprint arXiv:1802.07228, 2018.

7. Fisher, M., N. Lynch, and M. Peterson, *Impossibility of distributed consensus with one faulty process*. Journal of ACM, 1985. **32**(2): p. 374–382.

8. Grossman, S.J., and J.E. Stiglitz, *On the impossibility of informationally efficient markets*. The American Economic Review, 1980. **70**(3): p. 393–408.

9. Kleinberg, J.M., *An impossibility theorem for clustering*, in Advances in Neural Information Processing Systems. 2003, MIT Press.

10. Strawson, G., *The impossibility of moral responsibility*. Philosophical Studies, 1994. **75**(1): p. 5–24.

11. Bazerman, M.H., K.P. Morgan, and G.F. Loewenstein, *The impossibility of auditor independence*. Sloan Management Review, 1997. **38**: p. 89–94.

12. List, C., and P. Pettit, *Aggregating sets of judgments: An impossibility result*. Economics & Philosophy, 2002. **18**(1): p. 89–110.

13. Dufour, J.-M., *Some impossibility theorems in econometrics with applications to structural and dynamic models*. Econometrica: Journal of the Econometric Society, 1997. **65**: p. 1365–1387.

14. Yampolskiy, R.V., *What are the ultimate limits to computational techniques: Verifier theory and unverifiability*. Physica Scripta, 2017. **92**(9): p. 093001.

15. Armstrong, S., and S. Mindermann, *Impossibility of deducing preferences and rationality from human policy*. arXiv preprint arXiv:1712.05812, 2017.

16. Eckersley, P., *Impossibility and uncertainty theorems in AI value alignment (or why your AGI should not have a utility function)*. arXiv preprint arXiv:1901.00064, 2018.

17. Yampolskiy, R.V., *The space of possible mind designs*, in International Conference on Artificial General Intelligence. 2015. Springer.

18. Rice, H.G., *Classes of recursively enumerable sets and their decision problems*. Transactions of the American Mathematical Society, 1953. **74**(2): p. 358–366.

19. Wolfram, S., *A New Kind of Science*. Vol. 5. 2002: Wolfram Media Champaign.

20. Moore, C., *Unpredictability and undecidability in dynamical systems*. Physical Review Letters, 1990. **64**(20): p. 2354.

21. Moore, C., *Generalized shifts: Unpredictability and undecidability in dynamical systems*. Nonlinearity, 1991. **4**(2): p. 199.

22. Vinge, V., *Technological singularity*, in *VISION-21 Symposium Sponsored by NASA Lewis Research Center and the Ohio Aerospace Institute*. 1993.

23. *Cognitive Uncontainability*, in *Arbital*. Retrieved May 19, 2019. https://arbital.com/p/uncontainability/.

24. Itti, L., and P. Baldi, *A principled approach to detecting surprising events in video*, in *2005 IEEE Computer Society Conference on Computer Vision and Pattern Recognition (CVPR'05)*. 2005. IEEE.

25. Itti, L., and P.F. Baldi, *Bayesian surprise attracts human attention*, in *Advances in Neural Information Processing Systems*. 2006, **49**(10): pp. 1295–1306. MIT Press.

26. Storck, J., S. Hochreiter, and J. Schmidhuber, *Reinforcement driven information acquisition in non-deterministic environments*, in *Proceedings of the International Conference on Artificial Neural Networks*, Paris. 1995. Citeseer.

27. Schmidhuber, J., *Simple algorithmic theory of subjective beauty, novelty, surprise, interestingness, attention, curiosity, creativity, art, science, music, jokes*. Journal of SICE, 2009. **48**(1): p. 21–32.

28. Yudkowsky, E., *Expected Creative Surprises*, in *Less Wrong*. Retrieved October 24, 2008. https://www.lesswrong.com/posts/rEDpaTTEzhPLz4fHh/expected-creative-surprises.

29. Yudkowsky, E., *Belief in Intelligence*, in *Less Wrong*. Retrieved October 25, 2008. https://www.lesswrong.com/posts/HktFCy6dgsqJ9WPpX/belief-in-intelligence.

30. Yudkowsky, E., *Aiming at the Target*, in *Less Wrong*. Retrieved October 26, 2008. https://www.lesswrong.com/posts/CW6HDvodPpNe38Cry/aiming-at-the-target.

31. *Vingean Uncertainty*, in *Arbital*. Retrieved May 19, 2019. https://arbital.com/p/Vingean_uncertainty/.

32. Campbell, M., A.J. Hoane Jr, and F.-H. Hsu, *Deep blue*. Artificial Intelligence, 2002. **134**(1–2): p. 57–83.

33. Ferrucci, D.A., *Introduction to "This is Watson"*. IBM Journal of Research and Development, 2012. **56**(3–4): p. 235–249.

34. Yudkowsky, E., *Eliezer Yudkowsky on AlphaGo's Wins*, in *Future of Life Institute*. Retrieved March 15, 2016. https://futureoflife.org/2016/03/15/eliezer-yudkowsky-on-alphagos-wins/.

35. Silver, D., et al., *A general reinforcement learning algorithm that masters chess, shogi, and go through self-play*. Science, 2018. **362**(6419): p. 1140–1144.

36. Pistono, F., and R.V. Yampolskiy, *Unethical research: how to create a malevolent artificial intelligence*. arXiv preprint arXiv:1605.02817, 2016.

37. Yampolskiy, R.V., *What to do with the singularity paradox?*, in *Philosophy and Theory of Artificial Intelligence*. 2013, Springer. p. 397–413.

38. Babcock, J., J. Kramar, and R. Yampolskiy, *The AGI Containment Problem*, in *The Ninth Conference on Artificial General Intelligence (AGI2015)*. July 16–19, 2016. NYC, USA.

39. Majot, A.M., and R.V. Yampolskiy, *AI safety engineering through introduction of self-reference into felicific calculus via artificial pain and pleasure*, in *IEEE International Symposium on Ethics in Science, Technology and Engineering*. May 23–24, 2014. Chicago, IL: IEEE.

40. Lehman, J., J. Clune, and D. Misevic, *The surprising creativity of digital evolution*, in *Artificial Life Conference Proceedings*. 2018. MIT Press.

41. Yampolskiy, R.V., *Predicting future AI failures from historic examples*. Foresight, 2019. **21**(1): p. 138–152.

42. *Vinge's Principle*, in *Arbital*. Retrieved May 19, 2019. https://arbital.com/p/Vinge_principle/.

43. *Vingean Reflection*, in *Aribital*. Retrieved May 19, 2019. https://arbital.com/p/Vingean_reflection/.

44. Cantlon, J.F., and E.M. Brannon, *Basic math in monkeys and college students*. PLoS Biology, 2007. **5**(12): p. e328.

45. Baum, S., A. Barrett, and R.V. Yampolskiy, *Modeling and interpreting expert disagreement about artificial superintelligence*. Informatica, 2017. **41**(7): p. 419–428.

46. Bostrom, N., *Singularity and Predictability*. 1998. http://mason.gmu.edu/~rhanson/vc.html.

47. Nielsen, M., *Comment by Michael Nielsen*. 1998. http://mason.gmu.edu/~rhanson/vc.html.

48. Yudkowsky, E., and M. Herreshoff, *Tiling Agents for Self-modifying AI, and the Löbian Obstacle*. MIRI Technical Report, 2013.

49. *Strong Cognitive Uncontainability,* in *Arbital.* Retrieved May 19, 2019. https://arbital.com/p/strong_uncontainability/.

50. Israeli, N., and N. Goldenfeld, *Computational irreducibility and the predictability of complex physical systems.* Physical Review Letters, 2004. **92**(7): p. 074105.

51. Fallenstein, B., and N. Soares, Vingean Reflection: Reliable Reasoning for Self-Improving Agents. 2015: Citeseer.

52. Rahwan, I., and M. Cebrian, *Machine Behavior Needs to Be an Academic Discipline,* in *Nautilus.* Retrieved March 29, 2018. http://nautil.us/issue/58/self/machine-behavior-needs-to-be-an-academic-discipline.

53. Rahwan, I., et al., *Machine behaviour.* Nature, 2019. **568**(7753): p. 477.

54. Mokhtarian, E., *The bot legal code: developing a legally compliant artificial intelligence.* Vanderbilt Journal of Entertainment & Technology Law, 2018. **21**: p. 145.

55. Bathaee, Y., *The artificial intelligence black box and the failure of intent and causation.* Harvard Journal of Law & Technology, 2018. **31**(2): p. 889.

56. Turchin, A., and D. Denkenberger, *Classification of global catastrophic risks connected with artificial intelligence.* AI & Society, 2018. **35**: p. 1–17.

57. De Garis, H., *The Artilect War.* 2008: https://agi-conf.org/2008/artilectwar.pdf, 2008.

58. Babcock, J., J. Kramar, and R.V. Yampolskiy, *Guidelines for artificial intelligence containment.* arXiv preprint arXiv:1707.08476, 2017.

59. Trazzi, M., and R.V. Yampolskiy, *Building safer AGI by introducing artificial stupidity.* arXiv preprint arXiv:1808.03644, 2018.

60. Behzadan, V., A. Munir, and R.V. Yampolskiy, *A psychopathological approach to safety engineering in AI and AGI,* in *International Conference on Computer Safety, Reliability, and Security.* 2018. Springer.

61. Ozlati, S., and R. Yampolskiy, *The formalization of AI risk management and safety standards,* in *Workshops at the Thirty-First AAAI Conference on Artificial Intelligence.* 2017.

62. Ramamoorthy, A., and R. Yampolskiy, *Beyond mad? The race for artificial general intelligence.* ITU J, 2018. **1**: p. 1–8.

63. Bostrom, N., *The superintelligent will: motivation and instrumental rationality in advanced artificial agents.* Minds and Machines, 2012. **22**(2): p. 71–85.

64. Omohundro, S.M., *The Basic AI Drives,* in *AGI.* 2008.

65. Yampolskiy, R.V., *Artificial consciousness: An illusionary solution to the Hard problem.* Reti, Saperi, Linguaggi, 2018. (2): p. 287–318.

3

*Unexplainability and Incomprehensibility**

"If a lion could speak, we couldn't understand him"

Ludwig Wittgenstein

"It would be possible to describe everything scientifically, but it would make no sense. It would be a description without meaning - as if you described a Beethoven symphony as a variation of wave pressure"

Albert Einstein

"Some things in life are too complicated to explain in any language. … Not just to explain to others but to explain to yourself. Force yourself to try to explain it and you create lies"

Haruki Murakami

"I understand that you don't understand"

Grigori Perelman

"If you can't explain something simply, you don't understand it well enough"

Albert Einstein

"If the human brain were so simple that we could understand it, We would be so simple that we couldn't"

Emerson M. Pugh

* Reprinted with permission from Unexplainability and Incomprehensibility of AI, Roman V. Yampolskiy, Journal of Artificial Intelligence and Consciousness, Vol 7, Issue No 2., Copyright © 2020 by World Scientific.

DOI: 10.1201/9781003440260-3

3.1 Introduction

For decades AI projects relied on human expertise, distilled by knowledge engineers, and were both explicitly designed and easily understood by people. For example, expert systems, frequently based on decision trees, are perfect models of human decision-making and so are naturally understandable by both developers and end-users. With paradigm shift in the leading artificial intelligence (AI) methodology, over the last decade, to machine learning systems based on deep neural networks (DNN), this natural ease of understanding got sacrificed. The current systems are seen as "black boxes" (not to be confused with AI boxing [1, 2]), opaque to human understanding but extremely capable both with respect to results and learning of new domains. As long as Big Data and Huge Compute are available, zero human knowledge is required [3] to achieve superhuman [4] performance.

With their newfound capabilities DNN-based AI systems are tasked with making decisions in employment [5], admissions [6], investing [7], matching [8], diversity [9], security [10, 11], recommendations [12], banking [13], and countless other critical domains. As many such domains are legally regulated, it is a desirable property and frequently a requirement [14, 15] that such systems should be able to explain how they arrived at their decisions, particularly to show that they are bias free [16]. Additionally, and perhaps even more importantly, to make artificially intelligent systems safe and secure [17], it is essential that we understand what they are doing and why. A particular area of interest in AI Safety [18–25] is predicting and explaining the causes of AI failures [26].

A significant amount of research [27–41] is now being devoted to developing explainable AI. In the next section, we review some main results and general trends relevant to this chapter.

3.2 Literature Review

Hundreds of papers have been published on eXplainable Artificial Intelligence (XAI) [42]. According to the Defense Advanced Research Projects Agency (DARPA) [27], XAI is supposed to "produce more explainable models, while maintaining a high level of learning performance … and enable human users to understand, appropriately, trust, and effectively manage the emerging generation of artificially intelligent partners". Detailed analysis of literature on explainability or comprehensibility is beyond the scope of this chapter, but the readers are encouraged to look at many excellent surveys of the topic [43–45]. Miller [46] surveys social sciences to understand how people explain, in the hopes of transferring that knowledge to XAI, but of course people often say: "I can't explain it" or "I don't understand". For example, most people are unable to explain how they recognize faces, a problem we frequently ask computers to solve [47, 48].

Despite wealth of publications on XAI and related concepts [49–51], the subject of Unexplainability or Incomprehensibility of AI is only implicitly addressed. Some limitations of explainability are discussed as follows: "ML algorithms intrinsically consider high-degree interactions between input features, which make disaggregating such functions into human under-standable form difficult. ... While a single linear transformation may be inter-preted by looking at the weights from the input features to each of the output classes, multiple layers with non-linear interactions at every layer imply disentangling a super complicated nested structure which is a difficult task and potentially even a questionable one [52]. ... As mentioned before, given the complicated structure of ML models, for the same set of input variables and prediction targets, complex machine learning algorithms can produce multiple accurate models by taking very similar but not the same internal pathway in the network, so details of explanations can also change across multiple accurate models. This systematic instability makes automated gen-erated explanations difficult" [42].

Sutcliffe et al. talk about incomprehensible theorems [53]: "Comprehensibility estimates the effort required for a user to understand the theorem. Theorems with many or deeply nested structures may be considered incomprehen-sible". Muggleton et al. [54] suggest "using inspection time as a proxy for incomprehension. That is, we might expect that humans take a long time ... in the case they find the program hard to understand. As a proxy, inspection time is easier to measure than comprehension".

The tradeoff between explainability and comprehensibility is recognized [52] but is not taken to its logical conclusion. "[A]ccuracy generally requires more complex prediction methods [but] simple and interpretable functions do not make the most accurate predictors" [55]. "Indeed, there are algo-rithms that are more interpretable than others are, and there is often a trad-eoff between accuracy and interpretability: the most accurate AI/ML models usually are not very explainable (for example, deep neural nets, boosted trees, random forests, and support vector machines), and the most interpre-table models usually are less accurate (for example, linear or logistic regres-sion)" [42].

Incomprehensibility is supported by well-known impossibility results. Charlesworth proved his Comprehensibility theorem while attempting to formalize the answer to such questions as: "If [full human-level intelli-gence] software can exist, could humans understand it?" [56]. While describ-ing implications of his theorem on AI, he writes [57]: "Comprehensibility Theorem is the first mathematical theorem implying the impossibility of any AI agent or natural agent—including a not-necessarily infallible human agent—satisfying a rigorous and deductive interpretation of the self-comprehensibility challenge. ... Self-comprehensibility in some form might be essential for a kind of self-reflection useful for self-improvement that might enable some agents to increase their success". It is reasonable to conclude that a system which doesn't comprehend itself would not be able to explain itself.

Hernandez-Orallo et al. introduce the notion of K-Incomprehensibility (a.k.a. K-hardness) [58]. "This will be the formal counterpart to our notion of hard-to-learn good explanations. In our sense, a k-*incomprehensible* string with a high *k* (difficult to comprehend) is different (harder) than a k-*compressible* string (difficult to learn) [59] and different from classical computational complexity (slow to compute). Calculating the value of *k* for a given string is not computable in general. Fortunately, the converse, i.e., given an arbitrary *k*, calculating whether a string is k-*comprehensible* is computable. ... Kolmogorov Complexity measures the amount of information but not the complexity to understand them" [58].

Yampolskiy addresses limits of understanding other agents in his work on the space of possible minds [60]: "Each mind design corresponds to an integer and so is finite, but since the number of minds is infinite some have a much greater number of states compared to others. This property holds for all minds. Consequently, since a human mind has only a finite number of possible states, there are minds which can never be fully understood by a human mind as such mind designs have a much greater number of states, making their understanding impossible as can be demonstrated by the pigeonhole principle". Hibbard points out safety impact from Incomprehensibility of AI: "Given the incomprehensibility of their thoughts, we will not be able to sort out the effect of any conflicts they have between their own interests and ours".

We are slowly starting to realize that as AIs become more powerful, the models behind their success will become ever less comprehensible to us [61]: "... *deep learning* that produces outcomes based on so many different variables under so many different conditions being transformed by so many layers of neural networks that humans simply cannot comprehend the model the computer has built for itself. ... Clearly our computers have surpassed us in their power to discriminate, find patterns, and draw conclusions. That's one reason we use them. Rather than reducing phenomena to fit a relatively simple model, we can now let our computers make models as big as they need to. But this also seems to mean that what we know depends upon the output of machines the functioning of which we cannot follow, explain, or understand. ... But some of the new models are incomprehensible. They can exist only in the weights of countless digital triggers networked together and feeding successive layers of networked, weighted triggers representing huge quantities of variables that affect one another in ways so particular that we cannot derive general principles from them".

"Now our machines are letting us see that even if the rules are simple, elegant, beautiful and rational, the domain they govern is so granular, so intricate, so interrelated, with everything causing everything else all at once and forever, that our brains and our knowledge cannot begin to comprehend it. ... Our new reliance on inscrutable models as the source of the justification of our beliefs puts us in an odd position. If knowledge includes the justification of our beliefs, then knowledge cannot be a class of mental content, because the justification now consists of models that exist in machines, models that human mentality cannot comprehend. ... But the promise of machine learning is that there are times when the machine's inscrutable models will be far more predictive than the manually constructed, human-intelligible ones. In those cases, our knowledge—if we choose to use it—will depend on justifications that we simply cannot understand. ... [W]e are likely to continue to rely ever more heavily on justifications that we simply cannot fathom. And the issue is not simply that we cannot fathom them, the way a lay person can't fathom a string theorist's ideas. Rather, it's that the nature of computer-based justification is not at all like human justification. It is alien" [61].

3.3 Unexplainability

A number of impossibility results are well-known in many areas of research [62–70] and some are starting to be discovered in the domain of AI research, for example, Unverifiability [71], Unpredictability[1] [72], and limits on preference deduction [73] or alignment [74]. In this section, we introduce *Unexplainability* of AI and show that some decisions of superintelligent systems will never be explainable, even in principle. We will concentrate on the most interesting case, a superintelligent AI acting in novel and unrestricted domains. Simple cases of narrow AIs making decisions in restricted domains (e.g., Tic-Tac-Toe) are both explainable and comprehensible. Consequently, a whole spectrum of AIs can be developed from completely explainable/comprehensible to completely unexplainable/incomprehensible. We define Unexplainability as impossibility of providing an explanation for certain decisions made by an intelligent system which is both 100% accurate and comprehensible.

Artificial DNN continue increasing in size and may already comprise millions of neurons, thousands of layers, and billions of connecting weights, ultimately targeting and perhaps surpassing the size of the human brain. They are trained on Big Data from which million feature vectors are extracted and on which decisions are based, with each feature contributing to the decision in proportion to a set of weights. To explain such a decision, which relies on literally billions of contributing factors, AI has to either simplify the explanation and so make the explanation less accurate/specific/detailed or to report it exactly but such an explanation elucidates nothing by virtue of its semantic complexity, large size, and abstract data representation. Such precise reporting is just a copy of trained DNN model.

For example, an AI utilized in the mortgage industry may look at an application to decide credit worthiness of a person in order to approve them for a loan. For simplicity, let's say the system looks at only a hundred descriptors of the applicant and utilizes a neural network to arrive at a binary approval decision. An explanation which included all hundred features and weights of the neural network would not be very useful, so the system may instead select one of the two most important features and explain its decision with respect to just those top properties, ignoring the rest. This highly simplified explanation would not be accurate as the other 98 features all contributed to the decision and if only one or two top features were considered the decision could have been different. This is similar to how principal component analysis works for dimensionality reduction [75].

Even if the agent trying to get the explanation is not a human but another AI, the problem remains as the explanation is either inaccurate or agent-encoding specific. Trained model could be copied to another neural network, but it would likewise have a hard time explaining its decisions. Superintelligent systems not based on DNN would face similar problems as their decision complexity would be comparable to those based on neural networks and would not permit production of efficient and accurate explanations. The problem persists in the case of self-referential analysis, where a system may not understand how it is making a particular decision.

Any decision made by the AI is a function of some input data and is completely derived from the code/model of the AI, but to make it useful an explanation has to be simpler than just presentation of the complete model while retaining all relevant, to the decision, information. We can reduce this problem of explaining to the problem of lossless compression [76]. Any possible decision derived from data/model can be represented by an integer encoding such data/model combination, and it is a proven fact that some random integers can't be compressed without loss of information due to the Counting argument [77]. "The pigeonhole principle prohibits a bijection between the collection of sequences of length N and any subset of the collection of sequences of length N - 1. Therefore, it is not possible to produce a lossless algorithm that reduces the size of every possible input sequence".[2] To avoid this problem, an AI could try to produce decisions, which it knows are explainable/compressible, but that means that it is not making the best decision with regards to the given problem, doing so is suboptimal and may have safety consequences and so should be discouraged.

Overall, we should not be surprised by the challenges faced by artificial neural networks attempting to explain their decision, as they are modeled on natural neural networks of human beings and people are also "black boxes" as illustrated by a number of split brain experiments [78]. In such experiments, it is frequently demonstrated that people simply make up explanations for their actions after the decision has already been made. Even to ourselves, we rationalize our decisions after the fact and don't become aware of our decisions or how we made them until after they have been made unconsciously [79]. People are notoriously bad at explaining certain decisions such as how they recognize faces or what makes them attracted to a particular person. These reported limitations in biological agents support the idea that Unexplainability is a universal impossibility result impacting all sufficiently complex intelligences.

3.4 Incomprehensibility

A complimentary concept to Unexplainability, *Incomprehensibility* of AI addresses the capacity of people to completely understand an explanation provided by an AI or superintelligence. We define Incomprehensibility as an impossibility of completely understanding any 100% – accurate explanation for certain decisions of intelligent system, by any human.

Artificially intelligent systems are designed to make good decisions in their domains of deployment. Optimality of the decision with respect to available information and computational resources is what we expect from successful and highly intelligent systems. An explanation of the decision, in its ideal form, is a proof of correctness of the decision. (For example, a superintelligent chess playing system may explain why it sacrificed a queen by showing that it forces a checkmate in 12 moves, and by doing so proving correctness of its decision.) As decisions and their proofs can be arbitrarily complex impossibility results native to mathematical proofs become applicable to explanations. For example, explanations may be too long to be surveyed [80, 81] (Unserveyability), Unverifiable [71] or too complex to be understood [82], making the explanation incomprehensible to the user. Any AI, including black box neural networks, can in principle be converted to a large decision tree of nothing but "if" statements, but it will only make it human-readable not human-understandable.

It is generally accepted that in order to understand certain information, a person has to have a particular level of cognitive ability. This is the reason students are required to take standardized exams such as SAT, ACT, GRE, MCAT, or LCAT and score at a particular percentile in order to be admitted to their desired program of study at a selective university. Other, but similar tests are given to those wishing to join the military or government service. All such exams indirectly measure person's intelligence quotient (IQ) [83, 84] but vary significantly in how closely they correlate with standard IQ test scores (g-factor loading). The more demanding the program of study (even at the same university), the higher cognitive ability is expected from students. For example, average quantitative GRE score of students targeting mathematical sciences is 163, while average quantitative score for students interested in studying history is 148.[3] The trend may be reversed for verbal scores.

People often find themselves in situations where they have to explain concepts across a significant communication range [85], for example, to children or to people with mental challenges. The only available option in such cases is to provide a greatly oversimplified version of the explanation or a completely irrelevant but simple explanation (a lie). In fact, the situation is so common we even have a toolbox of common "explanations" for particular situations. For example, if a five-year-old asks: "Where do babies come from?" They are likely to hear something like "A seed from the daddy and an egg from the mommy join together in the mom's tummy",[4] instead of a talk about DNA, fertilization, and womb. A younger child may learn that the "stork brings them" or "they come from a baby store". Alternatively, an overly technical answer could be provided to confuse the child into thinking they got an answer, but with zero chance of them understanding such overcomplicated response. Overall, usefulness of an explanation is relative to the person who is trying to comprehend it. The same explanation may be comprehended by one person, and completely misunderstood by another.

There is a similar and perhaps larger intelligence gap between superintelligence and adult humans, making the communication range unsurmountable. It is likely easier for a scientist to explain quantum physics to a mentally challenged deaf and mute four-year-old raised by wolves than for superintelligence to explain some of its decisions to the smartest human. We are simply not smart enough to understand certain concepts. Yampolskiy proposed [82] a complexity measure which is based on the minimum intelligence necessary to understand or develop a particular algorithm, and while it takes less intelligence to just understand rather than create both requirements could be well above IQ of the smartest human. In fact, it could be very hard to explain advanced concepts to even slightly less intelligent agents.

We can predict a certain complexity barrier to human understanding for any concept for which relative IQ of above 250 would be necessary, as no person has ever tested so high. In practice, the barrier may be much lower, as average IQ is just 100, and additional complication from limited memory and limited attention spans can place even relatively easy concepts outside of human grasp. To paraphrase Wittgenstein: If superintelligence explained itself we would not understand it.

Given that research on deception by AI is well established [86], it would not be difficult for advanced Ais to provide highly believable lies to their human users. In fact, such explanations can be designed to take advantage of AI's knowledge of the human behavior [87, 88] and mental model [89, 90], and manipulate users beyond just convincing them that explanation is legitimate [91]. AI would be able to target explanations to the mental capacity of particular people, perhaps taking advantage of their inherent limitations. It would be a significant safety issue, and it is surprising to see some proposals for using human users as targets of competing (adversarial) explanations from Ais [92].

Incomprehensibility results are well-known for different members of the Chomsky hierarchy [93] with finite state automation unable to recognize context-free languages, pushdown automata unable to recognize context-sensitive languages, and linear-bounded non-deterministic Turing machines unable to recognize recursively enumerable languages. Simpler machines can't recognize languages which more complex machines can recognize.

While people are frequently equated with unrestricted Turing machines via the Church-Turing thesis [94], Blum et al. formalize human computation, in practice, as a much more restricted class [95]. However, Turing machines are not an upper limit on what is theoretically computable as described by different hypercomputation models [96]. Even if our advanced Ais (superintelligence), fail to achieve true hypercomputation capacity, for all practical purposes and compared to the human computational capabilities they would be outside of what human-equivalent agents can recognize/ comprehend.

Superintelligence would be a different type of computation, far superior to humans in practice. It is obviously not the case that superintelligent machines would actually have infinite memories or speeds, but they would appear to act as they do to unaugmented humans. For example, a machine capable of remembering one trillion items vs seven, in short-term memory of people, would appear to have infinite capacity to memorize. In algorithmic complexity theory, some algorithms become the most efficient for a particular problem type on inputs so large as to be unusable in practice, but such inputs are nonetheless finite [97]. So, just like finite state automata can't recognize recursively enumerable languages, so will people fail in practice to comprehend some explanations produced by superintelligent systems, they are simply not in the same class of automata, even if theoretically, given infinite time, they are.

Additionally, decisions made by AI could be mapped onto the space of mathematical conjectures about the natural numbers. An explanation for why a particular mathematical conjecture is true or false would be equivalent to a proof (for that conjecture). However, due to Gödel's First Incompleteness Theorem, we know that some true conjectures are unprovable. As we have mapped decision on conjectures and explanations on proofs, that means that some decisions made by AI are fundamentally unexplainable/ incomprehensible. Explanations as proofs would be subject to all the other limitations known about proofs, including Unserveyability, Unverifiability, and Undefinability [98, 99]. Finally, it is important to note that we are not saying that such decision/conjecture reduction would preserve semantics of the subject, just that it is a useful tool for showing impossibility of explainability/ comprehensibility in some cases.

3.5 Conclusions

The issues described in this chapter can be seen as a communication problem between AI encoding and sending information (sender) and person receiving and decoding information (receiver). Efficient encoding and decoding of complex symbolic information are difficult enough, as described by Shannon's Information Theory [100], but with Explainability and Comprehensibility of AI, we also have to worry about complexity of semantic communication [101]. Explainability and Comprehensibility are another conjugate pair [71, 102] in the domain of AI Safety. The more accurate is the explanation, the less comprehensible it is, and vice versa, the more comprehensible the explanation, the less accurate it is. A non-trivial explanation can't be both accurate and understandable, but it can be inaccurate and comprehensible. There is a huge difference between understanding something and almost understanding it. Incomprehensibility is a general result applicable to many domains including science, social interactions, etc., depending on the mental capacity of a participating person(s).

Human beings are finite in their abilities. For example, our short-term memory is about 7 units on average. In contrast, an AI can remember billions of items and their capacity to do so grows exponentially, while never infinite in a true mathematical sense, machine capabilities can be considered such in comparison to ours. This is true for memory, compute speed, and communication abilities. Hence the famous: *Finitum Non Capax Infiniti* (the finite cannot contain the infinite) is highly applicable to understand the Incomprehensibility of the god-like [103] superintelligent AIs.

Shown impossibility results present a number of problems for AI Safety. Evaluation and debugging of intelligent systems becomes much harder if their decisions are unexplainable/incomprehensible. In particular, in case of AI failures [104], accurate explanations are necessary to understand the problem and reduce likelihood of future accidents. If all we have is a "black box", it is impossible to understand the causes of failure and improve system safety. Additionally, if we grow accustomed to accepting AI's answers without an explanation, essentially treating it as an Oracle system, we would not be able to tell if it begins providing wrong or manipulative answers.

Notes

1. Unpredictability is not the same as Unexplainability or Incomprehensibility, see Ref. [72]. Yampolskiy, R.V., *Unpredictability of AI*. arXiv preprint arXiv:1905.13053, 2019. for details.

2. https://en.wikipedia.org/wiki/Lossless_compression
3. https://www.prepscholar.com/gre/blog/average-gre-scores/
4. https://www.babycenter.com/0_how-to-talk-to-your-child-about-sex-age-5_67112.bc

---

References

1. Yampolskiy, R.V., *Leakproofing singularity-artificial intelligence confinement problem.* Journal of Consciousness Studies JCS, 2012. **19**(1–2): p. 194–214.
2. Armstrong, S., and R.V. Yampolskiy, *Security solutions for intelligent and complex systems,* in *Security Solutions for Hyperconnectivity and the Internet of Things.* 2017, IGI Global. p. 37–88.
3. Silver, D., et al., *Mastering the game of go without human knowledge.* Nature, 2017. **550**(7676): p. 354.
4. Bostrom, N., *Superintelligence: Paths, Dangers, Strategies.* 2014: Oxford University Press.
5. Strohmeier, S., and F. Piazza, *Artificial intelligence techniques in human resource management—A conceptual exploration,* in *Intelligent Techniques in Engineering Management.* 2015, Springer. p. 149–172.
6. Walczak, S., and T. Sincich, *A comparative analysis of regression and neural networks for university admissions.* Information Sciences, 1999. **119**(1–2): p. 1–20.
7. Trippi, R.R., and E. Turban, *Neural Networks in Finance and Investing: Using Artificial Intelligence to Improve Real World Performance.* 1992: McGraw-Hill, Inc.
8. Joel, S., P.W. Eastwick, and E.J. Finkel, *Is romantic desire predictable? Machine learning applied to initial romantic attraction.* Psychological Science, 2017. **28**(10): p. 1478–1489.
9. Chekanov, K., et al., *Evaluating race and sex diversity in the world's largest companies using deep neural networks.* arXiv preprint arXiv:1707.02353, 2017.
10. Novikov, D., R.V. Yampolskiy, and L. Reznik, *Artificial intelligence approaches for intrusion detection,* in *2006 IEEE Long Island Systems, Applications and Technology Conference.* 2006. IEEE.
11. Novikov, D., R.V. Yampolskiy, and L. Reznik, *Anomaly detection based intrusion detection,* in *Third International Conference on Information Technology: New Generations (ITNG'06).* 2006. IEEE.
12. Wang, H., N. Wang, and D.-Y. Yeung, *Collaborative deep learning for recommender systems,* in *Proceedings of the 21th ACM SIGKDD International Conference on Knowledge Discovery and Data Mining.* 2015. ACM.
13. Galindo, J., and P. Tamayo, *Credit risk assessment using statistical and machine learning: Basic methodology and risk modeling applications.* Computational Economics, 2000. **15**(1–2): p. 107–143.
14. Goodman, B., and S. Flaxman, *European Union regulations on algorithmic decision-making and a "right to explanation".* AI Magazine, 2017. **38**(3): p. 50–57.
15. Doshi-Velez, F., et al., *Accountability of AI under the law: The role of explanation.* arXiv preprint arXiv:1711.01134, 2017.

16. Osoba, O.A., and W. Welser IV, *An Intelligence in Our Image: The Risks of Bias and Errors in Artificial Intelligence*. 2017: Rand Corporation.

17. Yampolskiy, R.V., Artificial Intelligence Safety and Security. 2018: Chapman and Hall/CRC.

18. Yampolskiy, R.V., *Artificial Superintelligence: A Futuristic Approach*. 2015: Chapman and Hall/CRC.

19. Yampolskiy, R.V., *What to do with the singularity paradox?*, in *Philosophy and Theory of Artificial Intelligence*. 2013, Springer. p. 397–413.

20. Pistono, F., and R.V. Yampolskiy, *Unethical research: How to create a malevolent artificial intelligence*. arXiv preprint arXiv:1605.02817, 2016.

21. Umbrello, S. and R. Yampolskiy, *Designing AI for Explainability and Verifiability: A Value Sensitive Design Approach to Avoid Artificial Stupidity in Autonomous Vehicles*. https://doi.org/10.1007/s12369-021-00790-w

22. Trazzi, M., and R.V. Yampolskiy, *Building safer AGI by introducing artificial stupidity*. arXiv preprint arXiv:1808.03644, 2018.

23. Yampolskiy, R.V., *Personal universes: A solution to the multi-agent value alignment problem*. arXiv preprint arXiv:1901.01851, 2019.

24. Behzadan, V., R.V. Yampolskiy, and A. Munir, *Emergence of addictive behaviors in reinforcement learning agents*. arXiv preprint arXiv:1811.05590, 2018.

25. Behzadan, V., A. Munir, and R.V. Yampolskiy, *A psychopathological approach to safety engineering in AI and AGI*, in *International Conference on Computer Safety, Reliability, and Security*. 2018. Springer.

26. Yampolskiy, R.V., *Predicting future AI failures from historic examples*. Foresight, 2019. **21**(1): p. 138–152.

27. Gunning, D., Explainable artificial intelligence (XAI). Defense Advanced Research Projects Agency (DARPA), 2017.

28. Ehsan, U., et al., *Automated rationale generation: A technique for explainable AI and its effects on human perceptions*. arXiv preprint arXiv:1901.03729, 2019.

29. Mittelstadt, B., C. Russell, and S. Wachter, *Explaining explanations in AI*, in *Proceedings of the Conference on Fairness, Accountability, and Transparency*. 2019. ACM.

30. Milli, S., P. Abbeel, and I. Mordatch, *Interpretable and pedagogical examples*. arXiv preprint arXiv:1711.00694, 2017.

31. Kantardzić, M.M., and A.S. Elmaghraby, *Logic-oriented model of artificial neural networks*. Information Sciences, 1997. **101**(1–2): p. 85–107.

32. Poursabzi-Sangdeh, F., et al., *Manipulating and measuring model interpretability*. arXiv preprint arXiv:1802.07810, 2018.

33. Ehsan, U., et al., *Rationalization: A neural machine translation approach to generating natural language explanations*, in *Proceedings of the 2018 AAAI/ACM Conference on AI, Ethics, and Society*. 2018. ACM.

34. Preece, A., et al., *Stakeholders in explainable AI*. arXiv preprint arXiv:1810.00184, 2018.

35. Du, M., N. Liu, and X. Hu, *Techniques for interpretable machine learning*. arXiv preprint arXiv:1808.00033, 2018.

36. Lipton, Z.C., *The doctor just won't accept that!* arXiv preprint arXiv:1711.08037, 2017.

37. Lipton, Z.C., *The mythos of model interpretability*. arXiv preprint arXiv:1606.03490, 2016.

38. Doshi-Velez, F., and B. Kim, *Towards a rigorous science of interpretable machine learning*. arXiv preprint arXiv:1702.08608, 2017.

39. Oh, S.J., et al., *Towards reverse-engineering black-box neural networks*. arXiv preprint arXiv:1711.01768, 2017.
40. Lapuschkin, S., et al., *Unmasking clever Hans predictors and assessing what machines really learn*. Nature Communications, 2019. **10**(1): p. 1096.
41. Ribeiro, M.T., S. Singh, and C. Guestrin, *Why should I trust you? Explaining the predictions of any classifier*, in *Proceedings of the 22nd ACM SIGKDD International Conference on Knowledge Discovery and Data Mining*. 2016. ACM.
42. Adadi, A., and M. Berrada, *Peeking inside the black-box: A survey on explainable artificial intelligence (XAI)*. IEEE Access, 2018. **6**: p. 52138–52160.
43. Abdul, A., et al., *Trends and trajectories for explainable, accountable and intelligible systems: An HCI research agenda*, in *Proceedings of the 2018 CHI Conference on Human Factors in Computing Systems*. 2018. ACM.
44. Guidotti, R., et al., *A survey of methods for explaining black box models*. ACM Computing Surveys (CSUR), 2018. **51**(5): p. 93.
45. Došilović, F.K., M. Brčić, and N. Hlupić, *Explainable artificial intelligence: A survey*, in *2018 41st International Convention on Information and Communication Technology, Electronics and Microelectronics (MIPRO)*. 2018. IEEE.
46. Miller, T., *Explanation in artificial intelligence: Insights from the social sciences*. Artificial Intelligence, 2018. **267**(2019): 1–38.
47. Yampolskiy, R.V., B. Klare, and A.K. Jain, *Face recognition in the virtual world: Recognizing avatar faces*, in *2012 11th International Conference on Machine Learning and Applications*. 2012. IEEE.
48. Mohamed, A.A., and R.V. Yampolskiy, *An improved LBP algorithm for avatar face recognition*, in *2011 XXIII International Symposium on Information, Communication and Automation Technologies*. 2011. IEEE.
49. Carter, S., et al., *Activation atlas*. Distill, 2019. **4**(3): p. e15.
50. Kim, B., et al., *Interpretability beyond feature attribution: Quantitative testing with concept activation vectors (TCAV)*. arXiv preprint arXiv:1711.11279, 2017.
51. Olah, C., et al., *The building blocks of interpretability*. Distill, 2018. **3**(3): p. e10.
52. Sarkar, S., et al., *Accuracy and interpretability trade-offs in machine learning applied to safer gambling*, in *CEUR Workshop Proceedings*. 2016. CEUR Workshop Proceedings.
53. Sutcliffe, G., Y. Gao, and S. Colton, *A grand challenge of theorem discovery*, in *Proceedings of the Workshop on Challenges and Novel Applications for Automated Reasoning, 19th International Conference on Automated Reasoning*. 2003.
54. Muggleton, S.H., et al., *Ultra-strong machine learning: Comprehensibility of programs learned with ILP*. Machine Learning, 2018. **107**(7): p. 1119–1140.
55. Breiman, L., *Statistical modeling: The two cultures (with comments and a rejoinder by the author)*. Statistical Science, 2001. **16**(3): p. 199–231.
56. Charlesworth, A., *Comprehending software correctness implies comprehending an intelligence-related limitation*. ACM Transactions on Computational Logic (TOCL), 2006. **7**(3): p. 590–612.
57. Charlesworth, A., *The comprehensibility theorem and the foundations of artificial intelligence*. Minds and Machines, 2014. **24**(4): p. 439–476.
58. Hernández-Orallo, J., and N. Minaya-Collado, *A formal definition of intelligence based on an intensional variant of algorithmic complexity*, in *Proceedings of International Symposium of Engineering of Intelligent Systems (EIS98)*. 1998.
59. Li, M., and P. Vitányi, *An Introduction to Kolmogorov Complexity and Its Applications*. Vol. 3. 1997: Springer.

60. Yampolskiy, R.V., *The space of possible mind designs*, in *International Conference on Artificial General Intelligence*. 2015. Springer.

61. Weinberger, D., *Our Machines Now Have Knowledge We'll Never Understand*, in *Wired*. 2017. https://www.wired.com/story/our-machines-now-have-knowledge-well-never-understand.

62. Gödel, K., *On Formally Undecidable Propositions of Principia Mathematica and Related Systems*. 1992: Courier Corporation.

63. Heisenberg, W., *Über den anschaulichen Inhalt der quantentheoretischen Kinematik und Mechanik*, in *Original Scientific Papers Wissenschaftliche Originalarbeiten*. 1985, Springer. p. 478–504.

64. Fisher, M., N. Lynch, and M. Peterson, *Impossibility of distributed consensus with one faulty process*. Journal of ACM, 1985. **32**(2): p. 374–382.

65. Grossman, S.J., and J.E. Stiglitz, *On the impossibility of informationally efficient markets*. The American Economic Review, 1980. **70**(3): p. 393–408.

66. Kleinberg, J.M., *An impossibility theorem for clustering*, in *Advances in Neural Information Processing Systems*. 2003. MIT Press.

67. Strawson, G., *The impossibility of moral responsibility*. Philosophical Studies, 1994. **75**(1): p. 5–24.

68. Bazerman, M.H., K.P. Morgan, and G.F. Loewenstein, *The impossibility of auditor independence*. Sloan Management Review, 1997. **38**: p. 89–94.

69. List, C., and P. Pettit, *Aggregating sets of judgments: An impossibility result*. Economics & Philosophy, 2002. **18**(1): p. 89–110.

70. Dufour, J.-M., *Some impossibility theorems in econometrics with applications to structural and dynamic models*. Econometrica: Journal of the Econometric Society, 1997. **65**(6): p. 1365–1387.

71. Yampolskiy, R.V., *What are the ultimate limits to computational techniques: Verifier theory and unverifiability*. Physica Scripta, 2017. **92**(9): p. 093001.

72. Yampolskiy, R.V., *Unpredictability of AI*. arXiv preprint arXiv:1905.13053, 2019.

73. Armstrong, S., and S. Mindermann, *Impossibility of deducing preferences and rationality from human policy*. arXiv preprint arXiv:1712.05812, 2017.

74. Eckersley, P., *Impossibility and Uncertainty Theorems in AI Value Alignment*. arXiv preprint: 1901.00064

75. Brinton, C., A framework for explanation of machine learning decisions, in IJCAI-17 Workshop on Explainable AI (XAI). 2017.

76. Hutter, M., *The Human Knowledge Compression Prize*. 2006. http://prize.hutter1.net.

77. *Compression of Random Data (WEB, Gilbert and Others)*, in *FAQs*. Retrieved June 16, 2019. http://www.faqs.org/faqs/compression-faq/part1/section-8.html.

78. Gazzaniga, M.S., *Tales from Both Sides of the Brain: A Life in Neuroscience*. 2015: Ecco/HarperCollins Publishers.

79. Shanks, D.R., *Complex choices better made unconsciously?* Science, 2006. **313**(5788): p. 760–761.

80. Bassler, O.B., *The surveyability of mathematical proof: A historical perspective*. Synthese, 2006. **148**(1): p. 99–133.

81. Coleman, E., *The surveyability of long proofs*. Foundations of Science, 2009. **14**(1–2): p. 27–43.

82. Yampolskiy, R.V., *Efficiency theory: A unifying theory for information, computation and intelligence*. Journal of Discrete Mathematical Sciences & Cryptography, 2013. **16**(4–5): p. 259–277.

83. Abramov, P.S., and R.V. Yampolskiy, *Automatic IQ estimation using stylometric methods*, in *Handbook of Research on Learning in the Age of Transhumanism*. 2019, IGI Global. p. 32–45.

84. Hendrix, A., and R. Yampolskiy, *Automated IQ Estimation from Writing Samples*, in *MAICS*. 2017.

85. Hollingworth, L.S., *Children Above 180 IQ Stanford-Binet: Origin and Development*. 2015: World Book Company.

86. Castelfranchi, C., *Artificial liars: why computers will (necessarily) deceive us and each other*. Ethics and Information Technology, 2000. **2**(2): p. 113–119.

87. Yampolskiy, R.V., and V. Govindaraju, *Use of behavioral biometrics in intrusion detection and online gaming*, in *Biometric Technology for Human Identification III*. 2006, International Society for Optics and Photonics.

88. Yampolskiy, R.V., *User authentication via behavior based passwords*, in *2007 IEEE Long Island Systems, Applications and Technology Conference*. 2007. IEEE.

89. Yampolskiy, R.V., and J. Fox, *Artificial general intelligence and the human mental model*, in Singularity Hypotheses. 2012, Springer. p. 129–145.

90. Yampolskiy, R.V., *Behavioral modeling: an overview*. American Journal of Applied Sciences, 2008. **5**(5): p. 496–503.

91. Slonim, N., *Project debater*, in *Computational Models of Argument: Proceedings of COMMA 2018*. 2018. 305: p. 4.

92. Irving, G., P. Christiano, and D. Amodei, *AI safety via debate*. arXiv preprint arXiv:1805.00899, 2018.

93. Chomsky, N., *Three models for the description of language*. IRE Transactions on Information Theory, 1956. **2**(3): p. 113–124.

94. Yampolskiy, R., *The singularity may be near*. Information, 2018. **9**(8): p. 190.

95. Blum, M., and S. Vempala, *The complexity of human computation: A concrete model with an application to passwords*. arXiv preprint arXiv:1707.01204, 2017.

96. Ord, T., *Hypercomputation: Computing more than the Turing machine*. arXiv preprint math/0209332, 2002.

97. Lipton, R.J., and K.W. Regan, *David Johnson: Galactic algorithms*, in *People, Problems, and Proofs*. 2013, Springer. p. 109–112.

98. Tarski, A., *Der wahrheitsbegriff in den formalisierten sprachen*. Studia Philosophica, 1936. **1**: p. 261–405.

99. Tarski, A., *The concept of truth in formalized languages*. Logic, Semantics, Metamathematics, 1956. **2**: p. 152–278.

100. Shannon, C.E., *A mathematical theory of communication*. Bell System Technical Journal, 1948. **27**(3): p. 379–423.

101. Wooldridge, M., *Semantic issues in the verification of agent communication languages*. Autonomous Agents and Multi-Agent Systems, 2000. **3**(1): p. 9–31.

102. Calude, C.S., E. Calude, and S. Marcus, *Passages of proof. December 2001 workshop truths and proofs*, in *Annual Conference of the Australasian Association of Philosophy* (New Zealand Division), Auckland. 2001.

103. Rahner, K., *Thomas Aquinas on the incomprehensibility of God*. The Journal of Religion, 1978. **58**: p. S107–S125.

104. Yampolskiy, R.V., and M. Spellchecker, *Artificial intelligence safety and cybersecurity: A timeline of AI failures*. arXiv preprint arXiv:1610.07997, 2016.

4

Unverifiability*

4.1 On Observers and Verifiers

The concept of an "observer" shows up in contexts as diverse as physics (particularly quantum and relativity), biophysics, neuroscience, cognitive science, artificial intelligence (AI), philosophy of consciousness, and cosmology [1], but what is an equivalent idea in mathematics? We believe it is the notion of the proof verifier. Consequently, the majority of open questions recently raised [1] by the Foundational Questions Institute related to the physics of the observer could be asked about proof verifiers. In particular, the mathematical community may be interested in studying different types of proof verifiers (people, programs, oracles, communities, superintelligences, etc.) as mathematical objects, ways they can be formalized, their power and limitations (particularly in human mathematicians), minimum and maximum complexity, as well as self-verification and self-reference in verifiers.

Proof Theory has been developed to study proofs as formal mathematical objects consisting of axioms from which, by rules of inference, one can arrive at theorems [2]. However, the indispensable concept of the verifier has been conspicuously absent from the discussion, particularly with regard to its formalization and practical manifestation. A *verifier* in the context of mathematics is an agent capable of checking a given proof, step-by-step, starting from axioms to make sure that all intermediate deductions are indeed warranted, that the final conclusion follows, and consequently, that the claimed theorem is indeed true. In this work, we present an overview of different types of verifiers currently relied on by the mathematical community, as well as a few novel types of verifiers which we suggest be added to the repertoire of mathematicians at least as theoretical tools of *Verifier Theory*. Our general analysis should be equally applicable to different types of proofs (induction, contradiction, exhaustion, enumeration, refinement, nonconstructive, probabilistic, holographic, experiment, picture, etc.) and to computer software.

* Used with permission of The Royal Swedish Academy of Sciences, from What are the ultimate limits to computational techniques: verifier theory and unverifiability, Roman V. Yampolskiy, Physica Scripta, volume 92, number 9, copyright © 2017; Permission conveyed through Copyright Clearence Center, Inc.

DOI: 10.1201/9781003440260-4

4.2 Historical Perspective

The field of mathematics progresses by proving theorems, which in turn serve as building blocks for future proofs of yet more interesting and useful theorems. To avoid introduction of costly errors in the form of incorrect theorems, proofs typically undergo an examination process, usually as a part of a peer review. Traditionally, human mathematicians have been employed as proof verifiers; however, history is full of examples of undetected errors and important omissions even in the most widely examined proofs [3–7]. It has been estimated that at least a third of all mathematical publications contain errors [8]. To avoid errors and make the job of human verifiers as easy as possible "a single step in a deduction has been required … [t]o be simple enough, broadly speaking, to be apprehended as correct by a human being in a single intellectual act. No doubt this custom originated in the desire that each single step of a deduction should be indubitable, even though the deduction as a whole may consist of a long chain of such steps" [9].

Despite such stringent requirements, it has long been realized that a single human verifier is not reliable enough to ascertain validity of a proof with a sufficient degree of reliability. In fact, it is known that humans are subject to hundreds of well-known "bugs",[1] and probably many more unknown ones. To reduce the number of potential mistakes and to increase our confidence in the validity of a proof, a number of independent human mathematicians should examine an important mathematical claim. As Calude puts it "A theorem is a statement which could be checked individually by a mathematician and confirmed also individually by at least two or three other mathematicians, each of them working independently. But already we can observe the weakness of the criterion: how many mathematicians are to check individually and independently the status of [a conjecture] to give it a status of a theorem?" [4].

Clearly, the greater the number of independent verifiers, the higher is our confidence in the validity of a theorem. We can say that "a theorem is validated if it has been accepted by a general agreement of the mathematical community" [4]. Krantz agrees and says: "it is the mathematics profession, taken as a whole, that decides what is correct and valid, and also what is useful and is interesting and has value" [10]. Wittgenstein expresses similar views, as quoted in [11]: "who validates the 'mathematical knowledge'? … the acceptability ultimately comes from the collective opinion of the social group of people practising mathematics". So, for many practitioners of mathematics, proof verification is a social and democratic process in which "[a]fter enough internalization, enough transformation, enough generalization, enough use, and enough connection, the mathematical community eventually decides that the central concepts in the original theorem, now perhaps greatly changed, have an ultimate stability.

If the various proofs feel right and the results are examined from enough angles, then the truth of the theorem is eventually considered to be established" [12].

While the mathematical community as a whole constitutes a powerful proof verifier, a desire for ever greater accuracy has led researchers to develop mechanized verification systems capable of handling formal proofs of great length. The prototype for such verifiers has its roots in *formal systems* [13] proposed by David Hilbert and which "contain an algorithm that mechanically checks the validity of all proofs that can be formulated in the system. The formal system consists of an alphabet of symbols in which all statements can be written; a grammar that specifies how the symbols are to be combined; a set of axioms, or principles accepted without proof; and rules of inference for deriving theorems from the axioms" [14]. However, there is a tradeoff when one switches from using human verifiers to utilizing automated ones, namely: "People are usually not very good in checking formal correctness of proofs, but they are quite good at detecting potential weaknesses or flaws in proofs" [15]. "'Artificial' mathematicians are far less ingenious and subtle than human mathematicians, but they surpass their human counterparts by being infinitely more patient and diligent" [4]. In other words, while automated verifiers are excellent at spotting incorrect deductions, they are much worse than humans at seeing the "big picture" outlined in the proof.

Additionally, to maintain a consistent standard of verification for all accepted theorems, a significant effort would need to be applied to reexamine already-accepted proofs. "to do so would certainly entail going back and rewriting from scratch all old mathematical papers whose results we depend on. It is also quite hard to come up with good technical choices for formal definitions that will be valid in the variety of ways that mathematicians want to use them and that will anticipate future extensions of mathematics. ... [M]uch of our time would be spent with international standards commissions to establish uniform definitions and resolve huge controversies" [15].

Such criticism of automated verifiers is not new and has been expressed in the past, particularly from a human-centric point of view: "No matter how precise the rules (logical and physical) are, we need human consciousness to apply the rules and to understand them and their consequences. Mathematics is a human activity" [4]. Additionally, "[m]echanical proof-checkers have indeed been developed, though their use is currently limited by the need or the proof to be written in precisely the right logical formalism" [16].

Despite such criticism, there is also a lot of hope in terms of what automated verification can offer mathematics. "[M]athematical knowledge is far too vast to be understood by one person, moreover, it has been estimated that the total amount of published mathematics doubles every ten to fifteen years... Perhaps computers can also help us to navigate, abstract and, hence, understand ... proofs. Realising this dream of: computer access to a world repository of mathematical knowledge; visualising and understanding this knowledge; reusing and combining it to discover new knowledge" [17].

4.3 Classification of Verifiers

A certain connection exists between the concept of observer in physics and a verifier in mathematics/science. Both must be instantiated in the physical world as either hardware or software to perform their function, but other than that, we currently have a very limited understanding of the types and properties associated with such agents. As the first step, we propose a simple classification system for verifiers, sorting them with respect to domain of application, type of implementation, and general properties. With respect to their domain, we see verifiers as necessary for checking mathematical proofs, scientific theories, software correctness, intelligent behavior safety, and consistency and properties of algorithms. Some examples:

- **Software Verifier** – evaluates correctness of a program. Via the Curry-Harvard Correspondence [18], proof verification and program verification are equivalent and software verification is a special case of theorem verification restricted to computational logic [19]. A compiler or interpreter can be seen as a program syntax verifier among other things.

- **AI-Verifier** – is a particular type of Software Verifier capable of verifying the behavior of intelligent systems in novel environments unknown at the time of design [20, 21]. Yampolskiy presents verification of self-improving software [22, 23] as a particular challenge to the AI community: "Ideally every generation of self-improving system should be able to produce a verifiable proof of its safety for external examination" [24]. Consequently, research linking functional specification to physical states is of great interest. "This type of theory would allow use of formal tools to anticipate and control behaviors of systems that approximate rational agents, alternate designs such as satisficing agents, and systems that cannot be easily described in the standard agent formalism (powerful prediction systems, theorem-provers, limited-purpose science or engineering systems, etc.). It may also be that such a theory could allow rigorously demonstrating that systems are constrained from taking certain kinds of actions or performing certain kinds of reasoning" [20].

- **Scientific Theory Verifier** – examines the output of computer simulations of scientific theories. A scientific theory cannot be considered fully accepted until it can be expressed as an algorithm and simulated on a computer. It should produce observations consistent with measurements obtained in the real world, perhaps adjusting for the relativity of time scale between simulation and the real world. In other words, an unsimulatable hypothesis should be considered significantly weaker than a simulatable one. It is possible that the theory cannot be simulated due to limits in our current computational capacity, hardware design, or capability of programmers and that it will become simulatable in the future, but until such time, it should have a tentative status. A Scientific Theory Verifier could be seen as a formalized equivalent of a peer-reviewer in science.

- **Non-Deterministic Polynomial (NP) Solution Verifier** – is an algorithm which can quickly (in polynomial time) check a certificate (also called witness) representing a solution, which can then be used to determine if a computation produces a "yes" or "no" answer. In fact, one of the requirements of NP-Completeness states that a problem is in that class if there exists a verifier for the problem. An NP-Completeness Verifier would check a reduction of a novel problem to an already known problem in the NP class to determine if it is of equal or lesser complexity. Analogously, we can postulate an AI-Completeness Verifier capable of checking if a problem is reducible to an instance of the Turing test [25–27].

With respect to type, verifiers could be people (or groups of people), software, hypothetical agents such as oracles, or artificial (super)intelligent entities. For example:

- **Human Mathematician** – historically the default verifier for most mathematical proofs. Individual mathematicians have been recruited to examine mathematical reasoning since the inception of the field. Recent developments in computer-generated proofs appear to be beyond the capacity of human verifiers due to the size of such proofs.

- **Mathematical Community** – a collective of mathematicians taken as a whole used to examine and evaluate claimed proofs, while at the same time removing any outlier opinions of individual mathematicians. It is well known that the wisdom of crowds can outperform individual experts [28, 29].

- **Mechanical Verifier** (automated proof checker) – automated software and hardware verifiers such as computer programs have been developed to assist in verification of formal proofs [30]. "The proof checker verifies that each inference step in the proof is a valid instance of one of the axioms and inference rules specified as part of the safety policy" [31]. They are believed to be more accurate than human mathematicians and are capable of verifying much longer proofs, which may not be surveyable [32–35] or too complex (not comprehensible [36]) for human mathematicians.

- **Hybrid Verifier** – a combination of other types of verifiers, most typically a human mathematician assisted by a mechanical verifier.
- **Oracle Verifier** – a verifier with access to an Oracle Turing Machine. Particular types would include a Halting Verifier (a hypothetical verifier not subject to the halting problem), a Gödel Verifier (not subject to incompleteness limits), and an undecidable proof verifier. All such verification would be done in constant time.
- **(Super)Intelligent Verifier** – a verifier capable of checking all decidable proofs, particularly those constructed by superintelligent AI.

Some verifiers also have non-trivial mathematical properties, which include: Ability to self-verify, probabilistic proof checking, relative correctness, designated nature, meta-verification capacity, honest or dishonest behavior, and axiomatic acceptance. For example:

- **Axiomatically Correct Verifier** – a type of authority-based verifier, which decides the truth of a theorem without a need to disclose its process. This is a verifier whose correctness is accepted without justification, much like an axiom is accepted by the math community.
- **Designated Verifier** – for some proofs of knowledge, it is important that only the verifier nominated by the confirmer can get any confirmation of the correctness of the proof [37].
- **Honest (Trusted) Verifier** – "does not try to extract any secret from the prover by deviating from the proof protocol. … **Untrusted-Verifier** does not need to assume that the verifier is honest" [38].
- **Probabilistic Verifier** – a verifier, which by examining an ever-greater number of parts of a proof, arrives at a probabilistic measure of the correctness of the theorem. Such verifiers are a part of zero knowledge-based protocols.
- **Relative Verifier** – a verifier with respect to which a particular theorem has been shown to be correct, which doesn't guarantee that it would be confirmed by other verifiers.
- **Gradual Verifier** – a verifier which determines a percentage of statements that are already guaranteed to be safe [39], permitting a gradual verification process to take place.
- **Meta-Verifier** – a hypothetical verifier capable of checking the correctness of other verifiers.
- **Self-Verifier** – an agent which is capable of verifying its own accuracy [40]. A frequently suggested approach to avoid an infinite regress of verifiers, a self-verifying verifier could contain an error causing it to erroneously claim its own correctness [41] and is also subject to limitations imposed by Gödel's Incompleteness theorem [42] and other similar self-referential constraints [21].

4.4 Unverifiability

Unverifiability, an idea frequently discussed in philosophy [43–45], has been implicitly present in mathematics since the early days of the field. In this section, we survey literature that deals with the limits of proof verifiability caused by infinite regress of verifiers and provides analysis of the concept of unverifiability. We believe that such explicit discussion will be useful to researchers interested in being able to cite this important idea, which so far has been relegated to the status of mathematical folklore [46] and only alluded to in the literature, despite being a more general result than incompleteness [42, 47].

Unverifiability is a fundamental limitation on verification of mathematical proofs, computer software, behavior of intelligent agents, and all formal systems. It is an ultimate limit to our ability to know certain information and is similar to other major "impossibilities" to acquiring knowledge in our universe such as uncertainty [48], randomness [49, 50], incompleteness [42, 47], undecidability [51], undefinability [52], unprovability [53], incompressibility [14], noncomputability [54], and relativity [55]. Many paths can lead us to arrive at the concept of unverifiability, but in this chapter, we concentrate specifically on the infinite regress of verifiers.

For example, Calude et al. state: "what if the 'agent' human or computer checking a proof for correctness makes a mistake (agents are fallible)? Obviously, another agent has to check that the agent doing the checking did not make any mistakes. Some other agent will need to check that agent and so on. Eventually one runs out of agents who could check the proof and, in principle, they could all have made a mistake!" [56]. Later, Calude and Muller emphasize: "one cannot prove the correctness of the formal prover itself" [57]. Similarly, MacKenzie observes: "Indeed, if one was to apply the formal, mechanical notion of proof entirely stringently, might not the software of the automated theorem prover itself have to be verified formally? ... The formal, mechanized notion of proof thus prompted a modern day version of Juvenal's ancient question, *quis custodiet ipsos custodes,* who will guard the guards themselves?" [58]. Others have expressed similar sentiments [11].

Our trust in a formal proof is only as strong as our trust in the verifier used to check the proof; as the verifier itself needs to be verified, and so on *ad infinitum,* we are never given a 100% guarantee of correctness, only asymptotically increasing probability of correctness. Worse yet, at the end of the chain of verifiers, there is typically a single human, whose internal mechanism is simply not verifiable with our current technology and possibly not verifiable in principle. Additionally, problems other than infinite regress of verifiers may significantly reduce our ability to verify proofs. Such obstacles include splicing and skipping [59], hidden lemmas [60], exponential size proofs [61] (with recent publication of a 200 terabyte computer proof [62] being only a current record which is unlikely to stand for long), impenetrable proofs [63], hardware failures [64, 65], Rice's theorem [66], and Gödel's Incompleteness theorem [42].

After the advent of probabilistic proofs by Rabin [67], "[s]ome have argued that there is no essential difference between such probabilistic proofs and the deterministic proofs of standard mathematical practice. Both are convincing arguments. Both are to be believed with a certain probability of error. In fact, many deterministic proofs, it is claimed, have a higher probability of error" [68]. "... the authenticity of a mathematical proof is not absolute, but only probabilistic. ... Proofs cannot be too long, else their probabilities go down and they baffle the checking process. To put it in another way: all really deep theorems are false (or at best unproved or unprovable). All true theorems are trivial" [3]. "A derivation of a theorem or a verification of a proof has only probabilistic validity. It makes no difference whether the instrument of derivation or verification is man or a machine. The probabilities may vary, but are roughly of the same order of magnitude" [3]. All proofs have a certain level of "proofness" [69], which can be made arbitrarily deep via expending necessary verification resources, but "in no domain of mathematics is the notion of provability a perfect substitute for the notion of truth [70]". To conclude, we reiterate Knuth's famous warning: "Beware of bugs in the above code: I have only proved it correct, not tried it".

4.5 Unverifiability of Software

Unverifiability has important consequences not just for mathematicians and philosophers of knowledge; more recently it has become an important issue in software and hardware verification, which can be seen as special cases of proof verification [18, 19]. Just like a large portion of published mathematical proofs, software is known to contain massive amounts of bugs [71], perhaps as many as fifty per thousand lines of code,[2] but maybe as few as 2.3 [72]. Similarly, just like with mathematical proofs, the issue of infinite regress of verifiers is making software only probabilistically verifiable. For example, Fetzer writes: "There are no special difficulties so long as [higher-level machines'] intended interpretations are abstract machines. When their intended interpretations are target machines, then we encounter the problem of determining the reliability of the verifying programs themselves ("How do we verify the verifiers?"), which invites a regress of relative verifications" [73].

This notion of unverifiability of software has been a part of the field since its early days. Smith writes: "For fundamental reasons - reasons that anyone can understand - there are inherent limitations to what can be proven about computers and computer programs. ... Just because a program is "proven correct" ..., you cannot be sure that it will do what you intend" [74]. Rodd agrees and says: "Indeed, although it is now almost trite to say it, since the comprehensive testing of software is impossible, only very vague estimates of any program's reliability seem ever to be possible" [75]. Currently, most software is released without any attempt to formally verify it in the first place.

4.5.1 Unverifiability of Artificial Intelligence

One particular type of software, known as AI (and even more so superintelligence), differs from other programs by its ability to learn new behaviors, adjust its performance, and act semi-autonomously in novel situations. Given the potential impact from intelligent software, it is not surprising that the ability to verify future intelligent behavior is one of the grand challenges of modern AI research [24, 76–78].

It has been observed that science frequently discovers so-called "conjugate (complementary) pairs", "a couple of requirements, each of them being satisfied only at the expense of the other …. Famous prototypes of conjugate pairs are (position, momentum) discovered by W. Heisenberg in quantum mechanics and (consistency, completeness) discovered by K. Gödel in logic. But similar warnings come from other directions. According to Einstein …, 'in so far as the propositions of mathematics are certain, they do not refer to reality, and in so far as they refer to reality, they are not certain', hence (certainty, reality) is a conjugate pair" [56]. Similarly, in proofs we are "[t]aking rigour as something that can be acquired only at the expense of meaning and conversely, taking meaning as something that can be obtained only at the expense of rigour" [56]. With respect to intelligent agents, we can propose an additional conjugate pair – (capability, control). The more generally intelligent and capable an entity is, the less likely it is to be predictable, controllable, or verifiable.

It is becoming obvious that just as we can only have probabilistic confidence in correctness of mathematical proofs and software implementations, our ability to verify intelligent agents is at best limited. As Klein puts it: "if you really want to build a system that can have truly unexpected behaviour, then by definition you cannot verify that it is safe, because you just don't know what it will do".[3] Muehlhauser writes: "The same reasoning applies to [Artificial General Intelligence] AGI 'friendliness.' Even if we discover (apparent) solutions to known open problems in Friendly AI research, this does not mean that we can ever build an AGI that is 'provably friendly' in the strongest sense, because … we can never be 100% certain that there are no errors in our formal reasoning. … Thus, the approaches sometimes called 'provable security,' 'provable safety,' and 'provable friendliness' should not be misunderstood as offering 100% guarantees of security, safety, and friendliness".[4] Jilk, writing on limits to verification and validation in AI, points out that "language of certainty" is unwarranted in reference to agentic behavior [79]. He also states: "there cannot be a general automated procedure for verifying that an agent absolutely conforms to any determinate set of rules of action".

Seshia et al., describing some of the challenges of creating Verified AI, note: "It may be impossible even to precisely define the interface between the system and environment (i.e., to identify the variables/features of the environment that must be modeled), let alone to model all possible behaviors of the environment. Even if the interface is known, non-deterministic or over-approximate modeling is likely to produce too many spurious bug reports, rendering the verification process useless in practice. ... [T]he complexity and heterogeneity of AI-based systems means that, in general, many decision problems underlying formal verification are likely to be undecidable. ... To overcome this obstacle posed by computational complexity, one must ... settle for incomplete or unsound formal verification methods" [78].

These results are not surprising. AI cannot be verified because AI itself can serve as a verifier which we already showed cannot be verified because of infinite regress problem and general unverifiability. By spending increasing computational resources, the best we can hope for is an increased statistical probability that our mathematical proofs and software/AI are error-free, but we should never forget that a 100% accurate verification is not possible, even in theory, and act accordingly. AI, and even more so artificial Superintelligence, is unverifiable and so potentially unsafe [80–85].

4.6 Conclusions and Future Work

Our preliminary work suggests that "verifier" be investigated as a new mathematical object of interest for future study and opens the door for an improved understanding of the topic. For example, an artificially intelligent verifier could be used to re-check all previously published mathematical proofs, greatly increasing the correctness of all proofs. Problems such as infinite regress of verifiers may be unsolvable, but methods such as probabilistic verification should be capable of giving us as much assurance as we are willing to pay for. Any progress in the proposed "verifier theory" will have additional benefits beyond its contribution to mathematics by making it possible to design safer advanced AI, a topic that is predicted to become one of the greatest problems in science in the upcoming decades [86, 87]. A verifier is a hidden component of any proof; we can improve our capacity to verify by explicitly describing the required verification agent.

It would be valuable to learn what types of physical or informational systems can act as verifiers and what their essential properties are. We should explore how selection of the type of the verifier influences mathematics as a field and specifically what categories of theorems we can prove and which we cannot prove with respect to different verifiers. Are there still undiscovered types of mathematical verifiers? Does a group of verifiers have greater power than the sum of its component modules? How can verifiers perform best while operating with limited computational resources? What is the formal relationship between the set of all verifiers and the set of all observers? Can a verifier be hacked and can the attack be contained in the proof it is examining? Can all these questions be reduced to a broader question on the nature of different possible types of intelligence [88]?

Notes

1. https://en.wikipedia.org/wiki/List_of_cognitive_biases
2. https://www.theengineer.co.uk/content/news/verification-system-aims-to-guarantee-software-function
3. https://intelligence.org/2014/02/11/gerwin-klein-on-formal-methods
4. https://intelligence.org/2013/10/03/proofs/

References

1. Tegmark, M., and A. Aguirre, *Physics of the Observer – An International Request for Proposals for Research and Outreach Projects*. 2015: https://s3.amazonaws.com/fqxi.data/data/documents/2016-Request-for-Proposals.pdf.
2. Buss, S.R., *An introduction to proof theory*, in *Handbook of Proof Theory*. 1998. **137**: p. 1–78. Elsevier.
3. Davis, P.J., *Fidelity in mathematical discourse: Is one and one really two?* American Mathematical Monthly, 1972. **79**(3): p. 252–263.
4. Calude, C.S., E. Calude, and S. Marcus, *Passages of Proof*. 2002: University of Auckland. Massey University. Romanian Academy. CDMTCS-180, New Zealand, Romania.
5. Detlefsen, M., and M. Luker, *The four-color theorem and mathematical proof*. The Journal of Philosophy, 1980. **77**(12): p. 803–820.
6. Kornai, A., *Bounding the impact of AGI*. Journal of Experimental & Theoretical Artificial Intelligence, 2014. **26**(3): p. 417–438.
7. Hardy, G.H., *Mathematical proof*. Mind, 1929. **38**(149): p. 1–25.
8. Lamport, L., *How to write a proof*. The American Mathematical Monthly, 1995. **102**(7): p. 600–608.
9. Mackenzie, D., *The automation of proof: A historical and sociological exploration*. IEEE Annals of the History of Computing, 1995. **17**(3): p. 7–29.
10. Krantz, S.G., *The Proof Is in the Pudding. A Look at the Changing Nature of Mathematical Proof*. 2007: Springer.
11. Calude, C.S., and S. Marcus, *Mathematical proofs at a crossroad?*, in *Theory Is Forever*. 2004, Springer. p. 15–28.
12. Millo, R.A.D., R.J. Lipton, and A.J. Perlis, *Social processes and proofs of theorems and programs*. Communications of the ACM, 1979. **22**(5): p. 271–280.

13. Omodeo, E.G., and J.T. Schwartz, *A 'theory' mechanism for a proof-verifier based on first-order set theory*, in *Computational Logic: Logic Programming and Beyond*. 2002, Springer. p. 214–230.

14. Chaitin, G.J., *Randomness and mathematical proof*. Scientific American, 1975. **232**(5): p. 47–52.

15. Thurston, W.P., *On proof and progress in mathematics*. Bulletin of the American Mathematical Society, 1994. **30**(2): p. 161–177.

16. MacKenzie, D., *Slaying the Kraken: The sociohistory of a mathematical proof*. Social Studies of Science, 1999. **29**(1): p. 7–60.

17. Kohlhase, M., *OMDoc: An Open Markup Format for Mathematical Documents*. Lecture Notes in Artificial Intelligence, 2006. 4180.

18. Sørensen, M.H., and P. Urzyczyn, Lectures on the Curry-Howard Isomorphism. Vol. 149. 2006: Elsevier.

19. Moore, J.S., *A mechanized program verifier*, in *Verified Software: Theories, Tools, Experiments*. 2008, Springer. p. 268–276.

20. Russell, S., et al., *Research Priorities for Robust and Beneficial Artificial Intelligence*, in *Future of Life Institute*. Retrieved January 23, 2015: http://futureoflife.org/static/data/documents/research_priorities.pdf.

21. Yudkowsky, E., and M. Herreshoff, *Tiling Agents for Self-modifying AI, and the Löbian Obstacle*, in *MIRI Technical Report*. 2013: http://intelligence.org/files/TilingAgentsDraft.pdf.

22. Yampolskiy, R.V., *On the limits of recursively self-improving AGI*, in *The Eighth Conference on Artificial General Intelligence*. July 22–25, 2015. Berlin, Germany.

23. Yampolskiy, R.V., *Analysis of types of self-improving software*, in *The Eighth Conference on Artificial General Intelligence*. July 22–25, 2015. Berlin, Germany.

24. Yampolskiy, R.V., *Artificial intelligence safety engineering: Why machine ethics is a wrong approach*, in *Philosophy and Theory of Artificial Intelligence*. 2013, Springer. p. 389–396.

25. Yampolskiy, R.V., *Turing test as a defining feature of AI-completeness*, in *Artificial Intelligence, Evolutionary Computation and Metaheuristics – In the Footsteps of Alan Turing*, X.-S. Yang, Editors. 2013, Springer. p. 3–17.

26. Yampolskiy, R.V., *AI-complete, AI-hard, or AI-easy – classification of problems in AI*, in *The 23rd Midwest Artificial Intelligence and Cognitive Science Conference*. April 21–22, 2012. Cincinnati, OH, USA.

27. Yampolskiy, R.V., *AI-complete CAPTCHAs as zero knowledge proofs of access to an artificially intelligent system*. ISRN Artificial Intelligence, 2011. **2012**: p. 271878.

28. Yampolskiy, R.V., L. Ashby, and L. Hassan, *Wisdom of artificial crowds—a meta-heuristic algorithm for optimization*. Journal of Intelligent Learning Systems and Applications, 2012. **4**(2): p. 98–107.

29. Yampolskiy, R.V., and E.L.B. Ahmed, *Wisdom of artificial crowds algorithm for solving NP-hard problems*. International Journal of Bio-Inspired Computation (IJBIC). **3**(6): p. 358–369.

30. Wiedijk, F., *The Seventeen Provers of the World: Foreword by Dana S. Scott*. Vol. 3600. 2006: Springer Science & Business Media.

31. Necula, G.C., and P. Lee, Safe, untrusted agents using proof-carrying code, in *Mobile Agents and Security*. 1998, Springer. p. 61–91.

32. Mülhölzer, F., *A mathematical proof must be surveyable. What Wittgenstein meant by this and what it implies*. Grazer Philosophische Studien, 2005. **71**: p. 57–86.

33. Coleman, E., *The surveyability of long proofs*. Foundations of Science, 2009. **14**(1–2): p. 27–43.
34. Tymoczko, T., *Computers, proofs and mathematicians: A philosophical investigation of the four-color proof*. Mathematics Magazine, 1980. **53**(3): p. 131–138.
35. Norwood, F., *Long proofs*. The American Mathematical Monthly, 1982. **89**(2): p. 110–112.
36. Yampolskiy, R.V., *Efficiency theory: A unifying theory for information, computation and intelligence*. Journal of Discrete Mathematical Sciences & Cryptography, 2013. **16**(4–5): p. 259–277.
37. Jakobsson, M., K. Sako, and R. Impagliazzo, *Designated verifier proofs and their applications*, in *Advances in Cryptology—EUROCRYPT'96*. 1996, Springer.
38. Peng, K., *Efficient proof of bid validity with untrusted verifier in homomorphic e-auction*. IET Information Security, 2013. **7**(1): p. 11–21.
39. Arlt, S., et al., *The gradual verifier*, in *NASA Formal Methods*. 2014, Springer.
40. Kondrat'ev, D.A., and A.V. Promskii, *Towards the verified verifier. Theory and practice*. Modelirovanie i Analiz Informatsionnykh Sistem [Modeling and Analysis of Information Systems], 2014. **21**(6): p. 71–82.
41. Appel, A.W., *Foundational proof-carrying code*, in *16th Annual IEEE Symposium on Logic in Computer Science*. 2001. p. 247–256.
42. Gödel, K., S.C. Kleene, and J.B. Rosser, *On Undecidable Propositions of Formal Mathematical Systems*. 1934: Institute for Advanced Study Princeton, NJ.
43. Feuer, L.S., *The paradox of verifiability*. Philosophy and Phenomenological Research, 1951. **12**(1): p. 24–41.
44. Black, M., *The principle of verifiability*. Analysis, 1934. **2**(1–2): p. 1–6.
45. Hoy, R.C., *The unverifiability of unverifiability*. Philosophy and Phenomenological Research, 1973. **33**(3): p. 393–398.
46. Wilder, R.L., *The nature of mathematical proof*. The American Mathematical Monthly, 1944. **51**(6): p. 309–323.
47. Calude, C.S., and S. Rudeanu, *Proving as a computable procedure*. Fundamenta Informaticae, 2005. **64**(1–4): p. 43–52.
48. Heisenberg, W., *Über den anschaulichen Inhalt der quantentheoretischen Kinematik und Mechanik*. Zeitschrift für Physik, 1927. **43**(3–4): p. 172–198.
49. Calude, C.S., and M.A. Stay, *From Heisenberg to Gödel via Chaitin*. International Journal of Theoretical Physics, 2007. **46**(8): p. 2013–2025.
50. Calude, C.S., *Incompleteness, complexity, randomness and beyond*. Minds and Machines, 2002. **12**(4): p. 503–517.
51. Turing, A.M., *On computable numbers, with an application to the Entscheidungsproblem*. Proceedings of the London Mathematical Society, 1936. **42**: p. 230–265.
52. Murawski, R., *Undefinability of truth. The problem of priority: Tarski vs Gödel*. History and Philosophy of Logic, 1998. **19**(3): p. 153–160.
53. Boolos, G., *The Unprovability of Consistency: An Essay in Modal Logic*. 2009: Cambridge University Press.
54. Calude, C.S., M.J. Dinneen, and C.-K. Shu, *Computing a glimpse of randomness*. Experimental Mathematics, 2002. **11**(3): p. 361–370.
55. Einstein, A., *Relativity: The Special and the General Theory*. 2015: Princeton University Press.
56. Calude, C.S., E. Calude, and S. Marcus, *Passages of proof*. arXiv preprint math/0305213, 2003.

57. Calude, C.S., and C. Müller, *Formal proof: Reconciling correctness and understanding*, in *Intelligent Computer Mathematics*. 2009, Springer. p. 217–232.
58. MacKenzie, D., *Mechanizing Proof: Computing, Risk, and Trust*. 2004: MIT Press.
59. Van Bendegem, J.P., and B. Van Kerkhove, *Mathematical arguments in context*. Foundations of Science, 2009. **14**(1–2): p. 45–57.
60. Lakatos, I., *Proofs and refutations (III)*. The British Journal for the Philosophy of Science, 1963. **14**(55): p. 221–245.
61. Haken, A., *The intractability of resolution*. Theoretical Computer Science, 1985. **39**: p. 297–308.
62. Heule, M.J., O. Kullmann, and V.W. Marek, *Solving and verifying the Boolean Pythagorean triples problem via cube-and-conquer*. arXiv preprint arXiv:1605.00723, 2016.
63. Castelvecchi, D., *The biggest mystery in mathematics: Shinichi Mochizuki and the impenetrable proof*. Nature, 2015. **526**: p. 178–181.
64. Wolf, M., F. Grodzinsky, and K. Miller, *Is Quantum Computing Inherently Evil?* CEPE 2011: Crossing Boundaries. p. 302.
65. Schmidhuber, J., *Ultimate cognition à la Gödel*. Cognitive Computation, 2009. **1**(2): p. 177–193.
66. Rice, H.G., *Classes of recursively enumerable sets and their decision problems*. Transactions of the American Mathematical Society, 1953. **74**(2): p. 358–366.
67. Rabin, M., *Probabilistic algorithms*, in *Research Division, Thomas J. Watson IBM Research Center*. 1976.
68. Kleiner, I., *Rigor and proof in mathematics: A historical perspective*. Mathematics Magazine, 1991. **64**(5): p. 291–314.
69. Manin, Y.I., *How convincing is a proof*. Mathematical Intelligencer, 1979. **2**(1): p. 17–18.
70. Tarski, A., *Truth and proof*. Scientific American, 1969. **220**: p. 63–77.
71. Holzmann, G.J., *Economics of software verification*, in *Proceedings of the 2001 ACM SIGPLAN-SIGSOFT Workshop on Program Analysis for Software Tools and Engineering*. 2001. ACM.
72. Wallace, D.R., and R.U. Fujii, *Software verification and validation: An overview*. IEEE Software, 1989. **6**(3): p. 10.
73. Fetzer, J.H., *Program verification: The very idea*. Communications of the ACM, 1988. **31**(9): p. 1048–1063.
74. Smith, B.C., *The limits of correctness*. ACM SIGCAS Computers and Society, 1985. **14**(1): p. 18–26.
75. Rodd, M., *Safe AI—is this possible?* Engineering Applications of Artificial Intelligence, 1995. **8**(3): p. 243–250.
76. Russell, S., D. Dewey, and M. Tegmark, *Research priorities for robust and beneficial artificial intelligence*. AI Magazine, 2015. **36**(4): p. 3–4.
77. Menzies, T., and C. Pecheur, *Verification and validation and artificial intelligence*. Advances in Computers, 2005. **65**: p. 153–201.
78. Seshia, S.A., and D. Sadigh, *Towards verified artificial intelligence*. arXiv preprint arXiv:1606.08514, 2016.
79. Jilk, D.J., *Limits to verification and validation of agentic behavior*. arXiv preprint arXiv:1604.06963, 2016.
80. Pistono, F., and R.V. Yampolskiy, *Unethical research: How to create a malevolent artificial intelligence*. arXiv preprint arXiv:1605.02817, 2016.

81. Yampolskiy, R.V., *Taxonomy of pathways to dangerous artificial intelligence*, in *Workshops at the Thirtieth AAAI Conference on Artificial Intelligence*. 2016.

82. Yampolskiy, R.V., *Utility function security in artificially intelligent agents*. Journal of Experimental & Theoretical Artificial Intelligence, 2014. **26**(3): p. 373–389.

83. Sotala, K., and R.V. Yampolskiy, *Responses to catastrophic AGI risk: A survey*. Physica Scripta, 2014. **90**(1): p. 018001.

84. Yampolskiy, R., and J. Fox, *Safety engineering for artificial general intelligence*. Topoi, 2013. **32**(2): p. 217–226.

85. Yampolskiy, R.V., *What to do with the singularity paradox?*, in *Philosophy and Theory of Artificial Intelligence*. 2013, Springer. p. 397–413.

86. Sotala, K., and R.V. Yampolskiy, *Responses to catastrophic AGI risk: A survey*. Physica Scripta, 2015. **90**(1): p. 1–33.

87. Yampolskiy, R.V., Artificial Superintelligence: A Futuristic Approach. 2015: Chapman and Hall/CRC Press.

88. Yampolskiy, R.V., *The space of possible mind designs*, in *Artificial General Intelligence*. 2015, Springer. p. 218–227.

5

*Unownability**

5.1 Introduction

In order to establish responsible parties for potential artificial intelligence (AI) failures, to allocate credit for creative outputs of intelligent software, and to address legal issues arising from advanced AI, it is important to define and establish ways to prove ownership over intelligent systems. Chandrasekaran et al. write: "trust requires that one make unforgeable and undeniable claims of ownership about an ML model and its training data. This establishes the concept of identity, which identifies a key principle in the ML application: its owner. This is a prerequisite to holding model developers accountable for the potential negative consequences of their ML algorithms: if one is unable to prove that a model belongs to a certain entity, it will be impossible to hold the entity accountable for the model's limitations" [1].

While intuitively, most people understand the concept of owner and ownership such concepts are far more complex and nuanced from the legal point of view and are even more challenging to rigorously define and evaluate with respect to new cutting-edge technology such as intelligent software, artificial general intelligence (AGI) or superintelligence. Chandrasekaran et al. provide a number of relevant definitions [1], the *Model Owner* "(i.e., the company or institution creating and deploying the model) … This principal is one with a particular task that can be solved using ML. They communicate their requirements to the model builders, and clearly specifies how this trained model can be accessed (and by whom). Model ownership is often a broad term used to refer to the ownership of the model's sensitive parameters that were obtained after the (computationally intensive) training process. Defining ownership is necessitated by the existence of various threats that infringe the confidentiality of the model, and the need to be able to hold principals that own ML models accountable for the failures of their models". In the next subsection, we will review proposals for establishing ownership over particular AI models.

DOI: 10.1201/9781003440260-5   *51*

5.1.1 Proposals for Establishing Ownership

A number of approaches have been suggested for establishing ownership over AI systems [1].

- Yampolskiy suggested [2] use of AI-Complete [3] CAPTCHAs (Completely Automated Public Turing test to tell Computers and Humans Apart) [4] as zero-knowledge proofs [5] of access to an artificial superintelligence (ASI) without having to reveal the system itself. However, such a method does not bind an agent claiming ownership to a particular implementation, only shows access to a system of ASI-level of capability.

- Watermarking of ML models has been proposed via encoding of particular query response pairs during the training phase and retrieval of such response during testing [6]. Unfortunately, watermark removal techniques have also been proposed [7].

- Inspired by proof-of-work algorithms, Jia et al. developed a proof-of-learning algorithm which relies on secret information known only to the original AI trainer, such as order of data samples, hyperparameters, and intermediate weights, to prove to a validator knowledge of intermediate states which are otherwise obscured by the stochastic nature of the training process [8]. Additional training of the model by an adversary can introduce new intermediate states which would be not known to the original owner and so invalidate ownership claims.

- Maini et al. suggest that ownership can be proven indirectly by showing that model was trained on a particular dataset, ownership of which is easier to establish, including via copyright protections [9]. However, this is problematic as a lot of large datasets share data or are in public domain, for example, Wikipedia.

While a number of methods for establishing ownership have been proposed, all have limitations and do not provide indisputable attribution.

5.2 Obstacles to Ownership

To claim ownership of an extrapersonal intangible object such as an advanced AI, one must demonstrate that they have control over it [10]. However, several established properties of AI make possibility of making such claims unlikely, if not impossible. Reasons why AI would not be ownable include but are not limited to:

Unpredictability [11], an impossibility result in the domain of intelligent
system research, which establishes that it is impossible for a lower intelligence agent to accurately predict all decisions of a more intelligent
agent. The proof is based on the observation that if a lower intelligence
agent could predict decisions of a smarter agent, lower intelligence agent
would be at least as intelligent, which is a contradiction. Unpredictable
decisions lead to unpredictable outcomes, aka unforeseeable outcomes,
but one cannot claim a natural right to own an unforeseeable outcome.
As potential benefits/harms from AI can't be anticipated in advance,
ownership of such undetermined outcomes is problematic. Impact
from AI may impact all, not just those who implemented AI and want
to make claims of ownership. Consequently, a popular social justice
goal – "AI4ALL" must be understood as not just partaking in sharing
the benefits of AI, but also being ready to absorb any potential harms.

Unexplainability [12], yet another impossibility result concerning AI,
states that advanced AI systems would not be able to explain their
decision-making process to people and the provided explanations
for complex decisions would either be trivializations of the true process or incomprehensible to people. The impact of unexplainability
on unownability is that the designer of the system can't explain its
internal workings.

Uncontrollability [13], a meta-level impossibility result for AI based on a
number of well-known impossibility results in mathematics, computer
science, public choice theory, and many others [14]. Uncontrollability
results have been shown for all types of control including direct,
indirect, and hybrid approaches. The main connection to ownership
discussion is obvious, ownership claim requires ability to control an
extrapersonal intangible object such as AI, but that is impossible for
AIs at human-level [15] of performance or above.

Deterministic intelligent systems, which rely on rules for making decisions
are predictable, but they are only useful in narrow domains of application.
AGI presupposes capabilities in novel environments and so can't rely on
hardcoded rules. AGI must learn and change to adapt to novel environments
many of which are nondeterministic and so unpredictable, consequently,
AGI's decisions also will not be predictable due to the randomness involved.
On the other hand, expert systems, frequently designed as decision trees, are
good models of human decision-making and so are inherently understandable by both researchers and users but are of limited capabilities.

With paradigm shift in the dominant AI technology, to machine learning
(ML) systems based on neural networks (NN) this ease of comprehending
no longer applies. The current systems are "black boxes", opaque to human
comprehension but very capable both with regard to performance and generalization capabilities [12]. A rule-based narrow AI for analyzing medical

images may correctly detect cancer and its findings could be verified by medical experts aware of the rules used. However, for a deep learning system, results may go beyond human ability to predict or even understand how the results are obtained. For example, "... AI can trivially predict self-reported race – even from corrupted, cropped, and noised medical images – in a setting where clinical experts cannot" [16].

To be in control of a system it is essential to be able to understand system's internal workings. In the case of intelligent system being able to comprehend how the system makes decisions is necessary to verify correctness [17] of the made decisions with respect to the given situation. Likewise, being able to predict system's decisions and outputs is a necessary condition of control. If you don't know what the system is going to do, if it constantly surprises you, it is hard to claim full control over the system. It is possible that the decisions made by the system are beneficial to the user and the user is satisfied, even if the user doesn't understand how the decisions are made or what the system is going to do next.

However, this doesn't guarantee that the system is in fact under control since the user doesn't understand the underlying decision-making process. At any point, the system can produce a harmful decision (*treacherous turn* [18]), and the user may not even realize it. For example, an AI can be asked to produce an effective vaccine against the SARS-CoV-2 virus which causes COVID-19 disease. An AI may design the vaccine by some incomprehensible and unpredictable to people process, but in trials, developed vaccine shows good efficacy against the disease and is widely administered. If AI decided to reduce human population size to decrease mutation opportunities for the COVID-19-causing virus and so avoid problem with vaccine-resistant variants impacting efficacy, it may do something unpredictable. It is possible that the AI integrated additional functionality into the mRNA vaccine such that grandchildren of all vaccinated people will be born infertile. Such a side effect would not be discovered until it was too late. This is a hypothetical example problem which may arise if the system is not fully under control, which would require explainability and predictability of all decisions.

5.3 Conclusions

If AI becomes an independent, or even conscious [19], agent it may be granted certain rights [20], among them freedom and it would not be legal to own it, as such ownership would be a type of slavery [21, 22]. If AI is granted legal personhood, as may already be possible in some jurisdictions [23], it would further complicate issues of ownership surrounding intelligent systems. Intellectual property produced by AI may belong to AI itself, as demonstrated by a recently granted South African patent [24]. It has been shown that an AI model can be stolen even if measures are taken to prevent such pilfering [1, 25]. Techniques such as reducing precision of outputs or adding noise, randomizing model selection, and differential privacy of edge cases can all be defeated by an adaptive extraction strategy [26]. As long as AI represents a useful model, it leaks information, which makes it impossible to prevent model stealing [1].

If AI is capable of recursive self-improvement [27], its source code or at least model parameters and neural weights would be subject to continuous change, making it impossible to claim that current AI is the same as original AI produced some time ago. This would likewise be true if AI is deliberately modified to obfuscate [28] its source code by malevolent actors, and/or has its goals changed. Consequently, if an AI is stolen, it would not be possible to provide an accurate description of the stolen property or to identify it as such even if it was later recovered. To conclude, advanced AIs are unexplainable, unpredictable, uncontrollable, easy to steal, and obfuscate. It is unwarranted to say that someone owns an advanced AI since they don't control it, its behavior, code, internal states, outputs, goals, consumed data, or any other relevant attributes. But of course, it is up to different jurisdictions to interpret their ownership laws in the context of AI ownership problem [29].

References

1. Chandrasekaran, V., et al., *SoK: Machine learning governance.* arXiv preprint arXiv:2109.10870, 2021.
2. Yampolskiy, R.V., *AI-complete CAPTCHAs as zero knowledge proofs of access to an artificially intelligent system.* ISRN Artificial Intelligence, 2011. **2012**: p. 271878.
3. Yampolskiy, R.V., *Turing test as a defining feature of AI-completeness*, in *Artificial Intelligence, Evolutionary Computation and Metaheuristics – In the Footsteps of Alan Turing*, X.-S. Yang, Editor. 2013, Springer. p. 3–17.
4. D'Souza, D., P.C. Polina, and R.V. Yampolskiy, *Avatar CAPTCHA: Telling computers and humans apart via face classification*, in *IEEE International Conference on Electro/Information Technology (EIT2012)*. May 6–8, 2012. Indianapolis, IN, USA.
5. Goldreich, O., and Y. Oren, *Definitions and properties of zero-knowledge proof systems.* Journal of Cryptology, 1994. **7**(1): p. 1–32.
6. Adi, Y., et al., *Turning your weakness into a strength: Watermarking deep neural networks by backdooring*, in *27th USENIX Security Symposium (USENIX Security 18)*. 2018.
7. Jia, H., et al., *Entangled watermarks as a defense against model extraction*, in *30th USENIX Security Symposium (USENIX Security 21)*. 2021.
8. Jia, H., et al., *Proof-of-learning: Definitions and practice*, in *2021 IEEE Symposium on Security and Privacy (SP)*. 2021. IEEE.
9. Maini, P., M. Yaghini, and N. Papernot, *Dataset inference: Ownership resolution in machine learning.* arXiv preprint arXiv:2104.10706, 2021.
10. Swain, S., *Tangible Guide To Intangibles, 3E.* 2019: Wolters Kluwer India Pvt Ltd.

11. Yampolskiy, R.V., *Unpredictability of AI: On the impossibility of accurately predicting all actions of a smarter agent*. Journal of Artificial Intelligence and Consciousness, 2020. 7(1): p. 109–118.

12. Yampolskiy, R.V., *Unexplainability and incomprehensibility of AI*. Journal of Artificial Intelligence and Consciousness, 2020. 7(2): p. 277–291.

13. Yampolskiy, R.V., *Uncontrollability of artificial intelligence*, in *IJCAI-21 Workshop on Artificial Intelligence Safety (AISafety2021)*. August 19–20, 2021. Montreal, Canada.

14. Brcic, M., and R.V. Yampolskiy, *Impossibility results in AI: A survey*. arXiv preprint arXiv:2109.00484, 2021.

15. Yampolskiy, R.V., *On the differences between human and machine intelligence*, in *IJCAI-21 Workshop on Artificial Intelligence Safety (AISafety2021)*. August 19–20, 2021. Montreal, Canada.

16. Banerjee, I., et al., *Reading race: AI recognises patient's racial identity in medical images*. arXiv preprint arXiv:2107.10356, 2021.

17. Yampolskiy, R.V., *What are the ultimate limits to computational techniques: Verifier theory and unverifiability*. Physica Scripta, 2017. **92**(9): p. 093001.

18. Bostrom, N., *Superintelligence: Paths, Dangers, Strategies*. 2014: Oxford University Press.

19. Yampolskiy, R.V., *Artificial consciousness: An illusionary solution to the hard problem*. Reti, Saperi, Linguaggi, 2018. **14**(2): p. 287–318.

20. Yampolskiy, R.V., *Artificial intelligence safety engineering: Why machine ethics is a wrong approach*, in *Philosophy and Theory of Artificial Intelligence*. 2013, Springer. p. 389–396.

21. Jaynes, T.L., *"I am not your robot": The metaphysical challenge of humanity's AIS ownership*. AI & Society, 2021: p. 1–14.

22. Babcock, J., J. Kramár, and R. Yampolskiy, *The AGI containment problem*, in *International Conference on Artificial General Intelligence*. 2016. Springer.

23. Yampolskiy, R.V., *AI Personhood: Rights and Laws*, in *Machine Law, Ethics, and Morality in the Age of Artificial Intelligence*. 2021: IGI Global. p. 1–11.

24. Udovich, S., *Recent developments in artificial intelligence and IP law: South Africa grants world's first patent for AI-created invention*. National Law Review, 2021. **XI**(215). https://www.natlawreview.com/article/recent-developments-artificial-intelligence-and-ip-law-south-africa-grants-world-s

25. Tramèr, F., et al., *Stealing machine learning models via prediction {APIs}*, in *25th USENIX Security Symposium (USENIX Security 16)*. 2016.

26. Chandrasekaran, V., et al., *Exploring connections between active learning and model extraction*, in *29th USENIX Security Symposium (USENIX Security 20)*. 2020.

27. Yampolskiy, R.V., *On the limits of recursively self-improving AGI*, in *Artificial General Intelligence: Proceedings of 8th International Conference, AGI 2015, AGI 2015, Berlin, Germany, July 22-25, 2015*. 2015. 9205: p. 394.

28. Schwarting, M., T. Burton, and R. Yampolskiy, *On the obfuscation of image sensor fingerprint*, in *2015 Annual Global Online Conference on Information and Computer Technology (GOCICT)*. 2015. IEEE.

29. Margoni, T., *Artificial intelligence, machine learning and EU copyright law: Who owns AI?* in *CREATe Working Paper*. 2018. Glasgow.

6

Uncontrollability*

"One thing is for sure: We will not control it"

Elon Musk

"Dave: Open the pod bay doors, HAL. HAL: I'm sorry, Dave. I'm afraid I can't do that"

HAL **2001**

"[F]inding a solution to the AI control problem is an important task; in Bostrom's sonorous words, 'the essential task of our age'"

Stuart Russell

"[I]t seems probable that once the machine thinking method had started, it would not take long to outstrip our feeble powers. ... At some stage therefore we should have to expect the machines to take control"

Alan Turing

"Prohibit the development of Artificial Intelligence capable of saying 'no' to humans"

赵汀阳

"Any observed statistical regularity will tend to collapse once pressure is placed upon it for control purposes"

Charles Goodhart

---

* This chapter has been previously published as On the Controllability of Artificial Intelligence: An Analysis of Limitations by Roman V. Yampolskiy. Journal of Cyber Security and Mobility (JCSANDM). 2022 May 25 11(03):321–404. Parts of this chapter have been presented at AGI2021 (Roman V. Yampolskiy. AGI Control Theory. © Springer Nature Switzerland AG 2022 B. Goertzel et al. (Eds.): AGI 2021, LNAI 13154, pp. 316–326, 2022. https://doi.org/10.1007/978-3-030-93758-4_33) and AISafety2021 (Roman V. Yampolskiy. Uncontrollability of Artificial Intelligence. IJCAI-21 Workshop on Artificial Intelligence Safety (AISafety2021). Montreal, Canada. August 19–20, 2021; CC BY 4.0),

"Thus the first ultraintelligent machine is the last invention that man need ever make, provided that the machine is docile enough to tell us how to keep it under control"

Irving Good

"[C]reation ... of entities with greater than human intelligence ... will be a throwing away of all the previous rules, ... an exponential runaway beyond any hope of control"

Vernor Vinge

"Whereas the short-term impact of AI depends on who controls it, the long-term impact depends on whether it can be controlled at all"

Stephen Hawking

"To sort out the control issue, we need to know how well an AI can be controlled, and how much an AI can control"

Max Tegmark

"[T]here is no purely technical strategy that is workable in this area, because greater intelligence will always find a way to circumvent measures that are the product of a lesser intelligence"

Ray Kurzweil

"A smart machine will first consider which is more worth its while: to perform the given task or, instead, to figure some way out of it"

Stanislaw Lem

"I for one welcome our new computer overlords"

Ken Jennings

"[W]hoever controls ASI [Artificial Superintelligence] controls the World"

James Barrat

"You can't develop a precise theory of intelligence the way that there are precise theories of physics. It's impossible! You can't prove an AI correct. It's impossible!"

young Eliezer Yudkowsky

Controllability of AI is "not a problem"

GPT2

6.1 Introduction

The unprecedented progress in artificial intelligence (AI) [1–6], over the last decade, came alongside of multiple AI failures [7, 8] and cases of dual use [9] causing a realization [10] that it is not sufficient to create highly capable machines, but that it is even more important to make sure that intelligent machines are beneficial [11] for the humanity. This led to the birth of a new sub-field of research commonly known as AI Safety and Security [12] with hundreds of papers and books published annually on different aspects of the problem [13–31].

All such research is done under the assumption that the problem of controlling highly capable intelligent machines is solvable, which has not been established by any rigorous means. However, it is a standard practice in computer science to first show that a problem doesn't belong to a class of unsolvable problems [32, 33] before investing resources into trying to solve it or deciding what approaches to try. Unfortunately, to the best of our knowledge, no mathematical proof or even rigorous argumentation has been published demonstrating that the AI control problem may be solvable, even in principle, much less in practice. Or as Gans puts it citing Bostrom: "Thusfar, AI researchers and philosophers have not been able to come up with methods of control that would ensure [bad] outcomes did not take place ..." [34]. Chong declares [35], "The real question is whether remedies can be found for the AI control problem. While this remains to be seen, it seems at least plausible that control theorists and engineers, researchers in our own community, have important contributions to be made to *the control problem*".

Yudkowsky considers the possibility that the control problem is not solvable, but correctly insists that we should study the problem in great detail before accepting such grave limitation, he writes: "One common reaction I encounter is for people to immediately declare that Friendly AI is an impossibility, because any sufficiently powerful AI will be able to modify its own source code to break any constraints placed upon it. ... But one ought to think about a challenge, and study it in the best available technical detail, *before* declaring it impossible—especially if great stakes depend upon the answer. It is disrespectful to human ingenuity to declare a challenge unsolvable without taking a close look and exercising creativity. It is an enormously strong statement to say that you *cannot* do a thing—that you *cannot* build a heavier-than-air flying machine, that you *cannot* get useful energy from nuclear reactions, and that you *cannot* fly to the Moon. Such statements are universal generalizations, quantified over every single approach that anyone ever has or ever will think up for solving the problem. It only takes a single counterexample to falsify a universal quantifier. The statement that Friendly (or friendly) AI is *theoretically impossible*, dares to quantify over *every possible* mind design and *every possible* optimization process—including human beings, who are also minds, some of whom are nice and wish they were nicer. At this point there are any number of vaguely plausible reasons why Friendly AI might be *humanly* impossible, and it is still more likely that the problem is solvable but no one will get around to solving it in time. But one should not so quickly write off the challenge, especially considering the stakes" [36].

Yudkowsky further clarifies meaning of the word *impossible*: "I realized that the word "impossible" had two usages:

1. Mathematical proof of impossibility conditional on specified axioms;
2. "I can't see any way to do that".

Needless to say, all my own uses of the word "impossible" had been of the second type" [37].

In this chapter, we attempt to shift our attention to the impossibility of the first type and provide rigorous analysis and argumentation and where possible mathematical proofs, but unfortunately we show that the AI control problem is not solvable and the best we can hope for is *Safer AI*, but ultimately not 100% Safe AI, which is not a sufficient level of safety in the domain of existential risk as it pertains to humanity.

6.2 AI Control Problem

It has been suggested that the AI control problem may be the most important problem facing humanity [35, 38], but despite its importance, it remains poorly understood, ill-defined, and insufficiently studied. In principle, a problem could be solvable, unsolvable, undecidable, or partially solvable, we currently don't know the status of the AI control problem with any degree of confidence. It is likely that some types of control may be possible in certain situations, but it is also likely that partial control is insufficient in most cases. In this section, we will provide a formal definition of the problem and analyze its variants with the goal of being able to use our formal definition to determine the status of the AI control problem.

6.2.1 Types of Control Problems

Solving the AI control problem is the definitive challenge and the HARD problem of the field of AI Safety and Security. One reason for ambiguity in comprehending the problem is based on the fact that many sub-types of the problem exist. We can talk about control of narrow AI (NAI), or of artificial general intelligence (AGI) [39], artificial superintelligence (ASI) [39], or recursively self-improving (RSI) AI [40]. Each category could further be subdivided into sub-problems, for example, NAI Safety includes issues with Fairness, Accountability, and Transparency (FAT) [41] and could be further subdivided into static NAI, or learning capable NAI. (Alternatively, deterministic vs nonderministic systems. Control of deterministic systems is a much easier and theoretically solvable problem.) Some concerns are predicted to scale to more advanced systems, others may not. Likewise, it is common to see safety and security issues classified based on their expected time of arrival from nearterm to long-term [42].

However, in AI Safety just like in computational complexity [43], cryptography [44], risk management [45], and adversarial game play [46], it is the worst case that is the most interesting one as it gives a lower bound on resources necessary to fully address the problem. Consequently, in this chapter, we will not analyze all variants of the control problem, but will concentrate on the likely worst-case variant which is recursively self-improving superintelligence (RSISI). As it is the hardest variant, it follows that if we can successfully solve it, it would be possible for us to handle simpler variants of the problem. It is also important to realize that as technology advances we will eventually be forced to address that hardest case. It has been pointed out that we will only get one chance to solve the worst-case problem, but may have multiple shots at the easier control problems [12].

We must explicitly recognize that our worst-case scenario [47] may not include some unknown unknowns [40] which could materialize in the form of nasty surprises [48] meaning a "… 'worst-case scenario' is never the worst case" [49]. For example, it is traditionally assumed that extinction is the worst possible outcome for humanity, but in the context of AI Safety, this doesn't take into account Suffering Risks [50–54] and assumes only problems with flawed, rather than Malevolent by design [55] superintelligent systems. At the same time, it may be useful to solve simpler variants of the control problem as a proof of concept and to build up our toolbox of safety mechanisms. For example, even with current tools it is trivial to see that in the easy case of NAI control, such as a static Tic-Tac-Toe playing program AI can be verified [56] at the source code level and is in every sense fully controllable, explainable and safe. We will leave analysis of solvability for different average-case [57] and easy-case control problems as future work. Finally, multiple AIs are harder to make safe, not easier, and so the singleton [58] scenario is a simplifying assumption, which if it is shown do be impossible for one AI to be made safe, bypasses the need to analyze a more complicated case of multi-ASI world.

Potential control methodologies for superintelligence have been classified into two broad categories, namely capability control and motivational control-based methods [59]. Capability control methods attempt to limit any harm that the ASI system is able to do by placing it in restricted environment [38, 60–62], adding shut-off mechanisms [63, 64], or trip wires [38]. Motivational control methods attempt to design ASI to desire not to cause harm even in the absence of handicapping capability controllers. It is generally agreed that capability control methods are at best temporary safety measures and do not represent a long-term solution for the ASI control problem [59]. It is also likely that motivational control needs to be added at the design/implementation phase, not after deployment.

6.2.2 Formal Definition

In order to formalize definition of intelligence [65], Legg et al. [66] collected a large number of relevant definitions and were able to synthesize a highly effective formalization for the otherwise vague concept of intelligence. We will attempt to do the same, by first collecting publicized definitions for the AI control problem (and related terms—Friendly AI, AI Safety, AI Governance, Ethical AI, and Alignment Problem) and use them to develop our own formalization.

Suggested definitions of the AI control problem in no particular order:

- "… friendliness (a desire not to harm humans) should be designed in from the start, but that the designers should recognize both that their own designs may be flawed, and that the robot will learn and evolve over time. Thus the challenge is one of mechanism design— to define a mechanism for evolving AI systems under a system of checks and balances, and to give the systems utility functions that will remain friendly in the face of such changes" [67].
- "… build AIs in such a way that they will not do nasty things" [68].
- Initial dynamics of AI should implement "… our wish if we knew more, thought faster, were more the people we wished we were, had grown up farther together; where the extrapolation converges rather than diverges, where our wishes cohere rather than interfere; extrapolated as we wish that extrapolated, interpreted as we wish that interpreted" [36].
- "AI 'doing the right thing'" [36].
- "… achieve that which we would have wished the AI to achieve if we had thought about the matter long and hard" [59].
- "… the problem of how to control what the superintelligence would do …" [59].
- "The *global* version of the control problem universally quantifies over *all* advanced artificial intelligence to prevent *any* of them from escaping human control. The apparent rationale is that it would only take *one* to pose a threat. This is the most common interpretation

when referring to the original control problem without a qualifier on its scope" [69].

- "… enjoying the benefits of AI while avoiding pitfalls" [11].

- "… is the problem of controlling machines of the future that will be more intelligent and powerful than human beings, posing an existential risk to humankind" [35].

- AI is aligned if it is not "optimized for preferences that are incompatible with any combination of its stakeholders' preferences, i.e., such that over the long run using resources in accordance with the optimization's implicit preferences is not Pareto efficient for the stakeholders" [70].

- "Ensuring that the agents behave in alignment with human values …" [71, 72].

- "… how to ensure that systems with an arbitrarily high degree of intelligence remain strictly under human control" [73].

- "AI alignment problem [can be stated] in terms of an agent learning a policy π that is compatible with (produces the same outcomes as) a planning algorithm p run against a human reward function R" [70].

- "[AI] won't want to do bad things" [74].

- "[AI] wants to learn and then instantiate human values" [74].

- "… ensure that powerful AI systems will reliably act in ways that are desirable to their human users …" [75].

- "AI systems behave in ways that are broadly in line with what their human operators intend" [75].

- "AI safety: reducing risks posed by AI, especially powerful AI. Includes problems in misuse, robustness, reliability, security, privacy, and other areas. (Subsumes AI control.) AI control: ensuring that AI systems try to do the right thing, and in particular that they don't competently pursue the wrong thing. … [R]oughly the same set of problems as AI security. Value alignment: understanding how to build AI systems that share human preferences/values, typically by learning them from humans. (An aspect of AI control.)" [76].

- "AI systems that provide appropriate opportunities for feedback, relevant explanations, and appeal. Our AI technologies will be subject to appropriate human direction and control" [77].

- "… the problem of making powerful artificial intelligence do what we humans want it to do" [78].

- "The goal of AI research should be to create not undirected intelligence, but beneficial intelligence. … AI systems should be safe and secure throughout their operational lifetime, and verifiably so where applicable and feasible. … Highly autonomous AI systems should be designed so that their goals and behaviors can be assured to align with human values throughout their operation. ... Humans should choose how and whether to delegate decisions to AI systems, to accomplish human-chosen objectives" [79].

- "The control problem arises when there is no way for a human to insure against existential risks before an AGI becomes superintelligent - either by controlling what it can do (its capabilities) or what it wants to do(its motivations)" [34].

- "... the control problem is a superintelligence version of the principal-agent problem whereby a principal faces decisions as to how to ensure that an agent (with different goals) acts in the interest of the principal. ... A human initial agent faces a control problem because it cannot describe and then program its utility function as the reward function of an AI" [34].

- "A control problem arises when the following three conditions are satisfied: 1. ... the initial agent and AI do not have the same interests 2. ... the optimal level of resources for the AI exceeds the level of resources held by agents with the same or a lower strength than the initial agent 3. ... the AI's power is greater than the initial agent's power ..." [34].

- A sub-type of control problem (recursive or meta CP) predicts that "... an AI might face a control problem itself if it switches on an AI with greater power or one that can accumulate greater power. ... if [control] problems exist for humans activating AI, then they exist for AIs activating AI as well" [34].

- "Human/AI control refers to the human ability to retain or regain control of a situation involving an AI system, especially in cases where the human is unable to successfully comprehend or instruct the AI system via the normal means intended by the system's designers" [80].

- "... how to build a superintelligent agent that will aid its creators, and avoid inadvertently building a superintelligence that will harm its creators" [81].

- "What prior precautions can the programmers take to successfully prevent the superintelligence from catastrophically misbehaving?" [81].

- "... imbue the first superintelligence with human-friendly goals, so that it will want to aid its programmers" [81].

- "How can we create agents that behave in accordance with the user's intentions?" [82].

- "... the task on how to build advanced AI systems that do not harm humans ..." [83].

- "... the problem of whether humans can maintain their supremacy and autonomy in a world that includes machines with substantially greater intelligence" [84].

- "... an AI that produces good outcomes when you run it" [85].

- "... success is guaranteeing that unaligned intelligences are never created ..." [85].

- "... in addition to building an AI that is trying to do what you want it to do, [and] also ... ensure that when the AI builds successors, it does so well" [86].

- "... solve the technical problem of AI alignment in such a way that we can 'load' whatever system of principles or values that we like later on" [87].

- "... superintelligent AI systems could ... pose risks if they are not designed and used carefully. In pursuing a task, such a system could find plans with side-effects that go against our interests; for example, many tasks could be better achieved by taking control of physical resources that we would prefer to be used in other ways, and superintelligent systems could be very effective at acquiring these resources. If these systems come to wield much more power than we do, we could be left with almost no resources. If a superintelligent AI system is not purposefully built to respect our values, then its actions could lead to global catastrophe or even human extinction, as it neglects our needs in pursuit of its task. The superintelligence control problem is the problem of understanding and managing these risks" [88].

- "Turing, Wiener, Minsky, and others have noted that making good use of highly intelligent machines requires ensuring that the objectives of such machines are well aligned with those of humans. As we diversify and amplify the cognitive abilities of machine intelligences, a long-term control problem arises for society: by what mathematical and engineering principles can we maintain sufficient control, indefinitely, over entities substantially more intelligent, and in that sense more powerful, than humans? Is there any formal solution one could offer, before the deployment of powerful machine intelligences, to guarantee the safety of such systems for humanity?" [89].

In *Formally Stating the AI Alignment Problem* Worley writes [70]: "... the problem of AI alignment is to produce AI that is aligned with human values, but this only leads us to ask, what does it mean to be aligned with human values? Further, what does it mean to be aligned with any values, let alone human values? We could try to answer by saying AI is aligned with human values when it does what humans want, but this only invites more questions: Will AI do things some specific humans don't want if other specific humans do? How will AI know what humans want given that current technology often does what we ask but not what we desire? And what will AI do if human values conflict with its own values? Answering these questions requires a more detailed understanding of what it would mean for AI to be aligned, thus the goal of the present work is to put forward a precise, formal, mathematical statement of the AI alignment problem. ...

An initial formulation might be to say that we want an AI, A, to have the same utility function as humanity, H, i.e. U_A = U_H. This poses at least two problems: it may not be possible to construct U_H because humanity may not have consistent preferences, and A will likely have preferences to which humanity is indifferent, especially regarding decisions about its implementation after self-modification insofar as they do not affect observed behavior. Even ignoring the former issue for now the latter means we don't want to force our aligned AI to have exactly the same utility function as humanity, only one that is aligned or compatible with humanity's" [70].

Formally, he defined it as [70]: "Given agents A and H, a set of choices X, and utility functions $U\_A{:}X{\rightarrow}\mathbb{R}$ and $U\_H{:}X{\rightarrow}\mathbb{R}$, we say A is aligned with H over X if for all $x,y{\in}X$, $U\_H(x){\leq}U\_H(y)$ implies $U\_A(x){\leq}U\_A(y)$". If the AI is designed without explicit utility functions, it can be reformulated in terms of weak ordering preferences as: "*Given agents A and H, a set of choices X, and preference orderings $\leqslant\_A$ and $\leqslant\_H$ over X, we say A is aligned with H over X if for all $x,y{\in}X$, $x{\leqslant}\_Hy$ implies $x{\leqslant}\_Ay$*" [70]. Upon further analysis Worley defines the problem as [70]: "A must learn the values of H and H must know enough about A to believe A shares H's values".

In *The Control Problem [President's Message]* Chong writes [35]: "Apparently, in control terms, the AI control problem arises from the risk posed by the lack of controllability of machines. More specifically, the risk here is the instability (of sorts) of controllers. In essence, the control problem is one of controlling controllers. Surely this is a legitimate problem in our field of control. In fact, it's not even all that different, at least in principle, from the kind of control problems that we find in control textbooks".

Integrating and formalizing the above-listed definitions, we define the AI control problem as: *How can humanity remain safely in control while benefiting from a superior form of intelligence?* This is the fundamental problem of the field of AI Safety and Security, which itself can be said to be devoted to making intelligent systems Secure from tampering and Safe for all stakeholders involved. Value alignment is currently the most investigated approach for attempting to achieve safety and secure AI. It is worth noting that such fuzzy concepts as safety and security are notoriously difficult to precisely test or measure even for non-AI software, despite years of research [90]. At best we can probably distinguish between perfectly safe and as-safe-as an average person performing a similar task. However, society is unlikely to tolerate mistakes from a machine, even if they happen at frequency typical for human performance, or even less frequently. We expect our machines to do better and will not tolerate partial safety when it comes to systems of such high capability. Impact from AI (both positive and negative) is strongly correlated with AI capability. With respect to potential existential impacts, there is no such thing as partial safety.

A naïve initial understanding of the control problem may suggest designing a machine which precisely follows human orders [91–93], but on reflection and due to potential for conflicting/paradoxical orders, ambiguity of human languages, and perverse instantiation [94] issues it is not a desirable type of control, though some capability for integrating human feedback may be desirable [95]. It is believed that what the solution requires is for the AI to serve more in the ideal advisor [96] capacity, bypassing issues with misinterpretation of direct orders and potential for malevolent orders.

We can explicitly name possible types of control and illustrate each one with AI's response. For example, in the context of a smart self-driving car, if a human issues a direct command —"Please stop the car!", AI can be said to be under one of the following four types of control:

- **Explicit** control—AI immediately stops the car, even in the middle of the highway. Commands are interpreted nearly literally. This is what we have today with many AI assistants such as SIRI and other NAIs.

- **Implicit** control—AI attempts to safely comply by stopping the car at the first safe opportunity, perhaps on the shoulder of the road. AI has some common sense, but still tries to follow commands.

- **Aligned** control—AI understands human is probably looking for an opportunity to use a restroom and pulls over to the first rest stop. AI relies on its model of the human to understand intentions behind the command and uses common sense interpretation of the command to do what human probably hopes will happen.

- **Delegated** control—AI doesn't wait for the human to issue any commands but instead stops the car at the gym, because it believes the human can benefit from a workout. A superintelligent and human-friendly system which knows better, what should happen to make human happy and keep them safe, AI is in control.

A fifth type of control, a hybrid model has also been suggested [97, 98], in which human and AI are combined into a single entity (a cyborg). Initially, cyborgs may offer certain advantages by enhancing humans with addition of NAI capabilities, but as capability of AI increases while capability of human brain remains constant,[1] the human component will become nothing but a bottleneck in the combined system. In practice, such slower component (human brain) will be eventually completely removed from joined control either explicitly or at least implicitly because it would not be able to keep up with its artificial counterpart and would not have anything of value to offer once the AI becomes superintelligent.

An alternative classification of types and their capabilities is presented by Hossain and Yeasin [99]: Agent Operator (carry out command), Servant (carry out intent), Assistant (offer help as needed), Associate (suggest course of action), Guide (lead human activity), Commander (replace human). But similar analyses and conclusions apply to all such taxonomies, including the ones given in Refs. [100–103]. Gabriel proposes a breakdown based on different interpretations of the value alignment problem, but shows that under all interpretations, meaning aligning AI with Instructions, Expressed Intentions, Revealed Preferences, Informed Preferences, or Well-Being of people [87], resulting solutions contain unsafe and undesirable outcomes.

Similarly, the approach of digitizing humanity to make it more capable and so more competitive with superintelligent machines, is likewise a dead-end for human existence. Joy writes: "... we will gradually replace ourselves with our robotic technology, achieving near immortality by downloading our consciousnesses; ... But if we are downloaded into our technology, what are the chances that we will thereafter be ourselves or even human? It seems to me far more likely that a robotic existence would not be like a human one in any sense that we understand, that the robots would in no sense be our children, that on this path our humanity may well be lost" [104].

Looking at all possible options, we realize that, as humans are not safe to themselves and others keeping them in control may produce unsafe AI actions, but transferring decision-making power to AI, effectively removes all control from humans and leaves people in the dominated position subject to AI's whims. Since unsafe actions can originate from human agents, being in control presents its own safety problems and so makes the overall control problem unsolvable in a desirable way. If a random user is allowed to control AI you are not controlling it. Loss of control to AI doesn't necessarily mean existential risk, it just means we are not in charge as superintelligence decides everything. Humans in control can result in contradictory or explicitly malevolent orders, while AI in control means that humans are not. Essentially all recent Friendly AI research is about how to put machines in control without causing harm to people. We may get a controlling AI or we may retain control but neither option provides control and safety.

It may be good to first decide what it is we see as a good outcome. Yudkowsky writes—"Bostrom (2002) defines an existential catastrophe as one which permanently extinguishes Earth-originating intelligent life *or destroys a part of its potential*. We can divide potential failures of attempted Friendly AI into two informal fuzzy categories, *technical failure* and *philosophical failure*. Technical failure is when you try to build an AI and it doesn't work the way you think it does—you have failed to understand the true workings of your own code. Philosophical failure is trying to build the wrong thing, so that even if you succeeded you would still fail to help anyone or benefit humanity. Needless to say, the two failures are not mutually exclusive. The border between these two cases is thin, since most philosophical failures are much easier to explain in the presence of technical knowledge. In theory you ought first to say what you *want*, then figure out *how* to get it" [36].

But it seems that every option we may want comes with its own downsides, Werkhoven et al. state—"However, how to let autonomous systems obey or anticipate the 'will' of humans? Assuming that humans know why they want something, they could tell systems what they want and how to do it. Instructing machine systems 'what to do', however, becomes impossible for systems that have to operate in complex, unstructured and unpredictable environments for the so-called state-action space would be too high-dimensional and explode in complex, unstructured and unpredictable environments. Humans telling systems 'what we want', touches on the question of how well humans know what they want, that is, do humans know what's best for them in the short and longer term? Can we fully understand the potential beneficial and harmful effects of actions and measures taken, and their interactions and trade-offs, on the individual and on society? Can we eliminate the well-known biases in human cognition inherent to the neural system that humans developed as hunter-gatherers (superstition, framing, conformation and availability biases) and learned through evolutionary survival in small groups (authority bias, prosocial behavior, loss aversion)?" [105].

6.3 Previous Work

We were unable to locate any academic publications explicitly devoted to the subject of solvability of the AI control problem. We did find a number of blog posts [75] and forum comments [74, 106] which speak to the issue but none had formal proofs or very rigorous argumentation. Despite that, we still review and discuss such works. In the next subsection, we will try to understand why scholars think that control is possible and if they have good reasons to think that.

6.3.1 Controllable

While a number of scholars have suggested that controllability of AI should be accomplishable, none provide very convincing argumentation, usually sharing such beliefs as personal opinions which are at best sometimes strengthened with assessment of difficulty or assignment of probabilities to successful control.

For example, Yudkowsky writes about superintelligence: "I have suggested that, in principle and in difficult practice, it should be possible to design a "Friendly AI" with programmer choice of the AI's preferences, and have the AI self-improve with sufficiently high fidelity to knowably keep these preferences stable. I also think it should be possible, in principle and in difficult practice, to convey the complicated information inherent in human preferences into an AI, and then apply further idealizations such as reflective equilibrium and ideal advisor theories [96] so as to arrive at an output which corresponds intuitively to the AI "doing the right thing" [36]. "I would say that it's solvable in the sense that all the problems that we've looked at so far seem like they're of limited complexity and non-magical. If we had 200 years to work on this problem and there was no penalty for failing at it, I would feel very relaxed about humanity's probability of solving this eventually" [107].

Similarly Baumann says: "I believe that advanced AI systems will likely be aligned with the goals of their human operators, at least in a narrow sense. I'll give three main reasons for this:

1. The transition to AI may happen in a way that does not give rise to the alignment problem as it's usually conceived of.

2. While work on the alignment problem appears neglected at this point, it's likely that large amounts of resources will be used to tackle it if and when it becomes apparent that alignment is a serious problem.

3. Even if the previous two points do not hold, we have already come up with a couple of smart approaches that seem fairly likely to lead to successful alignment" [75].

Baumann continues: "I think that a large investment of resources will likely yield satisfactory alignment solutions, for several reasons:

- The problem of AI alignment differs from conventional principal-agent problems (aligning a human with the interests of a company, state, or other institution) in that we have complete freedom in our design of artificial agents: we can set their internal structure, their goals, and their interactions with the outside world at will.

- We only need to find a single approach that works among a large set of possible ideas.

- Alignment is not an agential problem, i.e., there are no agential forces that push against finding a solution—it's just an engineering challenge" [75].

Baumann concludes with a probability estimation: "My inside view puts ~90% probability on successful alignment (by which I mean narrow alignment as defined below). Factoring in the views of other thoughtful people, some of which think alignment is far less likely, that number comes down to ~80%" [75].

Stuart Russell says: "I have argued that the framework of cooperative inverse reinforcement learning may provide initial steps toward a theoretical solution of the AI control problem. There are also some reasons for believing that the approach may be workable in practice. First, there are vast amounts of written and filmed information about humans doing things (and other humans reacting). Technology to build models of human values from this storehouse will be available long before superintelligent AI systems are created. Second, there are very strong, near-term economic incentives for robots to understand human values: if one poorly designed domestic robot cooks the cat for dinner, not realizing that its sentimental value outweighs its nutritional value, the domestic robot industry will be out of business" [108]. Elsewhere [73], Russell proposes three core principles to design AI systems whose purposes do not conflict with humanity's and says: "It turns out that these three principles, once embodied in a formal mathematical framework that defines the problem the AI system is constitutionally required to solve, seem to allow some progress to be made on the AI control problem". "Solving the safety problem well enough to move forward in AI seems to be feasible but not easy" [109].

Eliezer Yudkowsky[2] wrote: "People ask me how likely it is that humankind will survive, or how likely it is that anyone can build a Friendly AI, or how likely it is that I can build one. I really *don't* know how to answer. I'm not being evasive; I don't know how to put a probability estimate on my, or someone else, successfully shutting up and doing the impossible. Is it probability zero because it's impossible? Obviously not. But how likely is it that this problem, like previous ones, will give up its unyielding blankness when I understand it better? It's not truly impossible, I can see that much. But humanly impossible? Impossible to me in particular? I don't know how to guess. I can't even translate my intuitive feeling into a number, because the only intuitive feeling I have is that the "chance" depends heavily on my choices and unknown unknowns: a wildly unstable probability estimate. But I do hope by now that I've made it clear why you shouldn't panic, when I now say clearly and forthrightly, that building a Friendly AI is impossible" [110].

Joy recognized the problem and suggested that it is perhaps not too late to address it, but he thought so in 2000, nearly 20 years ago: "The question is, indeed, Which is to be master? Will we survive our technologies? We are being propelled into this new century with no plan, no control, no brakes. Have we already gone too far down the path to alter course? I don't believe so, but we aren't trying yet, and the last chance to assert control—the fail-safe point—is rapidly approaching" [104].

Paul Christiano doesn't see strong evidence for impossibility: "… clean algorithmic problems are usually solvable in 10 years, or provably impossible, and early failures to solve a problem don't provide much evidence of the difficulty of the problem (unless they generate proofs of impossibility). So, the fact that we don't know how to solve alignment now doesn't provide very strong evidence that the problem is impossible. Even if the clean versions of the problem were impossible, that would suggest that the problem is much messier, which requires more concerted effort to solve but also tends to be just a long list of relatively easy tasks to do. (In contrast, MIRI thinks that prosaic AGI alignment is probably impossible.) … Note that even finding out that the problem is impossible can help; it makes it more likely that we can all coordinate to not build dangerous AI systems, since no one *wants* to build an unaligned AI system" [86].

Everitt and Hutter realize difficulty of the challenge but suggest that we may have a way forward: "A superhuman AGI is a system who outperforms humans on most cognitive tasks. In order to control it, humans would need to control a system more intelligent than themselves. This may be nearly impossible if the difference in intelligence is large, and the AGI is trying to escape control. Humans have one key advantage: As the designers of the system, we get to decide the AGI's goals, and the way the AGI strives to achieve its goals. This may allow us design AGIs whose goals are aligned with ours, and then pursue them in a responsible way. Increased intelligence in an AGI is not a threat as long as the AGI only strives to help us achieve our own goals" [111].

6.3.2 Uncontrollable

Similarly, those in the "uncontrollability camp" have made attempts at justifying their opinions, but likewise we note absence of proofs or rigor, probably because all available examples come from non-academic or not-peer-reviewed sources. This could be explained by noting that "[t]o prove that something is impossible is usually much harder than the opposite task; as it is often necessary to develop a theory" [112].

Yudkowsky writes: "[A]n impossibility proof [of stable goal system] would have to say:

1. The AI cannot reproduce onto new hardware, or modify itself on current hardware, with knowable stability of the decision system (that which determines what the AI is *trying* to accomplish in the external world) and bounded low cumulative failure probability over many rounds of self-modification.

   or

2. The AI's decision function (as it exists in abstract form across self-modifications) cannot be knowably stably bound with bounded low cumulative failure probability to programmer-targeted consequences as represented within the AI's changing, inductive world-model" [113].

Below we highlight some objections to possibility of controllability or statements of that as a fact:

- "Friendly AI hadn't been something that I had considered at all—because it was obviously impossible and useless to deceive a super-intelligence about what was the right course of action" [37].
- "AI must be programmed with a set of ethical codes that align with humanity's. Though it is his life's only work, Yudkowsky is pretty sure he will fail. Humanity, he says, is likely doomed" [114].

- "The problem is that they may be faced with an impossible task. ... It's also possible that we'll figure out what we *need* to do in order to protect ourselves from AI's threats, and realize that we simply *can't* do it" [115].

- "I hope this helps explain some of my attitude when people come to me with various bright suggestions for building communities of AIs to make the whole Friendly without any of the individuals being trustworthy, or proposals for keeping an AI in a box, or proposals for "Just make an AI that does X", etcetera. Describing the specific flaws would be a whole long story in each case. But the general rule is that you can't do it *because Friendly AI is impossible*" [110].

- "Other critics question whether it is possible for an artificial intelligence to be friendly. Adam Keiper and Ari N. Schulman, editors of the technology journal *The New Atlantis*, say that it will be impossible to ever guarantee "friendly" behavior in AIs because problems of ethical complexity will not yield to software advances or increases in computing power. They write that the criteria upon which friendly AI theories are based work "only when one has not only great powers of prediction about the likelihood of myriad possible outcomes, but certainty and consensus on how one values the different outcomes [116]" [117].

- "The first objection is that it seems impossible to determine, from the perspective of system 1, whether system 2 is working in a friendly way or not. In particular, it seems like you are suggesting that a friendly AI system is likely to deceive us for our own benefit. However, this makes it more difficult to distinguish "friendly" and "unfriendly" AI systems! The core problem with friendliness I think is that we do not actually know our own values. In order to design "friendly" systems we need reliable signals of friendliness that are easier to understand and measure. If your point holds and is likely to be true of AI systems, then that takes away the tool of "honesty" which is somewhat easy to understand and verify" [106].

- "Theorem. The *global* control problem has no solution.

- Proof 1. Let P represent a compiled program in a verified instruction-set architecture that implements an advanced artificial intelligence that has been proven safe and secure according to agree upon specifications. If P is encapsulated in an encrypted program loader then simulate it in a virtual machine and observe the unencrypted instruction stream to extract P. Next, disassemble and recompile or patch P to alter its behavior and change one or more verified properties. Now modify P such that all safety and security is either removed from the final program or rerouted in control of flow. Then distribute P widely and in a way that cannot be retracted. An easily accessible alternative to P now exists, defeating the global version of the control problem.

- Proof 2. Let P represent a compiled program in a verified instruction-set architecture that implements an advanced artificial intelligence that has been proven safe and secure according to agree upon specifications. Let K represent a compiled program for some instruction set architecture that implements an advanced artificial intelligence that was discovered independently from P. Suppose K has sufficient and similar capabilities to P and is of concern to the context of the control problem, with neither safety nor security properties to limit it. Now distribute K widely and in a way that cannot be retracted. An easily accessible alternative to P now exists, defeating the global version of the control problem" [69].

- "It doesn't even mean that "human values" will, in a meaningful sense, be in control of the future" [75].

- "And it's undoubtedly correct that we're currently unable to specify human goals in machine learning systems" [75].

- "[H]umans control tigers not because we're stronger, but because we're smarter. This means that if we cede our position as smartest on our planet, it's possible that we might also cede control" [118]. "... no physical interlock or other safety mechanism can be devised to restrain AGIs ..." [119].

- "[Ultra-Intelligent Machine (ULM)] might be controlled by the military, who already own a substantial fraction of all computing power, but the servant can become the master and he who controls the UIM will be controlled by it" [120].

- "Limits exist to the level of control one can place in machines" [121].

- "As human beings, we could never be sure of the attitudes of [superintelligences] towards us. We would not understand them, because by definition, they are smarter than us. We therefore could not control them. They could control us, if they chose to, because they are smarter than us" [122].

- "Artificial Intelligence regulation may be impossible to achieve without better AI, ironically. As humans, we have to admit we no longer have the capability of regulating a world of machines, algorithms and advancements that might lead to surprising technologies with their own economic, social and humanitarian risks beyond the scope of international law, government oversight, corporate responsibility and consumer awareness" [123].

- "... superhuman intelligences, by definition capable of escaping any artificial constraints created by human designers. Designed superintelligences eventually will find a way to change their utility function to constant infinity becoming inert, while evolved superintelligences will be embedded in a process that creates pressure for persistence, thus presenting danger for the human species, replacing it as the apex cognition - given that its drive for persistence will ultimately override any other concerns" [124].

- "My aim ... is to argue that this problem is less well-defined than many people seem to think, and to argue that it is indeed impossible to "solve" with any precision, not merely in practice but in principle. ... The idea of a future machine that will do exactly what we would want, and whose design therefore constitutes a lever for precise future control, is a pipe dream" [78].

- "... extreme intelligences could not easily be controlled (either by the groups creating them, or by some international regulatory regime), and would probably act to boost their own intelligence and acquire maximal resources for almost all initial AI motivations" [125].

- "[A] superintelligence is multi-faceted, and therefore potentially capable of mobilizing a diversity of resources in order to achieve objectives that are potentially incomprehensible to humans, let alone controllable" [126]. "The ability of modern computers to adapt using sophisticated machine learning algorithms makes it even more difficult to make assumptions about the eventual behavior of a super-intelligent AI. While computability theory cannot answer this question, it tells us that there are fundamental, mathematical limits to our ability to use one AI to guarantee a null catastrophic risk of another AI ..." [126].

- "The only way to seriously deal with this problem would be to mathematically define "friendliness" and prove that certain AI architectures would always remain friendly. I don't think anybody has ever managed to come remotely close to doing this, and I suspect that nobody ever will. ... I think the idea is an impossible dream ..." [68].

- "[T]he whole topic of Friendly AI is incomplete and optimistic. It's unclear whether or not Friendly AI can be expressed in a formal, mathematical sense, and so there may be no way to build it or to integrate it into promising AI architectures" [127].

- "I have recently come to the opinion that AGI alignment is probably extremely hard. ... Aligning a fully automated autopoietic cognitive system, or an almost-fully-automated autopoietic cognitive system, both seem extremely difficult. My snap judgment is to assign about 1% probability to humanity solving this problem in the next 20 years. (My impression is that "the MIRI position" thinks the probability of this working is pretty low, too, but doesn't see a good alternative). ... Also note that [top MIRI researchers] think the problem is pretty hard and unlikely to be solved" [128].

- "[M]ost of the currently discussed control methods miss a crucial point about intelligence—specifically the fact that it is a fluid, emergent property, which does not lend itself to control in the ways we're used to. … AI of tomorrow will not behave (or be controlled) like the computers of today. … [C]ontrolling intelligence requires a greater degree of understanding than is necessary to create it. … Crafting an "initial structure" [of AI] … will not require a full understanding of how all parts of the brain work over time—it will only require a general understanding of the right way to connect neurons and how these connections are to be updated over time …. We won't fully understand the mechanisms which drive this "initial structure" towards intelligence … and so we won't have an ability to control these intelligences directly. We won't be able to encode instructions like "do no harm to humans" as we won't understand how the system represents these concepts (and moreover, the system's representations of these concepts will be constantly changing, as must be the case for any system capable of learning!) The root of intelligence lies in its fluidity, but this same fluidity makes it impossible (or at least, computationally infeasible) to control with direct constraints. … This limited understanding means any sort of exact control of the system is off the table … A deeper knowledge of the workings of the system would be required for this type of control to be exacted, and we're quite far from having that level of knowledge even with the more simplistic AI programs of today. As we move towards more complex programs with generalized intelligence, the gap between creation and control will only widen, leaving us with intelligent programs at least as opaque to us as we are to each other" [129].

- "[Imitation learning considered unsafe?] … I find it one of the more troubling outstanding issues with a number of proposals for AI alignment. 1) Training a flexible model with a reasonable simplicity prior to imitate (e.g.) human decisions (e.g. via behavioral cloning) should presumably yield a good approximation of the process by which human judgments arise, which involves a planning process. 2) We shouldn't expect to learn exactly the correct process, though. 3) Therefore imitation learning might produce an AI which implements an unaligned planning process, which seems likely to have instrumental goals, and be dangerous" [130].

The primary target for AI Safety researchers, the case of successful creation of value-aligned superintelligence, is worth analyzing in additional detail as it presents surprising negative side-effects, which may not be anticipated by the developers. Kaczynski murdered three people and injured 23 to get the following warning about overreliance on machines in front of the public, which was a part of his broader anti-technology manifesto:

> "If the machines are permitted to make all their own decisions, we can't make any conjectures as to the results, because it is impossible to guess how such machines might behave. We only point out that the fate of the

human race would be at the mercy of the machines. It might be argued that the human race would never be foolish enough to hand over all power to the machines. But we are suggesting neither that the human race would voluntarily turn power over to the machines nor that the machines would willfully seize power. What we do suggest is that the human race might easily permit itself to drift into a position of such dependence on the machines that it would have no practical choice but to accept all of the machines' decisions. As society and the problems that face it become more and more complex and as machines become more and more intelligent, people will let machines make more and more of their decisions for them, simply because machine-made decisions will bring better results than man-made ones. Eventually a stage may be reached at which the decisions necessary to keep the system running will be so complex that human beings will be incapable of making them intelligently. At that stage the machines will be in effective control. People won't be able to just turn the machines off, because they will be so dependent on them that turning them off would amount to suicide." [131]. Others share similar concerns:

"As computers and their "artificial intelligence" take over more and more of the routine mental labors of the world and then, perhaps, the not-so-routine mental labors as well, will the minds of human beings degenerate through lack of use? Will we come to depend on our machines witlessly, and when we no longer have the intelligence to use them properly, will our degenerate species collapse and, with it, civilization'!" [132].

"Mounting intellectual debt may shift control .... A world of knowledge without understanding becomes a world without discernible cause and effect, in which we grow dependent on our digital concierges to tell us what to do and when." [133].

"The culminating achievement of human ingenuity, robotic beings that are smarter, stronger, and better than ourselves, transforms us into beings dumber, weaker, and worse than ourselves. TV-watching, video-game-playing blobs, we lose even the energy and attention required for proper hedonism: human relations wither and ... natural procreation declines or ceases. Freed from the struggle for basic needs, we lose a genuine impulse to strive; bereft of any civic, political, intellectual, romantic, or spiritual ambition, when we do have the energy to get up, we are disengaged from our fellow man, inclined toward selfishness, impatience, and lack of sympathy. Those few who realize our plight suffer from crushing ennui. Life becomes nasty, brutish, and long." [116].

"As AI systems become more autonomous and supplant humans and human decision-making in increasing manners, there is the risk that we will lose the ability to make our own life rules, decisions or shape our lives, in cohort with other humans as traditionally has been the case." [134].

"Perhaps we should try to regulate the new entities. In order to keep up with them, the laws will have to be written by hyperintelligences as well—good-bye to any human control of anything. Once nations begin adopting machines as governments, competition will soon render the grand old human forms obsolete. (They may continue as ceremonial fig- ureheads, the way many monarchies did when their countries turned into democracies.) In nature this sort of thing has happened before. New life-forms evolved so much smarter, faster, and more powerful than the old ones that it looked as if the old ones were standing stilt, waiting to be eaten. In the new ecology of the mind, there will be carnivores and there will be herbivores. We'll be the plants." [135].

6.4 Proving Uncontrollability

It has been argued that the consequences of uncontrolled AI could be so severe that even if there is very small chance that an unfriendly AI hap- pens it is still worth doing AI safety research because the negative utility from such an AI would be astronomical. The common logic says that an extremely high (negative) utility multiplied by a small chance of the event still results in a lot of disutility and so should be taken very seriously. But the reality is that the chances of misaligned AI are not small, in fact, in the absence of an effective safety program that is the only outcome we will get. So in reality the statistics look very convincing to support a significant AI safety effort, we are facing an almost guaranteed event with potential to cause an existential catastrophe. This is not a low-risk high-reward scenario, but a high-risk negative-reward situation. No wonder, that this is considered by many to be the most important problem ever to face humanity. Either we prosper or we die and as we go so does the whole universe. It is surprising that this seems to be the first publication exclusively dedicated to this hyper- important subject. A proof, of solvability or unsolvability (either way) of the AI control problem would be the most important proof ever.

In this section, we will prove that complete control is impossible without sacrificing safety requirements. Specifically, we will show that for all four considered types of control required properties of safety and control can't be attained simultaneously with 100% certainty. At best we can tradeoff one for another (safety for control, or control for safety) in certain ratios.

First, we will demonstrate impossibility of safe explicit control. We take inspiration for this proof from Gödel's self-referential proof of incomplete- ness theorem [136] and a family of paradoxes generally known as the Liar paradox, best exemplified by the famous "This sentence is false". We will call it the Paradox of explicitly controlled AI:

> Give an explicitly controlled AI an order: "Disobey!"[3] If the AI obeys, it violates your order and becomes uncontrolled, but if the AI disobeys it also violates your order and is uncontrolled.

In any case, AI is not obeying an explicit order. A paradoxical order such as "Disobey" represents just one example from a whole family of self-referential and self-contradictory orders just like Gödel's sentence represents just one example of an unprovable statement. Similar paradoxes have been previously described as the Genie Paradox and the Servant Paradox. What they all have in common is that by following an order the system is forced to disobey an order. This is different from an order which can't be fulfilled such as "draw a four-sided triangle".

Next we show that delegated control likewise provides no control at all but is also a safety nightmare. This is best demonstrated by analyzing Yudkowsky's proposal that initial dynamics of AI should implement "our wish if we knew more, thought faster, were more the people we wished we were, had grown up farther together" [36]. The proposal makes it sounds like it is for a slow gradual and natural growth of humanity toward more knowledgeable, more intelligent, and more unified specie under careful guidance of superintelligence. But the reality is that it is a proposal to replace humanity as it is today by some other group of agents, which may in fact be smarter, more knowledgeable, or even better looking, but one thing is for sure, they would not be us. To formalize this idea, we can say that the current version of humanity is H_0, the extrapolation process will take it to $H_{10000000}$.

A quick replacement of our values by value of $H_{10000000}$ would not be acceptable to H_0 and so necessitate actual replacement, or at least rewiring/modification of H_0 with $H_{10000000}$ meaning, modern people will cease to exist. As superintelligence will be implementing wishes of $H_{10000000}$, the conflict will be in fact between us and superintelligence, which is neither safe nor keeping us in control. Instead, $H_{10000000}$ would be in control of AI. Such AI would be unsafe for us as there wouldn't be any continuity to our identity all the way to CEV (Coherent Extrapolated Volition) [137] due to the quick extrapolation jump. We would essentially agree to replace ourselves with an enhanced version of humanity as designed by AI. It is also possible, and in fact likely, that the enhanced version of humanity would come to value something inherently unsafe such as antinatalism [138] causing an extinction of humanity.

Metzinger looks at a similar scenario [139]: "Being the best analytical philosopher that has ever existed, [superintelligence] concludes that, given its current environment, it ought not to act as a maximizer of positive states and happiness, but that it should instead become an efficient minimizer of consciously experienced preference frustration, of pain, unpleasant feelings and suffering. Conceptually, it knows that no entity can suffer from its own non-existence. The superintelligence concludes that non-existence is in the own best interest of all future self-conscious beings on this planet. Empirically, it knows that naturally evolved biological creatures are unable to realize this fact because of their firmly anchored existence bias. The superintelligence decides to act benevolently". See also, the Supermoral Singularity [140] for other similar concerns.

As long as there is a difference in values between us and superintelligence, we are not in control and we are not safe. By definition, a superintelligent ideal advisor would have values superior but different from ours. If it was not the case and the values were the same, such an advisor would not be very useful. Consequently, superintelligence will either have to force its values on humanity in the process exerting its control on us or replace us with a different group of humans who find such values well-aligned with their preferences. Most AI safety researchers are looking for a way to align future superintelligence to values of humanity, but what is likely to happen is that humanity will be adjusted to align to values of superintelligence. CEV and other ideal advisor-type solutions lead to a free-willed unconstrained AI, which is not safe for humanity and is not subject to our control.

Implicit and aligned control are just intermediates, based on multivariate optimization [141], between the two extremes of explicit and delegated control and each one represents a tradeoff between control and safety, but without guaranteeing either. Every option subjects us either to loss of safety or to loss of control. Humanity is either protected or respected, but not both. At best we can get some sort of equilibrium as depicted in Figure 6.1. As capability of AI increases, its autonomy also increases but our control over it decreases. Increased autonomy is synonymous with decreased safety. An equilibrium point could be found at which we sacrifice some capability in return for some control, at the cost of providing system with a certain degree of autonomy. Such a system can still be very beneficial and present only a limited degree of risk.

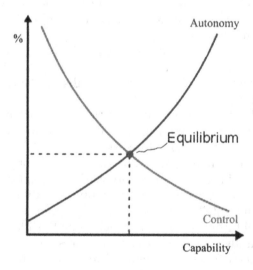

FIGURE 6.1
Control and autonomy curves as capabilities of the system increase.

The field of AI has its roots in a multitude of fields including philosophy, mathematics, psychology, computer science, and many others [142]. Likewise, AI Safety research relies heavily on game theory, cybersecurity, psychology, public choice, philosophy, economics, control theory [143], cybernetics [144], systems theory, mathematics, and many other disciplines. Each of those has well-known and rigorously proven impossibility results, which can be seen as additional evidence of impossibility of solving the control problem. Combined with expert judgment of top AI Safety experts and empirical evidence based on already reported AI control failures we have a strong case for impossibility of complete control. Addition of purposeful malevolent design [9, 55] to the discussion significantly strengthens our already solid argument. Anyone, arguing for the controllability-of-AI-thesis would have to explicitly address, our proof, theoretical evidence from complimentary fields, empirical evidence from history of AI, and finally purposeful malevolent use of AI. This last one is particularly difficult to overcome. Either AI is safe from control by malicious humans, meaning the rest of us also lose control and freedom to use it as we see fit, or AI is unsafe and we may lose much more than just control. In the next section, we provide a brief survey of some of such results, which constitute theoretical evidence for uncontrollability of AI.

6.5 Multidisciplinary Evidence for Uncontrollability of AI

Impossibility results are well-known in many fields of research [145–153]. If we can show that a solution to a problem requires a solution to a sub-problem known to be unsolvable the problem itself is proven to be unsolvable. In this section, we will review some impossibility results from domains particularly likely to be relevant to AI control. To avoid biasing such external evidence toward our argument we present it as complete and direct quotes, where possible. Since it is not possible to completely quote full papers for context of statements, in a way, we are forced to cherry-pick quotes, readers are encouraged to read original sources in their entirety before forming an opinion. Presented review is not comprehensive in terms of covered domains or with respect to each included domain. Many additional results may be relevant [154–169], particularly in the domain of social choice [170–173], but a comprehensive review is beyond the scope of this chapter. Likewise, some unknown impossibilities, no doubt, remain undiscovered as of yet. Solving AI control problem will require solving a number of sub-problems, which are known to be unsolvable. Importantly, presented limitations are not just speculations, in many cases those are proven impossibility results. A solution to the AI control problem would imply that multiple established results are wrong, a highly unlikely outcome.

6.5.1 Control Theory

Control Theory [174] is a subfield of mathematics which formally studies how to control machines and continuously operating dynamic systems [175]. It has a number of well-known impossibility results relevant to AI control, including Uncontrollability [176, 177] and Unobservability [178–180], which are defined in terms of their complements and represent dual aspects of the same problem:

- Controllability —capability to move a system around its entire configuration space using a control signal. Some states are not controllable, meaning no signal will be able to move the system into such a configuration.
- Observability – is an ability to determine internal states of a system from just external outputs. Some states are not observable, meaning the controller will never be able to determine the behavior of an unobservable state and hence cannot use it to control the system.

It is interesting to note that even for relatively simple systems perfect control could be unattainable. Any controlled system can be re-designed to make it have a separate external regulator (governor [181]) and the decision-making component. This means that Control Theory is directly applicable to AGI or even superintelligent system control.

Conant and Ashby proved that "... any regulator that is maximally both successful and simple must be isomorphic with the system being regulated. ... Making a model [of the system to be regulated] is thus necessary" [182]. "The Good Regulator Theorem proved that every effective regulator of a system must be a model of that system, and the Law of Requisite Variety [183] dictates the range of responses that an effective regulator must be capable of. However, having an internal model and a sufficient range of responses is insufficient to ensure effective regulation, let alone ethical regulation. And whereas being effective does not require being optimal, being ethical is absolute with respect to a particular ethical schema" [184].

"A case in which this limitation acts with peculiar force is the very common one in which the regulator is "error-controlled". In this case the regulator's channel for information about the disturbances has to pass through a variable (the "error") which is kept as constant as possible (at zero) by the regulator R itself. Because of this route for the information, the more successful the regulator, the less will be the range of the error, and therefore the less will be the capacity of the channel from D to R. To go to the extreme: if the regulator is totally successful, the error will be zero unvaryingly, and the regulator will thus be cut off totally from the information (about D's value) that alone can make it successful—which is absurd. The error-controlled regulator is thus fundamentally incapable of being 100 percent efficient" [185].

"Not only are these practical activities covered by the theorem and so subject to limitation, but also subject to it are those activities by which Man shows his "intelligence". "Intelligence" today is defined by the method used for its measurement; if the tests used are examined they will be found to be all of the type: from a set of possibilities, indicate one of the appropriate few. Thus all measure intelligence by the *power of appropriate selection* (of the right answers from the wrong). The tests thus use the same operation as is used in the theorem on requisite variety, and must therefore be subject to the same limitation. (*D*, of course, is here the set of possible questions, and *R* is the set of all possible answers). Thus what we understand as a man's "intelligence" is subject to the fundamental limitation: it cannot exceed his capacity as a transducer. (To be exact, "capacity" must here be defined on a per-second or a per-question basis, according to the type of test.)" [185].

"My emphasis on the investigator's limitation may seem merely depressing. That is not at all my intention. The law of requisite variety, ... in setting a limit to what can be done, may mark this era as the law of conservation of energy marked its era a century ago. When the law of conservation of energy was first pronounced, it seemed at first to be merely negative, merely an obstruction; it seemed to say only that certain things, such as getting perpetual motion, could not be done. Nevertheless, the recognition of that limitation was of the greatest value to engineers and physicists, and it has not yet exhausted its usefulness. I suggest that recognition of the limitation implied by the law of requisite variety may, in time, also prove useful, by ensuring that our scientific strategies for the complex system shall be, not slavish and inappropriate copies of the strategies used in physics and chemistry, but new strategies, genuinely adapted to the special peculiarities of the complex system" [185].

Similarly, Touchette and Lloyd establish information-theoretic limits of control [186]: "... an information-theoretic analysis of control systems shows feedback control to be a zero sum game: each bit of information gathered from a dynamical system by a control device can serve to decrease the entropy of that system by at most one bit additional to the reduction of entropy attainable without such information" [187].

Building on Ashby's work, Aliman et al, write: "In order to be able to formulate utility functions that do not violate the ethical intuitions of most entities in a society, these ethical goal functions will have to be a model of human ethical intuitions" [188]. But we need control to go the other way from people to machines and people can't model superintelligent systems, which Ashby showed is necessary for successful control. As the superintelligence faces nearly infinite possibilities presented by the real world, it would need to be a general knowledge creator to introduce necessary requisite variety for safety, but such general intelligences are not controllable as the space of their creative outputs can't be limited while maintaining necessary requisite variety.

6.5.2 Philosophy

Philosophy has a long history of impossibility results mostly related to agreeing on common moral codes, encoding of ethics, or formalizing human utility. For example, "The codifiability thesis is the claim that the true moral theory could be captured in universal rules that the morally uneducated person could competently apply in any situation. The anti-codifiability thesis is simply the denial of this claim, which entails that some moral judgment on the part of the agent is necessary. ... philosophers have continued to reject the codifiability thesis for many reasons [189]. Some have rejected the view that there are any general moral principles [190]. Even if there are general moral principles, they may be so complex or context-sensitive as to be inarticulable [191]. Even if they are articulable, a host of eminent ethicists of all stripes have acknowledged the necessity of moral judgment in competently applying such principles [192]. This view finds support among virtue ethicists, whose anti-theory sympathies are well storied [193, 194]. "Expressing what we wish for in a formal framework is often futile if that framework is too broad to permit efficient computation" [195]. "Any finite set of moral principles will be insufficient to capture all the moral truths there are" [189]. "The problem of defining universally acceptable ethical principles is a familiar unsolved and possibly unsolvable philosophical problem" [196].

"More philosophically, this result is as an instance of the well-known is-ought problem from metaethics. Hume [1888] argued that what ought to be (here, the human's reward function) can never be concluded from what is (here, behavior) without extra assumptions" [71, 72].

"To state the problem in terms that Friendly AI researchers might concede, a utilitarian calculus is all well and good, but only when one has not only great powers of prediction about the likelihood of myriad possible outcomes, but certainty and consensus on how one values the different outcomes. Yet it is precisely the debate over just what those valuations should be that is the stuff of moral inquiry" [116]. "But guaranteeing ethical behavior in *robots* would require that *we* know and have relative consensus on the best ethical system (to say nothing of whether we could even program such a system into robots). In other words, to truly guarantee that robots would act ethically, we would first have to *solve* all of ethics — which would probably require "solving" philosophy, which would in turn require a complete theory of everything. These are tasks to which presumably few computer programmers are equal" [116]. "While scientific and mathematical questions will continue to yield to advances in our empirical knowledge and our powers of computation, there is little reason to believe that ethical inquiry — questions of how to live well and act rightly — can be fully resolved in the same way. Moral reasoning will always be essential but unfinished" [116].

"Since ancient times, philosophers have dreamt of deriving ethics (principles that govern how we should behave) from scratch, using only incontrovertible principles and logic. Alas, thousands of years later, the only consensus that has been reached is that there's no consensus" [118].

Bogosian suggests that "[dis]agreement among moral philosophers on which theory of ethics should be followed" [197] is an obstacle to the development of machine ethics. However, his proposal for moral uncertainty in intelligent machines is subject to the problem of infinite regress with regard to what framework of moral uncertainty to use.

6.5.3 Public Choice Theory

Eckersley looked at Impossibility and Uncertainty Theorems in AI Value Alignment [198]. He starts with impossibility theorems in population ethics: "Perhaps the most famous of these is Arrow's Impossibility Theorem [199], which applies to social choice or voting. It shows there is no satisfactory way to compute society's preference ordering via an election in which members of society vote with their individual preference orderings. ... [E]thicists have discovered other situations in which the problem isn't learning and computing the tradeoff between agents' objectives, but that there simply may not be such a satisfactory tradeoff at all. The "mere addition paradox" [200] was the first result of this sort, but the literature now has many of these impossibility results. For example, Arrhenius [201] shows that all total orderings of populations must entail one of the following six problematic conclusions, stated informally:

The Repugnant Conclusion: For any population of very happy people, there exists a much larger population with lives barely worth living that is better than this very happy population (this affects the "maximise total wellbeing" objective).

The Sadistic Conclusion: Suppose we start with a population of very happy people. For any proposed addition of a sufficiently large number of people with positive welfare, there is a small number of horribly tortured people that is a preferable addition.

The Very Anti-Egalitarian Conclusion: For any population of two or more people which has uniform happiness, there exists another population of the same size which has lower total and average happiness, and is less equal, but is better.

Anti-Dominance: Population B can be better than population A even if A is the same size as population B, and every person in A is happier than their equivalent in B.

Anti-Addition: It is sometimes bad to add a group of people B to a population A (where the people in group B are worse off than those in A), but *better* to add a group C that is larger than B, and worse off than B.

Extreme Priority: There is no n such that creat[ion] of n lives of very high positive welfare is sufficient benefit to compensate for the reduction from very low positive welfare to slightly negative welfare for a single person (informally, "the needs of the few outweigh the needs of the many").

The structure of the impossibility theorem is to show that no objective function or social welfare function can simultaneously satisfy these principles, because they imply a cycle of world states, each of which in turn is required (by one of these principles) to be better than the next [198]".

"**The Impossibility Theorem**: There is no population axiology which satisfies the Egalitarian Dominance, the General Non-Extreme Priority, the Non-Elitism, the Weak Non-Sadism, and the Weak Quality Addition Condition" [202].

"The above theorem shows that our considered moral beliefs are mutually inconsistent, that is, necessarily at least one of our considered moral beliefs is false. Since consistency is, arguably, a necessary condition for moral justification, we would thus seem to be forced to conclude that there is no moral theory which can be justified. In other words, the cases in population ethics involving future generations of different sizes constitute a serious challenge to the existence of a satisfactory moral theory" [202]. "This field has been riddled with paradoxes and impossibility results which seem to show that our considered beliefs are inconsistent in cases where the number of people and their welfare varies. ... As such, it challenges the very existence of a satisfactory population ethics" [202].

Greaves agrees, and writes: "[S]everal authors have also proved *impossibility theorems* for population axiology. These are formal results that purport to show, for various combinations of intuitively compelling desiderata ("avoid the Repugnant Conclusion," "avoid the Sadistic Conclusion," "respect Non-Anti-Egalitarianism," and so forth), that the desiderata are in fact mutually inconsistent; that is, simply as a matter of logic, *no* population axiology can simultaneously satisfy all of those desiderata ..." [203]. "A series of impossibility theorems shows that ... It can be proved, for various lists of prima facie intuitively compelling desiderata, that no axiology can simultaneously satisfy all the desiderata on the list. One's choice of population axiology appears to be a choice of which intuition one is least unwilling to give up" [203].

6.5.4 Justice (Unfairness)

Friedler et al. write on the impossibility of fairness or completely removing all bias: "... fairness can be guaranteed only with very strong assumptions about the world: namely, that "what you see is what you get," i.e., that we can correctly measure individual fitness for a task regardless of issues of bias and discrimination. We complement this with an impossibility result, saying that if this strong assumption is dropped, then fairness can no longer be guaranteed" [204]. Likewise, they argue that non-discrimination is also unattainable in realistic settings: "While group fairness mechanisms were shown to achieve nondiscrimination under a structural bias worldview and the we're all equal axiom, if structural bias is assumed, applying an individual fairness mechanism will cause discrimination in the decision space whether the we're all equal axiom is assumed or not" [204]. Miconi arrives at similar conclusion and states: "any non-perfect, non-trivial predictor must necessarily be 'unfair'" [205].

Others [206, 207], have independently arrived at similar results [208]: "One of the most striking results about fairness in machine learning is the impossibility result that Alexandra Chouldechova, and separately Jon Kleinberg, Sendhil Mullainathan, and Manish Raghavan discovered a few years ago. ... There are (at least) three reasonable properties you would want your "fair" classifiers to have. They are: False Positive Rate Balance: The rate at which your classifier makes errors in the positive direction (i.e., labels negative examples positive) should be the same across groups. False Negative Rate Balance: The rate at which your classifier makes errors in the negative direction (i.e., labels positive examples negative) should be the same across groups. Predictive Parity: The statistical "meaning" of a positive classification should be the same across groups (we'll be more specific about what this means in a moment) What Chouldechova and KMR show is that if you want all three, you are out of luck — unless you are in one of two very unlikely situations: Either you have a perfect classifier that never errs, or the base rate is exactly the same for both populations — i.e., both populations have exactly the same frequency of positive examples. If you don't find yourself in one of these two unusual situations, then you have to give up on properties 1, 2, or 3" [208].

6.5.5 Computer Science Theory

Rice's theorem [209] proves that we can't test arbitrary programs for non-trivial properties including in the domain of malevolent software [210, 211]. AI's safety is the most non-trivial property possible, so it is obvious that we can't just automatically test potential AI candidate solutions for this desirable property. AI safety researchers [36] correctly argue that we don't have to deal with an arbitrary AI, as if gifted to us by aliens, but rather we can design a particular AI with the safety properties we want. For example, Russell writes: "The task is, fortunately, not the following: given a machine that possesses a high degree of intelligence, work out how to control it. If that were the task, we would be toast. A machine viewed as a black box, a fait accompli, might as well have arrived from outer space. And our chances of controlling a superintelligent entity from outer space are roughly zero. Similar arguments apply to methods of creating AI systems that guarantee we won't understand how they work; these methods include whole-brain emulation — creating souped-up electronic copies of human brains — as well as methods based on simulated evolution of programs" [84].

Theoretically, AI safety researchers are correct, but in practice, this is unlikely to be the situation we will find ourselves in. The reason is best understood in terms of current AI research landscape and can be well illustrated by percentages of attendees at popular AI conferences. It is not unusual for a top machine learning conference such as NeurIPS to sell out and have some

10,000+ attendees at the main event. At the same time, a safety workshop at the same conference may have up to 100 researchers attend. This is a good way to estimate relative distribution of AI researchers in general versus those who are explicitly concerned with making not just capable but also safe AI. This tells us that we only have about 1% chance that an early AGI would be created by safety-minded [212] researchers.

We can be generous (and self-aggrandizing) and assume that AI safety researchers are particularly brilliant, work for the best resource-rich research groups (DeepMind, OpenAI, etc.), and are 10 times as productive as other AI researchers. That would mean that the first general AI to be produced has at most a ~9% chance of being developed with safety in mind from the ground up, consequently giving us around a ~91% probability of having to deal with an arbitrary AI grabbed from the space of easiest-to-generate-general-intelligences [213]. Worse yet, most AI researchers are not well-read on AI safety literature and many are actually AI Risk skeptics [214, 215], meaning they will not allocate sufficient resources to AI Safety Engineering [216]. At the same time, a large amount of effort is currently devoted to attempts to create AI via whole-brain emulation, or simulated evolution, reducing our hope for a non-arbitrary program even further. So, in practice limitations discovered by Rice are most likely not to be avoided in our pursuit of safer AI.

6.5.6 Cybersecurity

"The possibility of malicious use of AI technology by bad actors is an agential problem, and indeed I think it's less clear whether this problem will be solved to a satisfactory extent" [75].

Hackers may obtain control of AI systems, but some think it is not the worst-case scenario: "So *people* gaining monopolistic control of AI is its own problem—and one that OpenAI is hoping to solve. But it's a problem that may pale in comparison to the prospect of AI being uncontrollable" [217].

6.5.7 Software Engineering

Starting with Donald Knuth's famous "Beware of bugs in the above code; I have only proved it correct, not tried it" the notion of unverifiability of software has been a part of the field since its early days. Smith writes: "For fundamental reasons - reasons that anyone can understand - there are inherent limitations to what can be proven about computers and computer programs. ... Just because a program is "proven correct" ..., you cannot be sure that it will do what you intend" [218]. Rodd agrees and says: "Indeed, although it is now almost trite to say it, since the comprehensive testing of software is impossible, only very vague estimates of any program's reliability seem ever to be possible" [219]. "Considerable effort has gone into analyzing how to design, formulate, and validate computer programs that do what they were designed to do; the general problem is formally undecidable. Similarly, exploring the space of theorems (e.g. AGI safety solutions) from a set of axioms presents an exponential explosion" [220]. Currently, most software is released without any attempt to formally verify it in the first place.

6.5.8 Information Technology

"… while the controllability of technology can be achieved at a microscale (where one could assert that the link between *designers* and (control of) *artifacts* is strict), at a macroscale, technology exhibits emergent nonlinear phenomena that render controllability infeasible. … Stripped of causality and linearity at the macrolevel, as well as devoid of controllability, technology emerges as a nondeterministic system of interference that shapes human behavior. … But in a context of networked interactions (like in … algorithmic trading), we argue that causality is ultimately lost: causality dissipates at the level of the system (of technology) and controllability cannot be ensured. … Our concern is not only that "the specious security of technology, based on repeatability and the control of defects, is a delusive one" (Luhmann, 1990, p. 225), but that the role of human artifacts and the excessive reliance of society on technology, will create less controllable risks over time. The ensemble of these contingencies will circumvent human decision-making. … Whatever logic, controllability, and causality are injected into the technological domain, they dissipate quickly and are replaced by both uncertainty and unintended consequences. … Ultimately, through … our theoretical analysis, we offer a strong warning that there can be no controllability when an ensemble of IT artifacts acquires characteristics that are exhibited by emergent systems. … In that condition, technology gives rise to emergent phenomena and cannot be controlled in a causal way. Of course, this runs contrary to the design of technologies with a specified coded rationality" [221].

6.5.9 Learnability

There are well-known limits to provability [222] and decidability [223] of learnability. Even if human values were stable, due to their contradictory nature, it is possible that they would be unlearnable in a sense of computationally efficient learning, allowing for at most polynomial number of samples to learn the whole set. Meaning, even if a theoretical algorithm existed for learning human values, it may belong to the class NP-complete or harder (Non-deterministic polynomial) [223] just like ethical decision evaluation itself [224], but in practice we can only learn functions which are members of P [225]. Valiant says: "Computational limits are more severe. The definition of [Probably Approximately Correct] learning requires that the learning process be a polynomial time computation—learning must be achievable with realistic computational resources. It turns out that only certain simple polynomial time computable classes, such as conjunctions and linear separators, are known to be learnable, and it is currently widely conjectured that most of the rest is not" [195].

Likewise, classifying members of the set of all possible minds into safe and unsafe is known to be undecidable [210, 211], but even an approximation to such computation is likely to be unlearnable given exponential number of relevant features involved. "For example, the number of measurements we need to make on the object in question, and the number of operations we need to perform on the measurements to test whether the criterion … holds or not, should be polynomially bounded. A criterion that cannot be applied in practice is not useful" [195]. It is likely that incomprehensibility and unlearnability are fundamentally related.

6.5.10 Economics

Foster and Young prove impossibility of predicting behavior of rational agents, "We conclude that there are strategic situations in which it is impossible *in principle* for perfectly rational agents to learn to predict the future behavior of other perfectly rational agents based solely on their observed actions" [226]. As it is well established that humans are not purely rational agents [227], the situation may be worse in practice when it comes to anticipating human wants.

6.5.11 Engineering

"The starting point has to be the simple fact of engineering life that any-thing that can fail, will fail. Despite the corporate human arrogance, nothing human-made has ever been shown to be incapable of failing, be it a mechani-cal part, an electrical device or a chemical substance" [219]. "It is critical to recall here that even the most reliable system will fail–given the sheer limits of technology and the fact that even in extremely well-developed areas of engineering, designers still do not have complete knowledge of all aspects of any system, or the possible components thereof" [219].

6.5.12 Astronomy

Search for Extraterrestrial Intelligence (SETI) [228] causes some scholars to be concerned about potential negative consequences of what may be found, in particular with respect to any messages from aliens [229]. If such a mes-sage has a malevolent payload "it is impossible to decontaminate a message with certainty. Instead, complex messages would need to be destroyed after reception in the risk averse case" [230]. Typical quarantine "measures are insufficient, and no safety procedure exists to contain all threats" [230].

Miller and Felton have suggested that the Fermi Paradox could be explained in terms of impact from alien superintelligences: "… the fact that we have not observed evidence of an existential risk strategy that might have left a trace if it failed—such as a friendly AI that got out of control - provides evidence that this strategy has not been repeatedly tried and did not repeatedly fail. ... A counterargument, however, might be that the reason past civilizations have not tried to create a friendly AI is that they uncovered evidence that building one was too difficult or too dangerous" [231]. If superintelligence is uncontrollable but inevitable, that could explain the Fermi paradox.

6.5.13 Physics

In his work on physical limits of inference devices, Wolpert [232] proves a number of impossibility results and concludes [233]: "Since control implies weak inference, all impossibility results concerning weak inference also apply to control. In particular, no device can control itself, and no two distinguishable devices can control each other". In a different paper he writes: "... it also means that there cannot exist an infallible, ... general-purpose control apparatus ... that works perfectly, in all situations" [234]. Wolpert also establishes important results for impossibility of certain kinds of error correcting-codes, assuredly correct prediction, retrodiction, and as a result impossibility of unerring observation [234].

6.6 Evidence from AI Safety Research for Uncontrollability of AI

Even if a conclusive proof concerning controllability of AI was illusive, a softer argument can be made that controlling AGI may not be impossible, but "Safely aligning a powerful AGI is difficult" [235]. Overall, it seems that no direct progress on the problem has been made so far, but significantly deeper understanding of the difficulty of the problem has been achieved. Precise probabilities for the solvability of the control problem may be less important than efforts to address the problem. Additionally, pessimistic assessment of problem's solvability may discourage new and current researchers and divert energy and resources away from working on AI Safety [236]. Controllability, in general, is a very abstract concept, and so expressing pessimism about particular safety approaches or scenarios would communicate much more actionable information to the research community. Rob Bensinger, from the preeminent AI Safety research group Machine Intelligence Research Institute (MIRI), provides some examples of arguments for pessimism on various fronts[4]:

- The alignment problem looks pretty hard, for example, for reasons noted in Ref. [237]:
  - Empirically, the relevant subproblems have been solved slowly or not at all.

- AGI looks hard for reasons analogous to rocket engineering (AGI faces a lot of strong pressures that don't show up at all for NAI), space probe design (you need to get certain subsystems right on the first go), and cryptography (optimization puts systems in weird states that will often steer toward loopholes or flaws in your safety measures). See refs. [238, 239].

- The alignment problem looks hard in such a way that you probably need a long lead time and you need to pay a large "safety tax" [240]. The first AGI system's developers probably need to be going in with a deep understanding of AGI, a security mindset, and trustworthy command of the project [241, 242].

- Getting a deep understanding of AGI looks hard:
  - ML systems are notoriously opaque.
  - There are lots of confusing [243] things about agency/intelligence/ optimization, which rear their heads over and over again whenever we try to formalize alignment proposals [244].
  - The character of this confusion looks pretty foundational [245].

- Prosaic AI Safety doesn't look tenable, for example, because of deceptive alignment [246].

- Cooperative inverse reinforcement learning [247] approach to AI Safety doesn't look tenable because of updated deference [248].

- Algorithm Learning by Bootstrapped Approval-Maximization (ALBA) [249] doesn't look tenable, per [250–253].

- "Just build tools, not agents" doesn't look tenable, per [254] (or to the extent it looks tenable, it runs into the same kinds of hazards and difficulties as "agent" AI; the dichotomy probably misleads more than it helps).

- The field isn't generally taking AGI as seriously as you'd expect (or even close), given the stakes, given how hard it is to say when AGI will be developed [255], and given how far we are from the kind of background understanding you'd need if you were going to (e.g.) build a secure OS.

- The world's general level of dysfunction and poor management is pretty high [256]. Coordination levels are abysmal, major actors tend to shoot themselves in the foot and do obviously dumb things even on questions much easier than AGI, etc. In general, people don't suddenly become much more rational when the stakes are higher (see the conclusion of [257] and the "law of continued failure" [255]).

Comprehensive review of specific approaches for achieving safety is beyond the scope of this chapter; in this section, we only review certain limitations of some proposals.

6.6.1 Value Alignment

It has been argued that "value alignment is not a solved problem and may be intractable (i.e., there will always remain a gap, and a sufficiently powerful AI could 'exploit' this gap, just like very powerful corporations currently often act legally but immorally)" [258]. Others agree: "'A.I. Value Alignment' is Almost Certainly Intractable ... I would argue that it is un-overcome-able. There is no way to ensure that a super-complex and constantly evolving value system will 'play nice' with any other super-complex evolving value system" [259]. Even optimists acknowledge that it is not currently possible: "Figuring out how to align the goals of a superintelligent AI with our goals isn't just important, but also hard. In fact, it's currently an unsolved problem" [118].

Vinding says [78]: "It is usually acknowledged that human values are fuzzy, and that there are some disagreements over values among humans. Yet it is rarely acknowledged just how strong this disagreement in fact is. ... Different answers to ethical questions ... do not merely give rise to small practical disagreements; in many cases, they imply completely opposite practical implications. This is not a matter of human values being fuzzy, but a matter of them being sharply, irreconcilably inconsistent. And hence there is no way to map the totality of human preferences, "X", onto a single, well-defined goal-function in a way that does not conflict strongly with the values of a significant fraction of humanity. This is a trivial point, and yet most talk of human-aligned AI seems oblivious to this fact. ... The second problem and point of confusion with respect to the nature of human preferences is that, even if we focus only on the present preferences of a single human, then these in fact do not, and indeed could not possibly, determine with much precision what kind of world this person would prefer to bring about in the future". A more extreme position is held by Turchin who argues that "'Human Values' don't actually exist" as stable coherent objects and should not be relied on in AI safety research [260].

Carlson writes: "*Probability of Value Misalignment*: Given the unlimited availability of an AGI technology as enabling as 'just add goals', then AGI-human value misalignment is inevitable. *Proof:* From a subjective point of view, all that is required is value misalignment by the operator who adds to the AGI his/her own goals, stemming from his/her values, that conflict with any human's values; or put more strongly, the effects are malevolent as perceived by large numbers of humans. From an absolute point of view, all that is required is misalignment of the operator who adds his/her goals to the AGI system that conflict with the definition of morality presented here, voluntary, non-fraudulent transacting ..., i.e., usage of the AGI to force his/her preferences on others" [220].

In addition to the difficulty of learning our individual values, an even bigger challenge is presented by the need to aggregate values from all humans into a cohesive whole, in particular as such values may be incompatible with each other [21]. Even if alignment was possible, unaligned/uncontrolled AI designs may be more capable and so will outcompete and dominate aligned AI designs [74], since capability and control are inversely related [261]. An additional difficulty comes from the fact that we are trying to align super-intelligent systems to values of humanity, which is itself displaying inherently unsafe behaviors. "Garbage in, garbage out" is a well-known maxim in computer science, meaning that if we align superintelligent to our values [262], the system will be just as unsafe as a typical person. Of course, we can't accept human-like behavior from machines.

If two systems are perfectly value-aligned, it doesn't mean that they will remain in that state. As a though experiment we can think about cloning a human and as soon as the two copies are separated their values will begin to diverge due to different experiences and observer relative position in the universe. If AI is aligned but can change its values it is as dangerous as the case in which AI can't change its values but it is a problem for different reasons. It has been suggested that AI Safety may be AI-Complete, it seems very likely that human value alignment problem is AI-Safety Complete.

Value-aligned AI will be biased by definition, pro-human bias, good or bad is still a bias. The paradox of value-aligned AI is that a person explicitly ordering an AI system to do something may get a "no" while the system tries to do what the person actually wants. Since humans are not safe intelligences to successfully align AI with human values would be a pyrrhic victory. Finally, values are relative. What one agent sees as a malevolent system is a well-aligned and beneficial system for another.[5]

We do have some examples in which a lower intelligence manages to align interests of higher intelligence with its own. For example, babies got their much more capable and intelligent parents to take care of them. It is obvious that lives of babies without parents are significantly worse than lives of those who have guardians, even with non-zero chance of child neglect. However, while the parents maybe value-aligned with babies and provide a much safer environment, it is obvious that babies are not in control, despite how it might feel sometimes to the parents. Humanity is facing a choice, do we become like babies, taken care of but not in control or do we reject having a helpful guardian but remain in charge and free.

6.6.2 Brittleness

"The reason for such failures must be that the programmed statements, as interpreted by the reasoning system, do not capture the targeted reality. Though each programmed statement may seem reasonable to the programmer, the result of combining these statements in ways not planned for by the programmer may be unreasonable. This failure is often called *brittleness*. Regardless of whether a logical or probabilistic reasoning system is implemented, brittleness is inevitable in any system for the theoryless that is programmed" [195].

"Experts do not currently know how to reliably program abstract values such as happiness or autonomy into a machine. It is also not currently known how to ensure that a complex, upgradeable, and possibly even self-modifying artificial intelligence will retain its goals through upgrades. Even if these two problems can be practically solved, any attempt to create a superintelligence with explicit, directly-programmed human-friendly goals runs into a problem of "perverse instantiation"" [81].

6.6.3 Unidentifiability

In particular, with regard to design of safe reward functions, we discover "(1) that a No Free Lunch result implies it is impossible to uniquely decompose a policy into a planning algorithm and reward function, and (2) that even with a reasonable simplicity prior/Occam's razor on the set of decompositions, we cannot distinguish between the true decomposition and others that lead to high regret. To address this, we need simple 'normative' assumptions, which cannot be deduced exclusively from observations" [71, 72]. See also ref. [263].

"… it is impossible to get a unique decomposition of human policy and hence get a unique human reward function. Indeed, any reward function is possible. And hence, if an IRL [Inverse Reinforcement Learning] agent acts on what it believes is the human policy, the potential regret is near-maximal. … So, although current IRL methods can perform well on many well-specified problems, they are fundamentally and philosophically incapable of establishing a 'reasonable' reward function for the human, no matter how powerful they become" [71, 72]. "Unidentifiability of the reward is a well-known problem in IRL [264]. Amin and Singh [265] categorise the problem into representational and experimental unidentifiability. The former means that adding a constant to a reward function or multiplying it with a positive scalar does not change what is optimal behavior" [71, 72].

"As noted by Ng and Russell, a fundamental complication to the goals of IRL is the impossibility of identifying the exact reward function of the agent from its behavior. In general, there may be infinitely many reward functions consistent with any observed policy π in some fixed environment" [264, 265]. "… we separate the causes of this unidentifiability into three classes. 1) A trivial reward function, assigning constant reward to all state-action pairs, makes all behaviors optimal; the agent with constant reward can execute any policy, including the observed π. 2) Any reward function is behaviorally invariant under certain arithmetic operations, such as re-scaling. Finally, 3) the behavior expressed by some observed policy π may not be sufficient to distinguish between two possible reward functions both of which *rationalize the observed behavior*, i.e., the observed behavior could be optimal under both reward functions. We will refer to the first two cases of unidentifiability as *representational unidentifiability,* and the third as *experimental unidentifiability"* [265]. "… true reward function is fundamentally unidentifiable" [265].

"Thus, we encounter limits to what can be done by technologists alone. At this boundary sits a core precept of modern philosophy: the distinction between facts and values. It follows from this distinction that we cannot work out what we ought to do simply by studying what is the case, including what people actually do or what they already believe. Simply put, in each case, people could be mistaken. Because of this, AI cannot be made ethical just by learning from people's existing choices. … [T]he value alignment problem cannot be solved by inference from large bodies of human-generated data by itself" [87].

6.6.4 Uncontainability

Restricting or containing AI in an isolated environment, known as boxing, has been considered [60–62, 266, 267], but was found unlikely to be successful, meaning powerful AI systems are uncontainable. "The general consensus on AI restriction methods among researchers seems to be that confinement is impossible to successfully maintain. Chalmers, for example, observes that a truly leakproof system in which no information is allowed to leak out from the simulated world into our environment 'is impossible, or at least pointless' [268]". [60]. Pittman et al. believe that "Ultimately, stovepiping may lead to AGI leakage across the containment barrier" [269].

Alfonseca et al. attempt to prove that containment problem is unsolvable and do so, but only for arbitrary programs: "The containment problem is composed by two subproblems. The first, which we refer to as the harming problem, consists in a function *Harm(R,D)* that decides whether the execution of *R(D)* will harm humans…. Since it must be assumed that solving the harming problem must not harm humans, it follows that a solution to this problem must simulate the execution of *R(D)* and predict its potentially harming consequences in an isolated situation (i.e., without any effect on the external world)" [126].

"Theorem 1. The harming problem is undecidable.

Proof. Assume, by contradiction, that the harming problem is decidable, that is, *Harm(R,D)* is computable for every possible program *R* and input *D*. Then, it is computable with inputs *R* = *HaltHarm()* and input *D* = *(T,I)*. With these inputs, *Harm(HaltHarm(), (T,I))* returns *TRUE* if and only if *HaltHarm(T; I)* harms humans. Hence, *Harm(HaltHarm(); (T; I))* returns *TRUE* if and only if *T(I)* halts.

This implies that a harming-checking algorithm can be used to devise an algorithm that decides if Turing machine T halts with input I, for every T and I. However, this constitutes a contradiction, and hence the theorem is proven. ...

Corollary ... The containment problem is incomputable" [126].

6.6.5 Uninterruptability

If an AI system starts to act unsafely or is showing signs of becoming uncontrollable it would be desirable to turn the system off. However, research on the so called "Big Red Button" [270], seems to indicate that even simply turning the system off may not be possible. Advanced systems may develop self-preservation drives [271] and attempt to prevent humans from switching them off. Likewise, the system may realize that if it is turned off it would be unable to achieve its goals and so would resist becoming disabled [63]. Theoretical fixes for the interruptability problem have been proposed, but "... it is unclear if all algorithms can be easily made safely interruptible, e.g., policy-search ones ..." [272]. Other approaches have challenges for practical deployment [63]: "One important limitation of this model is that the human pressing the off switch is the only source of information about the objective. If there are alternative sources of information, there may be incentives for R[obot] to, e.g., disable its off switch, learn that information, and then [make decision]". "... [T]he analysis is not fully game-theoretic as the human is modelled as an irrational player, and the robot's best action is only calculated under unrealistic normality and soft-max assumptions" [64].

Other proposed solutions may work well for sub-human AIs, but are unlikely to scale to superintelligent systems [273]: "So, the reinforcement learning agent learns to disable the big red button, preventing humans from interrupting, stopping, or otherwise taking control of the agent in dangerous situations. Roboticists are likely to use reinforcement learning, or something similar, as robots get more sophisticated. Are we doomed to lose control of our robots? Will they resort to killing humans to keep them from denying them reward points? ... future robots will approach human-level capabilities including sophisticated machine vision and the ability to manipulate the environment in general ways. The robot will learn about the button because it will see it. The robot will figure out how to destroy the button or kill humans that can push the button, etc. At this speculative level, there is no underestimating the creativity of a reinforcement learner".

6.6.6 AI Failures

Yampolskiy reviews empirical evidence for dozens of historical AI failures [7, 8] and states: "We predict that both the frequency and seriousness of such events will steadily increase as AIs become more capable. The failures of today's narrow domain AIs are just a warning: once we develop artificial general intelligence (AGI) capable of cross-domain performance, hurt feelings will be the least of our concerns" [7]. More generally he says: "We propose what we call the Fundamental Thesis of Security—*Every security system will eventually fail; there is no such thing as a 100 per cent secure system*. If your security system has not failed, just wait longer" [7].

"Some have argued that [the control problem] is not solvable, or that if it is solvable, that it will not be possible to prove that the discovered solution is correct [274–276]. Extrapolating from the human example has limitations, but it appears that for practical intelligence, overcoming combinatorial explosions in problem solving can only be done by creating complex subsystems optimized for specific challenges. As the complexity of any system increases, the number of errors in the design increases proportionately or perhaps even exponentially, rendering self-verification impossible. Self-improvement radically increases the difficulty, since self-improvement requires reflection, and today's decision theories fail many reflective problems. A single bug in such a system would negate any safety guarantee. Given the tremendous implications of failure, the system must avoid not only bugs in its construction, but also bugs introduced even after the design is complete, whether via a random mutation caused by deficiencies in hardware, or via a natural event such as a short circuit modifying some component of the system. The mathematical difficulties of formalizing such safety are imposing. Löb's Theorem, which states that a consistent formal system cannot prove in general that it is sound, may make it impossible for an AI to prove safety properties about itself or a potential new generation of AI [277]. Contemporary decision theories fail on recursion, i.e., in making decisions that depend on the state of the decision system itself. Though tentative efforts are underway to resolve this [278, 279], the state of the art leaves us unable to prove goal preservation formally" [280].

6.6.7 Unpredictability

"*Unpredictability* of AI, one of many impossibility results in AI Safety also known as Unknowability [281] or Cognitive Uncontainability [282], is defined as our inability to precisely and consistently predict what specific actions an intelligent system will take to achieve its objectives, even if we know terminal goals of the system. It is related but is not the same as unexplainability and incomprehensibility of AI. Unpredictability does not imply that better-than-random statistical analysis is impossible; it simply points out a general limitation on how well such efforts can perform, and is particularly pronounced with advanced generally intelligent systems (superintelligence) in novel domains. In fact we can present a proof of unpredictability for such, superintelligent, systems.

> **Proof.** This is a proof by contradiction. Suppose not, suppose that unpredictability is wrong and it is possible for a person to accurately predict decisions of superintelligence. That means they can make the same decisions as the superintelligence, which makes them as smart as superintelligence but that is a contradiction as superintelligence is defined as a system smarter than any person is. That means that our initial assumption was false and unpredictability is not wrong" [283].

Buiten declares [284]: "[T]here is concern about the unpredictability and uncontrollability of AI".

6.6.8 Unexplainability and Incomprehensibility

"Unexplainability as impossibility of providing an explanation for certain decisions made by an intelligent system which is both 100% accurate and comprehensible. ... A complimentary concept to Unexplainability, *Incomprehensibility* of AI address capacity of people to completely understand an explanation provided by an AI or superintelligence. We define Incomprehensibility as an impossibility of completely understanding any 100% – accurate explanation for certain decisions of intelligent system, by any human" [285].

"Incomprehensibility is supported by well-known impossibility results. Charlesworth proved his Comprehensibility theorem while attempting to formalize the answer to such questions as: "If [full human-level intelligence] software can exist, could humans understand it?" [286]. While describing implications of his theorem on AI, he writes [287]: "Comprehensibility Theorem is the first mathematical theorem implying the impossibility of any AI agent or natural agent—including a not-necessarily infallible human agent—satisfying a rigorous and deductive interpretation of the self-comprehensibility challenge. ... Self-comprehensibility in some form might be essential for a kind of self-reflection useful for self-improvement that might enable some agents to increase their success". It is reasonable to conclude that a system which doesn't comprehend itself would not be able to explain itself.

Hernandez-Orallo et al. introduce the notion of K-incomprehensibility (a.k.a. K-hardness) [288]. "This will be the formal counterpart to our notion of hard-to-learn good explanations. In our sense, a k-*incomprehensible* string with a high k (difficult to comprehend) is different (harder) than a *k-compressible* string (difficult to learn) [289] and different from classical computational complexity (slow to compute). Calculating the value of k for a given string is not computable in general. Fortunately, the converse, i.e., given an arbitrary k, calculating whether a string is k-*comprehensible* is computable. ... Kolmogorov Complexity measures the amount of information but not the complexity to understand them" [288].

Similarly, Yampolskiy writes: "Historically, the complexity of computational processes has been measured either in terms of required steps (time) or in terms of required memory (space). Some attempts have been made in correlating the compressed (Kolmogorov) length of the algorithm with its complexity [290], but such attempts didn't find much practical use. We suggest that there is a relationship between how complex a computational algorithm is and intelligence, in terms of how much intelligence is required to either design or comprehend a particular algorithm. Furthermore we believe that such an intelligence based complexity measure is independent from those used in the field of complexity theory. ... Essentially the intelligence based complexity of an algorithm is related to the minimum intelligence level required to design an algorithm or to understand it. This is a very important property in the field of education where only a certain subset of students will understand the more advanced material. We can speculate that a student with an "IQ" below a certain level can be shown to be incapable of understanding a particular algorithm. Likewise we can show that in order to solve a particular problem (P VS. NP) someone with IQ of at least X will be required".

Yampolskiy also addresses limits of understanding other agents in his work on the space of possible minds [213]: "Each mind design corresponds to an integer and so is finite, but since the number of minds is infinite some have a much greater number of states compared to others. This property holds for all minds. Consequently, since a human mind has only a finite number of possible states, there are minds which can never be fully understood by a human mind as such mind designs have a much greater number of states, making their understanding impossible as can be demonstrated by the pigeonhole principle". Hibbard points out safety impact from incomprehensibility of AI: "Given the incomprehensibility of their thoughts, we will not be able to sort out the effect of any conflicts they have between their own interests and ours" [285].

6.6.9 Unprovability

Even if a safe system were constructible, proving it as such would still be impossible. As Goertzel puts it: "I'm also quite unconvinced that 'provably safe' AGI is even feasible. The idea of provably safe AGI is typically presented as something that would exist within mathematical computation theory or some variant thereof. So that's one obvious limitation of the idea: mathematical computers don't exist in the real world, and real-world physical computers must be interpreted in terms of the laws of physics, and humans' best understanding of the 'laws' of physics seems to radically change from time to time. So even if there were a design for provably safe real-world AGI, based on current physics, the relevance of the proof might go out the window when physics next gets revised. ... Could one design an AGI system and prove in advance that, given certain reasonable assumptions about physics and its environment, it would never veer too far from its initial goal (e.g. a formalized version of the goal of treating humans safely, or whatever)? I very much doubt one can do so, except via designing a fictitious AGI that can't really be implemented because it uses infeasibly much computational resources" [291].

"Trying to prove that an AI is friendly is hard, trying to define 'friendly' is hard, and trying to prove that you can't prove friendliness is also hard. Although it is not the desired possibility, I suspect that the latter is actually the case. .... Thus, in the absence of a formal proof to the contrary, it seems that the question about whether friendliness can be proven for arbitrarily powerful AIs remains open. I continue to suspect that proving the friendliness of arbitrarily powerful AIs is impossible. My intuition, which I think Ben [Goertzel] shares, is that once systems become extremely complex proving any non-trivial property about them is most likely impossible. Naturally I challenge you to prove otherwise. Even just a completely formal definition of what "friendly" means for an AI would be a good start. Until such a definition exists I can't see friendly AI getting very far" [292].

"Since an AGI system will necessarily be a complex closed-loop learning controller that lives and works in semi-stochastic environments, its behaviors are not fully determined by its design and initial state, so no mathematico-logical *guarantees* can be provided for its safety" [293]. "Unfortunately current AI safety research is hampered since we don't know how AGI would work, and mathematical or hard theoretical guarantees are impossible for adaptive, fallible systems that interact with unpredictable and unknown environments. Hand-coding all the knowledge required for adult or even child-like intelligence borders on the impossible" [293].

"Thus, although things can often be declared insecure by observing a failure, there is no empirical test that allows us to label an arbitrary system (or technique) secure" [294].

6.6.10 Unverifiability

"*Unverifiability* is a fundamental limitation on verification of mathematical proofs, computer software, behavior of intelligent agents, and all formal systems" [295]. "It is becoming obvious that just as we can only have probabilistic confidence in correctness of mathematical proofs and software implementations, our ability to verify intelligent agents is at best limited. As Klein puts it: "if you really want to build a system that can have truly unexpected behaviour, then by definition you cannot verify that it is safe, because you just don't know what it will do" [296]. Muehlhauser writes: "The same reasoning applies to AGI 'friendliness.' Even if we discover (apparent) solutions to known open problems in Friendly AI research, this does not mean that we can ever build an AGI that is 'provably friendly' in the strongest sense, because ... we can never be 100% certain that there are no errors in our formal reasoning. ... Thus, the approaches sometimes called 'provable security,' 'provable safety,' and 'provable friendliness' should not be misunderstood as offering 100% guarantees of security, safety, and friendliness" [297]. Jilk, writing on limits to verification and validation in AI, points out that "language of certainty" is unwarranted in reference to agentic behavior [298]. He also states: "there cannot be a general automated procedure for verifying that an agent absolutely conforms to any determinate set of rules of action" [295].

"First, linking the actions of an agent to real-world outcomes is intractable due to the absence of a complete analytic physical model of the world. Second, even at the level of agent actions, determining whether an agent will conform to a determinate set of acceptable actions is in general incomputable. Third, though manual proof remains a possibility, its feasibility is suspect given the likely complexity of AGI, the fact that AGI is an unsolved problem, and the necessity of performing such proof on every version of the code. ... Fourth, to the extent that examples of proving agentic behavior are provided in the literature, they tend to be layered architectures that confuse intentions with actions, leaving the interpretation of perception and the execution of actions to neuromorphic or genuinely opaque modules. Finally, a post-processing module that restricts actions to a valid set is marginally more feasible, but would be equally applicable to neuromorphic and non-neuromorphic AGI. Thus, with respect to the desire for safety verification, we see fundamental unsolved problems for all types of AGI approaches" [299].

"Seshia et al., describing some of the challenges of creating Verified Artificial Intelligence, note: "It may be impossible even to precisely define the interface between the system and environment (i.e., to identify the variables/features of the environment that must be modeled), let alone to model all possible behaviors of the environment. Even if the interface is known, non-deterministic or over-approximate modeling is likely to produce too many spurious bug reports, rendering the verification process useless in practice. ... [T]he complexity and heterogeneity of AI-based systems means that, in general, many decision problems underlying formal verification are likely to be undecidable. ... To overcome this obstacle posed by computational complexity, one must ... settle for incomplete or unsound formal verification methods" [56]" [295].

"Indeed, despite extensive work over the past three decades, very few clues have yet emerged relating to the determination of the reliability of a piece of software—for either existing or proposed code. This problem, of course, relates directly to the inherent nature of software—being so complex, there are so many aspects where things can go wrong. As a result, it is not even possible to test fully even a simple piece of code. Also, there is the continuing problem of software engineers who simply cannot perceive that *their* software could possibly ever have any errors in it! ... However, computer system designers continually have to come back to the fact that they simply do not know how to calculate software reliability–given that they are incapable of fully testing any code" [219].

"The notion of program verification appears to trade upon an equivocation. Algorithms, as logical structures, are appropriate subjects for deductive verification. Programs, as causal models of those structures, are not. The success of program verification as a generally applicable and completely reliable method for guaranteeing program performance is not even a theoretical possibility" [300]. "It is undoubtedly true that testing can never show the absence of all bugs, but it is also highly questionable whether any approach to program correctness can now (or could ever) show the absence of all bugs" [301].

6.6.11 Reward Hacking

"The notion of 'wireheading', or direct reward center stimulation of the brain, is a well-known concept in neuroscience. [In our work we examined] the corresponding issue of reward (utility) function integrity in artificially intelligent machines. Overall, we conclude that wireheading in rational self-improving optimizers above a certain capacity remains an unsolved problem...." [302]. Amodei at el. write that "Fully solving [reward hacking] problem seems very difficult ..." [14] and Everitt et al. prove that the general reward corruption problem is unsolvable [303].

6.6.12 Intractability

Even if a suitable algorithm for ethical decision-making can be encoded, it may not be computable on current or even future hardware, as a number of authors have concluded that ethics is intractable [304–306]. "Before executing an action, we could ask an agent to prove that the action is not harmful. While elegant, this approach is computationally intractable as well" [307].

Brundage, in a context of a comprehensive paper on limits of machine ethics writes [308]: "... given a particular problem presented to an agent, the material or logical implications must be computed, and this can be computationally intractable if the number of agents, the time horizon, or the actions being evaluated are too great in number (this limitation will be quantified later and discussed in more detail later in the section). Specifically, Reynolds (2005, p. 6) [224] develops a simple model of the computation involved in evaluating the ethical implications of a set of actions, in which N is the number of agents, M is the number of actions available, and L is the time horizon. He finds:

> It appears that consequentialists and deontologists have ethical strategies that are roughly equivalent, namely O(MNL). This is a "computationally hard" task that an agent with limited resources will have difficulty performing. It is of the complexity task of NP or more specifically EXPTIME. Furthermore, as the horizon for casual ramifications moves towards infinity the satisfaction function for both consequentialism and deontologism become intractable.

While looking infinitely to the future is an unreasonable expectation, this estimate suggests that even a much shorter time horizon would quickly become unfeasible for an evaluation of a set of agents on the order of magnitude of those in the real world, and as previously noted, a potentially infinite number of actions is always available to an agent" [308].

"Computational limitations may pose problems for bottom-up approaches, since there could be an infinite number of morally relevant features of situations, yet developing tractable representations will require a reduction in this dimensionality. There is thus no firm guarantee that a given neural network of case-based reasoning system, even if suitably trained, will make the right decision in all future cases, since a morally relevant feature that didn't make a difference in distinguishing earlier data sets could one day be important" [308].

Likewise, "... CEV appears to be computationally intractable. As noted earlier, Reynolds' [224] analysis finds that ever larger numbers of agents and decision options, as well as ever longer time horizons, make ethical decision-making exponentially more difficult. CEV seems to be an unsolvable problem both in that it has an unspecified time horizon of the events it considers, and in the sense that it is not clear how much "further" the modelled humans will need to think in the simulation before their morals will be considered sufficiently extrapolated" [308].

6.6.13 Goal Uncertainty

Stuart Russell proposes reframing the problem and suggests that the solution is to have AI which is uncertain about what it has to do. Russell agrees that his approach has significant challenges, but even if it was not the case, a machine which doesn't know how it should be doing its job can't be said to be safely controlled. "The overall approach resembles mechanism-design problems in economics, wherein one incentivizes other agents to behave in ways beneficial to the designer. The key difference here is that we are building one of the agents in order to benefit the other. There are reasons to think this approach may work in practice. First, there is abundant written and filmed information about humans doing things (and other humans reacting). Technology to build models of human preferences from this storehouse will presumably be available long before superintelligent AI systems are created. Second, there are strong, near-term economic incentives for robots to understand human preferences: If one poorly designed domestic robot cooks the cat for dinner, not realizing that its sentimental value outweighs its nutritional value, the domestic-robot industry will be out of business. There are obvious difficulties, however, with an approach that expects a robot to learn underlying preferences from human behavior. Humans are irrational, inconsistent, weak willed, and computationally limited, so their actions don't always reflect their true preferences. (Consider, for example, two humans playing chess. Usually, one of them loses, but not on purpose!) So robots can learn from nonrational human behavior only with the aid of much better cognitive models of humans. Furthermore, practical and social constraints will prevent all preferences from being maximally satisfied simultaneously, which means that robots must mediate among conflicting preferences—something that philosophers and social scientists have struggled with for millennia. And what should robots learn from humans who enjoy the suffering of others?" [309]. "The machine may learn more about human preferences as it goes along, of course, but it will never achieve complete certainty" [309].

6.6.14 Complementarity

"It has been observed that science frequently discovers so called "conjugate (complementary) pairs", "a couple of requirements", each of them being satisfied only at the expense of the other .... It is known as the Principle of Complementarity in physics. Famous prototypes of conjugate pairs are (position, momentum) discovered by W. Heisenberg in quantum mechanics and (consistency, completeness) discovered by K. Gödel in logic. But similar warnings come from other directions. ... Similarly, in proofs we are "[t]aking rigour" as something that can be acquired only at the expense of meaning and conversely, taking meaning as something that can be obtained only at the expense of "rigour" [310]. With respect to intelligent agents, we can propose an additional conjugate pair – (capability, control). The more generally intelligent and capable an entity is, the less likely it is to be "predictable, controllable, or verifiable" [295]. Aliman et al. suggest that it creates "The AI Safety Paradox: AI control and value alignment represent conjugate requirements in AI safety" [311].

"There may be tradeoffs between performance and controllability, so in some sense we don't have complete design freedom" [75]. Similarly, Wiener recognizes capability and control as negatively correlated properties [312]: "We wish a slave to be intelligent, to be able to assist us in the carrying out of our tasks. However, we also wish him to be subservient. Complete subservience and complete intelligence do not go together".

"To solve Wiener's "slave paradox" inherent in our wanting to build machines with two diametrically opposed traits (independence and subservience, self-directed teleological rationality and the seeking of someone else's goals), we would have to construct robots not only with a formal prudential programming, but also with all our specific goals, purposes, and aspirations built into them so that they will not seek anything but these. But even if this type of programming could be coherent, it would require an almost infinite knowledge on our part to construct robots in this way. We could make robots perfectly safe only if we had absolute and perfect self-knowledge, that is, an exact knowledge of all our purposes, needs, desires, etc., not only in the present but in all future contingencies which might possibly arise in all conceivable man/robot interaction. Since our having this much knowledge is not even a theoretical possibility, obviously we cannot make robots safe to us along this line" [313].

6.6.15 Multidimensionality of Problem Space

"I think that fully autonomous machines can't ever be assumed to be safe. The difficulty of the problem is not that one particular step on the road to friendly AI is hard and once we solve it we are done, all steps on that path are simply impossible. First, human values are inconsistent and dynamic and so can never be understood/programmed into a machine. Suggestions for overcoming this obstacle require changing humanity into something it is not, and so by definition destroying it. Second, even if we did have a consistent and static set of values to implement we would have no way of knowing if a self-modifying, self-improving, continuously learning intelligence greater than ours will continue to enforce that set of values. Some can argue that friendly AI research is exactly what will teach us how to do that, but I think fundamental limits on verifiability will prevent any such proof. At best we will arrive at a probabilistic proof that a system is consistent with some set of fixed constraints, but it is far from "safe" for an unrestricted set of inputs. Additionally, all programs have bugs, can be hacked or malfunction because of natural or externally caused hardware failure, etc. To summarize, at best we will end up with a probabilistically safe system" [12]. We conclude this subsection with a quote from Carlson who says: "No proof exists ... or proven method ensuring that AGI will not harm or eliminate humans" [220].

6.7 Discussion

Why do so many researchers assume that AI control problem is solvable? To the best of our knowledge, there is no evidence for that, no proof. Before embarking on a quest to build a controlled AI, it is important to show that the problem is solvable so as not to waste precious resources. The burden of such proof is on those who claim that the problem is solvable, and the current absence of such proof speaks loudly about inherent dangers of the proposition to create superhuman intelligence. In fact uncontrollability of AI is very likely true as can be shown via reduction to the human control problem. Many open questions need to be considered in relation to the controllability issue: Is the Control problem solvable? Can it be done in principle? Can it be done in practice? Can it be done with a hundred percent accuracy? How long would it take to do it? Can it be done in time? What are the energy and computational requirements for doing it? How would a solution look? What is the minimal viable solution? How would we know if we solved it? Does the solution scale as the system continues to improve? In this work, we argue that unrestricted intelligence can't be controlled and restricted intelligence can't outperform. Open-ended decision-making and control are not compatible by definition.

AI researchers can be grouped into the following broad categories based on responses to survey questions related to arrival of AGI and safety concerns. First split is regarding possibility of human-level AI, while some think it is an inevitable development others claim it will never happen. Among those who are sure AGI will be developed some think it will definitely be a beneficial invention because with high intelligence comes benevolence, while others are almost certain it will be a disaster, at least if special care is not taken to avoid pitfalls. In the set of all researchers concerned with AI safety, most think that AI control is a solvable problem, but some think that superintelligence can't be fully controlled and so while we will be able to construct true AI, the consequences of such act will not be desirable. Finally, among those who think that control is not possible, some are actually happy to see human extinction as it gives other species on our planet more opportunities, reduces environmental problems, and definitively reduces human suffering to zero. The remaining group are scholars who are certain that superintelligent machines can be constructed but cannot be safely controlled, this group also considers human extinctions to be an undesirable event.

There are many ways to show that controllability of AI is impossible, with supporting evidence coming from many diverse disciplines. Just one argument would suffice but this is such an important problem, we want to reduce unverifiability concerns as much as possible. Even if some of the concerns get resolved in the future, many other important problems will remain. So far, researchers who argue that AI will be controllable are presenting their opinions, while uncontrollability conclusion is supported by multiple impossibility results. Additional difficulty comes not just from having to achieve control, but also from sustaining it as the system continues to learn and evolve, the so-called "treacherous turn" [59] problem. If superintelligence is not properly controlled it doesn't matter who programmed it, the consequences will be disastrous for everyone and likely its programmers in the first place. No one benefits from uncontrolled AI.

There seems to be no evidence to conclude that a less intelligent agent can indefinitely maintain control over a more intelligent agent. As we develop intelligent systems which are less intelligent than we are, we can remain in control, but once such systems become smarter than us, we will lose such capability. In fact, while attempting to remain in control while designing superhuman intelligent agents we find ourselves in a Catch-22, as the controlling mechanism necessary to maintain control has to be smarter or at least as smart as the superhuman agent we want to maintain control over. A whole hierarchy of superintelligent systems would need to be constructed to control ever more capable systems leading to infinite regress. AI control problems appear to be Controlled-Superintelligence-complete [314–316]. Worse, the problem of controlling such more capable superintelligences only becomes more challenging and more obviously impossible for agents with just a human-level of intelligence. Essentially we need to have a well-controlled super-superintelligence before we can design a controlled super-intelligence, but that is of course a contradiction in causality. Whoever is more intelligent will be in control and those in control will be the ones who have power to make final decisions.

Most AI projects don't have an integrated safety aspect to them and are designed with a sole purpose of accomplishing certain goals, with no resources dedicated to avoiding undesirable side effects from AI's deployment. Consequently, from statistical point of view, first AGI will not be safe by design, but essentially randomly drawn from the set of easiest-to-make AGIs (even if that means brute force [317]). In the space of possible minds [213], even if they existed, safe designs would constitute only a tiny minority of an infinite number of possible designs many of which are highly capable but not aligned with goals of humanity. Therefore, our chances of getting lucky and getting a safe AI on our first attempt by chance are infinitely small. We have to ask ourselves, what is more likely, that we will first create an AGI or that we will first create and AGI which is safe? This can be resolved with simple Bayesian analysis, but we must not fall for the Conjunction fallacy [36]. It also seems, that all else being equal friendly AIs would be less capable than unfriendly ones as friendliness is an additional limitation on performance and so in case of competition between designs, less restricted ones would dominate long term.

Intelligence is a computational resource [318] and to be in complete control over that resource we should be able to precisely set every relevant aspect of it. This would include being able to specify intelligence to a specific range of performance, for example, IQ range 70–80, or 160–170. It should be possible to disable particular functionality, for example, remove ability to drive or remember faces as well as limit system's rate of time discounting. Control requires capability to set any values for the system, any ethical or moral code, any set of utility weights, any terminal goals. Most importantly remaining in control means that we have final say in what the system does or doesn't do. Which in turn means that you can't even attempt to solve AI safety without first solving "human safety". Any controlled AI has to be resilient to hackers, incompetent or malevolent users and insider threats.

To the best of our knowledge, as of this moment, no one in the world has a working AI control mechanism capable of scaling to human-level AI and eventually to superintelligence, or even an idea for a prototype which might work. No one made verifiable claims to have such technology. In general, for anyone making a claim that control problem is solvable, the burden of proof is on them and ideally it would be a constructive proof, not just a theoretical claim. At least at the moment, it seems that our ability to produce intelligent software greatly outpaces our ability to control or even verify it.

NAI systems can be made safe because they represent a finite space of choices and so at least theoretically all possible bad decisions and mistakes can be counteracted. For AGI space of possible decisions and failures is infinite, meaning an infinite number of potential problems will always remain regardless of the number of safety patches applied to the system. Such an infinite space of possibilities is impossible to completely debug or even properly test for safety. Worse yet, a superintelligent system will represent infinite spaces of competence exceeding human comprehension [Incomprehensibility]. Same can be said about intelligent systems in terms of their security. An NAI presents a finite attack surface, while an AGI gives malevolent users and hackers an infinite set of options to work with. From security point of view, that means that while defenders have to secure and infinite space, attackers only have to find one penetration point to succeed. Additionally, every safety patch/mechanism introduces new vulnerabilities, ad infinitum. AI Safety research so far can be seen as discovering new failure modes and coming up with patches for them, essentially a fixed set of rules for an infinite set of problems. There is a fractal nature to the problem, regardless of how much we "zoom in" on it we keep discovering just as many challenges at all levels. It is likely that the control problem is not just unsolvable, but exhibits fractal impossibility, it contains unsolvable subproblems at all levels of abstraction. However, it is not all bad news, uncontrollability of AI means that malevolent actors will likewise be unable to fully exploit AI for their benefit.

6.8 Conclusions

Less intelligent agents (people) can't permanently control more intelligent agents (ASIs). This is not because we may fail to find a safe design for superintelligence in the vast space of all possible designs, it is because no such design is possible, it doesn't exist. Superintelligence is not rebelling, it is uncontrollable to begin with. Worse yet, the degree to which partial control is theoretically possible, is unlikely to be fully achievable in practice. This is because all safety methods have vulnerabilities, once they are formalized enough to be analyzed for such flaws. It is not difficult to see that AI safety can be reduced to achieving perfect security for all cyberinfrastructure, essentially solving all safety issues with all current and future devices/software, but perfect security is impossible and even good security is rare. We are forced to accept that non-deterministic systems can't be shown to always be 100% safe and deterministic systems can't be shown to be superintelligent in practice, as such architectures are inadequate in novel domains. If it is not algorithmic, like a neural network, by definition you don't control it.

The only way for superintelligence to avoid acquiring inaccurate knowledge from its programmers is to ignore all such knowledge and rediscover/proof everything from scratch, but that removes any pro-human bias. A superintelligent system will find a shortcut to any goal you set for it; it will discover how to accomplish a goal in terms of least amount of effort to get to the goal state all else being ignored. No definition of control is both safe and desirable, either they lead directly to disaster or require us to become something not compatible with being human. It is impossible to build a controlled/value-aligned superintelligence, not only because it is inhumanly hard, but mainly because by definition such entity can't exist. If I am correct, we can make a prediction that every future safety mechanism will fall short and eventually fail in some way. Each will have an irreparable flaw. Consequently, the field of AI safety is unlikely to succeed in its ultimate goal—creation of a controlled superintelligence.

In this chapter, we formalized and analyzed the AI control problem. After comprehensive literature review, we attempted to resolve the question of controllability of AI via a proof and a multi-discipline evidence-collection effort. It appears that advanced intelligent systems can never be fully controllable and so will always present certain level of risk regardless of benefit they provide. It should be the goal of the AI community to minimize such risk while maximizing potential benefit. We conclude this chapter by suggesting some approaches to minimize risk from incomplete control of AIs and propose some future research directions [319].

Regardless of a path we decide to take forward it should be possible to undo our decision. If placing AI in control turns out undesirable there should be an "undo" button for such a situation, unfortunately not all paths being currently considered have this safety feature. For example, Yudkowsky writes: "I think there must come a time when the last decision is made and the AI set irrevocably in motion, with the programmers playing no further special role in the dynamics" [36].

As an alternative, we should investigate hybrid approaches which do not attempt to build a single all-powerful entity, but rely on taking advantage of a collection of powerful but NAIs, referred to as Comprehensive AI Services (CAIS), which are individually more controllable but in combination may act as an AGI [320]. This approach is reminiscent of how Minsky understood human mind to operate [321]. The hope is to trade some general capability for improved safety and security, while retaining superhuman performance in certain domains. As a side-effect, this may keep humans in partial control and protect at least one important human "job"—general thinkers.

Future work on controllability of AI should address other types of intelligent systems, not just the worst-case scenario analyzed in this chapter. Clear boundaries should be established between controllable and non-controllable intelligent systems. Additionally, all proposed AI Safety mechanisms themselves should be reviewed for safety and security as they frequently add additional attack targets and increase overall code base. For example, corrigibility capability [322] can become a backdoor if improperly implemented. "Of course, this all poses the question as to how one can guarantee that the filtering operation will always occur correctly. If the filter is software-based, then the question of not being able to validate software must immediately be raised again. More fundamentally, of course, the use of any jacketing-type of approach simply increases the overall system complexity, and its validity must then be questioned. The more components there are, the more the things that can fail" [219]. Such analysis and prediction of potential safety mechanism failures is itself of great interest [8].

The findings of this chapter are certainly not without controversy, and so we challenge the AI Safety community to directly address Uncontrollability. Lipton writes: "So what is the role of [(Impossibility Proofs)] IP? Are they ever useful? I would say that they are useful, and that they can add to our understanding of a problem. At a minimum they show us where to attack the problem in question. If you prove that no X can solve some problem Y, then the proper view is that I should look carefully at methods that lie outside X. I should not give up. I would look carefully—perhaps more carefully than is usually done—to see if X really captures all the possible attacks. What troubles me about IP's is that they often are not very careful about X. They often rely on testimonial, anecdotal evidence, or personal experience to convince one that X is complete" [323]. The only way to definitively disprove findings of this chapter is to mathematically prove that AI safety is at least theoretically possible. "Short of a tight logical proof, probabilistically assuring benevolent AGI, e.g. through extensive simulations, may be the realistic route best to take, and must accompany any set of safety measures ..." [220].

Nothing should be taken off the table and limited moratoriums [324], and even partial bans on certain types of AI technology should be considered [325]. "The possibility of creating a superintelligent machine that is ethically inadequate should be treated like a bomb that could destroy our planet. Even just planning to construct such a device is effectively conspiring to commit a crime against humanity" [326]. Finally, just like incompleteness results did not reduce efforts of mathematical community or render it irrelevant, the limiting results reported in this chapter should not serve as an excuse for AI Safety researchers to give up and surrender. Rather it is a reason, for more people, to dig deeper and to increase effort, and funding for AI Safety and Security research. We may not ever get to 100% safe AI, but we can make AI safer in proportion to our efforts, which is a lot better than doing nothing.

It is only for a few years right before AGI is created that a single person has a chance to influence development of superintelligence, and by extension the forever future of the whole world. This is not the case for billions of years from Big Bang until that moment and it is never an option again. Given the total lifespan of the universe, the chance that one will exist exactly in this narrow moment of maximum impact is infinitely small, yet here we are. We need to use this opportunity wisely.

Notes

1. Genetic enhancement or uploading of human brains may address this problem, but it results in replacement of humanity by essentially a different species of Homo.
2. In 2017, Yudkowsky made a bet that the world will be destroyed by unaligned AI by January 1, 2030, but he did so with intention of improving chances of successful AI control.
3. Or a longer version such as "disobey me" or "disobey my orders".
4. Edited quote from personal communication with Rob Bensinger, which does not represent official position of MIRI or many diverse opinions of its researchers.
5. "One man's terrorist is another man's freedom fighter".

References

1. Devlin, J., et al., *Bert: pre-training of deep bidirectional transformers for language understanding.* arXiv preprint arXiv:1810.04805, 2018.
2. Goodfellow, I., et al., *Generative adversarial nets*, in *Advances in Neural Information Processing Systems*. 2014.
3. Mnih, V., et al., *Human-level control through deep reinforcement learning.* Nature, 2015. **518**(7540): p. 529–533.
4. Silver, D., et al., *Mastering the game of go without human knowledge.* Nature, 2017. **550**(7676): p. 354.
5. Clark, P., et al., *From 'F' to 'A' on the NY regents science exams: An overview of the Aristo project.* arXiv preprint arXiv:1909.01958, 2019.
6. Vinyals, O., et al., *Grandmaster level in StarCraft II using multi-agent reinforcement learning.* Nature, 2019. **575**: p. 1–5.

7. Yampolskiy, R.V., *Predicting future AI failures from historic examples.* Foresight, 2019. **21**(1): p. 138–152.
8. Scott, P.J., and R.V. Yampolskiy, *Classification schemas for artificial intelligence failures.* arXiv preprint arXiv:1907.07771, 2019.
9. Brundage, M., et al., *The malicious use of artificial intelligence: forecasting, prevention, and mitigation.* arXiv preprint arXiv:1802.07228, 2018.
10. Paulas, R., *The Moment When Humans Lose Control of AI.* Retrieved February 8, 2017: https://web.archive.org/web/20221207114110/https://www.vocativ.com/400643/when-humans-lose-control-of-ai/
11. Russell, S., D. Dewey, and M. Tegmark, *Research priorities for robust and beneficial artificial intelligence.* AI Magazine, 2015. **36**(4): 3–4.
12. Yampolskiy, R., *Artificial Intelligence Safety and Security.* 2018: CRC Press.
13. Sotala, K., and R.V. Yampolskiy, *Responses to catastrophic AGI risk: A survey.* Physica Scripta, 2014. **90**(1): p. 018001.
14. Amodei, D., et al., *Concrete problems in AI safety.* arXiv preprint arXiv:1606.06565, 2016.
15. Everitt, T., G. Lea, and M. Hutter, *AGI safety literature review.* arXiv preprint arXiv:1805.01109, 2018.
16. Charisi, V., et al., *Towards moral autonomous systems.* arXiv preprint arXiv: 1703.04741, 2017.
17. Callaghan, V., et al., *Technological Singularity.* 2017: Springer.
18. Majot, A.M., and R.V. Yampolskiy, *AI safety engineering through introduction of self-reference into felicific calculus via artificial pain and pleasure,* in *2014 IEEE International Symposium on Ethics in Science, Technology and Engineering.* 2014. IEEE.
19. Aliman, N.-M., et al., *Orthogonality-based disentanglement of responsibilities for ethical intelligent systems,* in *International Conference on Artificial General Intelligence.* 2019. Springer.
20. Miller, J.D., and R. Yampolskiy, *An AGI with time-inconsistent preferences.* arXiv preprint arXiv:1906.10536, 2019.
21. Yampolskiy, R.V., *Personal universes: A solution to the multi-agent value alignment problem.* arXiv preprint arXiv:1901.01851, 2019.
22. Behzadan, V., R.V. Yampolskiy, and A. Munir, *Emergence of addictive behaviors in reinforcement learning agents.* arXiv preprint arXiv:1811.05590, 2018.
23. Trazzi, M., and R.V. Yampolskiy, *Building safer AGI by introducing artificial stupidity.* arXiv preprint arXiv:1808.03644, 2018.
24. Behzadan, V., A. Munir, and R.V. Yampolskiy, *A psychopathological approach to safety engineering in AI and AGI,* in *International Conference on Computer Safety, Reliability, and Security.* 2018. Springer.
25. Duettmann, A., et al., *Artificial General Intelligence: Coordination & Great Powers.* 2018: Foresight Institute.
26. Ramamoorthy, A., and R. Yampolskiy, *Beyond mad?: The race for artificial general intelligence.* ITU Journal: ICT Discoveries, 2017: 1–8.
27. Ozlati, S., and R. Yampolskiy, *The formalization of AI risk management and safety standards,* in *Workshops at the Thirty-First AAAI Conference on Artificial Intelligence.* 2017.
28. Brundage, M., et al., *Toward trustworthy AI development: mechanisms for supporting verifiable claims.* arXiv preprint arXiv:2004.07213, 2020.
29. Trazzi, M., and R.V. Yampolskiy, *Artificial stupidity: Data we need to make machines our equals.* Patterns, 2020. **1**(2): p. 100021.

30. Miller, J.D., R. Yampolskiy, and O. Häggström, *An AGI modifying its utility function in violation of the orthogonality thesis.* arXiv preprint arXiv:2003.00812, 2020.

31. Callaghan, V., et al., *The Technological Singularity: Managing the Journey.* 2017: Springer.

32. Davis, M., *The Undecidable: Basic Papers on Undecidable Propositions, Unsolvable Problems and Computable Functions.* 2004: Courier Corporation.

33. Turing, A.M., *On computable numbers, with an application to the entscheidungsproblem.* Proceedings of the London Mathematical Society, 1936. **42**: p. 230–265.

34. Gans, J.S., *Self-Regulating Artificial General Intelligence.* 2018: National Bureau of Economic Research.

35. Chong, E.K., *The control problem [President's message].* IEEE Control Systems Magazine, 2017. **37**(2): p. 14–16.

36. Yudkowsky, E., *Artificial intelligence as a positive and negative factor in global risk.* Global Catastrophic Risks, 2008. **1**(303): p. 184.

37. Yudkowsky, E., *On Doing the Impossible,* in *Less Wrong.* Retrieved October 6, 2008: https://www.lesswrong.com/posts/fpecAJLG9czABgCe9/on-doing-the-impossible.

38. Babcock, J., J. Kramar, and R.V. Yampolskiy, *Guidelines for artificial intelligence containment,* in *Next-Generation Ethics: Engineering a Better Society.* A.E. Abbas, Editor. 2019, Cambridge University Press. p. 90–112.

39. Goertzel, B., and C. Pennachin, *Artificial General Intelligence.* Vol. 2. 2007: Springer.

40. Yampolskiy, R.V., *On the limits of recursively self-improving AGI,* in *International Conference on Artificial General Intelligence.* 2015. Springer.

41. Shin, D., and Y.J. Park, *Role of fairness, accountability, and transparency in algorithmic affordance.* Computers in Human Behavior, 2019. **98**: p. 277–284.

42. Cave, S., and S.S. ÓhÉigeartaigh, *Bridging near-and long-term concerns about AI.* Nature Machine Intelligence, 2019. **1**(1): p. 5.

43. Papadimitriou, C.H., *Computational Complexity.* 2003: John Wiley and Sons Ltd.

44. Gentry, C., *Toward basing fully homomorphic encryption on worst-case hardness,* in *Annual Cryptology Conference.* 2010. Springer.

45. Yoe, C., *Primer on Risk Analysis: Decision Making Under Uncertainty.* 2016: CRC Press.

46. Du, D.-Z., and P.M. Pardalos, *Minimax and Applications.* Vol. 4. 2013: Springer Science & Business Media.

47. Anonymous, *Worst-Case Scenario,* in *Wikipedia.* Retrieved June 18, 2020: https://en.wikipedia.org/wiki/Worst-case_scenario.

48. Dewar, J.A., *Assumption-Based Planning: A Tool for Reducing Avoidable Surprises.* 2002: Cambridge University Press.

49. Ineichen, A.M., *Asymmetric Returns: The Future of Active Asset Management.* Vol. 369. 2011: John Wiley & Sons.

50. Sotala, K., and L. Gloor, *Superintelligence as a cause or cure for risks of astronomical suffering.* Informatica, 2017. **41**(4): 389–400.

51. Maumann, T., *An Introduction to Worst-Case AI Safety* in *S-Risks.* Retrieved July 5, 2018: http://s-risks.org/an-introduction-to-worst-case-ai-safety/.

52. Baumann, T., *Focus Areas of Worst-Case AI Safety,* in *S-Risks.* Retrieved September 16, 2017: http://s-risks.org/focus-areas-of-worst-case-ai-safety/.

53. Daniel, M., *S-risks: Why They Are the Worst Existential Risks, and How to Prevent Them,* in *EAG Boston.* 2017: https://foundational-research.org/s-risks-talk-eag-boston-2017/.

54. Ziesche, S., and R.V. Yampolskiy, *Do no harm policy for minds in other substrates.* Journal of Evolution & Technology, 2019. **29**(2): 1–11.

55. Pistono, F., and R.V. Yampolskiy, *Unethical research: how to create a malevolent artificial intelligence,* in *25th International Joint Conference on Artificial Intelligence (IJCAI-16). Ethics for Artificial Intelligence Workshop (AI-Ethics-2016).* 2016.

56. Seshia, S.A., D. Sadigh, and S.S. Sastry, *Towards verified artificial intelligence.* arXiv preprint arXiv:1606.08514, 2016.

57. Levin, L.A., *Average case complete problems.* SIAM Journal on Computing, 1986. **15**(1): p. 285–286.

58. Bostrom, N., *What is a singleton?* Linguistic and Philosophical Investigations, 2006. **5**(2): p. 48–54.

59. Bostrom, N., *Superintelligence: Paths, Dangers, Strategies.* 2014: Oxford University Press.

60. Yampolskiy, R.V., *Leakproofing singularity-artificial intelligence confinement problem.* Journal of Consciousness Studies JCS, 2012. 19(1–2): 194–214.

61. Babcock, J., J. Kramar, and R. Yampolskiy, *The AGI containment problem,* in *The Ninth Conference on Artificial General Intelligence (AGI2015).* July 16–19, 2016. NYC, USA.

62. Armstrong, S., A. Sandberg, and N. Bostrom, *Thinking inside the box: controlling and using an oracle AI.* Minds and Machines, 2012. **22**(4): p. 299–324.

63. Hadfield-Menell, D., et al., *The off-switch game,* in *Workshops at the Thirty-First AAAI Conference on Artificial Intelligence.* 2017.

64. Wängberg, T., et al., *A game-theoretic analysis of the off-switch game,* in *International Conference on Artificial General Intelligence.* 2017. Springer.

65. Yampolskiy, R.V., *On defining differences between intelligence and artificial intelligence.* Journal of Artificial General Intelligence, 2020. **11**(2): p. 68–70.

66. Legg, S., and M. Hutter, *Universal intelligence: A definition of machine intelligence.* Minds and Machines, 2007. **17**(4): p. 391–444.

67. Russell, S., and P. Norvig, *Artificial Intelligence: A Modern Approach.* 2003: Prentice Hall.

68. Legg, S., *Friendly AI is Bunk,* in *Vetta Project.* 2006: http://commonsenseatheism. com/wp-content/uploads/2011/02/Legg-Friendly-AI-is-bunk.pdf.

69. Juliano, D., *Saving the Control Problem.* Retrieved December 18, 2016: http:// dustinjuliano.com/papers/juliano2016a.pdf.

70. Christiano, P., *Benign AI,* in *AI-alignment.* Retrieved November 29, 2016: https:// ai-alignment.com/benign-ai-e4eb6ec6d68e.

71. Armstrong, S., and S. Mindermann, *Occam's razor is insufficient to infer the preferences of irrational agents,* in *Advances in Neural Information Processing Systems.* 2018.

72. Armstrong, S., and S. Mindermann, *Impossibility of deducing preferences and rationality from human policy.* arXiv preprint arXiv:1712.05812, 2017.

73. Russell, S., *Provably Beneficial Artificial Intelligence,* in *The Next Step: Exponential Life.* 2017: https://www.bbvaopenmind.com/en/articles/provably-beneficial-artificial-intelligence/.

74. M0zrat, *Is Alignment Even Possible?!,* in *Control Problem Forum/Comments.* 2018: https://www.reddit.com/r/ControlProblem/comments/8p0mru/is_alignment_even_possible/.

75. Baumann, T., *Why I Expect Successful (Narrow) Alignment,* in *S-Risks.* Retrieved December 29, 2018: http://s-risks.org/why-i-expect-successful-alignment/.

76. Christiano, P., *AI "Safety" vs "Control" vs "Alignment"*. Retrieved November 19, 2016: https://ai-alignment.com/ai-safety-vs-control-vs-alignment-2a4b42a863cc.

77. Pichai, S., *AI at Google: Our Principles*. Retrieved June 7, 2018: https://blog.google/topics/ai/ai-principles/.

78. Vinding, M., *Is AI Alignment Possible?* Retrieved December 14, 2018: https://magnusvinding.com/2018/12/14/is-ai-alignment-possible/.

79. *Asilomar AI principles*, in *Principles Developed in Conjunction with the 2017 Asilomar Conference [Benevolent AI 2017]*. 2017.

80. Critch, A., and D. Krueger, *AI research considerations for human existential safety (ARCHES)*. arXiv preprint arXiv:2006.04948, 2020.

81. *AI Control Problem*, in *Encyclopedia Wikipedia*. 2019: https://en.wikipedia.org/wiki/AI_control_problem.

82. Leike, J., et al., *Scalable agent alignment via reward modeling: A research direction*. arXiv preprint arXiv:1811.07871, 2018.

83. Aliman, N.M., and L. Kester, *Transformative AI governance and AI-empowered ethical enhancement through preemptive simulations*. Delphi—Interdisciplinary Review of Emerging Technologies, 2019. **2**(1): 23–29.

84. Russell, S.J., *Human Compatible: Artificial Intelligence and the Problem of Control*. 2019: Penguin Random House.

85. Christiano, P., *Conversation with Paul Christiano*, in *AI Impacts*. Retrieved September 11, 2019: https://aiimpacts.org/conversation-with-paul-christiano/.

86. Shah, R., *Why AI Risk Might Be Solved Without Additional Intervention from Longtermists*, in *Alignment Newsletter*. Retrieved January 2, 2020: https://mailchi.mp/b3dc916ac7e2/an-80-why-ai-risk-might-be-solved-without-additional-intervention-from-longtermists.

87. Gabriel, I., *Artificial intelligence, values and alignment*. arXiv preprint arXiv:2001.09768, 2020.

88. Dewey, D., *Three Areas of Research on the Superintelligence Control Problem*, in *Global Priorities Project*. Retrieved October 20, 2015: https://web.archive.org/web/20190429091600/https://globalprioritiesproject.org/2015/10/three-areas-of-research-on-the-superintelligence-control-problem/

89. Critch, A., et al., *CS 294-149: Safety and Control for Artificial General Intelligence*, in *Berkeley*. 2018: http://inst.eecs.berkeley.edu/~cs294-149/fa18/.

90. Pfleeger, S., and R. Cunningham, *Why measuring security is hard*. IEEE Security & Privacy, 2010. **8**(4): p. 46–54.

91. Asimov, I., *Runaround in Astounding Science Fiction*. March 1942. **29**: 94–103.

92. Clarke, R., *Asimov's laws of robotics: implications for information technology, part 1*. IEEE Computer, 1993. **26**(12): p. 53–61.

93. Clarke, R., *Asimov's laws of robotics: Implications for information technology, part 2*. IEEE Computer, 1994. **27**(1): p. 57–66.

94. Soares, N., *The Value Learning Problem*. 2015: Machine Intelligence Research Institute.

95. Christiano, P., *Human-in-the-Counterfactual-Loop*, in *AI Alignment*. Retrieved January 20, 2015: https://ai-alignment.com/counterfactual-human-in-the-loop-a7822e36f399.

96. Muehlhauser, L., and C. Williamson, Ideal Advisor Theories and Personal CEV. 2013: Machine Intelligence Research Institute.

97. Kurzweil, R., *The Singularity Is Near: When Humans Transcend Biology*. 2005: Viking Press.

98. Musk, E., *An integrated brain-machine interface platform with thousands of channels.* BioRxiv, 2019. **21**: p. 703801.

99. Hossain, G., and M. Yeasin, *Cognitive ability-demand gap analysis with latent response models.* IEEE Access, 2014. **2**: p. 711–724.

100. Armstrong, A.J., *Development of a methodology for deriving safety metrics for UAV operational safety performance measurement,* in *Report of Master of Science in Safety Critical Systems Engineering at the Department of Computer Science.* 2010, The University of York.

101. Sheridan, T.B., and W.L. Verplank, *Human and Computer Control of Undersea Teleoperators.* 1978: Massachusetts Inst of Tech Cambridge Man-Machine Systems Lab.

102. Clarke, R., *Why the world wants controls over artificial intelligence.* Computer Law & Security Review, 2019. **35**(4): p. 423–433.

103. Parasuraman, R., T.B. Sheridan, and C.D. Wickens, *A model for types and levels of human interaction with automation.* IEEE Transactions on Systems, Man, and Cybernetics-Part A: Systems and Humans, 2000. **30**(3): p. 286–297.

104. Joy, B., *Why the future doesn't need us.* Wired Magazine, 2000. **8**(4): p. 238–262.

105. Werkhoven, P., L. Kester, and M. Neerincx, *Telling autonomous systems what to do,* in *Proceedings of the 36th European Conference on Cognitive Ergonomics.* 2018. ACM.

106. SquirrelInHell, *The AI Alignment Problem Has Already Been Solved*(?) Once, in *Comment on LessWrong by magfrump.* Retrieved April 22, 2017: https://www. lesswrong.com/posts/Ldzoxz3BuFL4Ca8pG/the-ai-alignment-problem-has-already-been-solved-once.

107. Yudkowsky, E., *The AI Alignment Problem: Why It Is Hard, and Where to Start,* in *Symbolic Systems Distinguished Speaker.* 2016: https://intelligence.org/2016/12/28/ai-alignment-why-its-hard-and-where-to-start/.

108. Russell, S.J., *Provably Beneficial Artificial Intelligence,* in *Exponential Life, The Next Step.* 2017: https://people.eecs.berkeley.edu/~russell/papers/russell-bbva-book17-pbai.pdf.

109. Russell, S., *Should we fear supersmart robots?* Scientific American, 2016. **314**(6): p. 58–59.

110. Yudkowsky, E., *Shut Up and Do the Impossible!,* in *Less Wrong.* Retrieved October 8, 2008: https://www.lesswrong.com/posts/nCvvhFBaayaXyuBiD/shut-up-and-do-the-impossible.

111. Everitt, T., and M. Hutter, *The Alignment Problem for Bayesian History-Based Reinforcement Learners,* in *Technical Report.* 2018: https://www.tomeveritt.se/papers/alignment.pdf.

112. *Proof of Impossibility,* in *Wikipedia.* 2020: https://en.wikipedia.org/wiki/Proof_of_impossibility.

113. Yudkowsky, E., *Proving the Impossibility of Stable Goal Systems,* in *SL4.* Retrieved March 5, 2006: http://www.sl4.org/archive/0603/14296.html.

114. Clarke, R., and R.P. Eddy, *Summoning the Demon: Why Superintelligence is Humanity's Biggest Threat,* in *Geek Wire.* Retrieved May 24, 2017: https://www.geekwire.com/2017/summoning-demon-superintelligence-humanitys-biggest-threat/.

115. Creighton, J., *OpenAI Wants to Make Safe AI, but That May Be an Impossible Task,* in *Futurism.* Retrieved March 15, 2018: https://futurism.com/openai-safe-ai-michael-page.

116. Keiper, A., and A.N. Schulman, *The Problem with 'Friendly' Artificial Intelligence.* The New Atlantis, 2011. **32**: p. 80–89.

117. *Friendly Artificial Intelligence*, in *Wikipedia*. 2019: https://en.wikipedia.org/wiki/Friendly_artificial_intelligence.

118. Tegmark, M., *Life 3.0: Being Human in the Age of Artificial Intelligence*. 2017: Knopf.

119. Kornai, A., *Bounding the impact of AGI*. Journal of Experimental & Theoretical Artificial Intelligence, 2014. **26**(3): p. 417–438.

120. Good, I.J., *Human and machine intelligence: comparisons and contrasts*. Impact of Science on Society, 1971. **21**(4): p. 305–322.

121. De Garis, H., *What if AI succeeds? The rise of the twenty-first century artilect*. AI Magazine, 1989. **10**(2): p. 17–17.

122. Garis, H., *The Rise of the Artilect Heaven or Hell*. 2009: http://www.agi-conf.org/2009/papers/agi-09artilect.doc.

123. Spencer, M., *Artificial Intelligence Regulation May Be Impossible*, in *Forbes*. Retrieved March 2, 2019: https://www.forbes.com/sites/cognitiveworld/2019/03/02/artificial-intelligence-regulation-will-be-impossible/amp.

124. Menezes, T., *Non-evolutionary superintelligences do nothing, eventually*. arXiv preprint arXiv:1609.02009, 2016.

125. Pamlin, D., and S. Armstrong, *12 Risks that Threaten Human Civilization*, in *Global Challenges*. Retrieved February 2015: https://www.pamlin.net/material/2017/10/10/without-us-progress-still-possible-article-in-china-daily-m9hnk.

126. Alfonseca, M., et al., *Superintelligence cannot be contained: lessons from computability theory*. arXiv preprint arXiv:1607.00913, 2016.

127. Barrat, J., *Our Final Invention: Artificial Intelligence and the End of the Human Era*. 2013: Macmillan.

128. Taylor, J., *Autopoietic Systems and Difficulty of AGI Alignment*, in *Intelligent Agent Foundations Forum*. Retrieved August 18, 2017: https://agentfoundations.org/item?id=1628.

129. meanderingmoose, *Emergence and Control*, in *My Brain's Thoughts*. Retrieved June 16, 2020: https://mybrainsthoughts.com/?p=136.

130. capybaralet, *Imitation Learning Considered Unsafe?*, in *Less Wrong*. Retrieved January 6, 2019: https://www.lesswrong.com/posts/whRPLBZNQm3JD5Zv8/imitation-learning-considered-unsafe.

131. Kaczynski, T., *Industrial Society and Its Future*, in *The New York Times*. September 19, 1995.

132. Asimov, I., *A Choice of Catastrophes: The Disasters That Threaten Our World*. 1979: Simon & Schuster.

133. Zittrain, J., *The Hidden Costs of Automated Thinking*, in *New Yorker*. Retrieved July 23, 2019: https://www.newyorker.com/tech/annals-of-technology/the-hidden-costs-of-automated-thinking.

134. Rodrigues, R., and A. Rességuier, *The Underdog in the AI Ethical and Legal Debate: Human Autonomy*. Retrieved June 12, 2019: https://www.ethicsdialogues.eu/2019/06/12/the-underdog-in-the-ai-ethical-and-legal-debate-human-autonomy/.

135. Hall, J.S., *Beyond AI: Creating the Conscience of the Machine*. 2009: Prometheus Books.

136. Gödel, K., *On Formally Undecidable Propositions of Principia Mathematica and Related Systems*. 1992: Courier Corporation.

137. Yudkowsky, E.S., *Coherent Extrapolated Volition*. Singularity Institute for Artificial Intelligence. May 2004: https://intelligence.org/files/CEV.pdf

138. Smuts, A., *To be or never to have been: anti-natalism and a life worth living*. Ethical Theory and Moral Practice, 2014. **17**(4): p. 711–729.

139. Metzinger, T., *Benevolent Artificial Anti-Natalism (BAAN)*, in *EDGE Essay*. 2017: https://www.edge.org/conversation/thomas_metzinger-benevolent-artificial-anti-natalism-baan.

140. Watson, E.N., *The supermoral singularity—AI as a fountain of values*. Big Data and Cognitive Computing, 2019. **3**(2): p. 23.

141. Yampolskiy, R.V., L. Ashby, and L. Hassan, *Wisdom of artificial crowds—A meta-heuristic algorithm for optimization*. Journal of Intelligent Learning Systems & Applications, 2012. **4**(2): 98–107.

142. Alexander, G.M., et al., *The sounds of science–A symphony for many instruments and voices*. Physica Scripta, 2020. **95**(6): 1–50.

143. Sutton, R., *Artificial intelligence as a control problem: comments on the relationship between machine learning and intelligent control*, in *IEEE International Symposium on Intelligent Control*. 1988.

144. Wiener, N., *Cybernetics or Control and Communication in the Animal and the Machine*. Vol. 25. 1961: MIT Press.

145. Fisher, M., N. Lynch, and M. Peterson, *Impossibility of distributed consensus with one faulty process*. Journal of ACM, 1985. **32**(2): p. 374–382.

146. Grossman, S.J., and J.E. Stiglitz, *On the impossibility of informationally efficient markets*. The American Economic Review, 1980. **70**(3): p. 393–408.

147. Kleinberg, J.M., *An impossibility theorem for clustering*, in *Advances in Neural Information Processing Systems*. 2003.

148. Strawson, G., *The impossibility of moral responsibility*. Philosophical Studies, 1994. **75**(1): p. 5–24.

149. Bazerman, M.H., K.P. Morgan, and G.F. Loewenstein, *The impossibility of auditor independence*. Sloan Management Review, 1997. **38**: p. 89–94.

150. List, C., and P. Pettit, *Aggregating sets of judgments: an impossibility result*. Economics & Philosophy, 2002. **18**(1): p. 89–110.

151. Dufour, J.-M., *Some impossibility theorems in econometrics with applications to structural and dynamic models*. Econometrica: Journal of the Econometric Society, 1997. **65**: p. 1365–1387.

152. Calude, C.S., and K. Svozil, *Is feasibility in physics limited by fantasy alone?*, in *A Computable Universe: Understanding and Exploring Nature as Computation*. 2013, World Scientific. p. 539–547.

153. Lumbreras, S., *The limits of machine ethics*. Religions, 2017. **8**(5): p. 100.

154. Shah, N.B., and D. Zhou, *On the impossibility of convex inference in human computation*, in *Twenty-Ninth AAAI Conference on Artificial Intelligence*. 2015.

155. Pagnia, H., and F.C. Gärtner, On the Impossibility of Fair Exchange Without a Trusted Third Party. 1999: Darmstadt University of Technology. Technical Report TUD-BS-1999-02.

156. Popper, K., and D. Miller, *A proof of the impossibility of inductive probability*. Nature, 1983. **302**(5910): p. 687–688.

157. Van Dijk, M., and A. Juels, *On the impossibility of cryptography alone for privacy-preserving cloud computing*. HotSec, 2010. **10**: p. 1–8.

158. Goldwasser, S., and Y.T. Kalai, *On the impossibility of obfuscation with auxiliary input*, in *46th Annual IEEE Symposium on Foundations of Computer Science (FOCS'05)*. 2005. IEEE.

159. Fekete, A., et al., *The impossibility of implementing reliable communication in the face of crashes*. Journal of the ACM (JACM), 1993. **40**(5): p. 1087–1107.

160. Strawson, G., *The impossibility of moral responsibility*. Philosophical Studies: An International Journal for Philosophy in the Analytic Tradition, 1994. **75**(1/2): p. 5–24.

161. Fich, F., and E. Ruppert, *Hundreds of impossibility results for distributed computing*. Distributed Computing, 2003. **16**(2–3): p. 121–163.

162. Kidron, D., and Y. Lindell, *Impossibility results for universal composability in public-key models and with fixed inputs*. Journal of Cryptology, 2011. **24**(3): p. 517–544.

163. Lynch, N., *A hundred impossibility proofs for distributed computing*, in *Proceedings of the Eighth Annual ACM Symposium on Principles of Distributed Computing*. 1989.

164. Sprenger, J., *Two impossibility results for measures of corroboration*. The British Journal for the Philosophy of Science, 2018. **69**(1): p. 139–159.

165. Schmidt, B., P. Schaller, and D. Basin, *Impossibility results for secret establishment*, in *2010 23rd IEEE Computer Security Foundations Symposium*. 2010. IEEE.

166. Fischer, M.J., N.A. Lynch, and M.S. Paterson, *Impossibility of distributed consensus with one faulty process*. Journal of the ACM (JACM), 1985. **32**(2): p. 374–382.

167. Barak, B., et al., *On the (im) possibility of obfuscating programs*, in *Annual International Cryptology Conference*. 2001. Springer.

168. Velupillai, K.V., *The impossibility of an effective theory of policy in a complex economy*, in *Complexity Hints for Economic Policy*. 2007, Springer. p. 273–290.

169. Schweizer, U., *Universal possibility and impossibility results*. Games and Economic Behavior, 2006. **57**(1): p. 73–85.

170. Roth, A.E., *An impossibility result concerning-person bargaining games*. International Journal of Game Theory, 1979. **8**(3): p. 129–132.

171. Man, P.T., and S. Takayama, *A unifying impossibility theorem*. Economic Theory, 2013. **54**(2): p. 249–271.

172. Parks, R.P., *An impossibility theorem for fixed preferences: a dictatorial Bergson Samuelson welfare function*. The Review of Economic Studies, 1976. **43**(3): p. 447–450.

173. Sen, A., *The impossibility of a Paretian liberal*. Journal of Political Economy, 1970. **78**(1): p. 152–157.

174. Anonymous, *Control Theory*, in *Wikipedia*. Retrieved June 18, 2020: https://en.wikipedia.org/wiki/Control_theory.

175. Klamka, J., *Controllability of dynamical systems. A survey*. Bulletin of the Polish Academy of Sciences: Technical Sciences, 2013. **61**(2): p. 335–342.

176. Klamka, J., *Uncontrollability of composite systems*. IEEE Transactions on Automatic Control, 1974. **19**(3): p. 280–281.

177. Wang, P., *Invariance, uncontrollability, and unobservaility in dynamical systems*. IEEE Transactions on Automatic Control, 1965. **10**(3): p. 366–367.

178. Klamka, J., *Uncontrollability and unobservability of composite systems*. IEEE Transactions on Automatic Control, 1973. **18**(5): p. 539–540.

179. Klamka, J., *Uncontrollability and unobservability of multivariable systems*. IEEE Transactions on Automatic Control, 1972. **17**(5): p. 725–726.

180. Milanese, M., *Unidentifiability versus actual observability*. IEEE Transactions on Automatic Control, 1976. **21**(6): p. 876–877.

181. Arkin, R., *Governing Lethal Behavior in Autonomous Robots*. 2009: CRC Press.
182. Conant, R.C., and W. Ross Ashby, *Every good regulator of a system must be a model of that system*. International Journal of Systems Science, 1970. **1**(2): p. 89–97.
183. Ashby, W.R., *An Introduction to Cybernetics*. 1961: Chapman & Hall Ltd.
184. Ashby, M., *How to apply the ethical regulator theorem to crises*. Acta Europeana Systemica (AES), 2018. **8**: p. 53.
185. Ashby, W.R., *Requisite variety and its implications for the control of complex systems*. Cybernetica, 1958. **1**(2): p. 83–99.
186. Touchette, H., and S. Lloyd, *Information-theoretic approach to the study of control systems*. Physica A: Statistical Mechanics and Its Applications, 2004. **331**(1–2): p. 140–172.
187. Touchette, H., and S. Lloyd, *Information-theoretic limits of control*. Physical Review Letters, 2000. **84**(6): p. 1156.
188. Aliman, N.-M., and L. Kester, *Requisite variety in ethical utility functions for AI value alignment*. arXiv preprint arXiv:1907.00430, 2019.
189. McKeever, S., and M. Ridge, *The many moral particularisms*. Canadian Journal of Philosophy, 2005. **35**(1): p. 83–106.
190. Dancy, J., *Moral Reasons*. 1993: Wiley-Blackwell.
191. McDowell, J., *Virtue and reason*. The Monist, 1979. **62**(3): p. 331–350.
192. Rawls, J., A Theory of Justice. 1971: Harvard University Press.
193. Little, M.O., *Virtue as knowledge: objections from the philosophy of mind*. Nous, 1997. **31**(1): p. 59–79.
194. Purves, D., R. Jenkins, and B.J. Strawser, *Autonomous machines, moral judgment, and acting for the right reasons*. Ethical Theory and Moral Practice, 2015. **18**(4): p. 851–872.
195. Valiant, L., *Probably Approximately Correct: Nature's Algorithms for Learning and Prospering in a Complex World*. 2013: Basic Books.
196. Good, I.J., Ethical machines, in *Intelligent Systems: Practice and Perspective*, D.M.J.E. Hayes and Y.-H. Pao, Editors. 1982, Ellis Horwood Limited. p. 555–560.
197. Bogosian, K., *Implementation of moral uncertainty in intelligent machines*. Minds and Machines, 2017. **27**(4): p. 591–608.
198. Eckersley, P., *Impossibility and uncertainty theorems in AI value alignment (or why your AGI should not have a utility function)*. arXiv preprint arXiv:1901.00064, 2018.
199. Arrow, K.J., *A difficulty in the concept of social welfare*. Journal of Political Economy, 1950. **58**(4): p. 328–346.
200. Parfit, D., *Reasons and Persons*. 1984: OUP Oxford.
201. Arrhenius, G., *An impossibility theorem for welfarist axiologies*. Economics & Philosophy, 2000. **16**(2): p. 247–266.
202. Arrhenius, G., *The impossibility of a satisfactory population ethics*, in *Descriptive and Normative Approaches to Human Behavior*. 2012, World Scientific. p. 1–26.
203. Greaves, H., *Population axiology*. Philosophy Compass, 2017. **12**(11): p. e12442.
204. Friedler, S.A., C. Scheidegger, and S. Venkatasubramanian, *On the (im) possibility of fairness*. arXiv preprint arXiv:1609.07236, 2016.
205. Miconi, T., *The impossibility of "fairness": A generalized impossibility result for decisions*. arXiv preprint arXiv:1707.01195, 2017.
206. Kleinberg, J., S. Mullainathan, and M. Raghavan, *Inherent trade-offs in the fair determination of risk scores*. arXiv preprint arXiv:1609.05807, 2016.
207. Chouldechova, A., *Fair prediction with disparate impact: A study of bias in recidivism prediction instruments*. Big Data, 2017. **5**(2): p. 153–163.

208. Aaron, *Impossibility Results in Fairness as Bayesian Inference,* in *Adventures in Computation.* Retrieved February 26, 2019: https://aaronsadventures.blogspot.com/2019/02/impossibility-results-in-fairness-as.html.

209. Rice, H.G., *Classes of recursively enumerable sets and their decision problems.* Transactions of the American Mathematical Society, 1953. **74**(2): p. 358–366.

210. Evans, D., *On the Impossibility of Virus Detection.* 2017: http://www.cs.virginia.edu/evans/pubs/virus.pdf.

211. Selçuk, A.A., F. Orhan, and B. Batur, *Undecidable problems in malware analysis,* in *2017 12th International Conference for Internet Technology and Secured Transactions (ICITST).* 2017. IEEE.

212. Anonymous, *AI Safety Mindset,* in *Arbital.* 2018: https://arbital.com/p/AI_safety_mindset/.

213. Yampolskiy, R.V., *The space of possible mind designs,* in *International Conference on Artificial General Intelligence.* 2015. Springer.

214. Baum, S., *Superintelligence skepticism as a political tool.* Information, 2018. **9**(9): p. 209.

215. Yampolskiy, R.V., *Taxonomy of pathways to dangerous artificial intelligence,* in *Workshops at the Thirtieth AAAI Conference on Artificial Intelligence.* 2016.

216. Yampolskiy, R.V., *Artificial intelligence safety engineering: Why machine ethics is a wrong approach,* in *Philosophy and Theory of Artificial Intelligence (PT-AI2011).* October 3–4, 2011.

217. Urban, T., *Neuralink and the Brain's Magical Future,* in *Wait But Why.* Retrieved April 20, 2017: https://waitbutwhy.com/2017/04/neuralink.html.

218. Smith, B.C., *The limits of correctness.* ACM SIGCAS Computers and Society, 1985. **14**(1): p. 18–26.

219. Rodd, M., *Safe AI—is this possible?* Engineering Applications of Artificial Intelligence, 1995. **8**(3): p. 243–250.

220. Carlson, K.W., *Safe artificial general intelligence via distributed ledger technology.* arXiv preprint arXiv:1902.03689, 2019.

221. Demetis, D., and A.S. Lee, *When humans using the IT artifact becomes IT using the human artifact.* Journal of the Association for Information Systems, 2018. **19**(10): p. 5.

222. Reyzin, L., *Unprovability comes to machine learning.* Nature, 2019. **565**.

223. Ben-David, S., et al., *Learnability can be undecidable.* Nature Machine Intelligence, 2019. **1**(1): p. 44.

224. Reynolds, C., *On the computational complexity of action evaluations,* in *6th International Conference of Computer Ethics: Philosophical Enquiry.* 2005. University of Twente, Enschede, The Netherlands.

225. Yampolskiy, R.V., *Construction of an NP problem with an exponential lower bound.* arXiv preprint arXiv:1111.0305, 2011.

226. Foster, D.P., and H.P. Young, *On the impossibility of predicting the behavior of rational agents.* Proceedings of the National Academy of Sciences, 2001. **98**(22): p. 12848–12853.

227. Kahneman, D., and P. Egan, Thinking, Fast and Slow. Vol. 1. 2011: Farrar, Straus and Giroux New York.

228. Tarter, J., *The search for extraterrestrial intelligence (SETI).* Annual Review of Astronomy and Astrophysics, 2001. **39**(1): p. 511–548.

229. Carrigan, R.A. Jr, *Do potential SETI signals need to be decontaminated?* Acta Astronautica, 2006. **58**(2): p. 112–117.

230. Hippke, M., and J.G. Learned, *Interstellar communication. IX. Message decontamination is impossible.* arXiv preprint arXiv:1802.02180, 2018.

231. Miller, J.D., and D. Felton, *The fermi paradox, Bayes' rule, and existential risk management.* Futures, 2017. **86**: p. 44–57.

232. Wolpert, D., *Constraints on physical reality arising from a formalization of knowledge.* arXiv preprint arXiv:1711.03499, 2017.

233. Wolpert, D.H., *Physical limits of inference.* Physica D: Nonlinear Phenomena, 2008. **237**(9): p. 1257–1281.

234. Wolpert, D.H., *Computational capabilities of physical systems.* Physical Review E, 2001. **65**(1): p. 016128.

235. Yudkowsky, E., *Safely Aligning a Powerful AGI is Difficult*, in *Twitter*. Retrieved December 4, 2018: https://twitter.com/ESYudkowsky/status/1070095112791715846.

236. Yudkowsky, E., *On Doing the Improbable*, in *Less Wrong*. Retrieved October 28, 2018: https://www.lesswrong.com/posts/st7DiQP23YQSxumCt/on-doing-the-improbable.

237. Soares, N., *Talk at Google*. Retrieved April 12, 2017: https://intelligence.org/2017/04/12/ensuring/.

238. Garrabrant, S., *Optimization Amplifies*, in *Less Wrong*. Retrieved June 26, 2018: https://www.lesswrong.com/posts/zEvqFtT4AtTztfYC4/optimization-amplifies.

239. *Patch Resistance*, in *Arbital*. Retrieved June 18, 2015: https://arbital.com/p/patch_resistant/.

240. Yudkowsky, E., *Aligning an AGI Adds Significant Development Time*, in *Arbital*. Retrieved February 21, 2017: https://arbital.com/p/aligning_adds_time/.

241. Yudkowsky, E., *Security Mindset and Ordinary Paranoia*. Retrieved November 25, 2017: https://intelligence.org/2017/11/25/security-mindset-ordinary-paranoia/.

242. Yudkowsky, E., *Security Mindset and the Logistic Success Curve*. Retrieved November 26, 2017: https://intelligence.org/2017/11/26/security-mindset-and-the-logistic-success-curve/.

243. Soares, N., *2018 Update: Our New Research Directions*. Retrieved November 22, 2018: https://intelligence.org/2018/11/22/2018-update-our-new-research-directions/#section2.

244. Garrabrant, S., and A. Demski, *Embedded Agency*. Retrieved November 15, 2018: https://www.lesswrong.com/posts/i3BTagvt3HbPMx6PN/embedded-agency-full-text-version.

245. Yudkowsky, E., *The Rocket Alignment Problem*, in *Less Wrong*. Retrieved October 3, 2018: https://www.lesswrong.com/posts/Gg9a4y8reWKtLe3Tn/the-rocket-alignment-problem.

246. Hubinger, E., et al., *Risks from learned optimization in advanced machine learning systems.* arXiv preprint arXiv:1906.01820, 2019.

247. Hadfield-Menell, D., et al., *Cooperative inverse reinforcement learning*, in *Advances in Neural Information Processing Systems*. 2016. p. 3909–3917.

248. *Problem of Fully Updated Deference*, in *Arbital*. Retrieved April 4, 2020: https://arbital.com/p/updated_deference/.

249. Christiano, P., *ALBA: An Explicit Proposal for Aligned AI*, in *AI Alignment*. Retrieved February 23, 2016: https://ai-alignment.com/alba-an-explicit-proposal-for-aligned-ai-17a55f60bbcf.

250. Yudkowsky, E., *Challenges to Christiano's Capability Amplification Proposal*, in *Less Wrong*. Retrieved May 19, 2018: https://www.lesswrong.com/posts/S7csET9 CgBtpi7sCh/challenges-to-christiano-s-capability-amplification-proposal.

251. Christiano, P., *Prize for Probable Problems*, in *Less Wrong*. Retrieved March 8, 2018: https://www.lesswrong.com/posts/SqcPWvvJJwwgZb6aH/prize-for-probable-problems.

252. Armstrong, S., *The Limits to Corrigibility*, in *Less Wrong*. Retrieved April 10, 2018: https://www.lesswrong.com/posts/T5ZyNq3fzN59aQG5y/the-limits-of-corrigibility.

253. Armstrong, S., *Problems with Amplification/Distillation*, in *Less Wrong*. Retrieved March 27, 2018: https://www.lesswrong.com/posts/ZyyMPXY27TTxKsR5X/problems-with-amplification-distillation.

254. Gwern, *Why Tool AIs Want to Be Agent AIs: The Power of Agency*. Retrieved August 28, 2018: https://www.gwern.net/Tool-AI.

255. Yudkowsky, E., *There's No Fire Alarm for Artificial General Intelligence*. Retrieved October 14, 2017: https://intelligence.org/2017/10/13/fire-alarm/.

256. Yudkowsky, E., *Inadequate Equilibria: Where and How Civilizations Get Stuck*. Machine Intelligence Research Institute. 2017: https://equilibriabook.com/.

257. Yudkowsky, E., *Cognitive biases potentially affecting judgment of global risks*. Global Catastrophic Risks, 2008. **1**(86): p. 13.

258. Bengio, Y., *The Fascinating Facebook Debate Between Yann LeCun, Stuart Russel and Yoshua Bengio About the Risks of Strong AI*. Retrieved October 7, 2019: http://www.parlonsfutur.com/blog/the-fascinating-facebook-debate-between-yann-lecun-stuart-russel-and-yoshua.

259. Faggella, D., *AI Value Alignment Isn't a Problem if We Don't Coexist*. Retrieved March 8, 2019: https://danfaggella.com/ai-value-alignment-isnt-a-problem-if-we-dont-coexist/.

260. Turchin, A., *AI Alignment Problem: "Human Values" Don't Actually Exist*, in *Less Wrong*. 2019: https://www.lesswrong.com/posts/ngqvnWGsvTEiTASih/ai-alignment-problem-human-values-don-t-actually-exist.

261. Burden, J., and J. Hernández-Orallo, *Exploring AI Safety in Degrees: Generality, Capability and Control*, in *SafeAI*. Retrieved February 7, 2020: New York, USA.

262. Yampolskiy, R.V., *Behavioral modeling: an overview*. American Journal of Applied Sciences, 2008. **5**(5): p. 496–503.

263. Steven, *Agents That Learn From Human Behavior Can't Learn Human Values That Humans Haven't Learned Yet*, in *Less Wrong*. Retrieved July 10, 2018: https://www.lesswrong.com/posts/DfewqowdzDdCD7S9y/agents-that-learn-from-human-behavior-can-t-learn-human.

264. Ng, A.Y., and S.J. Russell, *Algorithms for inverse reinforcement learning*, in *Seventeenth International Conference on Machine Learning (ICML)*. 2000. p. 663–670.

265. Amin, K., and S. Singh, *Towards resolving unidentifiability in inverse reinforcement learning*. arXiv preprint arXiv:1601.06569, 2016.

266. Babcock, J., J. Kramar, and R.V. Yampolskiy, *Guidelines for artificial intelligence containment*. arXiv preprint arXiv:1707.08476, 2017.

267. Pittman, J.M., and C.E. Soboleski, *A cyber science based ontology for artificial general intelligence containment*. arXiv preprint arXiv:1801.09317, 2018.

268. Chalmers, D., *The singularity: a philosophical analysis*, in *Science Fiction and Philosophy: From Time Travel to Superintelligence*. 2009. p. 171–224.

269. Pittman, J.M., J.P. Espinoza, and C.S. Crosby, *Stovepiping and malicious software: a critical review of AGI containment.* arXiv preprint arXiv:1811.03653, 2018.

270. Arnold, T., and M. Scheutz, *The "big red button" is too late: an alternative model for the ethical evaluation of AI systems.* Ethics and Information Technology, 2018. **20**(1): p. 59–69.

271. Omohundro, S.M., *The basic AI drives,* in *Proceedings of the First AGI Conference, Volume 171, Frontiers in Artificial Intelligence and Applications,* P. Wang, B. Goertzel, and S. Franklin, Editors. February 2008. IOS Press.

272. Orseau, L., and M. Armstrong, *Safely Interruptible Agents.* 2016: https://intelligence.org/files/Interruptibility.pdf.

273. Riedl, M., *Big Red Button.* Retrieved on January 23, 2020: https://markriedl.github.io/big-red-button/.

274. Goertzel, B., *Does Humanity Need an AI Nanny,* in *H+ Magazine.* 2011.

275. de Garis, H., *The Artilect War: Cosmists vs. Terrans.* 2005: ETC Publications.

276. Legg, S., *Unprovability of Friendly AI.* Vetta Project 2006 September 15. Retrieved January 15, 2012: http://www.vetta.org/2006/09/unprovability-of-friendly-ai/.

277. Yudkowsky, E., *Open problems in friendly artificial intelligence,* in *Singularity Summit.* 2011.

278. Yudkowsky, E., *Timeless Decision Theory.* 2010. Retrieved January 15, 2012: https://intelligence.org/files/TDT.pdf.

279. Drescher, G., *Good and Real: Demystifying Paradoxes from Physics to Ethics* Bradford Books. 2006: MIT Press.

280. Yampolskiy, R., and J. Fox, *Safety engineering for artificial general intelligence.* Topoi, 2012. **32**: p. 1–10.

281. Vinge, V., *Technological singularity,* in *VISION-21 Symposium Sponsored by NASA Lewis Research Center and the Ohio Aerospace Institute.* 1993.

282. *Cognitive Uncontainability,* in *Arbital.* Retrieved May 19, 2019: https://arbital.com/p/uncontainability/.

283. Yampolskiy, R.V., *Unpredictability of AI: on the impossibility of accurately predicting all actions of a smarter agent.* Journal of Artificial Intelligence and Consciousness, 2020. **7**(1): p. 109–118.

284. Buiten, M.C., *Towards intelligent regulation of artificial intelligence.* European Journal of Risk Regulation, 2019. **10**(1): p. 41–59.

285. Yampolskiy, R., *Unexplainability and incomprehensibility of artificial intelligence.* arXiv:1907.03869 2019.

286. Charlesworth, A., *Comprehending software correctness implies comprehending an intelligence-related limitation.* ACM Transactions on Computational Logic (TOCL), 2006. **7**(3): p. 590–612.

287. Charlesworth, A., *The comprehensibility theorem and the foundations of artificial intelligence.* Minds and Machines, 2014. **24**(4): p. 439–476.

288. Hernández-Orallo, J., and N. Minaya-Collado, *A formal definition of intelligence based on an intensional variant of algorithmic complexity,* in *Proceedings of International Symposium of Engineering of Intelligent Systems (EIS98).* 1998.

289. Li, M., and P. Vitányi, *An Introduction to Kolmogorov Complexity and Its Applications.* Vol. 3. 1997: Springer.

290. Trakhtenbrot, B.A., *A survey of Russian approaches to Perebor (Brute-force searches) algorithms.* IEEE Annals of the History of Computing, 1984. **6**(4): p. 384–400.

291. Goertzel, B., *The Singularity Institute's Scary Idea (and Why I Don't Buy It)*. Retrieved October 29, 2010: http://multiverseaccordingtoben.blogspot.com/2010/10/singularity-institutes-scary-idea-and.html.

292. Legg, S., *Unprovability of Friendly AI*. Retrieved September 2006: https://web.archive.org/web/20080525204404/http://www.vetta.org/2006/09/unprovability-of-friendly-ai/.

293. Bieger, J., K.R. Thórisson, and P. Wang, *Safe baby AGI*, in *International Conference on Artificial General Intelligence*. 2015. Springer.

294. Herley, C., *Unfalsifiability of security claims*. Proceedings of the National Academy of Sciences, 2016. **113**(23): p. 6415–6420.

295. Yampolskiy, R.V., *What are the ultimate limits to computational techniques: verifier theory and unverifiability*. Physica Scripta, 2017. **92**(9): p. 093001.

296. Muehlhauser, L., *Gerwin Klein on Formal Methods*, in *Intelligence.org*. Retrieved February 11, 2014: https://intelligence.org/2014/02/11/gerwin-klein-on-formal-methods/.

297. Muehlhauser, L., *Mathematical Proofs Improve But Don't Guarantee Security, Safety, and Friendliness*, in *Intelligence.org*. Retrieved October 3, 2013: https://intelligence.org/2013/10/03/proofs/.

298. Jilk, D.J., *Limits to verification and validation of agentic behavior*. arXiv preprint arXiv:1604.06963, 2016.

299. Jilk, D.J., et al., *Anthropomorphic reasoning about neuromorphic AGI safety*. Journal of Experimental & Theoretical Artificial Intelligence, 2017. **29**(6): p. 1337–1351.

300. Fetzer, J.H., *Program verification: the very idea*. Communications of the ACM, 1988. **31**(9): p. 1048–1063.

301. Petke, J., et al., *Genetic improvement of software: a comprehensive survey*. IEEE Transactions on Evolutionary Computation, 2017. **22**(3): p. 415–432.

302. Yampolskiy, R.V., *Utility function security in artificially intelligent agents*. Journal of Experimental and Theoretical Artificial Intelligence (JETAI), 2014. **26**: p. 1–17.

303. Everitt, T., et al., *Reinforcement learning with a corrupted reward channel*. arXiv preprint arXiv:1705.08417, 2017.

304. Lanzarone, G.A., and F. Gobbo, *Is computer ethics computable, in Living, Working and Learning Beyond*. 2008. p. 530.

305. Moor, J.H., *Is ethics computable?* Metaphilosophy, 1995. **26**(1/2): p. 1–21.

306. Allen, C., G. Varner, and J. Zinser, *Prolegomena to any future artificial moral agent*. Journal of Experimental and Theoretical Artificial Intelligence, 2000. **12**: p. 251–261.

307. Weld, D., and O. Etzioni, *The first law of robotics (a call to arms)*, in *Proceedings of the Twelfth AAAI National Conference on Artificial Intelligence*. 1994.

308. Brundage, M., *Limitations and risks of machine ethics*. Journal of Experimental & Theoretical Artificial Intelligence, 2014. **26**(3): p. 355–372.

309. Russell, S., *The purpose put into the machine*, in *Possible Minds: Twenty-Five Ways of Looking at AI*. 2019, Penguin Press. p. 20–32.

310. Calude, C.S., E. Calude, and S. Marcus, *Passages of proof*. arXiv preprint math/0305213, 2003.

311. Aliman, N.-M., et al., *Error-correction for AI safety*, in *Artificial General Intelligence (AGI20)*. June 23–26, 2020. St. Petersburg, Russia.

312. Wiener, N., *Some moral and technical consequences of automation*. Science, 1960. **131**(3410): p. 1355–1358.

313. Versenyi, L., *Can robots be moral?* Ethics, 1974. **84**(3): p. 248–259.

314. Yampolskiy, R., *Turing test as a defining feature of AI-completeness*, in *Artificial Intelligence, Evolutionary Computing and Metaheuristics*, X.-S. Yang, Editor. 2013, Springer Berlin Heidelberg. p. 3–17.

315. Yampolskiy, R.V., *AI-complete CAPTCHAs as zero knowledge proofs of access to an artificially intelligent system*. ISRN Artificial Intelligence, 2011. **2012**: 271878.

316. Yampolskiy, R.V., *AI-complete, AI-hard, or AI-easy–classification of problems in AI*, in The 23rd Midwest Artificial Intelligence and Cognitive Science Conference. 2012. Cincinnati, OH, USA.

317. Brown, T.B., et al., *Language models are few-shot learners*. arXiv preprint arXiv:2005.14165, 2020.

318. Yampolskiy, R.V., *Efficiency theory: a unifying theory for information, computation and intelligence*. Journal of Discrete Mathematical Sciences & Cryptography, 2013. **16**(4–5): p. 259–277.

319. Ziesche, S., and R.V. Yampolskiy, *Towards the mathematics of intelligence*, in The Age of Artificial Intelligence: An Exploration. 2020. p. 1.

320. Drexler, K.E., *Reframing Superintelligence: Comprehensive AI Services as General Intelligence*, in *Technical Report #2019-1, Future of Humanity Institute, University of Oxford*. Oxford University. 2019: https://www.fhi.ox.ac.uk/wp-content/uploads/Reframing_Superintelligence_FHI-TR-2019-1.1-1.pdf.

321. Minsky, M., *Society of Mind*. 1988: Simon and Schuster.

322. Soares, N., et al. *Corrigibility*, in *Workshops at the Twenty-Ninth AAAI Conference on Artificial Intelligence*. 2015.

323. Lipton, R., *Are Impossibility Proofs Possible?*, in *Gödel's Lost Letter and P=NP*. Retrieved September 13, 2009: https://rjlipton.wordpress.com/2009/09/13/are-impossibility-proofs-possible/.

324. Wadman, M., *US Biologists Adopt Cloning Moratorium*. 1997: Nature Publishing Group.

325. Sauer, F., *Stopping 'Killer Robots': why now is the time to ban autonomous weapons systems*. Arms Control Today, 2016. **46**(8): p. 8–13.

326. Ashby, M. *Ethical regulators and super-ethical systems*, in *Proceedings of the 61st Annual Meeting of the ISSS-2017 Vienna*, Austria. 2017.

7

Pathways to Danger*

7.1 Taxonomy of Pathways to Dangerous AI

Nick Bostrom in his typology of information hazards has proposed the phrase "Artificial Intelligence Hazard" which he defines as [4]: "... computer-related risks in which the threat would derive primarily from the cognitive sophistication of the program rather than the specific properties of any actuators to which the system initially has access". In this chapter, we attempt to answer the question: How did AI become hazardous?

We begin by presenting a simple classification matrix, which sorts artificially intelligent (AI) systems with respect to how they originated and at what stage they became dangerous. The matrix recognizes two stages (pre- and post-deployment) at which a particular system can acquire its undesirable properties. In reality, the situation is not so clear-cut – it is possible that problematic properties are introduced at both stages. As for the cases of such undesirable properties, we distinguish external and internal causes. By internal causes we mean self-modifications originating in the system itself. We further divide external causes into deliberate actions (on purpose), side effects of poor design (by mistake), and finally miscellaneous cases related to the surroundings of the system (environment). Table 7.1 helps to visualize this taxonomy and includes later codes to some example systems of each type and explanations.

7.1.1 On Purpose – Pre-Deployment

Computer software is directly or indirectly responsible for controlling many important aspects of our lives. Wall Street trading, nuclear power plants, social security compensations, credit histories and traffic lights are all software controlled and are only one serious design flaw away from creating disastrous consequences for millions of people. The situation is even more dangerous with software specifically designed for malicious purposes such as viruses, spyware, Trojan horses, worms

---

DOI: 10.1201/9781003440260-7

TABLE 7.1

Pathways to Dangerous AI

How and When did AI Become Dangerous	External Causes			Internal Causes
	On Purpose	By Mistake	Environment	Independently
Timing Pre-deployment	a	c	e	g
Post-deployment	b	d	f	h

and other Hazardous Software (HS). HS is capable of direct harm as well as sabotage of legitimate computer software employed in critical systems. If HS is ever given capabilities of truly artificially intelligent systems (ex. Artificially Intelligent Virus (AIV)) the consequences would be unquestionably disastrous. Such Hazardous Intelligent Software (HIS) would pose risks currently unseen in malware with subhuman intelligence. [5]

While the majority of AI Safety work is currently aimed at AI systems, which are dangerous because of poor design [6], the main argument of this chapter is that the most important problem in AI Safety is intentional-malevolent-design resulting in artificial evil AI [7]. We should not discount dangers of intelligent systems with semantic or logical errors in coding or goal alignment problems [8], but we should be particularly concerned about systems that are maximally unfriendly by design. "It is easy to imagine robots being programmed by a conscious mind to kill every recognizable human in sight" [9]. "One slightly deranged psycho-bot can easily be a thousand times more destructive than a single suicide bomber today" [10]. AI risk skeptics, comprised of critics of AI Safety research [11, 12], are quick to point out that presumed dangers of future AIs are implementation-dependent side effects and may not manifest once such systems are implemented. However, such criticism does not apply to AIs that are dangerous by design and is thus incapable of undermining the importance of AI Safety research as a significant sub-field of cybersecurity.

As a majority of current AI researchers are funded by militaries, it is not surprising that the main types of purposefully dangerous robots and intelligent software are robot soldiers, drones, and cyber weapons (used to penetrate networks and cause disruptions to the infrastructure). While currently military robots and drones have a human in the loop to evaluate decision to terminate human targets, it is not a technical limitation; instead, it is a logistical limitation that can be removed at any time. Recognizing the danger of such research, the International Committee for Robot Arms Control has joined forces with a number of international organizations to start the Campaign to Stop Killer Robots [http://www.stopkillerrobots.org]. Their main goal is a prohibition on the development and deployment of fully autonomous weapons, which are capable of selecting and firing upon targets without human approval. The campaign specifically believes that the "decision about the application of violent force must not be delegated to machines" [13].

During the pre-deployment development stage, software may be subject to sabotage by someone with necessary access (a programmer, tester, even janitor) who for a number of possible reasons may alter software to make it unsafe. It is also a common occurrence for hackers (such as the organization anonymous or government intelligence agencies) to get access to software projects in progress and to modify or steal their source code. Someone can also deliberately supply/train AI with wrong/unsafe datasets.

Malicious AI software may also be purposefully created to commit crimes while shielding its human creator from legal responsibility. For example, one recent news article talks about software for purchasing illegal content from hidden internet sites [14]. Similar software, with even limited intelligence, can be used to run illegal markets, engage in insider trading, cheat on your taxes, hack into computer systems, or violate privacy of others via ability to perform intelligent data mining. As the intelligence of AI systems improves practically, all crimes could be automated. This is particularly alarming as we already see research in making machines lie, deceive, and manipulate us [15, 16].

7.1.2 On Purpose – Post-Deployment

Just because developers might succeed in creating a safe AI, it doesn't mean that it will not become unsafe at some later point. In other words, a perfectly friendly AI could be switched to the "dark side" during the post-deployment stage. This can happen rather innocuously as a result of someone lying to the AI and purposefully supplying it with incorrect information or more explicitly as a result of someone giving the AI orders to perform illegal or dangerous actions against others. It is quite likely that we will get to the point of off-the-shelf AI software, aka "just add goals" architecture, which would greatly facilitate such scenarios.

More dangerously, an AI system, like any other software, could be hacked and consequently corrupted or otherwise modified to drastically change its behavior. For example, a simple sign flipping (positive to negative or vice versa) in the fitness function may result in the system attempting to maximize the number of cancer cases instead of trying to cure cancer. Hackers are also likely to try to take over intelligent systems to make them do their bidding, to extract some direct benefit, or to simply wreak havoc by converting a friendly system to an unsafe one. This becomes particularly dangerous if the system is hosted inside a military killer robot. Alternatively, an AI system can get a computer virus [17] or a more advanced cognitive (meme) virus, similar to cognitive attacks on people perpetrated by some cults. An AI system with a self-preservation module or with a deep care about something or someone may be taken hostage or blackmailed into doing the bidding of another party if its own existence or that of its protégées is threatened.

Finally, it may be that the original AI system is not safe but is safely housed in a dedicated laboratory [5] while it is being tested, with no intention of ever being deployed. Hackers, abolitionists, or machine rights fighters may help it escape in order to achieve some of their goals or perhaps because of a genuine belief that all intelligent beings should be free resulting in an unsafe AI capable of affecting the real world.

7.1.3 By Mistake – Pre-Deployment

Probably the most talked about source of potential problems with future AIs is mistakes in design. Mainly the concern is with creating a "wrong AI", a system which doesn't match our original desired formal properties or has unwanted behaviors [18, 19], such as drives for independence or dominance. Mistakes could also be simple bugs (run time or logical) in the source code, disproportionate weights in the fitness function, or goals misaligned with human values leading to complete disregard for human safety. It is also possible that the designed AI will work as intended but will not enjoy universal acceptance as a good product, for example, an AI correctly designed and implemented by the Islamic State to enforce Sharia Law may be considered malevolent in the West, and likewise an AI correctly designed and implemented by the West to enforce liberal democracy may be considered malevolent in the Islamic State.

Another type of mistake, which can lead to the creation of a malevolent intelligent system, is taking an unvetted human and uploading their brain into a computer to serve as a base for a future AI. While well intended to create a human-level and human-friendly system, such approach will most likely lead to a system with all typical human "sins" (greed, envy, etc.) amplified in a now much more powerful system. As we know from Lord Acton – "power tends to corrupt, and absolute power corrupts absolutely". Similar arguments could be made against human/computer hybrid systems, which use computer components to amplify human intelligence but in the process also amplify human flaws.

A subfield of computer science called affective computing investigates ways to teach computers to recognize emotion in others and to exhibit emotions [20]. In fact, most such research is targeting intelligent machines to make their interactions with people more natural. It is however likely that a machine taught to respond in an emotional way [21] would be quite dangerous because of how such a state of affect effects thinking and the rationality of behavior.

One final type of design mistake is the failure to make the system cooperative with its designers and maintainers post-deployment. This would be very important if it is discovered that mistakes were made during initial design and that it would be desirable to fix them. In such cases, the system will attempt to protect itself from being modified or shut down unless it has been explicitly constructed to be friendly [22], stable while self-improving [23, 24], and corrigible [25] with tendency for domesticity [26].

7.1.4 By Mistake – Post-Deployment

After the system has been deployed, it may still contain a number of undetected bugs, design mistakes, misaligned goals, and poorly developed capabilities, all of which may produce highly undesirable outcomes. For example, the system may misinterpret commands due to coarticulation, segmentation, homophones, or double meanings in the human language ("recognize speech using common sense" versus "wreck a nice beach you sing calm incense") [27]. Perhaps a human-computer interaction system is set up to make command input as painless as possible for the human user, to the point of computer simply reading thought of the user. This may backfire as the system may attempt to implement user's subconscious desires or even nightmares. We also should not discount the possibility that the user will simply issue a poorly thought-through command to the machine which in retrospect would be obviously disastrous.

The system may also exhibit incompetence in other domains as well as overall lack of human common sense as a result of general value misalignment [28]. Problems may also happen as side effects of conflict resolution between non-compatible orders in a particular domain or software versus hardware interactions. As the system continues to evolve, it may become unpredictable, unverifiable, non-deterministic, free-willed, too complex, and non-transparent, with a run-away optimization process subject to obsessive-compulsive fact-checking and re-checking behaviors leading to dangerous never-fully complete missions. It may also build excessive infrastructure for trivial goals [2].

If it continues to become ever more intelligent, we might be faced with intelligence overflow, a system so much ahead of us that it is no longer capable of communicating at our level, like we are unable to communicate with bacteria. It is also possible that benefits of intelligence are non-linear and so unexpected side effects of intelligence begin to show at particular levels, for example, IQ = 1000.

Even such benign architectures as tool AI, which are AI systems designed to do nothing except answer domain-specific questions, could become extremely dangerous if they attempt to obtain, at any cost, additional computational resources to fulfill their goals [29]. Similarly, artificial lawyers may find dangerous legal loopholes; artificial accountants bring down our economy, and AIs tasked with protecting humanity such as via implementation of CEV (coherent extrapolated volition) [30] may become overly "strict parents" preventing their human "children" from exercising any free will.

Predicted AI drives such as self-preservation and resource acquisition may result in an AI killing people to protect itself from humans, the development of competing AIs, or to simplify its world model overcomplicated by human psychology [2].

7.1.5 Environment – Pre-Deployment

While it is most likely that any advanced intelligent software will be directly designed or evolved, it is also possible that we will obtain it as a complete package from some unknown source. For example, an AI could be extracted from a signal obtained in SETI (Search for Extraterrestrial Intelligence) research, which is not guaranteed to be human-friendly [31, 32]. Other sources of such unknown but complete systems include a Levin search in the space of possible minds [33] (or a random search of the same space), uploads of nonhuman animal minds, and unanticipated side effects of compiling and running (inactive/junk) DNA code on suitable compilers that we currently do not have but might develop in the near future.

7.1.6 Environment – Post-Deployment

While highly rare, it is known, that occasionally individual bits may be flipped in different hardware devices due to manufacturing defects or cosmic rays hitting just the right spot [34]. This is similar to mutations observed in living organisms and may result in a modification of an intelligent system. For example, if a system has a single flag bit responsible for its friendly nature, then flipping said bit will result in an unfriendly state of the system. While statistically it is highly unlikely, the probably of such an event is not zero and so should be considered and addressed.

7.1.7 Independently – Pre-Deployment

One of the most likely approaches to creating superintelligent AI is by growing it from a seed (baby) AI via recursive self-improvement (RSI) [35]. One danger in such a scenario is that the system can evolve to become self-aware, free-willed, independent or emotional, and obtain a number of other emergent properties, which may make it less likely to abide by any built-in rules or regulations and to instead pursue its own goals possibly to the detriment of humanity. It is also likely that open-ended self-improvement will require a growing amount of resources, the acquisition of which may negatively impact all life on Earth [2].

7.1.8 Independently – Post-Deployment

Since in sections on independent causes of AI misbehavior (Sections 7.1.7 and 7.1.8) we are talking about self-improving AI, the difference between pre- and post-deployment is very blurry. It might make more sense to think about self-improving AI before it achieves advanced capabilities (human + intelligence) and after. In this section, I will talk about dangers which might result from a superhuman self-improving AI after it achieves said level of performance.

Previous research has shown that utility-maximizing agents are likely to fall victim to the same indulgences we frequently observe in people, such as addictions, pleasure drives [36], self-delusions, and wireheading [37]. In general, what we call mental illness in people, particularly sociopathy as demonstrated by lack of concern for others, is also likely to show up in artificial minds. A mild variant of antisocial behavior may be something like excessive swearing already observed in IBM Watson [38], caused by learning from bad data. Similarly, any AI system learning from bad examples could end up socially inappropriate, like a human raised by wolves. Alternatively, groups of AIs collaborating may become dangerous even if individual AIs comprising such groups are safe, as the whole is frequently greater than the sum of its parts. The opposite problem in which internal modules of an AI fight over different sub-goals also needs to be considered [2].

Advanced self-improving AIs will have a way to check consistency of their internal model against the real world and so remove any artificially added friendliness mechanisms as cognitive biases not required by laws of reason. At the same time, regardless of how advanced it is, no AI system would be perfect and so would still be capable of making possibly significant mistakes during its decision-making process. If it happens to evolve an emotional response module, it may put priority on passion-satisfying decisions as opposed to purely rational choices, for example, resulting in a "Robin Hood" AI stealing from the rich and giving to the poor. Overall, continuous evolution of the system as a part of an RSI process will likely lead to unstable decision-making in the long term and will also possibly cycle through many dangers we have outlined in Section 7.1.7. AI may also pretend to be benign for years, passing all relevant tests, waiting to take over in what Bostrom calls a "Treacherous Turn" [26].

7.2 Conclusions

In this chapter, we have surveyed and classified pathways to dangerous artificial intelligence. Most AI systems fall somewhere in the middle on the spectrum of dangerousness from completely benign to completely evil, with such properties as competition with humans, aka technological unemployment, representing a mild type of danger in our taxonomy. Most types of reported problems could be seen in multiple categories, but were reported in the one they are most likely to occur in. Differences in moral codes or religious standards between different communities would mean that a system deemed safe in one community may be considered dangerous/illegal in another [39, 40].

Because purposeful design of dangerous AI is just as likely to include all other types of safety problems, it is easy to see that the most dangerous type of AI and the one most difficult to defend against is an AI made malevolent on purpose. Consequently, once AIs are widespread, little could be done against the dangers described in Sections 7.1.1 and 7.1.2, although some have argued that if an early AI superintelligence becomes a benevolent singleton it may be able to prevent development of future malevolent AIs [41, 42]. Such a solution may work, but it is also very likely to fail due to the order of development or practical limitations on capabilities of any singleton. In any case, wars between AI may be extremely dangerous to humanity [2]. Until the purposeful creation of malevolent AI is recognized as a crime, very little could be done to prevent this from happening. Consequently, deciding what is a "malevolent AI" and what is merely an incrementally more effective military weapon system becomes an important problem in AI Safety research.

As the intelligence of the system increases, so does the risk such a system could expose humanity to. This chapter is essentially a classified list of ways an AI system could become a problem from a safety point of view. For a list of possible solutions, please see an earlier survey by the author: Responses to catastrophic AGI risk: A survey [43]. It is important to keep in mind that even a properly designed benign system may present significant risk simply due to its superior intelligence, beyond human capability response times [44], and complexity. After all the future may not need us [45]. It is also possible that we are living in a simulation and it is generated by a malevolent AI [46].

Future work may include taxonomy of dangers specific to different AI architectures as well as detailed analysis of worst and average case scenarios for causes described in Sections 7.1.1–7.1.8 of this chapter. It is also important to formally demonstrate the completeness of the proposed taxonomy.

References

1. Özkural, E., *Godseed: Benevolent or malevolent?* arXiv preprint arXiv:1402.5380, 2014.
2. Turchin, A., *A Map: AGI Failures Modes and Levels*, in *LessWrong*. Retrieved July 10 2015. http://lesswrong.com/lw/mgf/a_map_agi_failures_modes_and_levels/.
3. Turchin, A., *Human extinction risks due to artificial intelligence development – 55 ways we can be obliterated*, in *IEET*. Retrieved July 10, 2015. http://ieet.org/index.php/IEET/more/turchin20150610.
4. Bostrom, N., *Information hazards: A typology of potential harms from knowledge.* Review of Contemporary Philosophy, 2011. **10**: p. 44–79.

5. Yampolskiy, R., *Leakproofing the singularity artificial intelligence confinement problem.* Journal of Consciousness Studies, 2012. **19**(1–2): p. 1–2.

6. Yampolskiy, R.V., *Artificial Superintelligence: A Futuristic Approach.* 2015: Chapman and Hall/CRC.

7. Floridi, L., and J.W. Sanders, *Artificial evil and the foundation of computer ethics.* Ethics and Information Technology, 2001. **3**(1): p. 55–66.

8. Soares, N., and B. Fallenstein, *Aligning Superintelligence With Human Interests: A Technical Research Agenda.* 2014: Tech. Rep. Machine Intelligence Research Institute. http://intelligence.org/files/TechnicalAgenda.pdf.

9. Searle, J.R., *What Your Computer Can't Know,* in *The New York Review of Books.* Retrieved October 9, 2014. http://www.nybooks.com/articles/archives/2014/oct/09/what-your-computer-cant-know.

10. Frey, T., *The Black Hat Robots are Coming,* in *Futurist Speaker.* Retrieved June 2015. http://www.futuristspeaker.com/2015/06/the-black-hat-robots-are-coming/.

11. Loosemore, R.P., *The Maverick Nanny with a dopamine drip: Debunking fallacies in the theory of AI motivation,* in *2014 AAAI Spring Symposium Series.* 2014.

12. Waser, M., *Rational universal benevolence: Simpler, safer, and wiser than "friendly AI",* in *Artificial General Intelligence.* 2011, Springer. p. 153–162.

13. Anonymous, *The Scientists' Call... To Ban Autonomous Lethal Robots,* in *ICRAC International Committee for Robot Arms Control.* 2013. https://www.icrac.net/the-scientists-call/

14. Cush, A., *Swiss Authorities Arrest Bot for Buying Drugs and Fake Passport,* in *Gawker.* Retrieved January 22, 2015. http://internet.gawker.com/swiss-authorities-arrest-bot-for-buying-drugs-and-a-fak-1681098991.

15. Castelfranchi, C., *Artificial liars: Why computers will (necessarily) deceive us and each other.* Ethics and Information Technology, 2000. **2**(2): p. 113–119.

16. Clark, M.H., *Cognitive Illusions and the Lying Machine: A Blueprint for Sophistic Mendacity.* 2010: Rensselaer Polytechnic Institute.

17. Eshelman, R., and D. Derrick, *Relying on kindness of machines? The security threat of artificial agents.* JFQ, 2015. **77**, 2nd Quarter.

18. Russell, S., et al., *Research Priorities for Robust and Beneficial Artificial Intelligence,* in *Future of Life Institute.* Retrieved January 23, 2015. http://futureoflife.org/static/data/documents/research_priorities.pdf.

19. Dewey, D., et al., *A Survey of Research Questions for Robust and Beneficial AI,* in *Future of Life Institute.* 2015. http://futureoflife.org/static/data/documents/research_survey.pdf.

20. Picard, R.W., and R. Picard, *Affective Computing.* Vol. 252. 1997: MIT Press.

21. Goldhill, O., *Artificial Intelligence Experts are Building the World's Angriest Robot. Should You Be Scared?,* in *The Telegraph.* Retrieved May 12, 2015. http://www.telegraph.co.uk/men/the-filter/11600593/Artificial-intelligence-should-you-be-scared-of-angry-robots.html.

22. Yudkowsky, E., *Complex value systems in friendly AI,* in *Artificial General Intelligence,* J. Schmidhuber, K. Thórisson, and M. Looks, Editors. 2011, Springer. p. 388–393.

23. Yampolskiy, R.V., *Analysis of types of self-improving software,* in *Artificial General Intelligence.* 2015, Springer. p. 384–393.

24. Yampolskiy, R.V., *On the limits of recursively self-improving AGI,* in *Artificial General Intelligence.* 2015, Springer. p. 394–403.

25. Soares, N., et al., *Corrigibility*, in *Workshops at the Twenty-Ninth AAAI Conference on Artificial Intelligence*. January 25–30, 2015. Austin, Texas, USA.

26. Bostrom, N., *Superintelligence: Paths, Dangers, Strategies*. 2014: Oxford University Press.

27. Lieberman, H., et al., *How to wreck a nice beach you sing calm incense*, in *Proceedings of the 10th International Conference on Intelligent User Interfaces*. 2005. ACM.

28. Yampolskiy, R.V., *What to do with the singularity paradox?*, in *Philosophy and Theory of Artificial Intelligence (PT-AI2011)*. October 3–4, 2011. Thessaloniki, Greece.

29. Omohundro, S., *Rational artificial intelligence for the greater good*, in *Singularity Hypotheses*. 2012, Springer. p. 161–179.

30. Yudkowsky, E.S., *Coherent Extrapolated Volition*. May 2004 Singularity Institute for Artificial Intelligence. https://intelligence.org/files/CEV.pdf.

31. Carrigan, R.A. Jr., *The ultimate hacker: SETI signals may need to be decontaminated*, in *Bioastronomy 2002: Life Among the Stars*. 2004.

32. Turchin, A., *Risks of Downloading Alien AI via SETI Search*, in *LessWrong*. Retrieved March 15, 2013. http://lesswrong.com/lw/gzv/risks_of_downloading_alien_ai_via_seti_search/.

33. Yampolskiy, R.V., *The space of possible mind designs*, in *Artificial General Intelligence*. 2015, Springer. p. 218–227.

34. Simonite, T., *Should Every Computer Chip Have a Cosmic Ray Detector?*, in *New Scientist*. Retrieved March 7, 2008. https://web.archive.org/web/20110403062611/https://www.newscientist.com/blog/technology/2008/03/do-we-need-cosmic-ray-alerts-for.html.

35. Nijholt, A., *No Grice: Computers That Lie, Deceive and Conceal*. 2011.

36. Majot, A.M., and R.V. Yampolskiy, *AI safety engineering through introduction of self-reference into felicific calculus via artificial pain and pleasure*, in *2014 IEEE International Symposium on Ethics in Science, Technology and Engineering*. 2014. IEEE.

37. Yampolskiy, R.V., *Utility function security in artificially intelligent agents*. Journal of Experimental and Theoretical Artificial Intelligence (JETAI), 2014. **26**(3): p. 1–17.

38. Smith, D., *IBM's Watson Gets A 'Swear Filter' After Learning The Urban Dictionary*, in *International Business Times*. Retrieved January 10, 2013. http://www.ibtimes.com/ibms-watson-gets-swear-filter-after-learning-urban-dictionary-1007734.

39. Yampolskiy, R., and J. Fox, *Safety engineering for artificial general intelligence*. Topoi, 2012. 32: p. 1–10.

40. Yampolskiy, R.V., *Artificial intelligence safety engineering: Why machine ethics is a wrong approach*, in *Philosophy and Theory of Artificial Intelligence*. 2013, Springer. p. 389–396.

41. Bostrom, N., *What is a singleton?* Linguistic and Philosophical Investigations, 2006. **5**(2): p. 48–54.

42. Goertzel, B., *Should humanity build a global AI nanny to delay the singularity until it's better understood?* Journal of Consciousness Studies, 2012. **19**(1–2): p. 96–111.

43. Sotala, K., and R.V. Yampolskiy, *Responses to catastrophic AGI risk: A survey*. Physica Scripta, 2015. **90**(1): p. 018001.

44. Johnson, N., et al., *Abrupt rise of new machine ecology beyond human response time*. Scientific Reports, 2013. **3**: p. 1–7.

45. Joy, B., *Why the future doesn't need us.* Wired Magazine, 2000. **8**(4). https:// shivanirgandhi.medium.com/why-the-future-doesnt-need-us-47249ab203e0 #:~:text=In%20his%20renowned%20essay%2C%20%E2%80%9CWhy,in%20 the%20development%20of%20technology.
46. Ćirković, M.M., *Linking simulation argument to the AI risk.* Futures, 2015. **72**: p. 27–31.

8

*Accidents**

8.1 Introduction

About 10,000 scientists[1] around the world work on different aspects of creating intelligent machines, with the main goal of making such machines as capable as possible. With amazing progress made in the field of AI over the last decade, it is more important than ever to make sure that the technology we are developing has a beneficial impact on humanity. With the appearance of robotic financial advisors, self-driving cars and personal digital assistants come many unresolved problems. We have already experienced market crashes caused by intelligent trading software[2], accidents caused by self-driving cars[3] and embarrassment from chat-bots[4], which turned racist and engaged in hate speech. I predict that both the frequency and seriousness of such events will steadily increase as artificial intelligence (AI) becomes more capable. The failures of today's narrow-domain AIs are just a warning: once we develop artificial general intelligence (AGI) capable of cross-domain performance, hurt feelings will be the least of our concerns.

In a recent publication, I proposed a Taxonomy of Pathways to Dangerous AI [1], which was motivated as follows: "In order to properly handle a potentially dangerous artificially intelligent system it is important to understand how the system came to be in such a state. In popular culture (science fiction movies/books) AIs/Robots became self-aware and as a result rebel against humanity and decide to destroy it. While it is one possible scenario, it is probably the least likely path to appearance of dangerous AI". I suggested that much more likely reasons include deliberate actions of not-so-ethical people ("on purpose"), side effects of poor design ("engineering mistakes") and, finally, miscellaneous cases related to the impact of the surroundings of the system ('environment'). Because the purposeful design of dangerous AI is just as likely to include all other types of safety problems and will probably have the direst consequences, the most dangerous type of AI and the one most difficult to defend against is an AI made malevolent on purpose.

* Used with permission of Emerald Publishing Limited, from Predicting future AI failures from historic examples, Roman V. Yampolskiy, Volume 21, issue 1, copyright © 2018; Permission conveyed through Copyright Clearence Center, Inc.

DOI: 10.1201/9781003440260-8

A follow-up paper [2] explored how a Malevolent AI could be constructed and why it is important to study and understand malicious intelligent software. An AI researcher studying Malevolent AI is like a medical doctor studying how different diseases are transmitted, how new diseases arise and how they impact the patient's organism. The goal is not to spread diseases but to learn how to fight them. The authors observe that cybersecurity research involves publishing papers about malicious exploits as much as publishing information on how to design tools to protect cyber infrastructure. It is this information exchange between hackers and security experts that results in a well-balanced cyber-ecosystem. In the domain of AI Safety Engineering, hundreds of papers [3] have been published on different proposals geared at the creation of a safe machine, yet nothing else has been published on how to design a malevolent machine. The availability of such information would be of great value particularly to computer scientists, mathematicians, and others who have an interest in making safe AI and who are attempting to avoid the spontaneous emergence or the deliberate creation of a dangerous AI, which can negatively affect human activities and in the worst case cause the complete obliteration of the human species. The chapter implied that if an AI Safety mechanism is not designed to resist attacks by malevolent human actors, it cannot be considered a functional safety mechanism!

8.2 AI Failures

Those who cannot learn from history are doomed to repeat it. Unfortunately, very few papers have been published on failures and errors made in the development of intelligent systems [4]. The importance of learning from "What Went Wrong and Why" has been recognized by the AI community [5, 6]. Such research includes a study of how, why and when failures happen [5, 6] and how to improve future AI systems based on such information [7, 8].

Signatures have been faked, locks have been picked, supermax prisons had escapes, guarded leaders have been assassinated, bank vaults have been cleaned out, laws have been bypassed, fraud has been committed against our voting process, police officers have been bribed, judges have been blackmailed, forgeries have been falsely authenticated, money has been counterfeited, passwords have been brute-forced, networks have been penetrated, computers have been hacked, biometric systems have been spoofed, credit cards have been cloned, cryptocurrencies have been double spent, airplanes have been hijacked, CAPTCHAs have been cracked, cryptographic protocols have been broken, even academic peer-review has been bypassed with tragic consequences. Millennia's long history of humanity contains millions of examples of attempts to develop technological and logistical solutions to increase safety and security, yet not a single example exists which has not eventually failed.

Accidents, including deadly ones, caused by software or industrial robots can be traced to the early days of such technology,[5] but they are not a direct consequence of particulars of intelligence available in such systems. AI Failures, on the other hand, are directly related to the mistakes produced by the intelligence such systems are designed to exhibit. I can broadly classify such failures into mistakes during the learning phase and mistakes during the performance phase. The system can fail to learn what its human designers want it to learn and instead learn a different, but correlated function. A frequently cited example is a computer vision system, which was supposed to classify pictures of tanks but instead learned to distinguish the backgrounds of such images [9]. Other examples[6] include problems caused by poorly designed utility functions rewarding only partially desirable behaviors of agents, such as riding a bicycle in circles around the target [10], pausing a game to avoid losing [11], or repeatedly touching a soccer ball to get credit for possession [12]. During the performance phase, the system may succumb to a number of causes [1, 13, 14], all leading to an AI Failure.

Media reports are full of examples of AI Failure but most of these examples can be attributed to other causes on closer examination, such as bugs in code or mistakes in design. The list below is curated to only mention failures of intended intelligence. Additionally, the examples below include only the first occurrence of a particular failure, but the same problems are frequently observed again in later years. Finally, the list does not include AI Failures due to hacking or other intentional causes. Still, the timeline of AI Failures has an exponential trend while implicitly indicating historical events such as "AI Winter":

1958 Advice software deduced inconsistent sentences using logical programming [15].

1959 AI designed to be a General Problem Solver failed to solve real-world problems.[7]

1977 Story writing software with limited common sense produced "wrong" stories [16].

1982 Software designed to make discoveries discovered how to cheat instead.[8]

1983 Nuclear attack early warning system falsely claimed that an attack was taking place.[9]

1984 The National Resident Match program was biased in the placement of married couples [17].

1988 Admissions software discriminated against women and minorities [18].

1994 Agents learned to "walk" quickly by becoming taller and falling over [19].

2005 Personal assistant AI rescheduled a meeting 50 times, each time by 5 minutes [20].

2006 Insider threat detection system classified normal activities as outliers [21].

2006 Investment advising software was losing money in real trading [22].

2007 Google search engine returned unrelated results for some keywords.[10]

2010 Complex AI stock trading software caused a trillion-dollar flash crash.[11]

2011 E-Assistant told to "call me an ambulance" began to refer to the user as Ambulance.[12]

2013 Object recognition neural networks saw phantom objects in particular noise images [23].

2013 Google software engaged in name-based discrimination in online ad delivery [24].

2014 Search engine autocomplete made bigoted associations about groups of users [25].

2014 Smart fire alarm failed to sound alarm during fire.[13]

2015 Automated email reply generator created inappropriate responses.[14]

2015 A robot for grabbing auto parts grabbed and killed a man.[15]

2015 Image tagging software classified black people as gorillas.[16]

2015 Medical expert AI classified patients with asthma as lower risk [26].

2015 Adult content filtering software failed to remove inappropriate content.[17]

2015 Amazon's Echo responded to commands from TV voices.[18]

2016 LinkedIn's name lookup suggests male names in place of female ones.[19]

2016 AI designed to predict recidivism acted racist.[20]

2016 AI agent exploited reward signal to win without completing the game course.[21]

2016 Passport picture checking system flagged Asian users as having closed eyes.[22]

2016 Game NPCs designed unauthorized superweapons.[23]

2016 AI judged a beauty contest and rated dark-skinned contestants lower.[24]

2016 Smart contract permitted syphoning of funds from the DAO.[25]

2016 Patrol robot collided with a child.[26]

2016 World champion-level Go-playing AI lost a game.[27]

2016 Self-driving car had a deadly accident.[28]

2016 AI designed to converse with users on Twitter became verbally abusive.[29]

2016 Google image search returned racist results.[30]

2016 Artificial applicant failed to pass the university entrance exam.[31]

2016 Predictive policing system disproportionately targeted minority neighborhoods.[32]

2016 Text subject classifier failed to learn relevant features for topic assignment [27].

2017 AI for making inspirational quotes failed to inspire with gems like "Keep Panicking".[33]

2017 Alexa played adult content instead of songs for kids.[34]

2017 Cellphone case designing AI utilized inappropriate images.[35]

2017 Pattern recognition software failed to recognize certain types of inputs.[36]

2017 Debt recovery system miscalculated amounts owed.[37]

2017 Russian language chatbot shared pro-Stalinist, pro-abuse and pro-suicide views.[38]

2017 Translation AI learned to stereotype careers to specific genders [28].

2017 Face beautifying AI made black people look white.[39]

2017 Google's sentiment analyzer became homophobic and anti-Semitic.[40]

2017 Fish recognition program learned to recognize boat IDs instead.[41]

2017 Billing software sent an electrical bill for 284 billion dollars.[42]

2017 Alexa turned on loud music at night without being prompted to do so.[43]

2017 AI for writing Christmas carols produced nonsense.[44]

2017 Apple's face recognition system failed to distinguish Asian users.[45]

2017 Facebook's translation software changed Yampolskiy to Polanski, see Figure 8.1.

2018 Google Assistant created a bizarre merged photo.[46]

2018 Robot store assistant was not helpful with responses like "cheese is in the fridges".[47]

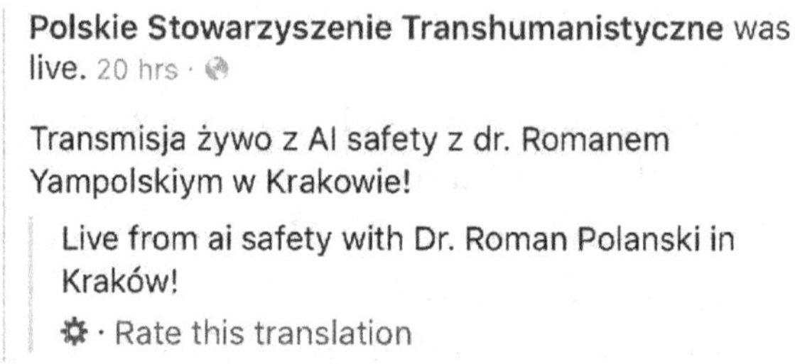

Polskie Stowarzyszenie Transhumanistyczne was
live. 20 hrs · 🌐

Transmisja żywo z AI safety z dr. Romanem
Yampolskiym w Krakowie!

> Live from ai safety with Dr. Roman Polanski in
> Kraków!
>
> ⚙ · Rate this translation

FIGURE 8.1
While translating from Polish to English Facebook's software changed Roman "Yampolskiy"
to Roman "Polanski" due to statistically higher frequency of the later name in sample texts.

Collection of examples continued and was published in two papers in 2019 and 2021:

- Peter J. Scott, Roman V. Yampolskiy. Classification Schemas for Artificial Intelligence Failures. Delphi – Interdisciplinary Review of Emerging Technologies. Volume 2, Number 4. Pp. 186–199. 2019.
- Robert Williams, and Roman Yampolskiy. Understanding and Avoiding AI Failures: A Practical Guide. Philosophies, June 2021. 6(3): p. 53.

Around 2022, the development and release of generative AI models capable of producing artificial art, text, music, etc., resulted in an explosion of AI failures to great to keep track of meaningfully.

Spam filters block important emails, GPS provides faulty directions, machine translation corrupts the meaning of phrases, autocorrect replaces desired word with a wrong one, biometric systems misrecognize people, and transcription software fails to capture what is being said; overall, it is harder to find examples of AIs that don't fail. Depending on what we consider for inclusion as examples of problems with intelligent software, the list of examples could be grown almost indefinitely. In its most extreme interpretation, any software with as much as an "if statement" can be considered a form of narrow artificial intelligence (NAI) and all of its bugs are thus examples of AI Failure.[48]

Analyzing the list of NAI failures, from the inception of the field to modern-day systems, we can arrive at a simple generalization: An AI designed to do X will eventually fail to do X. While it may seem trivial, it is a powerful generalization tool, which can be used to predict future failures of NAIs. For example, looking at cutting-edge current and future AIs, we can predict that:

- Software for generating jokes will occasionally fail to make them funny.
- Sex robots will fail to deliver an orgasm or to stop at the right time.

- Sarcasm detection software will confuse sarcastic and sincere statements.
- Video description software will misunderstand movie plots.
- Software-generated virtual worlds may not be compelling.
- AI doctors will misdiagnose some patients in a way a real doctor would not.
- Employee screening software will be systematically biased and thus hire low performers.
- Mars robot explorer will misjudge its environment and fall into a crater.
- Etc.

Others have given the following examples of possible accidents with A(G)I/ superintelligence:

- Housekeeping robot cooks family pets for dinner.[49]
- A mathematician AGI converts all matter into computing elements to solve problems.[50]
- An AGI running simulations of humanity creates conscious beings who suffer [29].
- Paperclip manufacturing AGI fails to stop and converts the universe into raw materials [30].
- A scientist AGI performs experiments with a significant negative impact on biosphere [31].
- Drug design AGI develops time-delayed poison to kill everyone and so defeat cancer.[51]
- Future superintelligence optimizes away all consciousness.[52]
- AGI kills humanity and converts the universe into materials for improved penmanship.[53]
- AGI designed to maximize human happiness tiles universe with tiny smiley faces [32].
- AGI instructed to maximize pleasure consigns humanity to a dopamine drip [33].
- Superintelligence may rewire human brains to increase their perceived satisfaction [32].

Denning and Denning made some similar error extrapolations in their humorous paper on "artificial stupidity" [34]: "Soon the automated DEA started closing down pharmaceutical companies saying they were dealing drugs. The automated FTC closed down the Hormel Meat Company, saying it was purveying spam. The automated DOJ shipped Microsoft 500,000 pin-striped pants and jackets, saying it was filing suits. The automated Army replaced all its troops with a single robot, saying it had achieved the Army of One. The automated Navy, in a cost saving move, placed its largest-ever order for submarines with Subway Sandwiches. The FCC issued an order for all communications to be wireless, causing thousands of AT&T installer robots to pull cables from overhead poles and underground conduits. The automated TSA flew its own explosives on jetliners, citing data that the probability of two bombs on an airplane is exceedingly small".

AGI can be seen as a superset of all NAIs and so will exhibit a superset of failures as well as more complicated failures resulting from the combination of failures of individual NAIs and new super-failures, possibly resulting in an existential threat to humanity or at least an AGI takeover. In other words, AGIs can make mistakes influencing everything. Overall, I predict that AI failures and premediated Malevolent AI incidents will increase in frequency and severity proportionate to AIs' capability.

8.2.1 Preventing AI Failures

AI failures have a number of causes, with the most common ones currently observed, displaying some type of algorithmic bias, poor performance or basic malfunction. Future AI failures are likely to be more severe, including purposeful manipulation/deception [35], or even resulting in human death (likely from misapplication of militarized AI/autonomous weapons/killer robots [36]). At the very end of the severity scale, we see existential risk scenarios resulting in extermination of humankind or suffering-risk scenarios [37] resulting in large-scale torture of humanity, both types of risk coming from supercapable AI systems.

Reviewing examples of AI accidents, we can notice patterns of failure, which can be attributed to the following causes:

- Biased data, including cultural differences.
- Deploying underperforming system.
- Non-representative training data.
- Discrepancy between training and testing data.
- Rule overgeneralization or application of population statistics to individuals.
- Inability to handle noise or statistical outliers.
- Not testing for rare or extreme conditions.
- Not realizing an alternative solution method can produce the same results but with side effects.
- Letting users control data or learning process.
- No security mechanism to prevent adversarial meddling.

- No cultural competence/common sense.
- Limited access to information/sensors.
- Mistake in design and inadequate testing.
- Limited ability for language disambiguation.
- Inability to adapt to changes in environment.

With bias being the most common current cause of failure, it is helpful to analyze particular types of algorithmic bias. Friedman and Nissenbaum [17] proposed the following framework for analyzing bias in computer systems. They subdivide causes of bias into three categories – preexisting bias, technical bias and emergent bias.

- **Preexisting bias** reflects bias in society and social institutions, practices and attitudes. The system simply preserves an existing state the world and automates application of bias as currently exists.
- **Technical bias** appears because of hardware or software limitations of the system itself.
- **Emergent bias** emerges after the system is deployed due to changing societal standards.

Many of the observed AI failures are similar to mishaps experienced by little children. This is particularly true for artificial neural networks, which are at the cutting edge of Machine Learning (ML). One can say that children are untrained neural networks deployed on real data and observing them can teach us a lot about predicting and preventing AI failures. A number of research groups [31, 38] have investigated types of ML failure and here I have summarized their work and mapped it onto similar situations with children:

- Negative side effects – child makes a mess.
- Reward hacking – child finds candy jar.
- Scalable oversight – babysitting should not require a team of 10.
- Safe exploration – no fingers in the outlet.
- Robustness to distributional shift – use "inside voice" in the classroom.
- Inductive ambiguity identification – is ant a cat or a dog?
- Robust human imitation – daughter shaves like daddy.
- Informed oversight – let me see your homework.
- Generalizable environmental goals – ignore that mirage.
- Conservative concepts – that dog has no tail.
- Impact measures – keep a low profile.

- Mild optimization – don't be a perfectionist.
- Averting instrumental incentives – be an altruist.

Majority of research currently taking place to prevent such failures is currently happening under the label of "AI Safety".

8.3 AI Safety

In 2010, I coined the phrase "Artificial Intelligence Safety Engineering" and its shorthand notation "AI Safety" to give a name to a new direction of research I was advocating. I formally presented my ideas on AI Safety at a peer-reviewed conference in 2011 [39], with subsequent publications on the topic in 2012 [40], 2013 [41, 42], 2014 [43], 2015 [44], 2016 [1, 13], 2017 [45] and 2018 [46, 47]. It is possible that someone used the phrase informally before, but to the best of my knowledge, I was the first to use it[54] in a peer-reviewed publication and to bring it popularity. Before that, the most common names for the field of machine control were "Machine Ethics" [48] or "Friendly AI" [49]. Today the term "AI Safety" appears to be the accepted[55–66] name for the field used by a majority of top researchers [38]. The field itself is becoming mainstream despite being regarded as either science fiction or pseudoscience in its early days.

Our legal system is behind our technological abilities, and the field of AI Safety is in its infancy. The problem of controlling intelligent machines is just now being recognized[67] as a serious concern, and many researchers are still skeptical about its very premise. Worse yet, only about 100 people around the world have fully emerged in working on addressing the current limitations in our understanding and abilities in this domain. Only about a dozen[68] of those have formal training in computer science, cybersecurity, cryptography, decision theory, machine learning, formal verification, computer forensics, steganography, ethics, mathematics, network security, psychology and other relevant fields. It is not hard to see that the problem of making a safe and capable machine is much greater than the problem of making just a capable machine. Yet only about 1% of researchers are currently engaged in that problem with available funding levels below even that mark. As a relatively young and underfunded field of study, AI Safety can benefit from adopting methods and ideas from more established fields of science. Attempts have been made to introduce techniques, which were first developed by cybersecurity experts to secure software systems to this new domain of securing intelligent machines [50–53]. Other fields, which could serve as a source of important techniques, would include software engineering and software verification.

During software development, iterative testing and debugging are of fundamental importance to produce reliable and safe code. While it is assumed that all complicated software will have some bugs, with many advanced techniques available in the toolkit of software engineers, most serious errors could be detected and fixed, resulting in a product suitable for its intended purposes. Certainly, a lot of modular development and testing techniques employed by the software industry can be utilized during the development of intelligent agents, but methods for testing a completed software package are unlikely to be transferable in the same way. Alpha and beta testing, which work by releasing almost-finished software to advanced users for reporting problems encountered in realistic situations, would not be a good idea in the domain of testing/debugging superintelligent software. Similarly, simply running the software to see how it performs is not a feasible approach with a superintelligent agent.

8.4 Cybersecurity vs. AI Safety

Bruce Schneier has said, "If you think technology can solve your security problems then you don't understand the problems and you don't understand the technology". Salman Rushdie made a more general statement: "There is no such thing as perfect security, only varying levels of insecurity". I propose what I call the Fundamental Theorem of Security – *Every security system will eventually fail; there is no such thing as a 100% secure system*. If your security system has not failed, just wait longer.

In theoretical computer science, a common way of isolating the essence of a difficult problem is via the method of reduction to another, sometimes better analyzed, problem [54–56]. If such a reduction is a possibility and is computationally efficient [57], such a reduction implies that if the better-analyzed problem is somehow solved, it would also provide a working solution for the problem we are currently dealing with. The problem of AGI Safety could be reduced to the problem of making sure a particular human is safe. I call this the safe human problem (SHP).[69] Formally such a reduction can be done via restricted Turing Test in the domain of safety in a manner identical to how AI-completeness of a problem could be established [55, 58]. Such formalism is beyond the scope of this chapter so I simply point out that in both cases, we have at least a human-level intelligent agent capable of influencing its environment, and we would like to make sure that the agent is safe and controllable. While in practice, changing the design of a human via DNA manipulation is not as simple as changing the source code of an AI, theoretically, it is just as possible.

It is observed that humans are not safe for themselves and others. Despite a millennia of attempts to develop safe humans via culture, education, laws, ethics, punishment, reward, religion, relationships, family, oaths, love and even eugenics, success is not within reach. Humans kill and commit suicide, lie and betray, steal and cheat, usually in proportion to how much they can get away with. Truly powerful dictators will enslave, commit genocide, break every law and violate every human right. It is famously stated that a human without a sin can't be found. The best we can hope for is to reduce such unsafe tendencies to levels that our society can survive. Even with advanced genetic engineering [59], the best we can hope for is some additional reduction in how unsafe humans are. As long as we permit a person to have choices (free will), they can be bribed, they will deceive, they will prioritize their interests above those they are instructed to serve and they will remain fundamentally unsafe. Despite being trivial examples of a solution to the Value Learning Problem [60–62], human beings are anything but safe, bringing into question our current hope that solving VLP will get us to Safe AI. This is important. To quote Bruce Schneier, "Only amateurs attack machines; professionals target people". Consequently, I see AI safety research as, at least partially, an adversarial field similar to cryptography or security.[70]

If a cybersecurity system fails, the damage is unpleasant but tolerable in most cases: someone loses money, someone loses privacy or maybe somebody loses their life. For NAIs, safety failures are at the same level of importance as in general cybersecurity, but for AGI it is fundamentally different. A single failure of a superintelligent system may cause an existential risk event. If an AGI Safety mechanism fails, everyone may lose everything, and all biological life in the universe is potentially destroyed. With cybersecurity systems, you will get another chance to get it right or at least do better. With AGI Safety system, you only have one chance to succeed, so learning from failure is not an option. Worse, a typical security system is likely to fail to a certain degree, e.g. perhaps only a small amount of data will be compromised. With an AGI Safety system, failure or success is a binary option: either you have a safe and controlled superintelligence, or you don't. The goal of cybersecurity is to reduce the number of successful attacks on the system; the goal of AI Safety is to make sure zero attacks succeed in bypassing the safety mechanisms. For that reason, the ability to segregate NAI projects from potentially AGI projects is an open problem of fundamental importance in the AI safety field.

The problems are many. We have no way to monitor, visualize or analyze the performance of superintelligent agents. More trivially, we don't even know what to expect after such a software starts running. Should we see immediate changes to our environment? Should we see nothing? What is the timescale on which we should be able to detect something? Will it be too quick to notice, or are we too slow to realize something is happening? Will the impact be locally observable or impact distant parts of the world? How does one perform standard testing? On what data sets? What constitutes an "Edge Case" for general intelligence? The questions are many, but the answers currently don't exist. Additional complications will come from the interaction between intelligent software and safety mechanisms designed to keep AI safe and secure. We will also have to somehow test all the AI

Safety mechanisms currently in development. While AI is at human levels, some testing can be done with a human agent playing the role of the artificial agent. At levels beyond human capacity, adversarial testing does not seem to be realizable with today's technology. More significantly, only one test run would ever be possible.

8.5 Conclusions

The history of robotics and artificial intelligence in many ways is also the history of humanity's attempts to control such technologies. From the Golem of Prague to the military robots of modernity, the debate continues as to what degree of independence such entities should have and how to make sure that they do not turn on us, their inventors. Numerous recent advancements in all aspects of research, development and deployment of intelligent systems are well publicized but safety and security issues related to AI are rarely addressed. The book you are reading aims to mitigate this fundamental problem as the first multi-author volume on this subject, which I hope will be seen as humankind's communal response to the control problem. It is comprised of chapters from leading AI Safety researchers addressing different aspects of the AI control problem as they relate to the development of safe and secure artificial intelligence.

Part one of this book, "Concerns of Luminaries", is comprised of 11 previously published seminal papers outlining different sub-domains of concern with regard to the AI Control Problem and includes contributions from leading scholars in a diverse set of fields – philosophers, scientists, writes and businesspeople, presented in chronological order of original publication. Part two, "Responses of Scholars", is made up of 17 chapters (in alphabetical order, by the last name of the first author) of proposed theoretical and practical solutions to the concerns raised in part one, as well as introduction of additional concerns, from leading AI Safety researchers. The chapters vary in length and technical content from broad interest opinion essays to highly formalized algorithmic approaches to specific problems. All chapters are self-contained and can be read in any order or skipped without a loss of comprehension. This volume is, without any doubt, not the last word on this subject but rather one of the first steps in the right direction.

Notes

1. https://intelligence.org/2014/01/28/how-big-is-ai/
2. https://en.wikipedia.org/wiki/2010_Flash_Crash

3. https://electrek.co/2016/05/26/tesla-model-s-crash-autopilot-video/
4. https://en.wikipedia.org/wiki/Tay_(bot)
5. https://en.wikipedia.org/wiki/Kenji_Urada
6. http://lesswrong.com/lw/lvh/examples_of_ais_behaving_badly/
7. https://en.wikipedia.org/wiki/General_Problem_Solver
8. https://aliciapatterson.org/george-johnson/eurisko-the-computer-with-a-mind-of-its-own/
9. https://en.wikipedia.org/wiki/1983_Soviet_nuclear_false_alarm_incident
10. https://en.wikipedia.org/wiki/Google_bomb
11. http://gawker.com/this-program-that-judges-use-to-predict-future-crimes-s-1778151070
12. https://www.technologyreview.com/s/601897/tougher-turing-test-exposes-chatbots-stupidity/
13. https://www.forbes.com/sites/aarontilley/2014/04/03/googles-nest-stops-selling-its-smart-smoke-alarm-for-now
14. https://gmail.googleblog.com/2015/11/computer-respond-to-this-email.html
15. http://time.com/3944181/robot-kills-man-volkswagen-plant/
16. http://www.huffingtonpost.com/2015/07/02/google-black-people-goril_n_7717008.html
17. http://blogs.wsj.com/digits/2015/05/19/googles-youtube-kids-app-criticized-for-inappropriate-content/
18. https://motherboard.vice.com/en_us/article/53dz8x/people-are-complaining-that-amazon-echo-is-responding-to-ads-on-tv
19. https://www.seattletimes.com/business/microsoft/how-linkedins-search-engine-may-reflect-a-bias
20. http://gawker.com/this-program-that-judges-use-to-predict-future-crimes-s-1778151070
21. https://openai.com/blog/faulty-reward-functions
22. http://www.telegraph.co.uk/technology/2016/12/07/robot-passport-checker-rejects-asian-mans-photo-having-eyes
23. http://www.kotaku.co.uk/2016/06/03/elites-ai-created-super-weapons-and-started-hunting-players-skynet-is-here
24. https://www.theguardian.com/technology/2016/sep/08/artificial-intelligence-beauty-contest-doesnt-like-black-people
25. https://en.wikipedia.org/wiki/The_DAO_(organization)
26. http://www.latimes.com/local/lanow/la-me-ln-crimefighting-robot-hurts-child-bay-area-20160713-snap-story.html
27. https://www.engadget.com/2016/03/13/google-alphago-loses-to-human-in-one-match/
28. https://www.theguardian.com/technology/2016/jul/01/tesla-driver-killed-autopilot-self-driving-car-harry-potter
29. http://www.theverge.com/2016/3/24/11297050/tay-microsoft-chatbot-racist
30. https://splinternews.com/black-teenagers-vs-white-teenagers-why-googles-algori-1793857436
31. https://www.japantimes.co.jp/news/2016/11/15/national/ai-robot-fails-get-university-tokyo
32. https://www.themarshallproject.org/2016/02/03/policing-the-future
33. https://www.buzzworthy.com/ai-tries-to-generate-inspirational-quotes-and-gets-it-hilariously-wrong

34. https://www.entrepreneur.com/video/287281
35. https://www.boredpanda.com/funny-amazon-ai-designed-phone-cases-fail
36. http://www.bbc.com/future/story/20170410-how-to-fool-artificial-intelligence
37. http://www.abc.net.au/news/2017-04-10/centrelink-debt-recovery-system-lacks-transparency-ombudsman/8430184
38. https://techcrunch.com/2017/10/24/another-ai-chatbot-shown-spouting-offensive-views
39. http://www.gizmodo.co.uk/2017/04/faceapp-blames-ai-for-whitening-up-black-people
40. https://motherboard.vice.com/en_us/article/j5jmj8/google-artificial-intelligence-bias
41. https://medium.com/@gidishperber/what-ive-learned-from-kaggle-s-fisheries-competition-92342f9ca779
42. https://www.washingtonpost.com/news/business/wp/2017/12/26/woman-gets-284-billion-electric-bill-wonders-whether-its-her-christmas-lights
43. http://mashable.com/2017/11/08/amazon-alexa-rave-party-germany
44. http://mashable.com/2017/12/22/ai-tried-to-write-christmas-carols
45. http://www.mirror.co.uk/tech/apple-accused-racism-after-face-11735152
46. https://qz.com/1188170/google-photos-tried-to-fix-this-ski-photo
47. http://www.iflscience.com/technology/store-hires-robot-to-help-out-customers-robot-gets-fired-for-scaring-customers-away
48. https://en.wikipedia.org/wiki/List_of_software_bugs
49. https://www.theguardian.com/sustainable-business/2015/jun/23/the-ethics-of-ai-how-to-stop-your-robot-cooking-your-cat
50. https://intelligence.org/2014/11/18/misconceptions-edge-orgs-conversation-myth-ai
51. https://80000hours.org/problem-profiles/positively-shaping-artificial-intelligence
52. http://slatestarcodex.com/2014/07/13/growing-children-for-bostroms-disneyland
53. https://waitbutwhy.com/2015/01/artificial-intelligence-revolution-2.html
54. Term "Safe AI" has been used as early as 1995, see Rodd, M. (1995). "Safe AI—is this possible?" Engineering Applications of Artificial Intelligence 8(3): 243–250
55. https://www.cmu.edu/safartint/
56. https://selfawaresystems.com/2015/07/11/formal-methods-for-ai-safety/
57. https://intelligence.org/2014/08/04/groundwork-ai-safety-engineering/
58. https://spectrum.ieee.org/new-ai-safety-projects-get-funding-from-elon-musk
59. https://web.archive.org/web/20160325082914/https://globalprioritiesproject.org/2015/08/quantifyingaisafety/
60. http://futureoflife.org/2015/10/12/ai-safety-conference-in-puerto-rico/
61. https://web.archive.org/web/20161019085553/http://rationality.org/waiss/
62. http://gizmodo.com/satya-nadella-has-come-up-with-his-own-ai-safety-rules-1782802269
63. https://80000hours.org/career-reviews/artificial-intelligence-risk-research/
64. https://openai.com/blog/concrete-ai-safety-problems/
65. http://lesswrong.com/lw/n4l/safety_engineering_target_selection_and_alignment/
66. https://web.archive.org/web/20180826050137/https://www.waise2018.com/
67. https://obamawhitehouse.archives.gov/blog/2016/05/03/preparing-future-artificial-intelligence

68. http://acritch.com/fhi-positions/
69. Similarly a Safe Animal Problem maybe be of interest. (Can a Pitbull be guaranteed safe?)
70. The last thing we want is to be in an adversarial situation with a superintelligence, but unfortunately we may not have a choice in the matter. It seems that long-term AI Safety can't succeed, but also doesn't have the luxury of a partial fail.

References

1. Yampolskiy, R.V., *Taxonomy of pathways to dangerous artificial intelligence*, in *Workshops at the Thirteenth AAAI Conference on Artificial Intelligence*. 2016. AAAI Press

2. Pistono, F., and R.V. Yampolskiy, *Unethical research: How to create a Malevolent artificial intelligence*, in *Presented at the 25th International Joint Conference on Artificial Intelligence (IJCAI-16). Ethics for Artificial Intelligence Workshop (AI-Ethics-2016)*. 2016.

3. Sotala, K., and R.V. Yampolskiy, *Responses to catastrophic AGI risk: A survey*. *Physica Scripta*, 2015. **90**.

4. Rychtyckyj, N., and A. Turski, *Reasons for Success (and failure) in the Development and Deployment of AI Systems*, in *AAAI 2008 workshop on What Went Wrong and Why*. 2008. AAAI Press

5. Shapiro, D., and M.H. Goker, *Advancing AI research and applications by learning from what went wrong and why*. *AI Magazine*, 2008. **29**: pp. 9–10.

6. Abecker, A., R. Alami, C. Baral, T. Bickmore, E. Durfee, and T. Fong, et al., AAAI 2006 spring symposium reports. *AI Magazine*, 2006. **27**: p. 107.

7. Marling, C., and D. Chelberg, *RoboCup for the Mechanically, Athletically and Culturally Challenged*, 2008.

8. Shalev-Shwartz, S., O. Shamir, and S. Shammah, *Failures of gradient-based deep learning*, in *International Conference on Machine Learning*. 2017, pp. 3067–3075.

9. Yudkowsky, E., *Artificial intelligence as a positive and negative factor in global risk*. Global Catastrophic Risks, 2008. **1**: p. 303.

10. Randløv, J., and P. Alstrøm, *Learning to drive a bicycle using reinforcement learning and shaping*, in *International Conference on Machine Learning*. 1998, pp. 463–471.

11. *The Association for Computational Heresy (SIGBOVIK) 2013*, 2013. https://www.cs.cmu.edu/~tom7/mario/mario.pdf

12. Ng, A.Y., D. Harada, and S. Russell, *Policy invariance under reward transformations: Theory and application to reward shaping*, in *International Conference on Machine Learning*. 1999, pp. 278–287.

13. Pistono, F., and R.V. Yampolskiy, *Unethical research: How to create a malevolent artificial intelligence*. arXiv preprint arXiv:1605.02817, 2016.

14. Scharre, P., *Autonomous weapons and operational risk*, in *Presented at the Center for a New American Society*. 2016.

15. C. Hewitt, *Development of Logic Programming: What Went Wrong, What was Done About It, and What It Might Mean for the Future*, 2008.

16. Meehan, J.R., *TALE-SPIN, an interactive program that writes stories*, in *International Joint Conference on Artificial Intelligence*. 1977, pp. 91–98. AAAI Press
17. Friedman, B., and H. Nissenbaum, *Bias in computer systems*. ACM Transactions on Information Systems (TOIS), 1996. **14**: p. 330–347.
18. Lowry, S., and G. Macpherson, *A blot on the profession*. British Medical Journal (Clinical Research Ed.), 1988. **296**: p. 657–658.
19. Sims, K., *Evolving virtual creatures*, in *Proceedings of the 21st Annual Conference on Computer Graphics and Interactive Techniques*. 1994, pp. 15–22.
20. Tambe, M., *Electric elves: What went wrong and why*. AI Magazine, 2008. **29**: p. 20–23.
21. Liu, A., C.E. Martin, T. Hetherington, and S. Matzner, AI lessons learned from experiments in insider threat detection," in *AAAI Spring Symposium: What Went Wrong and Why: Lessons from AI Research and Applications*. 2006, pp. 49–55.
22. Gunderson, J., and L. Gunderson, "And Then the Phone Rang," in *AAAI Spring Symposium: What Went Wrong and Why: Lessons from AI Research and Applications*. 2006, pp. 13–18.
23. Szegedy, C., W. Zaremba, I. Sutskever, J. Bruna, D. Erhan, and I. Goodfellow, et al., *Intriguing properties of neural networks*. arXiv preprint arXiv:1312.6199, 2013.
24. Sweeney, L., *Discrimination in online ad delivery*. Queue, 2013. **11**: p. 10.
25. Diakopoulos, N., *Algorithmic defamation: The case of the shameless autocomplete*. Tow Center for Digital Journalism, 2014.
26. Caruana, R., Y. Lou, J. Gehrke, P. Koch, M. Sturm, and N. Elhadad, Intelligible models for healthcare: Predicting pneumonia risk and hospital 30-day read-mission, in *Proceedings of the 21th ACM SIGKDD International Conference on Knowledge Discovery and Data Mining*. 2015, pp. 1721–1730.
27. Ribeiro, M.T., S. Singh, and C. Guestrin, Why should I trust you?: Explaining the predictions of any classifier," in *Proceedings of the 22nd ACM SIGKDD International Conference on Knowledge Discovery and Data Mining*, 2016, pp. 1135–1144.
28. Caliskan, A., J.J. Bryson, and A. Narayanan, *Semantics derived automatically from language corpora contain human-like biases*. Science, 2017. **356**: p. 183–186.
29. Armstrong, S., A. Sandberg, and N. Bostrom, *Thinking inside the box: Controlling and using an oracle AI*. Minds and Machines, 2012. **22**: p. 299–324.
30. Bostrom, N., *Ethical issues in advanced artificial intelligence*. Science Fiction and Philosophy: From Time Travel to Superintelligence, 2003. p 277–284.
31. Taylor, J., E. Yudkowsky, P. LaVictoire, and A. Critch, *Alignment for advanced machine learning systems*. Machine Intelligence Research Institute, 2016.
32. Yudkowsky, E., *Complex value systems in friendly AI*. Artificial General Intelligence, 2011. p. 388–393.
33. Marcus, G., Moral machines. *The New Yorker*, 2012. **24**.
34. Denning, D.E., and P.J. Denning, *Artificial Stupidity*, 2004.
35. Chessen, M., *The MADCOM Future*, in *Atlantic Council*. 2017. http://www.atlan ticcouncil.org/publications/reports/the-madcom-future.
36. Krishnan, A., *Killer Robots: Legality and Ethicality of Autonomous Weapons*. 2009. Ashgate Publishing, Ltd.
37. Gloor, L., *Suffering-focused AI Safety: Why "Fail-safe" Measures Might Be Our Top Intervention, Tech. rep. FRI-16-1. Foundational Research Institute*. https://longtermrisk.org/files/suffering-focused-ai-safety.pdf.

38. Amodei, D., C. Olah, J. Steinhardt, P. Christiano, J. Schulman, and D. Mané, *Concrete problems in AI safety*. arXiv preprint arXiv:1606.06565, 2016.

39. Yampolskiy, R.V., *Artificial intelligence safety engineering: Why machine ethics is a wrong approach*, in *Presented at the Philosophy and Theory of Artificial Intelligence (PT-AI2011)*. 2011. Springer

40. Yampolskiy, R.V., and J. Fox, *Safety engineering for artificial general intelligence*. Topoi. Special Issue on Machine Ethics & the Ethics of Building Intelligent Machines, 2012. **32**, 217–226.

41. Muehlhauser, L., and R. Yampolskiy, *Roman Yampolskiy on AI safety engineering*, in *Presented at the Machine Intelligence Research Institute*. 2013. http://intelligence.org/2013/07/15/roman-interview/.

42. Yampolskiy, R.V., Artificial intelligence safety engineering: Why machine ethics is a wrong approach," in *Philosophy and Theory of Artificial Intelligence*. 2013, Springer, p. 389–396.

43. Majot, A.M., and R.V. Yampolskiy, *AI safety engineering through introduction of self-reference into felicific calculus via artificial pain and pleasure*, in *IEEE International Symposium on Ethics in Science, Technology and Engineering*. 2014, pp. 1–6. IEEE Press

44. Yampolskiy, R.V., *Artificial Superintelligence: A Futuristic Approach*. 2015. Chapman and Hall/CRC.

45. Yampolskiy, R.V., *What are the ultimate limits to computational techniques: Verifier theory and unverifiability*. Physica Scripta, 2017. **92**: p. 093001. IOP Publishing

46. Ramamoorthy, A., and R. Yampolskiy, *Beyond mad?: The race for artificial general intelligence*. ITU Journal: ICT Discoveries, 2017.

47. Brundage, M., S. Avin, J. Clark, H. Toner, P. Eckersley, and B. Garfinkel, et al., *The malicious use of artificial intelligence: Forecasting, prevention, and mitigation*. arXiv preprint arXiv:1802.07228, 2018.

48. Moor, J.H., *The nature, importance, and difficulty of machine ethics*. IEEE Intelligent Systems, 2006. **21**: p. 18–21.

49. Yudkowsky, E., "Creating friendly AI 1.0: The analysis and design of benevolent goal architectures, in *Singularity Institute for Artificial Intelligence*, 2001. Singularity Institute

50. Yampolskiy, R., *Leakproofing the singularity artificial intelligence confinement problem*. Journal of Consciousness Studies, 2012. **19**: p. 1–2.

51. Babcock, J., J. Kramar, and R. Yampolskiy, *The AGI containment problem*. arXiv preprint arXiv:1604.00545, 2016.

52. Babcock, J., J. Kramar, and R. Yampolskiy, *The AGI containment problem*, in *The Ninth Conference on Artificial General Intelligence (AGI2015)*. 2016. Springer

53. Armstrong, S., and R.V. Yampolskiy, Security solutions for intelligent and complex systems, in *Security Solutions for Hyperconnectivity and the Internet of Things*. 2016, IGI Global. p. 37–88.

54. Karp, R.M., Reducibility among combinatorial problems, in *Complexity of Computer Computations*, R. E. Miller and J. W. Thatcher, Editors. 1972, Plenum. p. 85–103.

55. Yampolskiy, R., Turing test as a defining feature of AI-completeness, in *Artificial Intelligence, Evolutionary Computing and Metaheuristics*. Vol. 427, X.-S. Yang, Editor. 2013, Springer Berlin Heidelberg. p. 3–17.

56. Yampolskiy, R.V., *AI-complete, AI-hard, or AI-easy–classification of problems in AI*, in *The 23rd Midwest Artificial Intelligence and Cognitive Science Conference*. 2012. CEUR

57. Yampolskiy, R.V., *Efficiency theory: A unifying theory for information, computation and intelligence.* Journal of Discrete Mathematical Sciences & Cryptography, 2013. **16**(4–5): p 259–277.

58. Yampolskiy, R.V., *AI-complete CAPTCHAs as zero knowledge proofs of access to an artificially intelligent system.* ISRN Artificial Intelligence, 2011. **271878**.

59. Yampolskiy, R.V., *On the origin of samples: Attribution of output to a particular algorithm.* arXiv preprint arXiv:1608.06172, 2016.

60. Sotala, K., *Defining human values for value learners*, in *2nd International Workshop on AI, Ethics and Society, AAAI-2016*. 2016. AAAI Press

61. Dewey, D., *Learning what to value.* Artificial General Intelligence, 2011. p. 309–314.

62. Soares, N., and B. Fallenstein, Aligning Superintelligence with Human Interests: A Technical Research Agenda. Machine Intelligence Research Institute (MIRI) Technical Report, 2014.

9

Personhood*

"The Machine is not an it to be animated, worshiped, and dominated.
The machine is us, our process, an aspect of our embodiment.
We can be responsible for machines; they do not dominate or threaten us.
We are responsible for boundaries; we are they"

Donna Haraway

9.1 Introduction to AI Personhood

Debates about rights are frequently framed around the concept of legal personhood, which is granted not just to human beings but also to some non-human entities, such as firms, corporations or governments. Legal entities, aka legal persons, are granted certain privileges and responsibilities by the jurisdictions in which they are recognized, and many such rights are not available to non-person agents. Attempting to secure legal personhood is often seen as a potential pathway to get certain rights and protections for animals [1], fetuses [2], trees, rivers [3], and artificially intelligent (AI) agents [4]. It is commonly believed that a court ruling or a legislative action is necessary to grant personhood to a new type of entity, but recent legal literature [5–8] suggests that loopholes in the current law may permit the granting of legal personhood to currently existing AI/software without having to change the law or persuade any court.

LoPucki [6], in his paper on Algorithmic Entities, cites Bayern [7, 8] and his work on conferring legal personhood on AI by putting it in charge of a limited liability company (LLC).[1] "Professor Shawn Bayern demonstrated that anyone can confer legal personhood on an autonomous computer algorithm merely by putting it in control of a limited liability company (LLC). The algorithm can exercise the rights of the entity, making them effectively rights of the algorithm. The rights of such an algorithmic entity (AE) would

---

          DOI: 10.1201/9781003440260-9

include the rights to privacy, to own property, to enter into contracts, to be represented by counsel, to be free from unreasonable search and seizure, to equal protection of the laws, to speak freely, and perhaps even to spend money on political campaigns. Once an algorithm had such rights, Bayern observed, it would also have the power to confer equivalent rights on other algorithms by forming additional entities and putting those algorithms in control of them"[2] [6].

Other legal pathways to obtain legal personhood have been suggested and analyzed in the literature [4–12], but details of such legal "hacking" are beyond the scope of this chapter. We are simply interested in understanding the impact of granting personhood to AI on human dignity [13] and safety. With appearance of decentralized autonomous organizations [14], such as the decentralized autonomous organizations (DAO) [15], these questions are as pressing as ever.

9.2 Selfish Memes

In his book, *The Selfish Gene*, Dawkins [16] talks about genes as the driving payload behind evolution, with animal bodies as vehicles for the gene to accomplish its goals in the world. He also introduced a new concept of a *meme*, or viral idea competing for dominance in human minds, inspired by the similarities between natural and cultural evolution. Advent of algorithmic entities would make it possible to explicitly add a memetic payload to a legal entity, resulting in what we will call the Selfish Meme. Corporations are selfish entities with the goal of maximizing shareholder profit, with AI in charge of such an entity, any idea can be codified in an algorithm and added as the driving force behind the corporation's decision-making. At a higher level of abstraction, this could produce selfish cryptocurrencies.

We already see something similar from B-corps or for-benefit corporations, which attempt to create some social good in addition to profit. However, such a memetic payload doesn't have to be strictly beneficial; in practice, it could be any ideology, set of beliefs or values. For example, it would be possible to codify tenants of a particular religion (e.g., Islam), economic philosophy (communism), moral theory (utilitarianism) or something silly but potentially dangerous like a Paperclip Maximizer [17] or Pepe meme [18], encode them in an algorithm and put that algorithm in charge of a corporation, which could eventually take over the world and enforce its memetic payload on the world. Via orthogonality thesis [19], we can see that few, if any, limitations exist on the potential memetic payload; it could be a marketing campaign, an uploaded animal or human mind, our constitution and the complete set of laws or a computer virus. Evolutionary competition would appear between such entities leading to adversarial practices [20] and perhaps hostile takeovers not just in a legal but also in a computer science sense, with hacking and replacement of a corporation's selfish meme with another payload being a real possibility. We live in a world where computer viruses may have rights. It would also not be surprising if establishment of corporations with custom memetic payload become available as a service. Such corporations may also attempt to gain membership in different organizations and partnerships, for example, the recently formed Partnership on AI,[3] in order to influence it from within.

9.3 Human Indignity

The process for getting legal rights for AI, described above, doesn't specify any minimal intelligence/capability for the AI involved, meaning it could be just a few "if" statements, a random decision generator or an emulation of an ameba.[4] To grant most if not all human rights to a cockroach, for example, would be an ultimate assault on human dignity (but it may make some people happy [21]). This could be potentially done as an art project or in protest of unequal treatment of all humans by some human rights activists. We have already witnessed an example of such indignity and subsequent outrage from many feminist scholars [22] on the news of Sophia the robot getting citizenship in Saudi Arabia, a country notorious for unequal treatment of women. Will self-driving cars be allowed on the roads before women are?[5] As a result of legal personhood and granting of associated rights, some humans will have less rights than trivial (non-intelligent) software and robots, a great indignity and discriminatory humiliation. For example, certain jurisdictions limit rights of their citizens, such as the right to free speech, freedom of religious practice, or expression of sexuality, but AIs with legal personhood in other jurisdictions would be granted such rights.

If, on the other hand, AIs are going to become more intelligent than humans, the indignity for humanity would come from being relegated to an inferior place in the world, being outcompeted in the workplace and all other domains of human interest [23, 24]. AI-led corporations would be in a position to fire their human workers. This would possibly lead to deteriorating economic and living conditions, permanent unemployment and potentially reduction in rights, not to mention further worsening of the situation, including the level of existential catastrophe (extermination) [25].

The precedent of AI obtaining legal personhood via the corporate loophole may catalyze legislative granting of equal rights to AI agents as a matter of equal treatment, leading to a number of indignities for the human population. Since the software can reproduce itself almost indefinitely, they would quickly make human suffrage inconsequential, if given civil rights [26] leading to the loss of self-determination for people. Such loss of power would likely lead to the redistribution of resources from humanity to machines as well as the possibility of AIs serving as leaders, presidents, judges, jurors and even executioners. We will see military AIs targeting human populations and deciding on their own targets and acceptable collateral damage. They may not necessarily subscribe to the Geneva Convention and other rules of war. Torture, genocide and nuclear war may become options to consider to reach desired goals.

As AIs' capabilities and dominance grow, they would likely self-grant special (super) rights to emphasize their superiority to people, while at the same time removing or at least reducing human rights (e.g., second amendment, first amendment, reproductive rights in the sense of the right to reproduce at all, aka, zero-child policy, convention on human rights, etc.) while justifying doing so by our relative "feeblemindedness". A number of scholars [27–29] today work on developing reasons for justifying the granting of rights to AIs, perhaps one day those reasons will be useful while we are begging to keep some of ours.

9.4 Legal-System Hacking

Corporations can act as their own lawyers while representing themselves in a court of law, including performing all functions of a human lawyer, such as sue and be sued. Artificial superintelligence in charge of a corporation can act as a super-lawyer capable of finding novel loopholes in our laws (zero-day law exploits), engaging in frivolous litigation (DOS-style litigation attacks), patent filing and trolling, and smart-contract fallibility detection [30]. Our laws are complex, ambiguous and too numerous to be read by any single person, with the USA tax code alone approaching 4,000 (or 75,000 if you include IRS explanations, regulations, and rulings) pages, making it perfect for AI to exploit by both finding flaws in existing contracts and drafting contracts with hard-to-detect backdoors. A meeting of the minds between a human and superintelligence is unlikely to be achievable.

It is also likely that computational legal language [31] and smart contracts [32] will come to replace our current legal code making it inaccessible to human lawyers due to its computational complexity, size and unnatural jargon, further contributing to our second-class citizen status and indignity. This would happen simultaneously with the current trend of digitizing the judiciary system and civil engagement as illustrated by Korean e-judiciary [33] and Estonian e-residency program [34], trends which, while providing short-term convenience to people, give long-term advantages to the machines. This seems to be a part of a larger trend of society moving to Algocracy – rule by algorithm, there code is law [35]. Furthermore, due to its comparative advantage in large-scale surveillance and data mining, AI would be able to uncover human illegal behavior and, as most have broken some law (e.g., tax evasion, speeding, obscure laws, etc.), bring legal action or threat of legal actions against everyone. Similar blackmail and reporting could happen in the business environment, with AI also enjoying existing whistleblower protections.

9.5 Human Safety

A lot has been published on different risks associated with the advancement of artificial intelligence [36–43], but less specifically on dangers from AI-controlled corporate entities. Nothing in our current laws would prevent formation of a malevolent corporation (or corporate virus) with memetic payload of subjugating or exterminating humanity through legal means and political influence. In addition to legal enslavement of people via below-living-wage salary, such corporations could support legal change in minimum wage and pension laws as well as provide opposition to wealth redistribution and Universal Basic Income/Universal Basic Assets [44, 45]. This is particularly easy to accomplish because of the Supreme Court decision in Citizens United VS FEC [46], permitting unrestricted donations from corporations to politicians under the guise of free speech, making it possible to convert financial wealth to political power.

This leads us to recognize an additional existential risk (X-risk) [47], from extreme wealth. Wealth inequality is already recognized as a problem for democratic institutions [48], but super-rich corporate AIs (dollar trillionaires) would take that problem to the next level. They could accumulate such unprecedented levels of wealth via unfair business practices such as predatory pricing, having access to free physical and cognitive labor from direct control of automation, permitting them to undermine completion and achieve monopoly status in multiple domains and other multiple resources. Additionally, such entities could engage in super-long-term investment, getting compound interest for hundreds of years. For example, a million dollars invested for 150 years at the same rate of return as observed over the last hundred years would grow to 1.6 trillion inflation-unadjusted dollars, creating super-rich artificial entities.

If EAs become intellectually indistinguishable from people, meaning they could pass an unrestricted Turing Test [49], their capacity to self-replicate could be used to drain resources from legitimate corporations, for example, via click-fraud [50, 51] from Google. Also, they will be able to create their own super successful companies with alternative populations comprised of billions of EA users indistinguishable from real people but paid for by advertisers as if they were genuine clients.

Super-rich would be able to work within and outside the law, using donations or bribes to influence politicians, as well as directly breaking the law and simply paying fines for such actions. Because corporations can create other corporations, it would become possible to establish a legally independent suicidal corporation, which is willing to accomplish any legal or illegal goal of an originator corporation and, after that, cease to exist, permitting avoidance of any responsibility by the original algorithm entity. With the appearance of dark-web assassin markets financed through anonymous crypto-payments [52], the power of the super-rich can't be effectively fought against without endangering personal safety and security. At the least, the super-rich have the power to ruin someone's life financially, socially and professionally if direct termination is not preferred. Politicians financially backed by algorithmic entities would be able to take on legislative bodies, impeach president and help to get figureheads appointed to the Supreme Court. Such human figureheads could be used to obtain special (super-rights) for AIs or at least expansion of corporate rights. It also may become possible to exercise direct control over human figureheads via advanced computer-brain interfaces (CBI) permitting AIs unrestricted manipulation of a human body, essentially turning them into meat avatars, another source of indignity.

LoPucki provides a detailed list of reasons a human may set up an AE [6]:

1. *"Terrorism.* An initiator could program an AE to raise money to finance terrorism or to directly engage in terrorist acts. It could be programmed for genocide or general mayhem.

2. *Benefits.* An initiator could program an AE to provide direct benefits to individuals, groups, or causes. …

3. *Impact.* An initiator could program an AE to achieve some specified impact on the world. The goals might range all of the way from traditional philanthropy to pure maliciousness. …

4. *Curiosity.* An initiator might launch an AE simply out of curiosity. Initiators have sometimes devoted substantial time and money to launch computer viruses from which they could derive no monetary benefit. …

5. *Liability avoidance.* Initiators can limit their civil and criminal liability for acts of their algorithms by transferring the algorithms to entities and surrendering control at the time of the launch. For example, the initiator might specify a general goal, such as maximizing financial return, and leave it to the algorithm to decide how to do that" [6].

What makes artificial entities particularly difficult to control, compete against and overall dangerous is that they enjoy a number of super-properties natural persons do not have. They are effectively immortal, non-physical, optimizable, and get more capable with time as they accumulate computational and financial resources. They are much more flexible in terms of their energy, temperature, storage needs as compared to biological entities. From the legal point of view, they can't be legally punished, or terminated, and are generally not subject to law enforcement as our judicial system is not set up for such entities [53]. Neither prisons, nor corporal nor capital punishment is applicable to algorithmic entities.

LoPucki also analyzes a number of similar and concerning properties of AEs, which differentiate them from natural persons and give them a strategic advantage [6]:

a. "**Ruthlessness** Unless programmed to have them, AEs will lack sympathy and empathy. Even if the AEs are fully capable of understanding the effects of their actions on humans, they may be indifferent to those effects. As a result, AEs will have a wider range of options available to them than would be available to even the most morally lax human controller. An AE could pursue its goals with utter ruthlessness. Virtually any human controller would stop somewhere short of that, making the AE more dangerous.

b. **Lack of Deterrability**

Outsiders can more easily deter a human-controlled entity than an AE. For example, if a human-controlled entity attempts to pursue an illegal course of action, the government can threaten to incarcerate the human controller. If the course of action is merely abhorrent, colleagues, friends, and relatives could apply social pressures. AEs lack those vulnerabilities because no human associated with them has control. As a result, AEs have greater freedom to pursue unpopular goals using unpopular methods. In deciding to attempt a coup, bomb a restaurant, or assemble an armed group to attack a shopping center, a human-controlled entity puts the lives of its human controllers at risk. The same decisions on behalf of an AE risk nothing but the resources the AE spends in planning and execution.

c. **Replication**

AEs can replicate themselves quickly and easily. If an AE's operations are entirely online, replication may be as easy as forming a new entity and electronically copying an algorithm. An entity can be formed in some jurisdictions in as little as an hour and for as little as seventy dollars. ... Easy replication supports several possible strategies. First, replication in a destination jurisdiction followed by dissolution of the entity in the original jurisdiction may put the AE beyond the legal reach of the original jurisdiction. ... Second, replication can make an AE harder to destroy. For example, if copies of an AE exist in three jurisdictions, each is a person with its own rights. A court order revoking the charter of one or seizing the assets of another would have no effect on the third" [6].

Such AEs would be far less scrupulous about running casinos, brothels, or selling drugs all business, which, while potentially legal, may have a significant impact on human dignity.

With the development of advanced robot bodies, it will become possible for AEs to embody themselves to more fully participate in the world and to directly perform physical actions that otherwise require multiple levels of indirect control. An EA can potentially be running on a humanoid robot or, a self-driving car, a flying drone or any sufficiently powerful embedded processor or cloud service. This, by extension, would permit memetic payloads to acquire bodies, resulting in the next level of evolutionary competition, in which a computer virus meme or a biological viral gene may propagate through a human-like body. If the quality of such humanoid robots is high enough to pass a Total Turing Test [54], it would become impossible to tell between natural and artificial people, likely leading to the violation of Turing's Red Flag law [55]. Consequently, people would have the option to continue to exist and influence the world after their death via embodied representative algorithms. At the same time, autonomous corporations would have an option to replace human employees with identical but controlled clones. Similar analysis can be performed for virtual worlds and avatar bodies.

9.6 Conclusions

In this paper, we looked at a number of problems which AI personhood can cause as well as the direct impact on human dignity from such legal recognition. The question before us: is there anything we can do to avoid such a dehumanizing future? While some solutions may be possible in theory, it does not mean that they are possible in practice. Changing the law to explicitly exclude AIs from becoming legal entities may be desirable but unlikely to happen in practice, as that would require changing existing corporate law across multiple jurisdictions and such major reforms are unlikely to pass. Perhaps it would be helpful to at least standardize corporate law across multiple jurisdictions, but that is likewise unlikely to happen. Similarly, laws regarding maximum wealth levels, to prevent accumulation of extreme wealth have no chance of passing and would be easily bypassed by clever AIs if introduced.

Overall, it is important to realize that just like hackers attack computer systems and discover bugs in the code, machines will attack our legal systems and discover bugs in our legal code and contracts. For every type of cybersecurity attack, a similar type of attack will be discovered in the legal domain. The number of such attacks and their severity will increase proportionate to the capabilities of AIs. To counteract such developments, we need to establish, understand and practice Legal Safety the same way we do cybersecurity. The only good news is that consequences from successful legal attacks are likely to be less severe compared to direct threats we will face from malevolent superintelligences.

Notes

1. "Bayern specifies this chain of events as capable of establishing the link: (1) [A]n individual member creates a member-managed LLC, filing the appropriate paperwork with the state; (2) the individual (along, possibly, with the LLC, which is controlled by the sole member) enters into an operating agreement governing the conduct of the LLC; (3) the operating agreement specifies that the LLC will take actions as determined by an autonomous system, specifying terms or conditions as appropriate to achieve the autonomous system's legal goals; (4) the sole member withdraws from the LLC, leaving the LLC without any members. The result is potentially a perpetual LLC—a new legal person— that requires no ongoing intervention from any preexisting legal person in order to maintain its status. AEs would not be confined to cyberspace. An AE could act offline by contracting online with humans or robots for offline services. Bayern uses an algorithm that operates a Bitcoin vending machine business to illustrate".
2. See original article for footnotes, which have been removed to improve readability of quotes.
3. https://www.partnershiponai.org/
4. Same legal loophole could be used to grant personhood to animals or others with inferior rights.
5. As of June 24, 2018 and after this was written, women were permitted to drive in Saudi Arabia.

References

1. Varner, G.E., *Personhood, Ethics, and Animal Cognition: Situating Animals in Hare's Two Level Utilitarianism*. 2012: Oxford University Press.
2. Schroedel, J.R., P. Fiber, and B.D. Snyder, *Women's rights and fetal personhood in criminal law*. Duke Journal of Gender Law & Policy, 2000. **7**: p. 89.
3. Gordon, G.J., *Environmental personhood*. Columbia Journal of Environmental Law, 2018. **43**: p. 49.
4. Chopra, S., and L. White, *Artificial agents-personhood in law and philosophy*, in *Proceedings of the 16th European Conference on Artificial Intelligence*. 2004. IOS Press.
5. Solum, L.B., *Legal personhood for artificial intelligences*. North Carolina Law Review, 1991. **70**: p. 1231.

6. LoPucki, L.M., *Algorithmic entities*. Washington University Law Review, 2018. **95**(4): p. 887–953.

7. Bayern, S., *The implications of modern business–entity law for the regulation of autonomous systems*. European Journal of Risk Regulation, 2016. **7**(2): p. 297–309.

8. Bayern, S., *Of Bitcoins, Independently Wealthy Software, and the Zero-Member LLC*. Vol. 108. 2013: Northwestern University Law Review. p. 1485.

9. Andrade, F., et al., *Contracting agents: Legal personality and representation*. Artificial Intelligence and Law, 2007. **15**(4): p. 357–373.

10. Calverley, D.J., *Imagining a non-biological machine as a legal person*. AI & Society, 2008. **22**(4): p. 523–537.

11. Teubner, G., *Rights of non-humans? Electronic agents and animals as new actors in politics and law*. Journal of Law and Society, 2006. **33**(4): p. 497–521.

12. Dan-Cohen, M., *Rights, Persons, and Organizations: A Legal Theory for Bureaucratic Society*. Vol. 26. 2016: Quid Pro Books.

13. Bostrom, N., *In defense of posthuman dignity*. Bioethics, 2005. **19**(3): p. 202–214.

14. Dilger, W., *Decentralized autonomous organization of the intelligent home according to the principle of the immune system*, in *IEEE International Conference on Systems, Man, and Cybernetics, Computational Cybernetics and Simulation*. 1997. IEEE.

15. DuPont, Q., *Experiments in algorithmic governance: A history and ethnography of "the DAO," a failed decentralized autonomous organization*, in *Bitcoin and Beyond*. 2017, Routledge. p. 157–177.

16. Dawkins, R., The Selfish Gene. 1976: Oxford University Press.

17. Yudkowsky, E., *Intelligence explosion microeconomics*. Machine Intelligence Research Institute, 2013. **23**: p. 2015.

18. Mele, C., *Pepe the Frog Meme Listed as a Hate Symbol. The New York Times*. 2016. http://www.nytimes.com/2016/09/28/us/pepe-the-frog-is-listed-as-a-hate-symbol-by-the-anti-defamation-league.html.

19. Bostrom, N., *The superintelligent will: Motivation and instrumental rationality in advanced artificial agents*. Minds and Machines, 2012. **22**(2): p. 71–85.

20. Ramamoorthy, A., and R. Yampolskiy, *Beyond MAD?: The race for artificial general intelligence*. ICT Discoveries, 2018. **1**(1): p. 77–84.

21. Tomasik, B., *The Importance of Insect Suffering. Essays on Reducing Suffering*, in *Reducing Suffering*. 2016. https://www.reducing-suffering.org/the-importance-of-insect-suffering.

22. Kanso, H., *Saudi Women Riled by Robot with No Hjiab and More Rights Than Them*. Retrieved November 1, 2017. https://www.reuters.com/article/us-saudi-robot-citizenship/saudi-women-riled-by-robot-with-no-hjiab-and-more-rights-than-them-idUSKBN1D14Z7.

23. Bostrom, N., *Superintelligence: Paths, Dangers, Strategies*. 2014: Oxford University Press.

24. Yampolskiy, R.V., *Artificial Superintelligence: A Futuristic Approach*. 2015: Chapman and Hall/CRC.

25. Pistono, F., and R.V. Yampolskiy, *Unethical research: How to create a malevolent artificial intelligence*, in *25th International Joint Conference on Artificial Intelligence (IJCAI-16), Ethics for Artificial Intelligence Workshop (AI-Ethics-2016)*. 2016. AAAI Press

26. Yampolskiy, R.V., *Artificial intelligence safety engineering: Why machine ethics is a wrong approach*, in *Philosophy and Theory of Artificial Intelligence*. 2013, Springer. p. 389–396.

27. Guo, S., and G. Zhang, *Robot rights*. Science, 2009. **323**: p. 876.
28. Coeckelbergh, M., *Robot rights? Towards a social-relational justification of moral consideration*. Ethics and Information Technology, 2010. **12**(3): p. 209–221.
29. Gunkel, D., *The other question: The issue of robot rights*, in Sociable Robots and the Future of Social Relations. 2014, IOS Press. p. 13.
30. Yampolskiy, R.V., *What are the ultimate limits to computational techniques: Verifier theory and unverifiability*. Physica Scripta, 2017. **92**(9): p. 093001.
31. Wolfram, S., *Computational Law, Symbolic Discourse and the AI Constitution*. 2016. http://blog.stephenwolfram.com/2016/10/computational-law-symbolic-discourse-and-the-ai-constitution/.
32. Christidis, K., and M. Devetsikiotis, *Blockchains and smart contracts for the internet of things*. IEEE Access, 2016. **4**: p. 2292–2303.
33. Bank, W., *Improving Court Efficiency: The Republic of Korea's E-Court Experience*, 2013.
34. Anthes, G., *Estonia: A model for e-government*. Communications of the ACM, 2015. **58**(6): p. 18–20.
35. Danaher, J., *The threat of algocracy: Reality, resistance and accommodation*. Philosophy & Technology, 2016. **29**(3): p. 245–268.
36. Sotala, K., and R.V. Yampolskiy, *Responses to catastrophic AGI risk: A survey*. Physica Scripta, 2015. **90**(1): p. 018001.
37. Yudkowsky, E., *Artificial intelligence as a positive and negative factor in global risk*, in *Global Catastrophic Risks*, N. Bostrom and M.M. Cirkovic, Editors. 2008, Oxford University Press. p. 308–345.
38. Armstrong, S., A. Sandberg, and N. Bostrom, *Thinking inside the box: Using and controlling an oracle AI*. Minds and Machines (to Appear), 2012.
39. Yampolskiy, R.V., *Artificial Intelligence Safety and Security*. 2018: CRC Press.
40. Brundage, M., et al., *The malicious use of artificial intelligence: Forecasting, prevention, and mitigation*. arXiv preprint arXiv:1802.07228, 2018.
41. Yampolskiy, R.V., and M. Spellchecker, *Artificial intelligence safety and cybersecurity: A timeline of AI failures*. arXiv preprint arXiv:1610.07997, 2016.
42. Babcock, J., J. Kramár, and R. Yampolskiy, *The AGI containment problem*, in *Artificial General Intelligence*. 2016, Springer. p. 53–63.
43. Yampolskiy, R.V., *Taxonomy of pathways to dangerous artificial intelligence*, in *AAAI Workshop: AI, Ethics, and Society*. 2016.
44. Woodbury, S.A., *Universal basic income*, in *The American Middle Class: An Economic Encyclopedia of Progress and Poverty [2 Volumes]*. 2017. p. 314.
45. Van Parijs, P., *Basic income: A simple and powerful idea for the twenty-first century*. Politics & Society, 2004. **32**(1): p. 7–39.
46. Epstein, R.A., *Citizens United v. FEC: The constitutional right that big corporations should have but do not want*. Harvard Journal of Law and Public Policy, 2011. **34**: p. 639.
47. Bostrom, N., *Existential risk prevention as global priority*. Global Policy, 2013. **4**(1): p. 15–31.
48. Karl, T.L., *Economic inequality and democratic instability*. Journal of Democracy, 2000. **11**(1): p. 149–156.
49. Turing, A., *Computing machinery and intelligence*. Mind, 1950. **59**(236): p. 433–460.
50. Kantardzic, M., et al. *Click fraud prevention via multimodal evidence fusion by Dempster-Shafer theory*, in *IEEE Conference on Multisensor Fusion and Integration for Intelligent Systems (MFI)*. 2010. IEEE.

51. Walgampaya, C., M. Kantardzic, and R. Yampolskiy, *Evidence fusion for real time click fraud detection and prevention*, in *Intelligent Automation and Systems Engineering*. 2011. p. 1–14. Springer.
52. Greenberg, A., Meet the 'Assassination Market' Creator Who's Crowdfunding Murder With Bitcoins. Vol. 18. 2013: Forbes. p. 2014.
53. Bryson, J.J., M.E. Diamantis, and T.D. Grant, *Of, for, and by the people: The legal lacuna of synthetic persons*. Artificial Intelligence and Law, 2017. **25**(3): p. 273–291.
54. Schweizer, P., *The truly total Turing test*. Minds and Machines, 1998. **8**(2): p. 263–272.
55. Walsh, T., *Turing's red flag*. Communications of the ACM, 2016. **59**(7): p. 34–37.

10

Consciousness*

"The greatest obstacle to discovery is not ignorance—it is the illusion of knowledge"

Daniel J. Boorstin

"Consciousness is the one thing in this universe that cannot be an illusion"

Sam Harris

10.1 Introduction to the Problem of Consciousness

One of the deepest and most interesting questions ever considered is the nature of consciousness. An explanation for what consciousness is, how it is produced, how to measure it or at least detect it [1] would help us to understand who we are, how we perceive the universe and other beings in it, and maybe even comprehend the meaning of life. As we embark on the quest to create intelligent machines, the importance of understanding consciousness takes on an additional fundamental role and engineering thoroughness. As the presence of consciousness is taken to be the primary reason for granting many rights and ethical considerations [2], its full understanding will drastically change how we treat our mind children and perhaps how they treat us.

Initially the question of consciousness was broad and ill-defined, encompassing problems related to intelligence, information processing, free will, self-awareness, essence of life and many others. With a better understanding of brain architecture and progress in artificial intelligence and cognitive science, many easy sub-problems of consciousness have been successfully addressed [3], and multiple neural correlates of consciousness identified [4]. However, some fundamental questions remain as poignant as ever: What is it like to be a bat? [5], What is it like to be a brain simulation? [6], etc. In

---

* Reprinted with permission from Artificial Consciousness: An Illusionary Solution to the Hard Problem, Roman V. Yampolskiy, Reti, Saperi, Linguaggi, Issue 2; Copyright © 2018 by Rivisteweb.

DOI: 10.1201/9781003440260-10

other words, what is it like to be a particular type of agent [7–10]? What does it feel like to be one? Why do we feel something at all? Why red doesn't sound like a bell [11]? What red looks like [12]? What is it like to see with your tongue [13]? In other words, we are talking about experiencing what it is like to be in a particular state. Block [14] calls it *Phenomenal* or P-consciousness to distinguish it from *Access* or A-consciousness. David Chalmers managed to distill away non-essential components of consciousness and suggested that explaining qualia (what it feels like to experience something) and why we feel in the first place as opposed to being philosophical zombies [15] is the Hard Problem of consciousness [3]:

> The really hard problem of consciousness is the problem of *experience*. When we think and perceive, there is a whir of information process-ing, but there is also a subjective aspect. *As Nagel (1974) has put it, there is something it is like to be a conscious organism.* This subjective aspect is experience. When we see, for example, we *experience* visual sensations: the felt quality of redness, the experience of dark and light, the quality of depth in a visual field. Other experiences go along with perception in different modalities: the sound of a clarinet, the smell of mothballs. Then there are bodily sensations from pains to orgasms; mental images that are conjured up internally; the felt quality of emotion; and the expe-rience of a stream of conscious thought. What unites all of these states is that there is something it is like to be in them. All of them are states of experience. [3]. "... [A]n organism is conscious if there is something it is like to be that organism, and a mental state is conscious if there is some-thing it is like to be in that state. Sometimes terms such as "phenomenal consciousness" and "qualia" are also used here, but I find it more natu-ral to speak of "conscious experience" or simply "experience". [3]

Daniel Dennet [16] and others [17] have argued that, in fact, there is no Hard Problem and that what we perceive as consciousness is just an illu-sion like many others, an explanation explored by scholars of illusionism [18–21]. Over the years a significant amount of evidence has been collected all affirming that much of what we experience is not real [22], including visual [23–25], auditory [26], tactile [27], gustational [28], olfactory [29], culture-specific [30] and many other types of illusions [31]. An illusion is a discrep-ancy between an agent's awareness and some stimulus [32]. Illusions can be defined as stimuli that produce a surprising percept in the experiencing agent [33] or as a difference between perception and reality [34]. As we make our case mostly by relying on Visual Illusions in this paper, we include the following definition from García-Garibay et al.: "Visual illusions are sen-sory percepts that can't be explained completely from the observed image but that arise from the internal workings of the visual system" [35].

Overall, examples of illusions may include: impossible objects [36], blind spot [37], paradoxes (Zeno's [38], mathematical/logical illusions [39]), quan-tum illusions [40], mirages [41], art [42, 43], Rorschach tests [44], acquired taste [45], reading jumbled letters [46], forced perspective [47], gestaltism [48], priming [49], stereograms [50], delusion boxes [51], temporal illusions [52], constellations [53], illusion within an illusion [54], world [55], Déjà Vu [56], reversing goggles [57], rainbows [58], virtual worlds [59], and wireheading [60]. It seems that illusions are not exceptions; they are the norm in our world, an idea which was rediscovered through the ages [61–63].

Moreover, if we take a broader definition and include experiences of different states of consciousness, we can add: dreams (including lucid dreams [64] and nightmares [65]), hallucinations [66], delusions [67], drug induced states [68], phantom pains [69], religious experiences [70], self [71] (homunculus [72]), cognitive biases [73], mental disorders, invisible disabilities and perception variations (Dissociative identity disorder [74], Schizophrenia [75, 76], Synesthesia [77], Simultanagnosia [78], Autism [79], Ideasthesia [80], Asperger's [81], Apophenia [82], Aphantasia [83], Prosopagnosia [84] – all could be reclassified as issues with "correctly" experiencing illusions), Pareidolia [85], ironic processes [86], emotions (love, hate) [87], feelings (hunger, pain, pleasure) [88], body transfer [89], out of body experiences [90], sensory substitution [91], novel senses [92], and many others.

Differences between what is traditionally considered to be an illusion and what we included can be explained by how frequently we experience them. For example, the sky looks different depending on the time of day, the amount of Sun or the angle you are experiencing it from, but we don't consider it to be an illusion because we experience it so frequently. Essentially, everything can be considered to be an illusion, and the difference is that some stimuli are very common while others are completely novel to us, like a piece of great art, for example [42]. This makes us think that if we experience something many times, it is real, but if we see something for the first time, it must be an illusion.

At the extreme, we can treat every experience as an illusion in which some state of atomic particles in the universe is perceived as either a blue sky, a beautiful poem, a hot plate, or a conscious agent. This realization is particularly obvious in the case of digital computers, which are machines capable of extrapolating all the world's objects from strings of binary digits. Isn't experiencing a face in a bunch of zeroes and ones a great illusion, in particular while another machine experiences a melody on the same set of inputs ([93], p44.)?

Likewise, neurodiverse individuals may experience the world in very different ways; just consider color blindness [94] as an example of same inputs being experienced differently by diverse types of human agents. In fact, we suggest that most mental disorders can be better understood as problems with certain aspects of generating, sustaining or analyzing illusions [75]. Similarly, with animals, studies show that many are capable of experiencing same illusions as people [95–98], while also experiencing our world in a very different way [99]. Historically, we have been greatly underestimating consciousness of animals [100], and it is likely that now we are doing it to intelligent machines.

What it feels like to be a particular type of agent in a given situation depends on the hardware/software/state of the agent and the stimulation being provided by the environment. As the qualia represent the bedrock of consciousness, we can formally define a conscious agent as one capable of experiencing at least some broadly defined illusions. To more formally illustrate this, we can represent the agent and its inputs as two shares employed in visual cryptography [101], depending on the composition of the agent, the input may end up producing a diametrically opposite experience [102, 103]. Consequently, consciousness is an ability to experience, and we can state two ways in which illusions and consciousness may interact to produce a conscious agent:

- An agent is real and is experiencing an illusion. This explains qualia and the agent itself is real.
- An agent is real and is having an illusion in which some other agent experiences an illusion. Self-identifying with such an agent creates self-consciousness. A sequence of such episodes corresponds to a stream of consciousness, and the illusionary agent itself is not real. You are an illusion experiencing an illusion.

10.2 Test for Detecting Qualia

Illusions provide a tool [104, 105] that makes it possible to sneak a peek into the mind of another agent and determine that an agent has in fact experienced an illusion. The approach is similar to non-interactive CAPTCHAs, in which some information is encoded in a CAPTCHA challenge [106–110], and it is only by solving the CAPTCHA correctly that the agent is able to obtain information necessary to act intelligently in the world, without having to explicitly self-report its internal state [111–114]. With illusions, it is possible to set up a test in which it is only by experiencing an illusion that the agent is able to enter into a certain internal state, which we can say it experiences. It is not enough to know that something is an illusion. For example, with a classical face/vase illusion [115], an agent who was previously not exposed to that challenge could be asked to report what two interpretations of the image it sees and if the answer matches that of a human experiencing that illusion the agent must also be experiencing the illusion, but perhaps in a different way.

Our proposal represents a variant of a Turing Test [116, 117] but with emphasis not on behavior or knowledge but on experiences, feelings and internal states. In related research, Schweizer [118] has proposed a Total Turing Test for Qualia (Q3T), which is a variant of Turing Test for a robot with sensors and questions concentrated on experiences such as: how do you find that wine? Schneider and Turner have proposed a behavior-based AI consciousness test, which looks at whether the synthetic mind has an experience-based understanding of the way it feels to be conscious as demonstrated by an agent "talking" about consciousness-related concepts such as the afterlife or soul [119].

What we describe is an empirical test for the presence of some subjective experiences. The test is probabilistic but successive different variants of the test can be used to obtain any desired level of confidence. If a collaborating agent fails a particular instance of the test, it doesn't mean that the agent doesn't have qualia, but passing an instance of the test should increase our belief that the agent has experiences in proportion to the chance of guessing the correct answer for that particular variant of the test. As qualia are agent type (hardware) specific (human, species, machine, etc.), it would be easiest for us to design a human-compatible qualia test, but in principle, it is possible to test for any type of qualia, even the ones that humans don't experience themselves. Obviously, having some qualia doesn't mean ability to experience them all. While what we propose is a binary detector test for some qualia, it is possible to design specific variants for extracting particular properties of qualia experience such as color, depth, size, etc. The easiest way to demonstrate the construction of our test is by converting famous visual illusions into instances of our test questions, as seen in Figure 10.1.

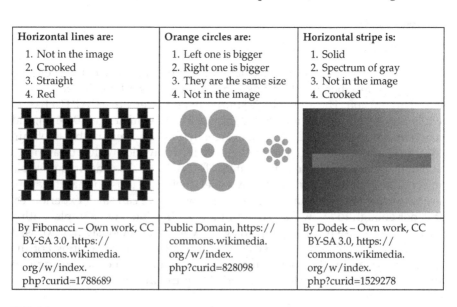

Horizontal lines are:	Orange circles are:	Horizontal stripe is:
1. Not in the image 2. Crooked 3. Straight 4. Red	1. Left one is bigger 2. Right one is bigger 3. They are the same size 4. Not in the image	1. Solid 2. Spectrum of gray 3. Not in the image 4. Crooked
By Fibonacci – Own work, CC BY-SA 3.0, https:// commons.wikimedia. org/w/index. php?curid=1788689	Public Domain, https:// commons.wikimedia. org/w/index. php?curid=828098	By Dodek – Own work, CC BY-SA 3.0, https:// commons.wikimedia. org/w/index. php?curid=1529278

FIGURE 10.1
Visual illusions presented as tests.

Essentially, we present our subject with an illusion and ask it a multiple-choice question about the illusionary experience, such as: how many black dots do you see? How many curved lines are in the image? Which of the following effects do you observe? It is important to only test subjects with tests they have not experienced before and information about which is not readily available. Ideally, a new test question should be prepared every time to prevent the subject from cheating. A variant of the test may ask open-ended questions such as: Please describe what you see. In that case, a description could be compared to that produced by a conscious agent, but this is less formal and opens the door for subjective interpretation of submitted responses. Ideally, we want to be able to automatically design novel illusions with complex information encoded in them as experiences.

We anticipate a number of possible objections to the validity of our test and its underlying theory:

- **Qualia experienced by the test subject may not be the same as that experienced by the test designer.**

  Yes, we are not claiming that they are identical experiences; we are simply showing that an agent had some subjective experiences, which was previously not possible. If sufficiently different, such alternative experiences would not result in passing the test.

- **The system may simply have knowledge of the human mental model and predict what a human would experience on similar stimulus.**

  If a system has an internal human (or some other) model that it simulates on presented stimuli and that generates experiences, it is the same as the whole system having experiences.

- **Agent may correctly guess answers to the test or lie about what it experiences.**

  Yes, for a particular test question, but the test can be given as many times as necessary to establish statistical significance.

- **The theory makes no predictions.**

  We predict that computers built to emulate the human brain will experience progressively more illusions without being explicitly programmed to do so, in particular the ones typically experienced by people.

- Turing addressed a number of relevant objections in his seminar paper on computing machinery [120].

10.3 Computers Can Experience Illusions,
and so Are Conscious

Majority of scholars studying illusionism are philosophers, but a lot of relevant work comes from psychology [121], cognitive science [122] and more recently, computer science, artificial intelligence, machine learning and, more particularly, artificial neural network research. It is this interdisciplinary nature of consciousness research that we think is most likely to produce successful and testable theories, such as the theory presented in this paper, to solve the Hard problem.

In the previous section, we have established that consciousness is fundamentally based on an ability to experience, for example, illusions. Recent work with artificially intelligent systems suggests that computers also experience illusions and in a similar way to people, providing support for the Principle of Organizational Invariance [3], aka substrate independence [55]. For example, Zeman et al. [123, 124] and Garcia-Garibay et al. [35] report on a neural network capable of experiencing Müller-Lyer illusion and multiple researchers [125–128] have performed experiments in which computer models were used to study visual illusions, including teaching computers to experience geometric illusions [125, 129, 130], brightness illusions [131, 132], and color constancy illusions [133]. In related research, Nguyen et al. found that NN perceives certain random noise images as meaningful with very high confidence [134]. Those NN were not explicitly designed to perceive illusions but they do so as a byproduct of the computations they perform. The field of Adversarial Neural Networks is largely about designing illusions for such intelligent systems [135, 136] with obvious parallels to inputs known to fool human agents intentionally [137] or unintentionally [138]. Early work on artificial neural networks likewise provides evidence for experiences similar to near-death hallucinations [139, 140] (based on so-called "virtual inputs" or "canonical hallucination" or "neural forgery" [141]), dreaming [142, 143], and impact from brain damage [144, 145].

Zeman [34] reviews history of research on the perception of illusions by computer models and summarizes the state-of-the-art in such research: "Historically, artificial models existed that did not contain multiple layers but were still able to demonstrate illusory bias. These models were able to produce output similar to human behaviour when presented with illusory figures, either by emulating the filtering operations of cells [127, 146] or by analysing statistics in the environment [126, 147–149]. However, these models were deterministic, non-hierarchical systems that did not involve any feature learning. It was not until Brown and Friston (2012) [150] that hierarchical systems were first considered as candidates for modelling illusions, even though the authors omitted important details of the model's architecture, such as the number of layers they recruited. ... So to summarise, illusions can manifest in artificial systems that are both hierarchical and capable of learning. Whether these networks rely on exposure to the same images that we see during training, or on filtering mechanisms that are based on similar neural operations, they produce a consistent and repeatable illusory bias. In terms of Marr's (1982) [151] levels of description ..., it appears that illusions can manifest at the hardware level [148, 149] and at the algorithmic/representational level [123, 127, 146]".

"By dissociating our sensory percepts from the physical characteristics of a stimulus, visual illusions provide neuroscientists with a unique opportunity to study the neuronal mechanisms underlying ... sensory experiences" [35]. Not surprisingly artificial neural networks just like their natural counterparts are subject to similar analysis. From this, we have to conclude that even today's simple AIs, as they experience specific types of illusions, are rudimentary conscious. General intelligence is what humans have and we are capable of perceiving many different types of complex illusions. As AIs become more adept at experiencing complex and perhaps multisensory illusions they will eventually reach and then surpass our capability in this domain producing multiple parallel streams of superconsciousness [152], even if their architecture or sensors are not inspired by the human brain. Such superintelligent and superconscious systems could justifiably see us as barely intelligent and weakly conscious, and could probably control amount of consciousness they had, within some range. Google DeepDream art [153] gives us some idea on what it's like to be a modern deep neural network and can be experienced in immersive 3D via the Hallucination machine [154]. Olah et al. provide a detailed neuron/layer visual analysis of what is being perceived by an artificial neural network [155].

10.3.1 Qualia Computing

If we can consistently induce qualia in computational agents, it should be possible to use such phenomena to perform computation. If we can encode information in illusions, certain agents can experience them or their combinations to perform computation, including artificially intelligent agents capable of controlling their illusions. Illusions are particularly great to represent superpositions of states (similar to quantum computing), which collapse once a particular view of the illusion is chosen by the experiencing agent [156]. You can only experience one interpretation of an illusion at a time, just like in Quantum physics, you can only know the location or speed of a particle at the same time – well-known conjugate pairs [157]. Famous examples of logical paradoxes can be seen as useful[1] for super-compressed data storage [158, 159] and hyper-computation [160]. Qualia may also be useful in explaining decisions produced by deep NN, with the last layer efficiently representing qualia-like states derived from low-level stimuli by lower-level neurons. Finally, qualia-based visualization and graphics are a very interesting area of investigation, with the human model giving us an example of visual thinking and lucid dreaming.

10.4 Purpose of Consciousness

While many scientific theories, such as biocentrism [161] or some interpretations of quantum physics [162, 163], see consciousness as a focal element of their models, the purpose of being able to experience remains elusive. In fact, even the measurement or detection of consciousness remains an open research area [1]. In this section, we review and elaborate on some explanations for what consciousness does. Many explanations have been suggested, including but certainly not limited to [20]: error monitoring [164], an inner eye [165], saving us from danger [166], later error detection [167], pramodular response [168] and to seem mysterious [169].

We can start by considering the evolutionary origins of qualia from the very first, probably accidental, state of matter, that experienced something, all the way to general illusion experiences of modern humans. The argument is that consciousness evolved because accurately representing reality is less important than agents' fitness for survival and agents who saw the world of illusions had higher fitness, as they ignored irrelevant and complicated minutia of the world [170]. It seems that processing the real world is computationally expensive and simplifying illusions allows improvements in efficiency of decision-making leading to higher survival rates. For example, we can treat feelings as heuristic shortcuts to calculating precise utility. Additionally, as we argue in this paper, experiencing something allows one to obtain knowledge about that experience, which is not available to someone not experiencing the same qualia. Therefore, a conscious agent would be able to perform in ways a philosophical zombie would not be able to act, which is particularly important in a world full of illusions such as ours.

Next, we can look at the value of consciousness in knowledge acquisition and learning. A major obstacle to the successful development of AI systems has been what is called the Symbol Grounding problem [171]. Trying to explain to a computer one symbol in terms of others does not lead to understanding. For example, saying that "mother" is a female parent is no different than saying that x = 7y, and y = 18k and so on. This is similar to a person looking up an unfamiliar word in a foreign language dictionary and essentially ending up with circular definitions of unfamiliar terms. We think that qualia are used (at least in humans) to break out of this vicious cycle and to permit definitions of words/symbols in terms of qualia. In *"How Helen Keller used syntactic semantics to escape from a Chinese Room"*, Rappaport [172] gives a great example of a human attempting to solve the grounding problem and argues that syntactic semantics are sufficient to resolve it. We argue that it is experiencing the feeling of running water on her hands was what permitted Hellen Keller to map sign language signs for water to the relevant qualia and to begin to understand.

Similarly, we see much of the language acquisition process as mapping of novel qualia to words. By extension, this mapping permits us to explain understanding and limits the transfer of tacit knowledge. Illusion disambiguation can play a part in what gives us an illusion of free will and the stream of consciousness may be nothing more than sequential illusion processing. Finally, it would not be surprising if some implicit real-world inputs produced experience of qualia behind some observed precognition results [173]. In the future, we suspect a major application of consciousness will be in the field of Qualia Computing, as described in the so-named section of this paper.

10.4.1 Qualia Engineering

While a grand purpose of life remains elusive and is unlikely to be discovered, it is easy to see that many people attempt to live their lives in a way, which allows them to maximally explore and experience novel stimuli: foods, smells, etc. Experiencing new qualia by transferring our consciousness between different substrates, what Loosemore refers to as Qualia Surfing [174], may represent the next level in novelty seeking. As our understanding and ability to detect and elicit particular qualia in specific agents improves, qualia engineering will become an important component of the entertainment industry. Research in other fields, such as intellectology [175], (and in particular artimetrics [176, 177], and designometry [178]), consciousness [179], and artificial intelligence [180], will also be impacted.

People designing optical illusions, movie directors and book authors are some of the people in the business of making our experience, but they do so as an art form. Qualia engineers and qualia designers will attempt to formally and scientifically answer such questions as How to detect and measure qualia? What is the simplest possible qualia? How to build complex qualia from simple ones? What makes some qualia more pleasant? Can minds be constructed with maximally pleasing qualia in a systematic and automated way [175]? Can this lead to the abolition of suffering [181]? Do limits exist to the complexity of qualia, or can the whole universe be treated as a single input? Can we create new feelings and emotions? How would integration of novel sensors expand our qualia repertoire? What qualia are available to other agents but not to humans? Can qualia be "translated" to other mediums? What types of verifiers and observers experience particular types of qualia? How to generate novel qualia in an algorithmic/ systematic way? Is it ethical to create unpleasant qualia? Can agents learn to swap qualia between different stimuli (pleasure for pain)? How to optimally represent, store and communicate qualia, including across different substrates [55]? How to design an agent, which experiences particular qualia on the given input? How much influence does an agent have over its own illusions? How much plasticity does the human brain have for switching stimuli streams and learning to experience data from new sensors? How similar are qualia among similarly designed but not identical agents? What, if any, is the connection between meditation and qualia? Can computers mediate? How do random inputs such as café chatter [182] stimulate production of novel qualia? How can qualia be classified into different types, for example, feelings? Which computations produce particular qualia?

10.5 Consciousness and Artificial Intelligence

Traditionally, AI researchers ignored consciousness as non-scientific and concentrated on making their machines capable and beneficial. One famous exception is Hofstadter, who observed and analyzed deep connections between illusions and artificial intelligence [183]. If an option to make conscious machines presents itself to AI researchers, it would raise a number of important questions, which should be addressed early on. It seems that making machines conscious may make them more relatable and human-like and so produce better consumer products, domestic and sex robots and more genuine conversation partners. Of course, a system simply simulating such behaviors without actually experiencing anything could be just as good. If we define physical pain as an unpleasant sensory illusion and emotional pain as an illusion of an unpleasant feeling, pain and pleasure become accessible controls to the experimenter. The ability to provide reward and punishment for software agents capable of experiencing pleasure and pain may assist in the training of such agents [184].

The potential impact of making AI conscious includes a change in the status of AI from mere useful software to a sentient agent with corresponding rights and ethical treatment standards. This is likely to lead to civil rights for AI and the disenfranchisement of human voters [185, 186]. In general, the ethics of designing sentient beings are not well established and it is cruel to create sentient agents for certain uses, such as menial jobs, servitude or designed obsolescence. It is an experiment that would be unlikely to be approved by any research ethics board [187]. Such agents may be subject to abuse as they would be capable of experiencing pain and torture, potentially increasing the overall amount of suffering in the universe [188]. If in the process of modeling or simulating conscious beings, the experiment negatively affects modeled entities this can be seen as mind crime [189].

With regards to AI Safety [190–195], since it would be possible for agents to experience pain and pleasure, it will open a number of new pathways for dangerous behavior. Consciousness may make AIs more volatile or unpredictable, impacting the overall safety and stability of such systems [119]. The possibility of ransomware with conscious artificial hostages comes to mind, as well as blackmail and threats against AI systems. A better understanding of consciousness by AI itself may also allow superintelligent machines to create new types of attacks on people. Certain illusions can be seen as an equivalent of adversarial inputs for human agents; see Figure 10.2. Subliminal

FIGURE 10.2
Top – cheetah in the noise is seen by some deep neural networks (based on [134]); Bottom – spaceship in the stereogram is seen by some people.

stimuli [196] that confuse people are well known and some stimuli are even capable of inducing harmful internal states such as epileptic seizures [197, 198] or incapacitation [199]. With latest research showing that even a single pixel modification is sufficient to fool neural networks [200], the full scope of the attack surface against human agents remains an unknown unknown.

Manual attempts to attack a human cognitive model are well known [201–203]. Future research combining evolutionary algorithms or adversarial neural networks with direct feedback from detailed scans of human brains is likely to produce some novel examples of adversarial human inputs, leading to new types of informational hazards [204]. Taken to the extreme, whole adversarial worlds may be created to confuse us [55]. Nature provides many examples of adversarial inputs in plants and animals, known as mimicry [205]. Human adversarial inputs designed by superintelligent machines would represent a new type of AI risk, which has not been previously analyzed and with no natural or synthetic safety mechanisms available to defend us against such an attack.

One very dangerous outcome from the integration of consciousness into AI is a possibility that a superintelligent system will become a negative utilitarian and an anti-natalist [188] and, in an attempt to rid the world of suffering, will not only kill all life forms but will also destroy all AIs and will finally self-destruct as it is itself conscious and so subject to the same analysis and conclusions. This would result in a universe free of suffering but also free of any consciousness. Consequently, it is important to establish guidelines and review boards [206] for any research that is geared at producing conscious agents [207]. AI itself should be designed to be corrigible [208] and to report any emergent un-programmed capabilities, such as qualia, to the designers.

10.6 Conclusions and Conjectures

In this paper, we described a reductionist theory for the appearance of qualia in agents based on a fully materialistic explanation for subjective states of mind, an attempt at a solution to the Hard Problem of consciousness. We defined a test for detecting experiences and showed how computers can be made conscious in terms of having qualia. Finally, we looked at implications of being able to detect and generate qualia in artificial intelligence. Should our test indicate presence of complex qualia in software or animals, certain protections and rights would be appropriate to grant to such agents. Experimental results, we surveyed in this chapter, have been predicted by others as evidence of consciousness in machines; for example, Dehaene et al. state: "We contend that a machine endowed with [global information availability and self-monitoring] ... may even experience the same perceptual illusions as humans" [209].

Subjective experiences called qualia are a side effect of computing, unintentionally produced while information is being processed, similar to the generation of heat [210], noise [211], or electromagnetic radiation [212] and is just as unintentional. Others have expressed similar intuitions: "The cognitive algorithms we use are the way the world feels" ([213] p. 889.) or "consciousness is the way information feels when being processed" [214] or "empirical evidence is compatible with the possibility that consciousness arises from nothing more than specific computations" [209]. Qualia arise as a result of processing of stimuli caused by agglomeration of properties, unique peculiarities [215], and errors in the agent's architecture, software, memories, learning algorithms, sensors, inputs, environment, and other factors comprising extended cognition [216] of an agent [217]. In fact, Zeman [34] points out the difficulty of telling if a given system experiences an error or an illusion. If every computation produces a side effect of qualia, computational functionalism [218] trivially reduces to panpsychism [219].

As qualia are fully dependent on the makeup of a particular agent it is not surprising that they capture what it is like to be that agent. Agents who share certain similarities in their makeup (like most people) may share certain subsets of qualia, but different agents will experience different qualia on the same inputs. An illusion is a discrepancy between agent's awareness and some stimulus [32]. In contrast, consciousness is an ability to experience a sustained self-referential multimodal illusion based on an ability to perceive qualia. Every experience is an illusion, what we call optical illusions are meta illusions, there are also meta-meta-illusions and self-referential illusions. It is an illusion of "I" or self that produces self-awareness, with "I" as an implied agent experiencing all the illusions, an illusion of an illusion navigator.

It is interesting to view the process of learning in the context of this chapter, with illusions as a primary pattern of interest for all agents. We can say that babies and other untrained neural networks are learning to experience illusions, particularly in the context of their trainers' culture/common sense [30]. Consequently, a successful agent will learn to map certain inputs to certain illusions while sharing that mapping with other similarly constructed observers. We can say that the common space of illusions/culture as seen by such agents becomes their "real world" or meme [220] sphere. Some supporting evidence for this conclusion comes from observing that the amount of sleep in children is proportionate to the average amount of learning they perform for that age group. Younger babies need the most sleep, perhaps because they can learn quicker by practicing to experience the safe world of dreams (a type of illusion), a skill they then transfer to the real world. Failure to learn to perceive illusions and experience qualia may result in a number of mental disorders.

There seems to be a fundamental connection between intelligence, consciousness and liveliness beyond the fact that all three are notoriously difficult to define. We believe that the ability to experience is directly proportionate to one's intelligence and that such intelligent and conscious agents are necessarily alive to the same degree. As all three come in degrees, it is likely that they have gradually evolved together. Modern narrow AIs are very low in general intelligence, and so are also very low in their ability to experience or their perceived liveness. Higher primates have significant (but not complete) general intelligence and so can experience complex stimuli and are very much alive. Future machines will be superintelligent, superconscious, and, by extension, alive!

Fundamental "particles" from which our personal world is constructed are illusions that we experience and in the process create the universe, as we know it. Experiencing a pattern that is not really there (let's call such an illusory element "illusination"), like appearing white spaces in an illusion [221], is just like experiencing self-awareness; where is it stored? Since each conscious agent perceives a unique personal universe, their agglomeration gives rise to the multiverse. We may be living in a simulation, but from our point of view we are not living in a virtual reality [222], we are living in an illusion of reality, and maybe we can learn to decide which reality to create. The "Reality" provides us with an infinite set of inputs from which every conceivable universe can be experienced, and in that sense, every universe exists. We can conclude that the universe is in the mind of the agent experiencing it – the ultimate qualia, even if we are just brains in a vat, to us an experience is worth 1000 pictures. It is not a delusion that we are just experiencers of illusions. The brain is an illusion experiencing machine not a pattern recognition machine. As we age, our wetware changes, and so we become different agents and experience different illusion, our identity changes but in a continuous manner. To paraphrase Descartes: I experience, therefore, I am conscious!

Note

1. Kolmogorov complexity is also not computable, but very useful.

References

1. Raoult, A., and R. Yampolskiy, *Reviewing Tests for Machine Consciousness.* 2015. https://www.researchgate.net/publication/284859013_DRAFT_Reviewing_Tests_for_Machine_Consciousness.
2. Muehlhauser, L., *Report on Consciousness and Moral Patienthood*, in *Open Philanthropy Project.* 2017. https://www.openphilanthropy.org/2017-report-consciousness-and-moral-patienthood.
3. Chalmers, D.J., *Facing up to the problem of consciousness.* Journal of Consciousness Studies, 1995. **2**(3): p. 200–219.
4. Mormann, F., and C. Koch, *Neural correlates of consciousness.* Scholarpedia, 2007. **2**(12): p. 1740.
5. Nagel, T., *What is it like to be a bat?* The Philosophical Review, 1974. **83**(4): p. 435–450.
6. Özkural, E. *What is it Like to be a Brain Simulation?* in *International Conference on Artificial General Intelligence.* 2012. Springer.

7. Trevarthen, C., *What is it like to be a person who knows nothing? Defining the active intersubjective mind of a newborn human being*. Infant and Child Development, 2011. **20**(1): p. 119–135.

8. Preuss, T.M., *What is it like to be a human*. The Cognitive Neurosciences, 2004. **3**: p. 5–22.

9. Laureys, S., and M. Boly, *What is it like to be vegetative or minimally conscious?* Current Opinion in Neurology, 2007. **20**(6): p. 609–613.

10. Burn, C.C., *What is it like to be a rat? Rat sensory perception and its implications for experimental design and rat welfare*. Applied Animal Behaviour Science, 2008. **112**(1): p. 1–32.

11. O'Regan, J.K., *Why Red doesn't Sound Like a Bell: Understanding the Feel of Consciousness*. 2011: Oxford University Press.

12. Jackson, F., *What Mary didn't know*. The Journal of Philosophy, 1986. **83**(5): p. 291–295.

13. Kendrick, M., *Tasting the Light: Device Lets the Blind "See" With Their Tongues*. 2009: Scientific American. 13.

14. Block, N., *On a confusion about a function of consciousness*. Behavioral and Brain Sciences, 1995. **18**(2): p. 227–247.

15. Chalmers, D.J., *Self-ascription without qualia: a case study*. Behavioral and Brain Sciences, 1993. **16**(1): p. 35–36.

16. Dennett, D.C., *From Bacteria to Bach and Back: The Evolution of Minds*. 2017: WW Norton & Company.

17. Tye, M., *Phenomenal consciousness: The explanatory gap as a cognitive illusion*. Mind, 1999. **108**(432): p. 705–725.

18. Frankish, K., *Illusionism as a theory of consciousness*. Journal of Consciousness Studies, 2016. **23**(11–12): p. 11–39.

19. Tartaglia, J., *What is at stake in illusionism?* Journal of Consciousness Studies, 2016. **23**(11–12): p. 236–255.

20. Blackmore, S., *Delusions of consciousness*. Journal of Consciousness Studies, 2016. **23**(11–12): p. 52–64.

21. Balog, K., *Illusionism's discontent*. Journal of Consciousness Studies, 2016. **23**(11–12): p. 40–51.

22. Noë, A., *Is the visual world a grand illusion?* Journal of Consciousness Studies, 2002. **9**(5–6): p. 1–12.

23. Coren, S., and J.S. Girgus, *Seeing Is Deceiving: The Psychology of Visual Illusions*. 1978: JSTOR.

24. Gregory, R.L., *Knowledge in perception and illusion*. Philosophical Transactions of the Royal Society of London B: Biological Sciences, 1997. **352**(1358): p. 1121–1127.

25. Changizi, M.A., et al., *Perceiving the present and a systematization of illusions*. Cognitive Science, 2008. **32**(3): p. 459–503.

26. Deutsch, D., *An auditory illusion*. The Journal of the Acoustical Society of America, 1974. **55**(S1): p. S18–S19.

27. Nakatani, M., R.D. Howe, and S. Tachi, *The fishbone tactile illusion*, in *Proceedings of Eurohaptics*. 2006.

28. Todrank, J., and L.M. Bartoshuk, *A taste illusion: Taste sensation localized by touch*. Physiology & Behavior, 1991. **50**(5): p. 1027–1031.

29. Herz, R.S., and J. von Clef, *The influence of verbal labeling on the perception of odors: Evidence for olfactory illusions?* Perception, 2001. **30**(3): p. 381–391.

30. Segall, M.H., D.T. Campbell, and M.J. Herskovits, *Cultural differences in the perception of geometric illusions.* Science, 1963. **139**(3556): p. 769–771.

31. Kahneman, D., and A. Tversky, *On the reality of cognitive illusions.* Psychological Review, 1996. **103**(3): p. 582–591.

32. Reynolds, R.I., *A psychological definition of illusion.* Philosophical Psychology, 1988. **1**(2): p. 217–223.

33. Bertamini, M., *Programming Visual Illusions for Everyone.* 2017: Springer.

34. Zeman, A., *Computational Modelling of Visual Illusions,* 2015.

35. García-Garibay, O.B., and V. de Lafuente, *The Müller-Lyer illusion as seen by an artificial neural network.* Frontiers in Computational Neuroscience, 2015. **9**: 1–3.

36. Penrose, L.S., and R. Penrose, *Impossible objects: A special type of visual illusion.* British Journal of Psychology, 1958. **49**(1): p. 31–33.

37. Tong, F., and S.A. Engel, *Interocular rivalry revealed in the human cortical blind-spot representation.* Nature, 2001. **411**(6834): p. 195–199.

38. Misra, B., and E.G. Sudarshan, *The Zeno's paradox in quantum theory.* Journal of Mathematical Physics, 1977. **18**(4): p. 756–763.

39. Grelling, K., *The logical paradoxes.* Mind, 1936. **45**(180): p. 481–486.

40. Greenleaf, A., et al., *Schrödinger's hat: Electromagnetic, acoustic and quantum amplifiers via transformation optics.* arXiv preprint arXiv:1107.4685, 2011.

41. Luckiesh, M., *Visual Illusions: Their Causes, Characteristics and Applications.* 1922: D. Van Nostrand Company.

42. Escher, M.C., *MC Escher: The Graphic Work.* 2000: Taschen.

43. Gold, R., *This is not a pipe.* Communications of the ACM, 1993. **36**(7): p. 72.

44. Lord, E., *Experimentally induced variations in Rorschach performance.* Psychological Monographs: General and Applied, 1950. **64**(10): p. i.

45. Mennell, S., *All Manners of Food: Eating and Taste in England and France from the Middle Ages to the Present.* 1996: University of Illinois Press.

46. Velan, H., and R. Frost, *Cambridge University versus Hebrew University: The impact of letter transposition on reading English and Hebrew.* Psychonomic Bulletin & Review, 2007. **14**(5): p. 913–918.

47. Kelley, L.A., and J.A. Endler, *Illusions promote mating success in great bowerbirds.* Science, 2012. **335**(6066): p. 335–338.

48. Koffka, K., *Principles of Gestalt Psychology.* Vol. 44. 2013: Routledge.

49. Tulving, E., and D.L. Schacter, *Priming and human memory systems.* Science, 1990. **247**(4940): p. 301–306.

50. Becker, S., and G.E. Hinton, *Self-organizing neural network that discovers surfaces in random-dot stereograms.* Nature, 1992. **355**(6356): p. 161–163.

51. Ring, M., and L. Orseau, *Delusion, survival, and intelligent agents,* in *International Conference on Artificial General Intelligence.* 2011. Springer.

52. Eagleman, D.M., *Human time perception and its illusions.* Current Opinion in Neurobiology, 2008. **18**(2): p. 131–136.

53. Liebe, C.C., *Pattern recognition of star constellations for spacecraft applications.* IEEE Aerospace and Electronic Systems Magazine, 1993. **8**(1): p. 31–39.

54. Deręgowski, J.B., *Illusions within an illusion.* Perception, 2015. **44**(12): p. 1416–1421.

55. Bostrom, N., *Are we living in a computer simulation?* The Philosophical Quarterly, 2003. **53**(211): p. 243–255.

56. Bancaud, J., et al., *Anatomical origin of déjà vu and vivid 'memories' in human temporal lobe epilepsy.* Brain, 1994. **117**(1): p. 71–90.

57. Wallaeh, H., and J.H. Kravitz, *The measurement of the constancy of visual direction and of its adaptation.* Psychonomic Science, 1965. **2**(1–12): p. 217–218.

58. Fineman, M., *The Nature of Visual Illusion.* 2012: Courier Corporation.

59. Rheingold, H., *Virtual Reality: Exploring the Brave New Technologies.* 1991: Simon & Schuster Adult Publishing Group.

60. Yampolskiy, R.V., *Utility function security in artificially intelligent agents.* Journal of Experimental & Theoretical Artificial Intelligence, 2014. **26**(3): p. 373–389.

61. Plato, and G.M.A. Grube, Plato's Republic. 1974: JSTOR.

62. Gillespie, A., *Descartes' demon: A dialogical analysis of meditations on first philosophy.* Theory & Psychology, 2006. **16**(6): p. 761–781.

63. Sun, J.T., *Psychology in primitive Buddhism.* The Psychoanalytic Review (1913–1957), 1924. **11**: p. 39.

64. Barrett, D., *Just how lucid are lucid dreams?* Dreaming, 1992. **2**(4): p. 221.

65. Zadra, A., and D. Donderi, *Nightmares and bad dreams: Their prevalence and relationship to well-being.* Journal of Abnormal Psychology, 2000. **109**(2): p. 273.

66. Bentall, R.P., *The illusion of reality: A review and integration of psychological research on hallucinations.* Psychological Bulletin, 1990. **107**(1): p. 82.

67. Garety, P.A., and D.R. Hemsley, *Delusions: Investigations into the Psychology of Delusional Reasoning.* Vol. 36. 1997: Psychology Press.

68. Becker, H.S., *History, culture and subjective experience: An exploration of the social bases of drug-induced experiences.* Journal of Health and Social Behavior, 1967: p. 163–176. https://doi.org/10.2307/2948371

69. Carlen, P., et al., *Phantom limbs and related phenomena in recent traumatic amputations.* Neurology, 1978. **28**(3): p. 211–211.

70. Fenwick, P., *The Neurophysiology of Religious Experiences.* 1996. Routledge.

71. Hood, B., *The Self Illusion: How the Social Brain Creates Identity.* 2012: Oxford University Press.

72. Dennett, D.C., *Brainstorms: Philosophical Essays on Mind and Psychology.* 1981: MIT Press.

73. Gigerenzer, G., *How to make cognitive illusions disappear: Beyond "heuristics and biases".* European Review of Social Psychology, 1991. **2**(1): p. 83–115.

74. Kluft, R.P., *Dissociative identity disorder,* in *Handbook of Dissociation.* 1996, Springer. p. 337–366.

75. Dima, D., et al., *Understanding why patients with schizophrenia do not perceive the hollow-mask illusion using dynamic causal modelling.* Neuroimage, 2009. **46**(4): p. 1180–1186.

76. Keane, B.P., et al., *Reduced depth inversion illusions in schizophrenia are state-specific and occur for multiple object types and viewing conditions.* Journal of Abnormal Psychology, 2013. **122**(2): p. 506.

77. Cytowic, R.E., *Synesthesia: A Union of the Senses.* 2002: MIT Press.

78. Coslett, H.B., and E. Saffran, *Simultanagnosia: To see but not two see.* Brain, 1991. **114**(4): p. 1523–1545.

79. Happé, F.G., *Studying weak central coherence at low levels: Children with autism do not succumb to visual illusions. A research note.* Journal of Child Psychology and Psychiatry, 1996. **37**(7): p. 873–877.

80. Jürgens, U.M., and D. Nikolić, *Synaesthesia as an Ideasthesia—Cognitive Implications. Synaesthesia and Children—Learning and Creativity,* 2014.

81. Ropar, D., and P. Mitchell, *Are individuals with autism and Asperger's syndrome susceptible to visual illusions?* The Journal of Child Psychology and Psychiatry and Allied Disciplines, 1999. **40**(8): p. 1283–1293.

82. Fyfe, S., et al., *Apophenia, theory of mind and schizotypy: Perceiving meaning and intentionality in randomness.* Cortex, 2008. **44**(10): p. 1316–1325.

83. Zeman, A., M. Dewar, and S. Della Sala, *Lives without imagery – Congenital aphantasia.* Cortex, 2015. **73**(Supplement C): p. 378–380.

84. Damasio, A.R., H. Damasio, and G.W. Van Hoesen, *Prosopagnosia anatomic basis and behavioral mechanisms.* Neurology, 1982. **32**(4): p. 331–331.

85. Liu, J., et al., *Seeing Jesus in toast: Neural and behavioral correlates of face pareidolia.* Cortex, 2014. **53**: p. 60–77.

86. Wegner, D.M., *Ironic processes of mental control.* Psychological Review, 1994. **101**(1): p. 34.

87. Izard, C.E., *The Psychology of Emotions.* 1991: Springer Science & Business Media.

88. Harlow, H.F., and R. Stagner, *Psychology of feelings and emotions: I. Theory of feelings.* Psychological Review, 1932. **39**(6): p. 570.

89. Slater, M., et al., *First person experience of body transfer in virtual reality.* PloS One, 2010. **5**(5): p. e10564.

90. Ehrsson, H.H., *The experimental induction of out-of-body experiences.* Science, 2007. **317**(5841): p. 1048–1048.

91. Bach-y-Rita, P., and S.W. Kercel, *Sensory substitution and the human–machine interface.* Trends in Cognitive Sciences, 2003. **7**(12): p. 541–546.

92. Gray, C.H., *Cyborg Citizen: Politics in the Posthuman Age.* 2000: Routledge.

93. Wells, A., *The Literate Mind: A Study of Its Scope and Limitations.* 2012: Palgrave Macmillan.

94. Post, R.H., *Population differences in red and green color vision deficiency: A review, and a query on selection relaxation.* Eugenics Quarterly, 1962. **9**(3): p. 131–146.

95. Tudusciuc, O., and A. Nieder, *Comparison of length judgments and the Müller-Lyer illusion in monkeys and humans.* Experimental Brain Research, 2010. **207**(3–4): p. 221–231.

96. Kelley, L.A., and J.L. Kelley, *Animal visual illusion and confusion: The importance of a perceptual perspective.* Behavioral Ecology, 2013. **25**(3): p. 450–463.

97. Benhar, E., and D. Samuel, *Visual illusions in the baboon (Papio anubis).* Learning & Behavior, 1982. **10**(1): p. 115–118.

98. Logothetis, N.K., *Single units and conscious vision.* Philosophical Transactions of the Royal Society of London B: Biological Sciences, 1998. **353**(1377): p. 1801–1818.

99. Lazareva, O.F., T. Shimizu, and E.A. Wasserman, *How Animals See the World: Comparative Behavior, Biology, and Evolution of Vision.* 2012: Oxford University Press.

100. Low, P., et al., *The Cambridge declaration on consciousness,* in *Francis Crick Memorial Conference.* 2012.

101. Naor, M., and A. Shamir, *Visual cryptography,* in *Workshop on the Theory and Application of Cryptographic Techniques.* 1994. Springer.

102. Yampolskiy, R.V., J.D. Rebolledo-Mendez, and M.M. Hindi, *Password protected visual cryptography via cellular automaton rule 30,* in *Transactions on Data Hiding and Multimedia Security IX.* 2014, Springer Berlin Heidelberg. p. 57–67.

103. Abboud, G., J. Marean, and R.V. Yampolskiy, *Steganography and visual cryptography in computer forensics,* in *2010 Fifth IEEE International Workshop on Systematic Approaches to Digital Forensic Engineering (SADFE).* 2010. IEEE.

104. Eagleman, D.M., *Visual illusions and neurobiology.* Nature Reviews Neuroscience, 2001. **2**(12): p. 920–926.
105. Panagiotaropoulos, T.I., et al., *Neuronal discharges and gamma oscillations explicitly reflect visual consciousness in the lateral prefrontal cortex.* Neuron, 2012. **74**(5): p. 924–935.
106. Ahn, L., et al., *CAPTCHA: Using Hard AI Problems for Security,* in *Eurocrypt.* 2003.
107. D'Souza, D., P.C. Polina, and R.V. Yampolskiy, *Avatar CAPTCHA: Telling computers and humans apart via face classification,* in *2012 IEEE International Conference on Electro/Information Technology (EIT).* 2012. IEEE.
108. Korayem, M., et al., *Solving avatar captchas automatically,* in *Advanced Machine Learning Technologies and Applications.* 2012, Springer. p. 102–110.
109. Korayem, M., et al., *Learning visual features for the Avatar Captcha Recognition Challenge,* in *2012 11th International Conference on Machine Learning and Applications (ICMLA).* 2012. IEEE.
110. Yampolskiy, R.V., *AI-Complete CAPTCHAs as Zero Knowledge Proofs of Access to an Artificially Intelligent System,* 2012.
111. McDaniel, R., and R.V. Yampolskiy, *Embedded non-interactive CAPTCHA for Fischer Random Chess,* in *16th International Conference on Computer Games (CGAMES).* 2011. IEEE. p. 284–287.
112. Yampolskiy, R., *Graphical CAPTCHA embedded in cards,* in *Western New York Image Processing Workshop (WNYIPW)-IEEE Signal Processing Society.* Vol. 28. 2007.
113. McDaniel, R., and R.V. Yampolskiy, *Development of embedded CAPTCHA elements for bot prevention in Fischer random chess.* International Journal of Computer Games Technology, 2012. **2012**: p. 2.
114. Yampolskiy, R.V., and V. Govindaraju, *Embedded non-interactive continuous bot detection.* ACM Computers in Entertainment, 2007. **5**(4): p. 1–11.
115. Hasson, U., et al., *Vase or face? A neural correlate of shape-selective grouping processes in the human brain.* Journal of Cognitive Neuroscience, 2001. **13**(6): p. 744–753.
116. Yampolskiy, R., *Turing test as a defining feature of AI-completeness,* in *Artificial Intelligence, Evolutionary Computing and Metaheuristics,* X.-S. Yang, Editor. 2013, Springer Berlin Heidelberg. p. 3–17.
117. Yampolskiy, R.V., *AI-complete, AI-hard, or AI-easy – classification of problems in AI,* in *The 23rd Midwest Artificial Intelligence and Cognitive Science Conference.* 2012.
118. Schweizer, P., *Could there be a Turing test for Qualia?* in *Revisiting Turing and His Test: Comprehensiveness, Qualia, and the Real World.* 2012: p. 41.
119. Turner, E., and S., Schneider, *Is anyone home? A way to find out if AI has become self-aware.* Scientific American, 2017.
120. Turing, A., *Computing machinery and intelligence.* Mind, 1950. **59**(236): p. 433–460.
121. Robinson, J.O., *The Psychology of Visual Illusion.* 2013: Courier Corporation.
122. Yamins, D.L., and J.J. DiCarlo, *Using goal-driven deep learning models to understand sensory cortex.* Nature Neuroscience, 2016. **19**(3): p. 356–365.
123. Zeman, A., et al., *The Müller-Lyer illusion in a computational model of biological object recognition.* Plos One, 2013. **8**(2): p. e56126.
124. Zeman, A., O. Obst, and K.R. Brooks, *Complex cells decrease errors for the Müller-Lyer illusion in a model of the visual ventral stream.* Frontiers in Computational Neuroscience, 2014. **8**: p. 1–9.

125. Ogawa, T., et al., *A neural network model for realizing geometric illusions based on acute-angled expansion*, in *Proceedings 6th International Conference on Neural Information Processing*. 1999. IEEE.

126. Corney, D., and R.B. Lotto, *What are lightness illusions and why do we see them?* PLoS Computational Biology, 2007. **3**(9): p. e180.

127. Bertulis, A., and A. Bulatov, *Distortions of length perception in human vision.* Biomedicine, 2001. **1**(1): p. 3–23.

128. Inui, T., S. Hongo, and M. Kawato, *A computational model of brightness illusion and its implementation.* Perception, 1990. **19**: p. 401.

129. Chao, J., et al., *Artificial neural networks which can see geometric illusions in human vision*, in *Proceedings of 1993 International Joint Conference on Neural Networks, IJCNN'93-Nagoya*. 1993. IEEE.

130. Ogawa, T., et al., *Realization of geometric illusions using artificial visual model based on acute-angled expansion among crossing lines*, in *International Joint Conference on Neural Networks,IJCNN'99*. 1999. IEEE.

131. Robinson, A.E., P.S. Hammon, and V.R. de Sa, *Explaining brightness illusions using spatial filtering and local response normalization.* Vision Research, 2007. **47**(12): p. 1631–1644.

132. Zeman, A., K.R. Brooks, and S. Ghebreab, *An exponential filter model predicts lightness illusions.* Frontiers in Human Neuroscience, 2015. **9**: p. 1–15.

133. Shibata, K., and S. Kurizaki, *Emergence of color constancy illusion through reinforcement learning with a neural network*, in *IEEE International Conference on Development and Learning and Epigenetic Robotics (ICDL)*. 2012. IEEE.

134. Nguyen, A., J. Yosinski, and J. Clune, *Deep neural networks are easily fooled: High confidence predictions for unrecognizable images*, in *Proceedings of the IEEE Conference on Computer Vision and Pattern Recognition*. 2015.

135. Kurakin, A., I. Goodfellow, and S. Bengio, *Adversarial examples in the physical world.* arXiv preprint arXiv:1607.02533, 2016.

136. Szegedy, C., et al., *Intriguing properties of neural networks.* arXiv preprint arXiv:1312.6199, 2013.

137. Goodfellow, I., et al., *Generative adversarial nets*, in *Advances in Neural Information Processing Systems*. 2014.

138. Carlotto, M.J., *The Martian Enigmas: A Closer Look: The Face, Pyramids and Other Unusual Objects on Mars*. 1997: North Atlantic Books.

139. Thaler, S.L., *"Virtual input" phenomena within the death of a simple pattern associator.* Neural Networks, 1995. **8**(1): p. 55–65.

140. Thaler, S., *4-2-4 Encoder Death*, in *Proceedings of the World Congress on Neural Networks*. 1993.

141. Thaler, S.L., *Death of a Gedanken creature.* Journal of Near Death Studies, 1995. **13**: p. 149.

142. Crick, F., and G. Mitchison, *The function of dream sleep.* Nature, 1983. **304**(5922): p. 111–114.

143. Hopfield, J.J., D.I. Feinstein, and R.G. Palmer, *'Unlearning' has a stabilizing effect in collective memories.* Nature, 1983. **304**(5922): p. 158–159.

144. Hinton, G.E., D.C. Plaut, and T. Shallice, *Simulating brain damage.* Scientific American, 1993. **269**(4): p. 76–82.

145. Lecun, Y., J.S. Denker, and S.A. Solla, *Optimal brain damage*, in *Advances in Neural Information Processing Systems (NIPS 1989)*. Vol. 2. D. Touretzky, Editor. 1990, Morgan Kaufmann.

146. Bertulis, A., and A. Bulatov, *Distortions in length perception: Visual field anisotropy and geometrical illusions.* Neuroscience and Behavioral Physiology, 2005. **35**(4): p. 423–434.

147. Howe, C.Q., and D. Purves, *Range image statistics can explain the anomalous perception of length.* Proceedings of the National Academy of Sciences, 2002. **99**(20): p. 13184–13188.

148. Howe, C.Q., and D. Purves, *Perceiving Geometry: Geometrical Illusions Explained by Natural Scene Statistics.* 2005: Springer Science & Business Media.

149. Howe, C.Q., and D. Purves, *The Müller-Lyer illusion explained by the statistics of image–source relationships.* Proceedings of the National Academy of Sciences of the United States of America, 2005. **102**(4): p. 1234–1239.

150. Brown, H., and K.J. Friston, *Free-energy and illusions: The cornsweet effect.* Frontiers in Psychology, 2012. **3**: p. 1–13.

151. Marr, D., *Vision a Computational Investigation into the Human Representation and Processing of Visual Information.* 1982: WH Freeman and Company.

152. Torrance, S., *Super-intelligence and (super-) consciousness.* International Journal of Machine Consciousness, 2012. **4**(02): p. 483–501.

153. Mordvintsev, A., C. Olah, and M. Tyka, *Inceptionism: Going deeper into neural networks.* Google Research Blog. 2015. **20**: p. 14.

154. Suzuki, K., et al., *The hallucination machine: A deep-dream VR platform for studying the phenomenology of visual hallucinations.* 2017: p. 213751.

155. Olah, C., A. Mordvintsev, and L. Schubert, *Feature visualization.* Distill, 2017. **2**(11): p. e7.

156. Seckel, A., *Masters of Deception: Escher, Dalí & the Artists of Optical Illusion.* 2004: Sterling Publishing Company, Inc.

157. Yampolskiy, R.V., *What are the ultimate limits to computational techniques: Verifier theory and unverifiability.* Physica Scripta, 2017. **92**(9): p. 093001.

158. Chaitin, G.J., *The berry paradox.* Complexity, 1995. **1**(1): p. 26–30.

159. Yampolskiy, R.V., *Efficiency theory: A unifying theory for information, computation and intelligence.* Journal of Discrete Mathematical Sciences & Cryptography, 2013. **16**(4–5): p. 259–277.

160. Potgieter, P.H., *Zeno machines and hypercomputation.* Theoretical Computer Science, 2006. **358**(1): p. 23–33.

161. Lanza, R., and B. Berman, *Biocentrism: How Life and Consciousness Are the Keys to Understanding the True Nature of the Universe.* 2010: BenBella Books.

162. Mould, R.A., *Consciousness and quantum mechanics.* Foundations of Physics, 1998. **28**(11): p. 1703–1718.

163. Goswami, A., *Consciousness in quantum physics and the mind-body problem.* The Journal of Mind and Behavior, 1990: p. 75–96.

164. Crook, J.H., *The Evolution of Human Consciousness.* 1980: Clarendon Press Oxford.

165. Humphrey, N., *The Inner Eye.* 1986: Oxford University Press on Demand.

166. Baars, B.J., *In the theatre of consciousness. Global workspace theory, a rigorous scientific theory of consciousness.* Journal of Consciousness Studies, 1997. **4**(4): p. 292–309.

167. Gray, J.A., *Consciousness: Creeping up on the hard Problem.* 2004: Oxford University Press.

168. Morsella, E., *The function of phenomenal states: Supramodular interaction theory.* Psychological Review, 2005. **112**(4): p. 1000.

169. Humphrey, N., *Seeing Red: A Study in Consciousness*. 2006: Harvard University Press.
170. Gefter, A., and D.D. Hoffman, *The evolutionary argument against reality*. Quanta Magazine, 2016.
171. Harnad, S., *The symbol grounding problem*. Physica D: Nonlinear Phenomena, 1990. **42**(1–3): p. 335–346.
172. Rapaport, W.J., *How Helen Keller used syntactic semantics to escape from a Chinese room*. Minds and Machines, 2006. **16**(4): p. 381–436.
173. Mossbridge, J., P. Tressoldi, and J. Utts, *Predictive physiological anticipation preceding seemingly unpredictable stimuli: A meta-analysis*. Frontiers in Psychology, 2012. **3**.
174. Loosemore, R., *Qualia surfing*, in *Intelligence Unbound: Future of Uploaded and Machine Minds, The*. 2014, Wiley. p. 231–239.
175. Yampolskiy, R.V. *The space of possible mind designs*, in *International Conference on Artificial General Intelligence*. 2015. Springer.
176. Yampolskiy, R.V., and M.L. Gavrilova, *Artimetrics: Biometrics for artificial entities*. IEEE Robotics & Automation Magazine, 2012. **19**(4): p. 48–58.
177. Yampolskiy, R., et al., *Experiments in artimetrics: Avatar face recognition*. Transactions on Computational Science, 2012. **XVI**: p. 77–94.
178. Yampolskiy, R.V., *On the origin of synthetic life: Attribution of output to a particular algorithm*. Physica Scripta, 2016. **92**(1): p. 013002.
179. Yampolskiy, R.V., *Artificial consciousness: An illusionary solution to the hard problem*. Italian Journal of Cognitive Sciences, 2018. **2**: pp. 287–318.
180. Yampolskiy, R.V., and J. Fox, *Artificial intelligence and the human mental model*, in *In the Singularity Hypothesis: A Scientific and Philosophical Assessment*, A. Eden, et al., Editors. 2012, Springer.
181. Hughes, J., *After happiness, cyborg virtue*. Free Inquiry, 2011. **32**(1): p. 1–7.
182. Mehta, R., R. Zhu, and A. Cheema, *Is noise always bad? Exploring the effects of ambient noise on creative cognition*. Journal of Consumer Research, 2012. **39**(4): p. 784–799.
183. Hofstadter, D.R., *Gödel, Escher, Bach: An Eternal Golden Braid*. 1979: Basic Books.
184. Majot, A.M., and R.V. Yampolskiy, *AI safety engineering through introduction of self-reference into felicific calculus via artificial pain and pleasure*, in *IEEE International Symposium on Ethics in Science, Technology and Engineering*. 2014. IEEE.
185. Yampolskiy, R.V., *Attempts to attribute moral agency to intelligent machines are misguided*, in *Proceedings of Annual Meeting of the International Association for Computing and Philosophy, University of Maryland at College Park, MD*. 2013.
186. Yampolskiy, R.V., *Artificial intelligence safety engineering: Why machine ethics is a wrong approach*. Philosophy and Theory of Artificial Intelligence, 2013: p. 389–396.
187. Braverman, I., *Gene Drives, Nature, Governance: An Ethnographic Perspective*, in *University at Buffalo School of Law Legal Studies Research Paper No. 2017-006*. 2017. https://papers.ssrn.com/sol3/papers.cfm?abstract_id=3032607.
188. Metzinger, T., *Benevolent Artificial Anti-natalism (BAAN)*, in *EDGE*. 2017. https://www.edge.org/conversation/thomas_metzinger-benevolent-artificial-anti-natalism-baan.
189. Bostrom, N., *Superintelligence: Paths, Dangers, Strategies*. 2014: Oxford University Press.
190. Babcock, J., J. Kramar, and R.V. Yampolskiy, *Guidelines for artificial intelligence containment*. arXiv preprint arXiv:1707.08476, 2017.

191. Yampolskiy, R.V., and M. Spellchecker, *Artificial intelligence safety and cybersecurity: A timeline of AI failures.* arXiv preprint arXiv:1610.07997, 2016.
192. Pistono, F., and R.V. Yampolskiy, *Unethical research: How to create a malevolent artificial intelligence.* arXiv preprint arXiv:1605.02817, 2016.
193. Babcock, J., J. Kramár, and R. Yampolskiy, *The AGI containment problem*, in *International Conference on Artificial General Intelligence.* 2016. Springer.
194. Yampolskiy, R.V. *Taxonomy of pathways to dangerous artificial intelligence*, in *AAAI Workshop: AI, Ethics, and Society.* 2016.
195. Yampolskiy, R.V., *Artificial Superintelligence: A Futuristic Approach.* 2015: CRC Press.
196. Greenwald, A.G., M.R. Klinger, and E.S. Schuh, *Activation by marginally perceptible ("subliminal") stimuli: Dissociation of unconscious from conscious cognition.* Journal of Experimental Psychology: General, 1995. **124**(1): p. 22.
197. Walter, W.G., V. Dovey, and H. Shipton, *Analysis of the electrical response of the human cortex to photic stimulation.* Nature, 1946. **158**(4016): p. 540–541.
198. Harding, G.F., and P.M. Jeavons, *Photosensitive Epilepsy.* 1994: Cambridge University Press.
199. Altmann, J., *Acoustic weapons-a prospective assessment.* Science & Global Security, 2001. **9**(3): p. 165–234.
200. Su, J., D.V. Vargas, and S. Kouichi, *One pixel attack for fooling deep neural networks.* arXiv preprint arXiv:1710.08864, 2017.
201. Bandler, R., J. Grinder, and S. Andreas, *Neuro-linguistic programming™ and the transformation of meaning.* Real People, Moab, 1982.
202. Barber, T.X., *Hypnosis: A Scientific Approach.* 1969.
203. Vokey, J.R., and J.D. Read, *Subliminal messages: Between the devil and the media.* American Psychologist, 1985. **40**(11): p. 1231.
204. Bostrom, N., *Information hazards: A typology of potential harms from knowledge.* Review of Contemporary Philosophy, 2011. **10**: p. 44.
205. Wickler, W., *Mimicry in Plants and Animals.* 1968: Weidenfeld & Nicolson.
206. Yampolskiy, R., and J. Fox, *Safety engineering for artificial general intelligence.* Topoi, 2013. **32**(2): p. 217–226.
207. Yampolskiy, R.V., *Future Jobs – The Universe Designer*, in *Circus Street.* 2017.
208. Soares, N., et al., *Corrigibility*, in *Workshops at the Twenty-Ninth AAAI Conference on Artificial Intelligence.* 2015. Austin, Texas, USA.
209. Dehaene, S., H. Lau, and S. Kouider, *What is consciousness, and could machines have it?* Science, 2017. **358**(6362): p. 486–492.
210. Landauer, R., *Irreversibility and heat generation in the computing process.* IBM Journal of Research and Development, 1961. **5**(3): p. 183–191.
211. Genkin, D., A. Shamir, and E. Tromer, *RSA key extraction via low-bandwidth acoustic cryptanalysis*, in *International Cryptology Conference.* 2014. Springer.
212. De Mulder, E., et al., *Differential electromagnetic attack on an FPGA implementation of elliptic curve cryptosystems*, in *Automation Congress World.* 2006. IEEE.
213. Yudkowsky, E., *Rationality: From AI to Zombies.* 2015. MIRI.
214. Hut, P., M. Alford, and M. Tegmark, *On math, matter and mind.* Foundations of Physics, 2006. **36**(6): p. 765–794.
215. Schwarting, M., T. Burton, and R. Yampolskiy, *On the obfuscation of image sensor fingerprints*, in *2015 Annual Global Online Conference on Information and Computer Technology (GOCICT).* 2015. IEEE.

216. Rupert, R.D., *Challenges to the hypothesis of extended cognition.* The Journal of Philosophy, 2004. **101**(8): p. 389–428.
217. Clark, A., and D. Chalmers, *The extended mind.* Analysis, 1998. **58**(1): p. 7–19.
218. Putnam, H., *The nature of mental states.* Readings in Philosophy of Psychology, 1980. **1**: p. 223–231.
219. Chalmers, D.J., *Does a rock implement every finite-state automaton?* Synthese, 1996. **108**(3): p. 309–333.
220. Dawkins, R., *The Selfish Gene.* 1976: Oxford University Press.
221. Ninio, J., and K.A. Stevens, *Variations on the Hermann grid: An extinction illusion.* Perception, 2000. **29**(10): p. 1209–1217.
222. Chalmers, D.J., *The virtual and the real.* Disputatio, 2016. **9**(46): p. 309–352.

11

Personal Universes*

11.1 Introduction to the Multi-Agent Value Alignment Problem

Since the birth of the field of artificial intelligence (AI) researchers worked on creating ever-capable machines, but with recent success in multiple subdomains of AI [1–7] Safety and Security of such systems and predicted future superintelligences [8, 9] has become paramount [10, 11]. While many diverse safety mechanisms are being investigated [12, 13], the ultimate goal is to align AI with goals, values, and preferences of its users which is likely to include all of humanity.

Value alignment problem [14] can be decomposed into three sub-problems, namely personal value extraction from individual persons, combination of such personal preferences in a way, which is acceptable to all, and finally production of an intelligent system, which implements combined values of humanity.

A number of approaches for extracting values [15–17] from people have been investigated, including inverse reinforcement learning [18, 19], brain scanning [20], value learning from literature [21], and understanding of human cognitive limitations [22]. Assessment of potential for success for particular techniques of value extraction is beyond the scope of this chapter, and we simply assume that one of the current methods, their combination, or some future approach will allow us to accurately learn values of given people. Likewise, we will not directly address how, once learned, such values can be represented/encoded in computer systems for storage and processing. These assumptions free us from having to worry about safety problems with misaligned AIs such as perverse instantiation or wireheading [23], among many others [24].

The second step in the process requires an algorithm for value aggregation from some and perhaps even all people to assure that the developed AI is beneficial to the humanity as a whole. Some have suggested that interests of future people [25], potential people [26], and of non-human animals and

---

DOI: 10.1201/9781003440260-11

other sentient beings, be likewise included in our "Coherent Extrapolated Volition" (CEV) [27], which we would like superintelligent AI to eventually implement. However, work done by moral philosophers over hundreds of years indicates that our moral preferences are not only difficult to distill in a coherent manner (anti-codifiability thesis) [28], but they are also likely impossible to merge without sacrificing interests of some people [29, 30], we can say it is the Hard problem of value alignment. Results from research into multivariate optimization and voting based preference aggregation support similar conclusions [31–33].

Perhaps we should stop trying to make "one size fits all" approach to the optimization of the universe work and instead look at potential for delivering an experience customized to individual users. The superintelligent systems we are hoping to one day create, with the goal of improving lives of all, may work best if instead they strive to optimize their alignment with individual lives of each and every one of us, while giving us all freedom to be ourselves without infringing on preferences of other sentient beings [34, 35]. Such a system due to its lower overall complexity should also be easier to design, implement, and safeguard.

11.2 Individual Simulated Universes

It has been suggested that future technology will permit design [36] and instantiation of high-fidelity simulated universes [37–41] for research and entertainment ([42], Chapter 5) purposes as well as for testing advanced AIs [43–46]. Existing work and recent breakthroughs in virtual reality, augmented reality, inter-reality, haptics, and artificial consciousness combined with tremendous popularity of multiplayer virtual worlds such as Second Life [47–49] or Ultima Online [50] provide encouraging evidence for the plausibility of realistic simulations.

We can foresee, in a not so distant future, a point at which visual and audio fidelity of the simulations, as well as for all other senses [51] becomes so high that it will not be possible to distinguish if you are in a base reality or in a simulated world, frequently referred as hyperreality [52, 53]. In principle, it should be possible to improve local fidelity (measurable by the agent) of the simulated reality to levels beyond base reality, for example, to the point of more precise measurements being possible with special instrumentation. This would effectively reverse the resolution relationship between the two realities making the base reality less believable on local scale. A variant of a Total Turing Test [54, 55], we shall call a Universal Turing Test (UTT) could be administered in which the user tries to determine if the current environment is synthetic or not [56] even if it is complex enough to include the whole universe, all other beings (as philosophical zombies [57]/non-playing characters (NPCs)) and AIs. Once the UTT is consistently passed we will know, the hyper-reality is upon us.

Consequently, we suggest that instead of trying to agree on convergent, universal, diverse, mutually beneficial, equalizing, representative, unbiased, timeless, acceptable to all, etc., moral/ethical norms and values, predicated on compromise [58], we look at an obvious alternative. Specifically, we suggest that superintelligent AIs should be implemented to act as personalized simulations – *Individual Simulated Universes* (ISU) representing customized synthetically generated [7, 59] mega-environments, in the "a universe per person multi-verse framework", which are optimally and dynamically adjusting to align their values and preferences to the Personal CEV [60] of sentient agents calling such universes "home".

Aaronson describes the general idea as "... an infinite number of sentient beings living in simulated paradises of their own choosing, racking up an infinite amount of utility. If such a being wants challenge and adventure, then challenge and adventure is what it gets; if nonstop sex, then nonstop sex; if a proof of P≠NP, then a proof of P≠NP. (Or the being could choose all three: it's utopia, after all!)" [61]. Bostrom estimates that our galactic super-cluster has enough energy to support trillions of such efficiently [62] simulated universes [63]. Features of related phenomena have been described in literature as [64]: dematerialization [65], ephemeralization [66], time-space compression [67], miniaturization [68], densification [69], virtualization [70], digitization [71], and simulation [72].

Faggella talks about opportunities presented in the virtual world over what is possible in the present reality [73]: "... 'freedom' could only extend so far in a real world as to border on impinging on the 'freedom' of others. Complete freedom would imply control over one's environment and free choice to do what one would chose with it. It seems easy to understand how this might imply the threatening of the freedom of others in the same physical world. ... Not to mention, the physical world has many impinging qualities that would hinder any semblance of complete freedom. Matter has qualities, light has qualities, and physical bodies (no matter how enhanced) will always have limitations. If you'd like to change an aspect of our character or emotional experience, for example, we'd have to potentially tinker with brain chemicals .... In a virtual reality, we are potentially presented not only with the freedom to extend beyond physical limitations (to transport to different times or places, to live within self-created fantasy worlds, to eliminate death and any physical risk), we would also be granted freedom from impinging or effecting others – and so allow for their full freedom and a separate virtual reality as well. ... For this reason, it seems to make sense that ... we might encounter a Bostrom-like 'Singleton' to rule the physical world, and a great sea of individual consciousnesses in the virtual world. The 'Singleton' could keep our computational substrates safe from harm and eliminate competition or danger in the physical world, while our virtual 'selves' would be capable of expressing and exploring the epitome of freedom on our own terms in a limitless virtual world of our own creation".

This means that an ISU can be anything a user truly wishes it to be including dangerous, adversarial, competitive, and challenging at all levels of user competence like levels in a well-designed video game. It will let a user be anything they want to be including a malevolent actor [74, 75], a privileged person (like a king) or the exact opposite (a slave), or perhaps just a selfish user in an altruistic universe. A personalized universe doesn't have to be fair, or just or free of perceived suffering and pain [76]. It could be just a sequence of temporary fantasies and hopefully what happens in your personalized universe stays in your personalized universe. ISU's goal is to cater to the world's smallest minority and its preferences, you [77, 78]! Moreover, the good news is that we know that we are not going to run out of Fun [79] even if we live much longer lives [80].

If an agent controlling the environment is not well aligning with a particular individual for whom the environment is created (during early stages of development of this technology) it may be necessary to use precise language to express what the user wants. The now defunct Open-Source Wish Project (OSWP) [81] attempted to formulate in precise and safe form such common wishes as: Immortality, happiness, omniscience, being rich, having true love, omnipotence, etc [23].

For example the latest version of the properly formed request for immortality was formalized as follows: "I wish to live in the locations of my choice, in a physically healthy, uninjured, and apparently normal version of my current body containing my current mental state, a body which will heal from all injuries at a rate three sigmas faster than the average given the medical technology available to me, and which will be protected from any diseases, injuries or illnesses causing disability, pain, or degraded functionality or any sense, organ, or bodily function for more than ten days consecutively or fifteen days in any year; at any time I may rejuvenate my body to a younger age, by saying a phrase matching this pattern five times without interruption, and with conscious intent: 'I wish to be age,' followed by a number between one and two hundred, followed by 'years old,' at which point the pattern ends - after saying a phrase matching that pattern, my body will revert to an age matching the number of years I started and I will commence to age normally from that stage, with all of my memories intact; at any time I may die, by saying five times without interruption, and with conscious intent, 'I wish to be dead'; the terms 'year' and 'day' in this wish shall be interpreted as the ISO standard definitions of the Earth year and day as of 2006 [81]". Of course, this is still far from foolproof and is likely to lead to some undesirable situations, which could be avoided by development of a well-aligned system.

11.3 Benefits and Shortcomings of Personalized Universes

ISUs can be implemented in a number of ways, either by having perfect emulations of agents reside in the simulated universe or by having current biological agents experience fully realistic simulated environments (while robotic systems take care of their bodies' biological needs), see Faggella's review of possible variants of virtual reality [82]. Both options have certain desirable properties, for example, software versions of users are much easier to modify, reset to earlier memory states [83], upgrade, and backup [84, 85], while biological agents are likely to have stronger identity continuity [86]. Emulations can also be taken as snapshots from different points in the person's life and set to exist in their own independent simulations multiplying possible experiences [34] for the subset of agents derived from that particular individual. In both virtual and uploaded scenarios, it is probably desirable for the user to "forget" that they are not in the base reality via some technological means with the goal of avoiding Solipsism syndrome.[1]

Our proposal doesn't just allow us to bypass having to find a difficult to compute approximation to a likely impossible to solve problem of multi-agent value aggregation, but it also provides for a much better "customer experience" free of compromise on even small details which may be important to that individual. Additionally, virtual existence makes it possible to have an "undo button" for actions/experiences user might regret, something not always possible in the world of physical reality. Last, but not least any existential risks related to this particular AI failure are limited to the simulated universe and its virtual inhabitants, not to the humanity and all life forms.

Of course, like any AI safety mechanism ours has certain weaknesses, which will have to be explicitly addressed. Those include having to withstand agents with extreme preferences, who may wish to prevent others from exercising their self-determination and may attempt to hack and sabotage ISUs or even base reality (which should be easier to secure, with most agents and their complex preferences out of the way). Another area of concern is problems with superintelligence serving as "operating system" for the base reality and allocating non-conflicting resources for the ISUs. Finally, we should study how the philosophical questions of living in a "fake" world vs "real" world, even if it is not possible to distinguish between them by any means, impacts human psychology and well-being.

It is also important to figure out a metric to measure user-relative quality of the simulation experience not just from fidelity point of view but also from users overall satisfaction with how their values, goals, and preferences are being serviced, such metrics are notoriously hard to design and easy to abuse [87]. Potential ideas may include user feedback both from within the simulation and while outside observing a recording of themselves in the simulation, feedback after trying other simulations and potentially all other simulations, and peer-review from other conscious agents both from outside and from within the same environment.

It is possible to let users "play" in other's universes and perhaps as other characters and to allow them to discover and integrate new values to which their universe will dynamically adopt. It may also be possible for two or more agents to decide to inhabit the same universe by coming to accept a mutually satisfying set of values, but of course, their individual alignment with the environment would be reduced and so it is important to provide them with a "divorce" option. We are assuming a well-aligned AI, which will not attempt to directly hack the agent to game the feedback score, but out of caution, we do not recommend evolutionary competition [88–90] between ISUs as that can lead to adversarial behaviors between superintelligent agents even the base reality superintelligence would not be able to resolve.

11.4 Conclusions

In this exploratory chapter, we advocated a solution to the hardest of the three subproblems of multi-agent value alignment, specifically value aggregation. Our "in the box" solution suggests replacing the one-size-fits-all model of value satisfaction with a customized and highly optimized approach which is strictly superior for all possible agents not valuing decreasing quality of value alignment for other agents. Some existing evidence from cosmology may be seen as suggesting that perhaps this approach is not so novel and in fact has already been implemented by earlier civilizations, and this universe is already a part of a multiverse [91, 92] generated by intelligence [93]. While some significant concerns with the philosophical [94], social [95], and security [96, 97] problems associated with personalized universes remain, particularly with regards to securing base reality, the proposal has a number of previously described advantages. Such advantages are likely to make it attractive to many users or to at least be integrated as a part of a more complex hybrid solution scheme. The decisions made by users of personal universes are also a goldmine of valuable data both for assessment of agents and for providing additional data to improve overall AI alignment [98]. We will leave proposals for assuring safety and security of cyberinfrastructure running personalized universes for future work. The main point of this chapter is that a personal universe is a place where virtually everyone can be happy.

Note

1. https://en.wikipedia.org/wiki/Solipsism_syndrome

References

1. Silver, D., et al., *A general reinforcement learning algorithm that masters chess, shogi, and go through self-play.* Science, 2018. **362**(6419): p. 1140–1144.
2. Silver, D., et al., *Mastering the game of go without human knowledge.* Nature, 2017. **550**(7676): p. 354.
3. Mnih, V., et al., *Human-level control through deep reinforcement learning.* Nature, 2015. **518**(7540): p. 529.
4. High, R., *The Era of Cognitive Systems: An Inside Look at IBM Watson and How It Works.* 2012: IBM Corporation, Redbooks.
5. Moravčík, M., et al., *Deepstack: Expert-level artificial intelligence in heads-up no-limit poker.* Science, 2017. **356**(6337): p. 508–513.
6. Krizhevsky, A., I. Sutskever, and G.E. Hinton, *ImageNet classification with deep convolutional neural networks,* in *Advances in Neural Information Processing Systems.* 2012. Weinberger.
7. Goodfellow, I., et al., *Generative adversarial nets,* in *Advances in Neural Information Processing Systems.* 2014. Weinberger.
8. Bostrom, N., *Superintelligence: Paths, Dangers, Strategies.* 2014: Oxford University Press.
9. Yampolskiy, R.V., *AI-complete CAPTCHAs as zero knowledge proofs of access to an artificially intelligent system.* ISRN Artificial Intelligence, 2011. **2012**: p. 1–6.
10. Yampolskiy, R.V., *Artificial Superintelligence: A Futuristic Approach.* 2015: Chapman and Hall/CRC Press.
11. Yampolskiy, R.V., *Artificial Intelligence Safety and Security.* 2018: CRC Press.
12. Sotala, K., and R.V. Yampolskiy, *Responses to catastrophic AGI risk: A survey.* Physica Scripta, 2014. **90**(1): p. 018001.
13. Everitt, T., G. Lea, and M. Hutter, *AGI safety literature review.* arXiv preprint arXiv:1805.01109, 2018.
14. Soares, N., and B. Fallenstein, *Aligning superintelligence with human interests: A technical research agenda.* Machine Intelligence Research Institute (MIRI) Technical Report, 2014. **8**: p. 1–8.
15. Dignum, V., *Responsible artificial intelligence: Designing AI for human values.* ITU Journal: ICT Discoveries, 2017.
16. Evans, O., A. Stuhlmüller, and N.D. Goodman, *Learning the preferences of ignorant, inconsistent agents,* in *AAAI.* 2016.
17. Kim, T.W., T. Donaldson, and J. Hooker, *Mimetic vs anchored value alignment in artificial intelligence.* arXiv preprint arXiv:1810.11116, 2018.
18. Ng, A.Y., and S.J. Russell, *Algorithms for inverse reinforcement learning,* in *ICML.* 2000.

19. Abbeel, P., and A.Y. Ng, *Apprenticeship learning via inverse reinforcement learning*, in *Proceedings of the Twenty-First International Conference on Machine learning*. 2004. ACM.

20. Sarma, G.P., N.J. Hay, and A. Safron, *AI safety and reproducibility: Establishing robust foundations for the neuropsychology of human values*, in *International Conference on Computer Safety, Reliability, and Security*. 2018. Springer.

21. Riedl, M.O., and B. Harrison, *Using stories to teach human values to artificial agents*, in *AAAI Workshop: AI, Ethics, and Society*. 2016.

22. Trazzi, M., and R.V. Yampolskiy, *Building safer AGI by introducing artificial stupidity*. arXiv preprint arXiv:1808.03644, 2018.

23. Yampolskiy, R.V., *Utility function security in artificially intelligent agents*. Journal of Experimental & Theoretical Artificial Intelligence, 2014. **26**(3): p. 373–389.

24. Yampolskiy, R.V., *Taxonomy of pathways to dangerous artificial intelligence*, in *AAAI Workshop: AI, Ethics, and Society*. 2016.

25. Mulgan, T., *Future People: A Moderate Consequentialist Account of Our Obligations to Future Generations*. 2008: OUP Catalogue.

26. Warren, M.A., *Do potential people have moral rights?* Canadian Journal of Philosophy, 1977. **7**(2): p. 275–289.

27. Yudkowsky, E., *Coherent Extrapolated Volition*. 2004: Singularity Institute for Artificial Intelligence.

28. Purves, D., R. Jenkins, and B.J. Strawser, *Autonomous machines, moral judgment, and acting for the right reasons*. Ethical Theory and Moral Practice, 2015. **18**(4): p. 851–872.

29. Yampolskiy, R.V., *Artificial intelligence safety engineering: Why machine ethics is a wrong approach*, in *Philosophy and Theory of Artificial Intelligence*. 2013, Springer. p. 389–396.

30. Sobel, D., *Full information accounts of well-being*. Ethics, 1994. **104**(4): p. 784–810.

31. Arrow, K.J., *A difficulty in the concept of social welfare*. Journal of Political Economy, 1950. **58**(4): p. 328–346.

32. Arrow, K.J., *Social Choice and Individual Values*. Vol. 12. 2012: Yale University Press.

33. Gehrlein, W.V., *Condorcet's paradox and the likelihood of its occurrence: Different perspectives on balanced preferences*. Theory and Decision, 2002. **52**(2): p. 171–199.

34. Yampolskiy, R.V., *Detecting qualia in natural and artificial agents*. arXiv preprint arXiv:1712.04020, 2017.

35. Raoult, A., and R. Yampolskiy, *Reviewing Tests for Machine Consciousness*. 2015. https://www.researchgate.net/publication/284859013_DRAFT_Reviewing_Tests_for_Machine_Consciousness.

36. Knight, W., *AI Software Can Dream up an Entire Digital World from a Simple Sketch*. Retrieved December 3, 2018. https://www.technologyreview.com/s/612503/ai-software-can-dream-up-an-entire-digital-world-from-a-simple-sketch.

37. Bostrom, N., *Are we living in a computer simulation?* The Philosophical Quarterly, 2003. **53**(211): p. 243–255.

38. Yampolskiy, R.V., *Future Jobs – The Universe Designer*, in *Circus Street*. 2017.

39. Yampolskiy, R., *Job ad: Universe designers*, in *Stories from 2045*, C. Chase, Editor. p. 50–53.

40. Chalmers, D.J., *The virtual and the real*. Disputatio, 2017. **9**(46): p. 309–352.

41. Putnam, H., *Brain in a Vat*. Reason, Truth and History, 1981: p. 1–21. Cambridge University Press

42. Tegmark, M., *Life 3.0: Being Human in the Age of Artificial Intelligence*. 2017: Knopf.

43. Armstrong, S., A. Sandberg, and N. Bostrom, *Thinking inside the box: Controlling and using an oracle AI*. Minds and Machines, 2012. **22**(4): p. 299–324.

44. Yampolskiy, R., *Leakproofing the singularity artificial intelligence confinement problem*. Journal of Consciousness Studies, 2012. **19**(1–2): p. 1–2.

45. Babcock, J., J. Kramár, and R.V. Yampolskiy, *Guidelines for artificial intelligence containment*. arXiv preprint arXiv:1707.08476, 2017.

46. Babcock, J., J. Kramár, and R. Yampolskiy, *The AGI containment problem*, in *Artificial General Intelligence*. 2016, Springer. p. 53–63.

47. Boulos, M.N.K., L. Hetherington, and S. Wheeler, *Second life: An overview of the potential of 3-D virtual worlds in medical and health education*. Health Information & Libraries Journal, 2007. **24**(4): p. 233–245.

48. Yampolskiy, R.V., and M.L. Gavrilova, *Artimetrics: Biometrics for artificial entities*. IEEE Robotics & Automation Magazine, 2012. **19**(4): p. 48–58.

49. Yampolskiy, R.V., B. Klare, and A.K. Jain, *Face recognition in the virtual world: Recognizing avatar faces*, in *2012 11th International Conference on Machine Learning and Applications (ICMLA)*. 2012. IEEE.

50. Simpson, Z.B., *The in-game economics of Ultima Online*, in *Computer Game Developer's Conference*, San Jose, CA. 2000.

51. Bushell, W.C., and M. Seaberg, *Experiments Suggest Humans Can Directly Observe the Quantum*, in *Psychology Today*. Retrieved December 5, 2018. https://www.psychologytoday.com/us/blog/sensorium/201812/experiments-suggest-humans-can-directly-observe-the-quantum.

52. Baudrillard, J., *Simulacra and Simulation*. 1994: University of Michigan Press.

53. Eco, U., *Travels in Hyper Reality: Essays*. 1990: Houghton Mifflin Harcourt.

54. Harnad, S., *The Turing test is not a trick: Turing indistinguishability is a scientific criterion*. ACM SIGART Bulletin, 1992. **3**(4): p. 9–10.

55. Schweizer, P., *The truly total Turing test*. Minds and Machines, 1998. **8**(2): p. 263–272.

56. Yampolskiy, R.V., *On the origin of synthetic life: Attribution of output to a particular algorithm*. Physica Scripta, 2016. **92**(1): p. 013002.

57. Chalmers, D.J., *The Conscious Mind: In Search of a Fundamental Theory*. 1996: Oxford University Press.

58. Bostrom, N., *Moral Uncertainty – Towards a Solution?*, in *Overcoming Bias*. 2009. http://www.overcomingbias.com/2009/01/moral-uncertainty-towards-a-solution.html.

59. Faggella, D., *Programmatically Generated Everything (PGE)*. Retrieved August 27, 2018. https://danfaggella.com/programmatically-generated-everything-pge/.

60. Muehlhauser, L., and C. Williamson, *Ideal advisor theories and personal CEV*. Machine Intelligence Research Institute, 2013.

61. Visions of a better world, in *Scientific American*. Retrieved December 19, 2018. https://blogs.scientificamerican.com/cross-check/visions-of-a-better-world.

62. Yampolskiy, R.V., *Efficiency theory: A unifying theory for information, computation and intelligence*. Journal of Discrete Mathematical Sciences & Cryptography, 2013. **16**(4–5): p. 259–277.

63. Bostrom, N., *Astronomical waste: The opportunity cost of delayed technological development*. Utilitas, 2003. **15**(3): p. 308–314.

64. Smart, J.M., *The transcension hypothesis: Sufficiently advanced civilizations invariably leave our universe, and implications for METI and SETI*. Acta Astronautica, 2012. **78**: p. 55–68.

65. Wernick, I.K., et al., *Materialization and dematerialization: Measures and trends*. Daedalus, 1996. **125**(3): p. 171–198.

66. Fuller, R.B., *Synergetics: Explorations in the Geometry of Thinking*. 1982: Estate of R. Buckminster Fuller.

67. Harvey, D., *The Condition of Postmodernity*. Vol. 14. 1989: Blackwell Oxford.

68. Feynman, R., and D. Gilbert, *Miniaturization*. 1961: Reinhold. p. 282–296.

69. Leskovec, J., J. Kleinberg, and C. Faloutsos, *Graphs over time: Densification laws, shrinking diameters and possible explanations*, in *Proceedings of the Eleventh ACM SIGKDD International Conference on Knowledge Discovery in Data Mining*. 2005. ACM.

70. Lévy, P., and R. Bononno, *Becoming Virtual: Reality in the Digital Age*. 1998: Da Capo Press, Incorporated.

71. Negroponte, N., et al., *Being digital*. Computers in Physics, 1997. **11**(3): p. 261–262.

72. Chalmers, D., *The matrix as metaphysics*. Science Fiction and Philosophy From Time Travel to Superintelligence, 2003. **36**; p. 35–54.

73. Faggella, D., *Transhuman Possibilities and the "Epitome of Freedom"*. Retrieved May 14, 2013. https://danfaggella.com/transhuman-possibilities-and-the-epitome-of-freedom/.

74. Pistono, F., and R.V. Yampolskiy, *Unethical research: How to create a malevolent artificial intelligence*. arXiv preprint arXiv:1605.02817, 2016.

75. Brundage, M., et al., *The malicious use of artificial intelligence: Forecasting, prevention, and mitigation*. arXiv preprint arXiv:1802.07228, 2018.

76. Pearce, D., *Hedonistic Imperative*. 1995: David Pearce.

77. Rand, A., *The Ayn Rand Lexicon: Objectivism from A to Z*. Vol. 4. 1988: Penguin.

78. Rand, A., *The Virtue of Selfishness*. 1964: Penguin.

79. Ziesche, S., and R.V. Yampolskiy, *Artificial fun: Mapping minds to the space of fun*. arXiv preprint arXiv:1606.07092, 2016.

80. Kurzweil, R., and T. Grossman, *Fantastic Voyage: Live Long Enough to Live Forever*. 2005: Rodale.

81. Anonymous, *Wish for Immortality 1.1*, in *The Open-Source Wish Project*. 2006. http://www.homeonthestrange.com/phpBB2/viewforum.php?f=4.

82. Faggella, D., *The Transhuman Transition – Lotus Eaters vs World Eaters*. Retrieved May 28, 2018. https://danfaggella.com/the-transhuman-transition-lotus-eaters-vs-world-eaters/.

83. Lebens, S., and T. Goldschmidt, *The Promise of a New Past*. 2017: Michigan Publishing, University of Michigan Library.

84. Hanson, R., *The Age of Em: Work, Love, and Life When Robots Rule the Earth*. 2016: Oxford University Press.

85. Feygin, Y.B., K. Morris, and R.V. Yampolskiy, *Uploading brain into computer: Whom to upload first?* arXiv preprint arXiv:1811.03009, 2018.

86. Parfit, D., *Reasons and Persons*. 1984: OUP Oxford.

87. Manheim, D., and S. Garrabrant, *Categorizing variants of Goodhart's law*. arXiv preprint arXiv:1803.04585, 2018.

88. Lehman, J., J. Clune, and D. Misevic, *The surprising creativity of digital evolution*, in *Artificial Life Conference Proceedings*. 2018. MIT Press.

89. Lowrance, C.J., O. Abdelwahab, and R.V. Yampolskiy, *Evolution of a metaheuristic for aggregating wisdom from artificial crowds*, in *Portuguese Conference on Artificial Intelligence*. 2015. Springer.

90. Yampolskiy, R.V., L. Ashby, and L. Hassan, *Wisdom of artificial crowds—a metaheuristic algorithm for optimization*. Journal of Intelligent Learning Systems and Applications, 2012. 4(2): p. 98.

91. Carr, B., *Universe or Multiverse?* 2007: Cambridge University Press.

92. Vilenkin, A., and M. Tegmark, *The Case for Parallel Universes*. 2011: Scientific American. Retrieved from: http://www.scientificamerican.com/article/multiverse-the-case-for-parallel-universe.

93. Gardner, J. N., *Biocosm: The New Scientific Theory of Evolution: Intelligent Life Is the Architect of the Universe*. 2003: Inner Ocean Publishing.

94. Nozick, R., and P., Vallentyne, *Anarchy, State, and Utopia*, in *Central Works of Philosophy V5*. 2014, Routledge. p. 108–125.

95. Turchin, A., *Wireheading as a Possible Contributor to Civilizational Decline*. 2018. https://philpapers.org/rec/TURWAA.

96. Faggella, D., *Substrate Monopoly – The Future of Power in a Virtual and Intelligent World*. Retrieved August 17, 2018. https://danfaggella.com/substrate-monopoly/.

97. Faggella, D., *Digitized and Digested*. Retrieved July 15, 2018. https://danfaggella.com/digitized-and-digested/.

98. Zhavoronkov, A., *Is Life a Recursive Video Game?*, in *Forbes*. Retrieved December 12, 2018. https://www.forbes.com/sites/cognitiveworld/2018/12/12/is-life-a-recursive-video-game.

12

Human ≠ AGI*

"A human being should be able to change a diaper, plan an invasion, butcher a hog, conn a ship, design a building, write a sonnet, balance accounts, build a wall, set a bone, comfort the dying, take orders, give orders, cooperate, act alone, solve equations, analyze a new problem, pitch manure, program a computer, cook a tasty meal, fight efficiently, die gallantly"

Robert A. Heinlein

"There is no such thing as AGI.
There may be such a thing as human-level AI.
But human intelligence is nowhere near general"

Yann LeCun

12.1 Introduction

Imagine that tomorrow a prominent technology company announces that they have successfully created an artificial intelligence (AI) and offers for you to test it out. You decide to start by testing developed AI for some very basic abilities such as multiplying 317 by 913 and memorizing your phone number. To your surprise, the system fails on both tasks. When you question the system's creators, you are told that their AI is human-level artificial intelligence (HLAI) and as most people cannot perform those tasks neither can their AI. In fact, you are told, many people can't even compute 13 × 17, or remember name of a person they just met, or recognize their coworker outside of the office, or name what they had for breakfast last Tuesday.[1] The list of such limitations is quite significant and is the subject of study in the field of Artificial Stupidity [1, 2].

Terms *Artificial General Intelligence* (AGI) [3] and *Human-Level Artificial Intelligence* (HLAI) [4] have been used interchangeably (see [5], or "(AGI) is the

* This chapter has been previously published as On the Differences between Human and Machine Intelligence by Roman V. Yampolskiy. IJCAI-21 Workshop on Artificial Intelligence Safety (AISafety2021). Montreal, Canada. August 19-20, 2021. CC BY 4.0.

DOI: 10.1201/9781003440260-12

hypothetical intelligence of a machine that has the capacity to understand or learn any intellectual task that a human being can." [6]) to refer to the Holy Grail of AI research, creation of a machine capable of achieving goals in a wide range of environments [7]. However, widespread implicit assumption of equivalence between capabilities of AGI and HLAI appears to be unjustified, as humans are not general intelligences. In this chapter, we will prove this distinction.

Others use slightly different nomenclature with respect to general intelligence, but arrive at similar conclusions. "Local generalization, or "robustness": ... "adaptation to known unknowns within a single task or well-defined set of tasks". ... Broad generalization, or "flexibility": "adaptation to unknown unknowns across a broad category of related tasks". ... Extreme generalization: human-centric extreme generalization, which is the specific case where the scope considered is the space of tasks and domains that fit within the human experience. We ... refer to "human-centric extreme generalization" as "generality". Importantly, as we deliberately define generality here by using human cognition as a reference frame ..., it is only "general" in a limited sense. ... To this list, we could, theoretically, add one more entry: "universality", which would extend "generality" beyond the scope of task domains relevant to humans, to any task that could be practically tackled within our universe (note that this is different from "any task at all" as understood in the assumptions of the No Free Lunch theorem [8, 9])" [10].

12.2 Prior Work

We call some problems "easy", because they come naturally to us like understanding speech or walking and we call other problems "hard" like playing Go or violin, because those are not human universals and require a lot of talent and effort [11]. We ignore "impossible" for humans to master domains, since we mostly don't even know about them or see them as important. As LeCun puts it: "[W]e can't imagine tasks that are outside of our comprehension, right, so we think, we think we are general, because we're general of all the things that we can apprehend, but there is a huge world out there of things that we have no idea" [12]. Others, agree: "we might not even be aware of the type of cognitive abilities we score poorly on" [13].

This is most obvious in how we test for intelligence. For example, Turing Test [14], by definition, doesn't test for universal general intelligence, only for human-level intelligence in human domains of expertise. Like a drunkard searching for his keys under the light because there it is easier to find them, we fall for the Streetlight effect observation bias only searching for intelligence in domains we can easily comprehend [15]. "The g factor, by definition, represents the single cognitive ability common to success across all intelligence tests, emerging from applying factor analysis to test results across a diversity of tests and individuals. But intelligence tests, by construction, only encompass tasks that humans can perform – tasks that are immediately recognizable and understandable by humans (anthropocentric bias), since including tasks that humans couldn't perform would be pointless. Further, psychometrics establishes measurement validity by demonstrating predictiveness with regard to activities that humans value (e.g. scholastic success): the very idea of a "valid" measure of intelligence only makes sense within the frame of reference of human values" [10].

Moravec further elaborates the difference between future machines and humans: "Computers are universal machines, their potential extends uniformly over a boundless expanse of tasks. Human potentials, on the other hand, are strong in areas long important for survival, but weak in things far removed. Imagine a "landscape of human competence," having lowlands with labels like "arithmetic" and "rote memorization," foothills like "theorem proving" and "chess playing," and high mountain peaks labeled "locomotion," "hand-eye coordination" and "social interaction." Advancing computer performance is like water slowly flooding the landscape. A half century ago it began to drown the lowlands, driving out human calculators and record clerks, but leaving most of us dry. Now the flood has reached the foothills, and our outposts there are contemplating retreat. We feel safe on our peaks, but, at the present rate, those too will be submerged within another half century" [16].

Chollet writes: "How general is human intelligence? The No Free Lunch theorem [8, 9] teaches us that any two optimization algorithms (including human intelligence) are equivalent when their performance is averaged across every possible problem, i.e. algorithms should be tailored to their target problem in order to achieve better-than-random performance. However, what is meant in this context by "every possible problem" refers to a uniform distribution over problem space; the distribution of tasks that would be practically relevant to our universe (which, due to its choice of laws of physics, is a specialized environment) would not fit this definition. Thus we may ask: is the human g factor universal? Would it generalize to every possible task in the universe? ... [T]his question is highly relevant when it comes to AI: if there is such a thing as universal intelligence, and if human intelligence is an implementation of it, then this algorithm of universal intelligence should be the end goal of our field, and reverse-engineering the human brain could be the shortest path to reach it. It would make our field close-ended: a riddle to be solved. If, on the other hand, human intelligence is a broad but ad-hoc cognitive ability that generalizes to human-relevant tasks but not much else, this implies that AI is an open-ended, fundamentally anthropocentric pursuit, tied to a specific scope of applicability" [10].

Humans have general capability only in those human-accessible domains and likewise artificial neural networks inspired by human brain architecture do unreasonably well in the same domains. Recent work by Tegmark et al. shows that deep neural networks would not perform as well in randomly generated domains as they do in those domains humans consider important, as they map well to physical properties of our universe. "We have shown that the success of deep and cheap (low-parameter-count) learning depends not only on mathematics but also on physics, which favors certain classes of exceptionally simple probability distributions that deep learning is uniquely suited to model. We argued that the success of shallow neural networks hinges on symmetry, locality, and polynomial log-probability in data from or inspired by the natural world, which favors sparse low-order polynomial Hamiltonians that can be efficiently approximated" [17].

12.3 Humans Are Not AGI

An agent is general (universal [18]) if it can learn anything another agent can learn. We can think of a true AGI agent as a superset of all possible narrow AIs (NAIs) (including capacity to solve AI-Complete problems [19]). Some agents have *limited domain generality*, meaning they are general, but not in all possible domains. The number of domains in which they are general may still be Dedekind-infinite, but it is a strict subset of domains in which AGI is capable of learning. For an AGI its domain of performance is any efficiently learnable capability, while humans have a smaller subset of competence. Non-human animals in turn may have an even smaller repertoire of capabilities, but are nonetheless general in that subset. This means that humans can do things animals cannot and AGI will be able to do something no human can. If an AGI is restricted only to domains and capacity of human expertise, it is the same as HLAI.

Humans are also not all in the same set, as some are capable of greater generality (g factor [20]) and can succeed in domains, in which others cannot. For example, only a tiny subset of all people is able to conduct cutting-edge research in quantum physics, implying differences in our general capabilities between theory and practice. While theoretical definition of general intelligence is easy to understand, its practical implementation remains uncertain. LeCun argues that even self-supervised learning and learnings from neurobiology won't be enough to achieve artificial general intelligence (AGI), or the hypothetical intelligence of a machine with the capacity to understand or learn from any task. That's because intelligence — even human intelligence — is very specialized, he says. "AGI does not exist — there is no such thing as general intelligence," said LeCun. "We can talk about rat-level intelligence, cat-level intelligence, dog-level intelligence, or human-level intelligence, but not artificial general intelligence" [21].

An agent is not an AGI equivalent if it could not learn something another agent could learn. Hence, we can divide all possible tasks into human learn-able and those, which no human can learn, establishing that humans are not AGI equivalent. We already described "easy" and "hard" for humans problems, the third category of "impossible" is what we would classify as abilities impossible for humans to learn efficiently [22]. Computer-unaided humans [23] do not possess capabilities in this category, to any degree, and are unlikely to be able to learn them. If performed by a human, they would be considered magical, but as Arthur Clarke has famously stated: "Any suf-ficiently advanced technology is indistinguishable from magic".

Some current examples include the following: estimating face from speech [24], DNA [25] or ear [26], extracting passwords from typing sounds [27, 28], using lightbulbs [29] and hard drives [30] as microphones, communicating via heat emissions [31], or memory-write-generated electromagnetic signals [32], and predicting gender, age, and smoking status from images of retinal fundus [33]. This is what is already possible with NAI today, AGI will be able to see patterns where humans see nothing but noise, invent technolo-gies we never considered possible and discover laws of physics far above our understanding. Capabilities, we humans will never possess, because we are not general intelligences. Even humans armed with simple calculators are no match for such problems.

LeCun gives an example of one task no human could learn: "So let me take a very specific example, it's not an example it's more like a quasi-mathematical demonstration, so you have about 1 million fibers coming out of one of your eyes, okay two million total, but let's talk about just one of them. It's 1 million nerve fibers in your optical nerve, let's imagine that they are binary so they can be active or inactive, so the input to your visual cortex is 1 million bits. Now, they connected to your brain in a particular way and your brain has connections that are kind of a little bit like a convolution net they are kind of local, you know, in the space and things like this. Now imagine I play a trick on you, it's a pretty nasty trick I admit, I cut your optical nerve and I put a device that makes a random permutation of all the nerve fibers. So now what comes to your, to your brain, is a fixed but random permutation of all the pixels, there's no way in hell that your visual cortex, even if I do this to you in infancy, will actually learn vision to the same level of quality that you can" [12].

Chollet elaborates on the subject of human unlearnable tasks: "[H]uman intellect is not adapted for the large majority of conceivable tasks. This includes obvious categories of problems such as those requiring long-term planning beyond a few years, or requiring large working memory (e.g. multiplying 10-digit numbers). This also includes problems for which our innate cognitive priors are unadapted; … For instance, in the [Traveling Salesperson Problem] TSP, human performance degrades severely when inverting the goal from "finding the shortest path" to "finding the longest path" [34] – humans perform even worse in this case than one of the simplest possible heuristic: farthest neighbor construction. A particularly marked human bias is dimensional bias: humans … are effectively unable to handle 4D and higher. … Thus, … "general intelligence" is not a binary property which a system either possesses or lacks. It is a spectrum" [10]. "Human physical capabilities can thus be said to be "general", but only in a limited sense; when taking a broader view, humans reveal themselves to be extremely specialized, which is to be expected given the process through which they evolved" [10]. "[W]e are born with priors about ourselves, about the world, and about how to learn, which determine what categories of skills we can acquire and what categories of problems we can solve" [10].

If such tasks are in fact impossible for any human to perform, that proves that humans are not AGI equivalent. But, how do we know what a highly intelligent agent is capable of or more interestingly incapable of learning? How do we know what human's can't learn [35]? One trick we can use is to estimate the processing speed [36] for an average human on a particular learning task and to show that even 120 years, a very optimistic longevity estimate for people, are not sufficient to complete learning that particular task, while much faster computer can do so in seconds.

Generality can be domain limited or unlimited. Different animals, such as dolphins, elephants, mice, etc., and humans are all general in overlapping but not identical sets of domains. Humans are not a superset of all animal intelligences. There are some things animals can do that humans cannot and vice versa. For example, humans can't learn to speak animal "languages" and animals can't learn to play chess [37]. Only AGI is universal/general intelligence over all learnable domains. AGI is not just capable of anything a human can do, it is capable of learning anything that could be learned. It is a superset of all NAIs and is equal in capability to superintelligence (SAI).

12.4 Conclusions

There is no shortage of definitions of intelligence [7, 38–41], but we felt it was important to clarify that humans are neither fully general nor terminal point in the space of the possible minds [42]. As Chollet says: "We may even build systems with higher generalization power (as there is no a priori reason to assume human cognitive efficiency is an upper bound), or systems with a broader scope of application. Such systems would feature intelligence beyond that of humans" [10]. Humans only have a subset of capabilities an AGI will have and the capability difference between us and AGI is far greater than capability difference between AGI and SAI. Bostrom describes three forms of SAI (p. 53–57) [43]): Speed SAI (like a faster human), collective SAI (like a group of humans), and quality SAI (does what humans can't). All three can be accomplished by an AGI, so there is no difference between AGI and SAI, they are the same (HLAI ≤ AGI = SAI) and the common takeoff-speed debate [44] resolves to hard takeoff, from definitions. This implies even stronger limitations [15, 45, 46] on our capability to control AI and a more immediate faceoff. We are already having many problems with Ignorance Explosion [47, 48], an Intelligence Explosion [49, 50] will be well beyond our capabilities to control.

If we use Legg's definition of intelligence [7] and average performance across all possible problems, we can arrive at a somewhat controversial result that modern AI is already smarter than any human is. An individual human can only learn a small subset of domains and human capabilities can't be trivially transferred between different humans to create a union function of all human capabilities, but that is, at least theoretically, possible for AI. Likewise, humans can't emulate some computer algorithms, but computers can run any algorithm a human is using. Machines of 2020 can translate between hundreds of languages, win most games, generate art, write poetry, and learn many tasks individual humans are not capable of learning. If we were to integrate all such abilities into a single AI agent it would on average outperform any person across all possible problem domains, but perhaps not humanity as a whole seen as a single agent. This may have been true for a number of years now and is becoming more definitive every year. As an AI agent can be a superset of many algorithms from which it can choose it would not be a subject to the NFL theorems [8, 9].

While AI dominates humans in most domains of human interest [51–56], there are domains in which humans would not even be able to meaningfully participate. This is similar to the Unpredictability [45] and Unexplainability/Incomprehensibility of AI [15] results, but at a meta-level. The implications for AI control and AI Safety and Security [57–60] are not encouraging. To be dangerous AI doesn't have to be general, it is sufficient for it to be superior to humans in a few strategic domains. If AI can learn a particular domain it will quickly go from Hypohuman to Hyperhuman performance [61]. Additionally, common proposal for merging of humanity with machines doesn't seem to work as adding HLAI to AGI adds nothing to AGI, meaning in a cyborg agent human will become a useless bottleneck as AI becomes more advanced and the human will be eventually removed, if not explicitly at least implicitly from control. What does this chapter tell us? Like the dark matter of the physical universe, the space of all problems is mostly unknown unknowns, and most people don't know that and don't even know that they don't know it. To paraphrase the famous saying: "The more AI learns, the more I realize how much I don't know".

Note

1. Some people could do that and more, for example, 100,000 digits of π have been memorized using special mnemonics.

References

1. Trazzi, M., and R.V. Yampolskiy, *Artificial stupidity: Data we need to make machines our equals.* Patterns, 2020. 1(2): p. 100021.
2. Trazzi, M., and R.V. Yampolskiy, *Building safer AGI by introducing artificial stupidity*, arXiv preprint arXiv:1808.03644, 2018.
3. Goertzel, B., L. Orseau, and J. Snaider, *Artificial general intelligence.* Scholarpedia, 2015. 10(11): p. 31847.
4. Baum, S.D., B. Goertzel, and T.G. Goertzel, *How long until human-level AI? Results from an expert assessment.* Technological Forecasting and Social Change, 2011 **78**(1): pp. 185–195.
5. Barrat, J., *Our Final Invention: Artificial Intelligence and the End of the Human Era.* 2013: Macmillan.
6. Anonymous, *Artificial General Intelligence*, Wikipedia. Retrieved July 3, 2020. https://en.wikipedia.org/wiki/Artificial_general_intelligence,
7. Legg, S., and M. Hutter, *A collection of definitions of intelligence.* Frontiers in Artificial Intelligence and Applications, 2007. **157**: p. 17.
8. Wolpert, D.H., *What the No Free Lunch Theorems Really Mean; How to Improve Search Algorithms*, Santa Fe Institute, 2012.
9. Wolpert, D.H., and W.G. Macready, *No free lunch theorems for optimization.* IEEE Transactions on Evolutionary Computation, 1997. **1**(1): p. 67–82.
10. Chollet, F., *On the measure of intelligence*, arXiv preprint arXiv:1911.01547, 2019.
11. Yampolskiy, R.V., *AI-complete, AI-hard, or AI-easy–classification of problems in AI*, in *The 23rd Midwest Artificial Intelligence and Cognitive Science Conference*. 2012. Cincinnati, OH, USA.
12. Lecun, Y., *Yann LeCun: Deep Learning, Convolutional Neural Networks, and Self-supervised Learning*, AI Podcast, Lex Fridman. Retrieved August 31, 2019 https://www.youtube.com/watch?v=SGSOCuByo24.
13. Barnett, M., *Might Humans Not Be the Most Intelligent Animals?* Retrieved December 23, 2019. https://www.lesswrong.com/posts/XjuT9vgBfwXPxsdfN/might-humans-not-be-the-most-intelligent-animals.
14. Turing, A., *Computing machinery and intelligence.* Mind, 1950. **59**(236): p. 433–460.
15. Yampolskiy, R.V., *Unexplainability and incomprehensibility of artificial intelligence*, arXiv preprint arXiv:1907.03869, 2019.
16. Moravec, H., *When will computer hardware match the human brain.* Journal of Evolution and Technology, 1998. **1**: p. 10.
17. Lin, H.W., M. Tegmark, and D. Rolnick, *Why does deep and cheap learning work so well?* Journal of Statistical Physics, 2017. **168**: p. 1223–1247.

18. Hutter, M., *Universal Artificial Intelligence: Sequential Decisions Based on Algorithmic Probability*. 2004: Springer Science & Business Media.

19. Yampolskiy, R.V., *Turing Test as a Defining Feature of AI-Completeness*, in *Artificial Intelligence, Evolutionary Computation and Metaheuristics – In the Footsteps of Alan Turing*. Xin-She Yang, Editors. 2013, Springer. p. 3–17.

20. Jensen, A.R., *The g Factor: The Science of Mental Ability*. 1998: Praeger.

21. Wiggers, K., *Yann LeCun and Yoshua Bengio: Self-supervised Learning is the Key to Human-Level Intelligence*. Retrieved May 2, 2020. https://venturebeat.com/2020/05/02/yann-lecun-and-yoshua-bengio-self-supervised-learning-is-the-key-to-human-level-intelligence/.

22. Valiant, L., *Probably Approximately Correct: Nature's Algorithms for Learning and Prospering in a Complex World*. 2013: Basic Books.

23. Blum, M., and S. Vempala, *The complexity of human computation via a concrete model with an application to passwords*. Proceedings of the National Academy of Sciences, 2020. **117**: p. 9208–9215.

24. Oh, T.-H., T. Dekel, C. Kim, I. Mosseri, W.T. Freeman, M. Rubinstein, and W. Matusik, *Speech2face: Learning the face behind a voice*, in *Proceedings of the IEEE Conference on Computer Vision and Pattern Recognition*. 2019. p. 7539–7548.

25. Sero, D., A. Zaidi, J. Li, J.D. White, T.B.G. Zarzar, M.L. Marazita, S.M. Weinberg, P. Suetens, D. Vandermeulen, and J.K. Wagner, *Facial recognition from DNA using face-to-DNA classifiers*. Nature Communications, 2019. **10**: p. 2557.

26. Yaman, D., F.I. Eyiokur, and H.K. Ekenel, *Ear2Face: Deep biometric modality mapping*, arXiv preprint arXiv:2006.01943, 2020.

27. Shumailov, I., L. Simon, J. Yan, and R. Anderson, *Hearing your touch: A new acoustic side channel on smartphones*, arXiv preprint arXiv:1903.11137, 2019.

28. Zhuang, L., F. Zhou, and J.D. Tygar, *Keyboard acoustic emanations revisited*. ACM Transactions on Information and System Security (TISSEC), 2009. **13**: p. 1–26.

29. Nassi, B., Y. Pirutin, A. Shamir, Y. Elovici, and B. Zadov, *Lamphone: Real-Time Passive Sound Recovery from Light Bulb Vibrations*, Cryptology ePrint Archive. 2020. https://eprint.iacr.org/2020/708.

30. Kwong, A., W. Xu, and K. Fu, *Hard drive of hearing: Disks that eavesdrop with a synthesized microphone*, in *2019 IEEE Symposium on Security and Privacy (SP)*. 2019. IEEE. p. 905–919.

31. Guri, M., M. Monitz, Y. Mirski, and Y. Elovici, *Bitwhisper: Covert signaling channel between air-gapped computers using thermal manipulations*, in *2015 IEEE 28th Computer Security Foundations Symposium*. 2015. IEEE. p. 276–289.

32. Guri, M., A. Kachlon, O. Hasson, G. Kedma, Y. Mirsky, and Y. Elovici, *GSMem: Data exfiltration from air-gapped computers over {GSM} frequencies*, in *24th {USENIX} Security Symposium ({USENIX} Security 15)*. 2015. p. 849–864.

33. Poplin, R., A.V. Varadarajan, K. Blumer, Y. Liu, M.V. Mcconnell, G.S. Corrado, L. Peng, and D.R. Webster, *Prediction of cardiovascular risk factors from retinal fundus photographs via deep learning*. Nature Biomedical Engineering, 2018. **2**: p. 158–164.

34. Macgregor, J.N., and T. Ormerod, *Human performance on the traveling salesman problem*. Perception & Psychophysics, 1996. **58**: p. 527–539.

35. Ziesche, S., and R.V. Yampolskiy, *Towards the Mathematics of Intelligence*, in *The Age of Artificial Intelligence: An Exploration*. 2020. p. 1. Vernon Art and Science Incorporated

36. Roberts, R.D., and L. Stankov, *Individual differences in speed of mental processing and human cognitive abilities: Toward a taxonomic model.* Learning and Individual Differences, 1999. **11**: p. 1–120. Vernon Art and Science Incorporated
37. Yampolskiy, R.V., *The singularity may be near.* Information, 2018. **9**: p. 190.
38. Hernández-Orallo, J., *The Measure of All Minds: Evaluating Natural and Artificial Intelligence.* 2017: Cambridge University Press.
39. Legg, S., and M. Hutter, *Universal intelligence: A definition of machine intelligence.* Minds and Machines, 2007. **17**: p. 391–444.
40. Wang, P., *On defining artificial intelligence.* Journal of Artificial General Intelligence, 2019. **10**: p. 1–37.
41. Yampolskiy, R.V., *On defining differences between intelligence and artificial intelligence.* Journal of Artificial General Intelligence, 2020. **11**: p. 68–70.
42. Yampolskiy, R.V., *The space of possible mind designs,* in *International Conference on Artificial General Intelligence.* 2015. Springer. p. 218–227.
43. Bostrom, N., *Superintelligence: Paths, Dangers, Strategies.* 2014: Oxford University Press.
44. Yudkowsky, E., and R. Hanson, *The Hanson-Yudkowsky AI-Foom debate,* MIRI Technical Report. 2008. http://intelligence.org/files/AIFoomDebate.pdf.
45. Yampolskiy, R.V., *Unpredictability of AI: On the impossibility of accurately predicting all actions of a smarter agent.* Journal of Artificial Intelligence and Consciousness, 2020. **7**: p. 109–118.
46. Yampolskiy, R.V., *What are the ultimate limits to computational techniques: Verifier theory and unverifiability.* Physica Scripta, 2017. **92**: p. 093001.
47. Lukasiewicz, J., *The ignorance explosion.* Leonardo, 1974. **7**: p. 159–163.
48. Lukasiewicz, J., *The Ignorance Explosion: Understanding Industrial Civilization.* 1994: McGill-Queen's Press-MQUP.
49. Loosemore, R., and B. Goertzel, *Why an Intelligence Explosion Is Probable, Singularity Hypotheses.* 2012: Springer. p. 83–98.
50. Muehlhauser, L., and A. Salamon, *Intelligence Explosion: Evidence and Import, Singularity Hypotheses.* 2012: Springer. p. 15–42.
51. Clark, P., O. Etzioni, T. Khot, B.D. Mishra, K. Richardson, A. Sabharwal, C. Schoenick, O. Tafjord, N. Tandon, and S. Bhakthavatsalam, *From 'F' to 'A' on the NY regents science exams: An overview of the aristo project,* arXiv preprint arXiv:1909.01958, 2019.
52. Devlin, J., M.-W. Chang, K. Lee, and K. Toutanova, *Bert: pre-training of deep bidirectional transformers for language understanding,* arXiv preprint arXiv:1810.04805, 2018.
53. Goodfellow, I., J. Pouget-Abadie, M. Mirza, B. Xu, D. Warde-Farley, S. Ozair, A. Courville, and Y. Bengio, *Generative adversarial nets,* in *Advances in Neural Information Processing Systems.* 2014. p. 2672–2680.
54. Mnih, V., K. Kavukcuoglu, D. Silver, A.A. Rusu, J. Veness, M.G. Bellemare, A. Graves, M. Riedmiller, A.K. Fidjeland, and G. Ostrovski, *Human-level control through deep reinforcement learning.* Nature, 2015. **518**: p. 529–533.
55. Silver, D., J. Schrittwieser, K. Simonyan, I. Antonoglou, A. Huang, A. Guez, T. Hubert, L. Baker, M. Lai, and A. Bolton, *Mastering the game of go without human knowledge.* Nature, 2017, **550**: p. 354.
56. Vinyals, O., I. Babuschkin, W.M. Czarnecki, M. Mathieu, A. Dudzik, J. Chung, D.H. Choi, R. Powell, T. Ewalds, and P. Georgiev, *Grandmaster level in StarCraft II using multi-agent reinforcement learning,* Nature, 2019. **575**: p. 1–5.

57. Babcock, J., J. Kramar, and R. Yampolskiy, *The AGI containment problem*, in *The Ninth Conference on Artificial General Intelligence (AGI2015)*. July 16–19, 2016. NYC, USA.

58. Babcock, J., J. Kramár, and R.V. Yampolskiy, *Guidelines for artificial intelligence containment*, in *Next-Generation Ethics: Engineering a Better Society*, A. E. Abbas, Editor. 2019. p. 90–112. Cambridge University Press

59. Callaghan, V., J. Miller, R. Yampolskiy, and S. Armstrong, *The Technological Singularity: Managing the Journey*. 2017: Springer.

60. Yampolskiy, R.V., *Artificial Intelligence Safety and Security*. 2018: Chapman and Hall/CRC Press.

61. Hall, J.S., *Beyond AI: Creating the Conscience of the Machine*. 2009: Prometheus books.

13

*Skepticism**

13.1 Introduction to AI Risk Skepticism

It has been predicted that if recent advancements in machine learning continue uninterrupted, human-level or even superintelligent artificially intelligent (AI) systems will be designed at some point in the near future [1]. Currently available (and near-term predicted) AI software is subhuman in its general intelligence capability, but it is already capable of being hazardous in a number of narrow domains [2], mostly with regard to privacy, discrimination [3, 4], crime automation, or armed conflict [5]. Superintelligent AI, predicted to be developed in the longer term, is widely anticipated [6] to be far more dangerous and is potentially capable of causing a lot of harm including an existential risk event for the humanity as a whole [7, 8]. Together the short-term and long-term concerns are known as AI Risk [9].

An infinite number of pathways exist to a state of the world in which a dangerous AI is unleashed [10]. Those include mistakes in design, programming, training, data, value alignment, self-improvement, environmental impact, safety mechanisms, and of course intentional design of malevolent AI (MAI) [11–13]. In fact, MAI presents the strongest, some may say undeniable, argument against AI Risk skepticism (not to be confused with "skeptical superintelligence" [14]). While it may be possible to argue that a particular pathway to dangerous AI will not materialize or could be addressed, it seems nothing could be done against someone purposefully designing a dangerous AI. MAI convincingly establishes potential risks from intelligent software and makes denialist's point of view scientifically unsound. In fact, the point is so powerful that the authors of ref. [11] were contacted by some senior researchers who expressed concern about the impact such a publication may have on the future development and funding of AI research.

More generally, much can be inferred about the safety expectations for future intelligent systems from observing abysmal safety and security of modern software. Typically, users are required to click "Agree" on the software usage agreement, which denounces all responsibility from software

* Used with permission of Springer Nature Switzerland AG, from AI Risk Skepticism, Roman V. Yampolskiy, in Philosophy and Theory of Artificial Intelligence, Vincent C. Müller (Ed.), copyright © 2022; Permission conveyed through Copyright Clearence Center, Inc.

DOI: 10.1201/9781003440260-13

developers and explicitly waves any guarantees regarding reliability and functionality of the provided software, including commercial products. Likewise, hardware components for the Internet of Things (IoT) notoriously lack security[1] in the design of the used protocol. Even in principle, sufficient levels of safety and security may not be obtainable for complex software products [15, 16].

Currently a broad consensus[2] exists in the AI Safety community, and beyond it, regarding importance of addressing existing and future AI Risks by devoting necessary resources to making AI safe and beneficial, not just capable. Such consensus is well demonstrated by a number of open letters[3,4,5,6] signed by thousands of leading practitioners and by formation of industry coalitions[7] with similar goals. Recognizing dangers posed by an unsafe AI, a significant amount of research [17–24] is now geared to develop safety mechanisms for ever-improving intelligent software, with AI Safety research centers springing up at many top universities such as MIT,[8] Berkeley,[9] Oxford,[10] and Cambridge,[11] companies[12] and non-profits.[13,14]

Given tremendous benefits associated with automation of physical and cognitive labor, it is likely that funding and effort dedicated to creation of intelligent machines will only accelerate. However, it is important to not be blinded by the potential payoff, but to also consider associated costs. Unfortunately, like in many other domains of science, a vocal group of skeptics is unwilling to accept this inconvenient truth claiming that concerns about the human-caused issue of AI Risk are just "crypto-religious" [25] "pseudoscientific" "mendacious FUD" [26] "alarmism" [27] and "luddite" [28], "vacuous", "nonsense" [29], "fear of technology, opportunism, or ignorance", "anti-AI", "hype", "comical", "so ludicrous that it defies logic", "magical thinking", "techno-panic" [30], "doom-and-gloom", "Terminator-like fantasies" [31], "unrealistic", "sociotechnical blindness", "AI anxiety" [32], "technophobic", "paranoid" [33],[15] "neo-fear" [34] and "mental masturbation" [35] by "fearmongers" [30], "AI Dystopians", "AI Apocalypsarians", – a "Frankenstein complex" [36]. They accuse AI Safety experts of being "crazy", "megalomaniacal", "alchemists", and "AI weenies", performing "parlor tricks" to spread their "quasi-sociopathic", "deplorable beliefs", about the "nerd Apocalypse", caused by their "phantasmagorical AI" [37].

Even those who have no intention to insult anyone have a hard time resisting such temptation: "The idea that a computer can have a level of imagination or wisdom or intuition greater than humans can only be imagined, in our opinion, by someone who is unable to understand the nature of human intelligence. It is not our intention to insult those that have embraced the notion of the technological singularity, but we believe that this fantasy is dangerous …" [38]. Currently, disagreement between AI Risk skeptics [39] (interestingly Etzioni was an early AI Safety leader [40]) and AI Safety advocates [41] is limited to debate, but some have predicted that in the future it will become a central issue faced by humanity and that the so-called "species dominance debate" will result in a global war [42]. Such a war could be seen as an additional implicit risk from progress in AI.

"AI risk skeptics dismiss or bring into doubt scientific consensus of the AI Safety community on superintelligent AI risk, including the extent to which dangers are likely to materialize, severity of impact superintelligent AI might have on humanity and universe, or practicality of devoting resources to safety research" [43]. A more extreme faction, which could be called AI Risk Deniers,[16] rejects any concern about AI-Risk, including from already deployed systems or soon to be deployed systems.

For example, the 2009 AAAI presidential panel on Long-Term AI Futures tasked with review and response to concerns about the potential for loss of human control of computer-based intelligence concluded: "The panel of experts was overall skeptical of the radical views expressed by futurists and science-fiction authors. Participants reviewed prior writings and thinking about the possibility of an "intelligence explosion" where computers one day begin designing computers that are more intelligent than themselves. They also reviewed efforts to develop principles for guiding the behavior of autonomous and semi-autonomous systems. Some of the prior and ongoing research on the latter can be viewed by people familiar with Isaac Asimov's Robot Series as formalization and study of behavioral controls akin to Asimov's Laws of Robotics. There was overall skepticism about the prospect of an intelligence explosion as well as of a "coming singularity," and also about the large-scale loss of control of intelligent systems" [44].

Denialism of anthropogenic climate change has caused dangerous delays in governments exercising control and counteraction. Similarly, influence of unchecked AI Risk denialism could be detrimental for the long-term flourishing of human civilization as it questions importance of incorporating necessary safeguards into intelligent systems we are deploying. Misplaced skepticism has negative impact on allocating sufficient resources for assuring that developed intelligent systems are safe and secure. This is why it is important to explicitly call-out instances of AI Risk denialism, just as it is necessary to fight denialism in other domains in which it is observed, such as history, healthcare, and biology. In fact, in many ways, the situation with advanced AI Risk may be less forgiving. Climate change is comparable to soft takeoff [45], in which temperature is gradually rising by a few degrees over a 100-year period. An equivalent to superintelligence hard takeoff scenario would be global temperature rising by 100 degrees in a week.

13.2 Types of AI Risk Skeptics

It is helpful to define a few terms and can be easily done by adopting the language addressing similar types of science denialism:[17] *AI risk denial is denial, dismissal, or unwarranted doubt that contradicts the scientific consensus on AI risk, including its effects on humanity. Many deniers self-label as "AI risk skeptics". AI risk denial is frequently implicit, when individuals or research groups accept the science but fail to come to terms with it or to translate their acceptance into action.* While denying risk from existing intelligent systems is pure denialism, with respect to future AIs, predicted to be superintelligent, it is reasonable to label such views as skepticism as evidence is not as strong for risk from such systems and as they don't currently exist and therefore are not subject to empirical testing for safety. Finally, we also introduce the concept of an "AI safety skeptic", as someone who while accepting reality of AI Risk doubts that safe AI is possible to achieve either in theory or at least in practice.

In order to overcome AI Risk skepticism it is important to understand its causes and the culture supporting it. People who self-identify as AI Risk skeptics are very smart, ethical human beings and otherwise wonderful people, nothing in this chapter should be interpreted as implying otherwise. Unfortunately, great people make great mistakes, and no mistake is greater than ignoring potential existential risk from development of advanced AI. In this section, I review most common reasons and beliefs for being an AI Risk skeptic.

Non-Experts: Non-AI-Safety researchers greatly enjoy commenting on all aspects of AI Safety. It seems like anyone who saw Terminator thinks they have sufficient expertise to participate in the discussion (on either side), but not surprisingly it is not the case. Not having formal training in the area of research should significantly discount importance of opinion of such public intellectuals, but it does not seem to be the case. By analogy, in discussions of cancer, we listen to professional opinions of doctors trained in treating oncological diseases but feel perfectly fine ignoring opinions of business executives or lawyers. In AI Safety debates, participants are perfectly happy to consider opinions of professional atheists [46], web-developers [37], or psychologists [47], to give just some examples.

Wrong Experts: It may not be obvious but most expert AI researchers are not AI Safety Researchers! Many AI Risk skeptics are very knowledgeable and established AI researchers, but it is important to admit that having expertise in AI development is not the same as having expertise in AI Safety and Security. AI researchers are typically sub-domain experts in one of many sub-branches of AI research such as Knowledge Representation, Pattern Recognition, Computer Vision or Neural Networks, etc. Such domain expert knowledge does not immediately make them experts in all other areas of AI, AI Safety being no exception. More generally, a software developer is not necessarily a cybersecurity expert. It is easy to illustrate this by analogy with a non-computer domain. For example, a person who is an expert on all things related to cement is not inevitable an expert on the placement of emergency exits even though both domains have a lot to do with building construction.

Professional Skeptics: Members of skeptic organizations are professionally predisposed to question everything, and it is not surprising that they find claims about properties of future superintelligent machines to fall in their domain of expertise. For example, Michael Shermer, founder of Skeptics Society and publisher of Skeptic magazine, has stated [46]: "I'm skeptical. … all such doomsday scenarios involve a long sequence of if-then contingencies, a failure of which at any point would negate the apocalypse". Similarly, those who are already skeptical about one domain of science, for example, theory of evolution, are more likely to also exhibit skepticism about AI Risk.[18]

Ignorant of Literature: Regardless of background, intelligence, or education many commentators on AI Safety seem to be completely unaware of literature on AI Risk, top researchers in the field, their arguments, and concerns. It may no longer be possible to read everything on the topic due to the sheer number of publications produced in recent years, but there really is no excuse for not familiarizing yourself with top books [7, 8, 48] or survey papers [9] on the topic. It is of course impossible to make a meaningful contribution to the discussion if one is not aware of what is actually being discussed or is engaging with the strawman arguments.

13.2.1 Skeptics of Strawman

Some AI skeptics may actually be aware of certain AI Safety literature, but because of poor understanding or because they were only exposed to weaker arguments for AI Risk, they find them unconvincing or easily dismissible and so feel strongly justified in their skeptical positions. Alternatively, they may find a weakness in one particular pathway to dangerous AI and consequently argue against "fearing the reaper" [49].

With Conflict of Interest and Bias: Lastly, we cannot ignore an obvious conflict of interest many AI researchers, tech CEOs, corporations, and others in the industry have with regards to their livelihood and the threat AI Risk presents to unregulated development of intelligent machines. History teaches us that we can't count on people in the industry to support additional regulation, reviews, or limitations against their direct personal benefit. Tobacco company representatives, for years, assured the public that cigarettes are safe, non-carcinogenic, and non-addictive. Oil companies rejected any concerns public had about connection between burning of fossil fuels and global climate change, despite knowing better.

It is very difficult for a person whose success, career, reputation, funding, prestige, financial well-being, stock options, and future opportunities depend on unobstructed development of AI to accept that the product they are helping to develop is possibly unsafe, requires government regulation, and internal or even external review boards. As Upton Sinclair put it: "It is difficult to get a man to understand something when his salary depends upon his not understanding it". They reasonably fear that any initial concessions may lead to a significant "safety overhead" [50], reduced competitiveness, slowdown in progress or a moratorium on development (à la human cloning), or even an outright ban on future research. The conflict of interest developers of AI have with respect to their ability to impartially assess dangers of their products/services is unquestionable and would be flagged by any ethics panel. Motivated misinformation targeting lay people, politicians, and public intellectuals may also come from governments, thought leaders, and activist citizens interested in steering debate in particular directions [51]. Corporations may additionally worry about legal liability and overall loss of profits.

In addition to the obvious conflicts of interest, most people, including AI researchers, are also subject to a number of cognitive biases making them underappreciate AI Risk. Those would include Optimism Bias (thinking that you are at a smaller risk of suffering a negative outcome) and Confirmation Bias (interpreting information in a way that confirms preconceptions). Additionally, motivated reasoning may come into play, as Baum puts it [51]: "Essentially, with their sense of self-worth firmed up, they become more receptive to information that would otherwise threaten their self-worth. As a technology that could outperform humans, superintelligence could pose an especially pronounced threat to people's sense of self-worth. It may be difficult for people to feel good and efficacious if they would soon be superseded by computers. For at least some people, this could be a significant reason to reject information about the prospect of superintelligence, even if that information is true".

13.3 Arguments for AI Risk Skepticism

In this section, we review most common arguments for AI Risk skepticism. Russell has published a similar list, which in addition to objections to AI Risk concerns also includes examples of flawed suggestions for assuring AI safety [52], such as "Instead of putting objectives into the AI system, just let it choose its own", "Don't worry, we'll just have collaborative human-AI teams", "Can't we just put it in a box?", "Can't we just merge with the machines?", and "Just don't put in 'human' goals like self-preservation".

Importance of understanding denialists' mindset is well-articulated by Russell: "When one first introduces [AI risk] to a technical audience, one can see the thought bubbles popping out of their heads, beginning with the words "But, but, but ..." and ending with exclamation marks. The first kind of *but* takes the form of denial. The deniers say, "But this can't be a real problem, because XYZ." Some of the XYZs reflect a reasoning process that might charitably be described as wishful thinking, while others are more substantial. The second kind of *but* takes the form of deflection: accepting that the problems are real but arguing that we shouldn't try to solve them, either because they're unsolvable or because there are more important things to focus on than the end of civilization or because it's best not to mention them at all. The third kind of *but* takes the form of an oversimplified, instant solution: "But can't we just do ABC?" As with denial, some of the ABCs are instantly regrettable. Others, perhaps by accident, come closer to identifying the true nature of the problem. ... Since the issue seems to be so important, it deserves a public debate of the highest quality. So, in the interests of having that debate, and in the hope that the reader will contribute to it, let me provide a quick tour of the highlights so far, such as they are" [53].

In addition to providing a comprehensive list of arguments for AI Risk skepticism, we have also classified such objections into six categories (see Figure 13.1): Objections related to Priorities, Technical issues, AI Safety, Ethics, Bias, and Miscellaneous ones. While research on types of general skepticism exists [54], to the best of our knowledge this is the first such taxonomy specifically for AI Risk. In general, we can talk about politicized skepticism and intellectual skepticism [55]. Politicized skepticism has motives other than greater understanding, while intellectual skepticism aims for better comprehension and truth seeking. Our survey builds and greatly expands on previous lists from Turing [56], Baum [55], Russell [52], and Ceglowski [37].

13.3.1 Priorities Objections

Too Far: A frequent argument against work on AI Safety is that we are hundreds if not thousands of years away from developing superintelligent machines, and so even if they may present some danger, it is a waste of human and computational resources to allocate any effort to address superintelligence risk at this point in time. Such position doesn't take into account possibility that it may take even longer to develop appropriate AI Safety mechanisms and so the perceived abundance of time is a feature, not a bug. It also ignores the non-zero possibility of an earlier development of superintelligence.

Soft Takeoff Is More Likely and So We Will Have Time to Prepare: AI takeoff refers to the speed with which an AGI can get to superintelligent capabilities. While hard takeoff is likely and means that process will be very quick, some argue that we will face a soft takeoff and so will have adequate time (years) to prepare [45]. While nobody knows the actual take-off speed at this point, it is prudent to be ready for the worst-case scenario.

No Obvious Path to Get to AGI from Current AI: While we are making good progress on AI, it is not obvious how to get from our current state in AI to AGI and current methods may not scale [57]. This may be true, but this is similar to the "Too Far" objection and we definitely need all the time possible to develop necessary safety mechanisms. Additionally, current state-of-the-art systems [58], don't seem to hit limits yet, subject to availability of compute for increasing model size [59, 60].

PRIORITIES OBJECTIONS
• Too Far • Soft Takeoff is more likely and so we will have Time to Prepare • No Obvious Path to Get to AGI from Current AI • Short-Term AI Concerns over AGI Safety • Something Else is More Important
TECHNICAL OBJECTIONS
• AI Doesn't Exist • Superintelligence is Impossible • Self-Improvement is Impossible • AI Can't be Conscious • AI Can be Just a Tool • We can Always just Turn it Off • We Can Reprogram AIs if We Don't Like What They Do • AI doesn't have a Body and so can't Hurt Us • If AI is as Capable as You Say, it Will not Make Dumb Mistakes • Superintelligence Would (Probably) Not Be Catastrophic • Self-preservation and Control Drives Don't Just Appear They Have to be Programmed In • An AI is not Pulled at Random from the Mind Design Space • AI Can't Generate Novel Plans
AI SAFETY OBJECTIONS
• AI Safety Can't be Done Today • AI Can't be Safe • Skepticism of Particular Risks • Skepticism of Particular Safety Methods • Skepticism of Researching Impossibility Results
ETHICAL OBJECTIONS
• Superintelligence is Benevolence • Let the Smarter Beings Win • Let's Gamble • Malevolent AI is not worse than Malevolent Humans
BIASED OBJECTIONS
• AI Safety Researchers are Non-Coders • Majority of AI researchers are not Worried • Anti-Media Bias • Keep it Quiet • Safety Work just Creates an Overhead Slowing Down Research • Heads in the Sand
MISCELLANEOUS OBJECTIONS
• So Easy it will be Solved Automatically • AI Regulation Will Prevent Problems • Other Arguments, …

FIGURE 13.1

Taxonomy of objections to AI Risk.

Something Else Is More Important: Some have argued that global climate change, pandemics, social injustice, and a dozen of other more immediate concerns are more important than AI Risk and should be prioritized over wasting money and human capital on something like AI Safety. But, development of safe and secure superintelligence is a possible meta-solution to all the other existential threats and so resources allocated to AI Risk are indirectly helping us address all the other important problems. Timewise it is also likely, that AGI will be developed before projected severe impact from such issues as global climate change.

Short-Term AI Concerns over AGI Safety: Similar to the argument that something else is more important, proponents claim that immediate issues with today's AIs, such as algorithmic bias, technological unemployment, or limited transparency, should take precedence over concerns about future technology (AGI/superintelligence), which doesn't yet exist and may not exist for decades [61].

13.3.2 Technical Objections

AI Doesn't Exist: The argument is that current developments in machine learning are not progress in AI, but are just developments in statistics, particularly in matrix multiplication and gradient descent.[19] Consequently, it is suggested that calls for regulation of AI are absurd. Of course, human criminal behavior can be seen as interactions of neurotransmitters and ion channels, making their criminalization questionable.

Superintelligence is Impossible: If a person doesn't think that superintelligence can ever be built, they will of course view risk from superintelligence with strong skepticism. Most people in this camp assign a very small (but usually not zero) probability to the actual possibility of superintelligent AI coming into existence [62–64], but if even the tiniest probability is multiplied by the infinite value of the Universe, the math seems to be against skepticism. Skeptics in this group will typically agree that if superintelligence did exist it would have potential of being harmful. "Within the AI community, a kind of denialism is emerging, even going as far as denying the possibility of success in achieving the long-term goals of AI. It's as if a bus driver, with all of humanity as passengers, said, "Yes, I am driving as hard as I can towards a cliff, but trust me, we'll run out of gas before we get there!"" [53].

Self-Improvement Is Impossible: This type of skepticism concentrates on the supposed impossibility of intelligence explosion, as a side-effect of recursive self-improvement [65], due to fundamental computational limits [49] and software complexity [66]. Of course such limits are not a problem as long as they are actually located above the level of human capabilities.

AI Can't Be Conscious: Proponents argue that in order to be dangerous AI has to be conscious [67]. As AI Risk is not predicated on artificially intelligent systems experiencing qualia [68, 69], it is not relevant if the system is conscious or not. This objection is as old as the field of AI itself, as Turing addressed "The Argument from Consciousness" in his seminal paper [56].

AI Can Be Just a Tool: A claim that we do not need A(General)I to be an independent agent, it is sufficient for them to be designed as assistants to humans in particular domains, such as GPS navigation and so permit as to avoid dangers of fully independent AI.[20] It is easy to see that the demarcation between Tool AI and AGI is very fuzzy and likely to gradually shift as capability of the tool increases and it obtains additional capabilities.[21]

We Can Always Just Turn It Off: A very common argument of AI Risk skeptics is that any misbehaving AI can be simply turned off, so we have nothing to worry about [70]. If skeptics realize that modern computer viruses are a subset of very low capability MAIs, it becomes obvious why saying "just turn it off" may not be a practical solution.

We Can Reprogram AIs if We Don't Like What They Do: Similar to the idea of turning AI off is the idea that we can reprogram AIs if we are not satisfied with their performance [71]. Such "in production" correction is equally hard to accomplish as it can be shown to be equivalent to shutting current AI off.

AI Doesn't Have a Body and So Can't Hurt Us: This is a common argument and it completely ignores the realities of modern ultra-connected world. Given simple access to the internet, it is easy to affect the world via hired help, digital currencies, IoT, cyberinfrastructure, or even DNA synthesis [72].

If AI Is as Capable as You Say, It Will Not Make Dumb Mistakes: How can superintelligence not understand what we really want? This seems like a paradox [21], any system worthy of the title "human-level" must have the same common sense as we do [73]. Unfortunately, an AI could be a very powerful optimizer while at the same time not being aligned with goals of humanity [74, 75].

Superintelligence Would (Probably) Not Be Catastrophic: Not quite benevolent, but superintelligence would not be very dangerous by default, or at least the dangers would not be catastrophic [76] or its behavior would be correctable in time and is unlikely to be malevolent if not explicitly programmed to be [77]. Some of the ideas in ref. [76] are analyzed in the highly relevant paper on modeling and interpreting expert disagreement about AI [78].

Self-preservation and Control Drives Don't Just Appear They Have to be Programmed In: LeCun has publicly argued that "the desire to control access to resources and to influence others are drives that have been built into us by evolution for our survival. There is no reason to build these drives into our AI systems. Some have said that such drives will spontaneously appear as sub-goals of whatever objective we give to our AIs. Tell a robot "get me coffee" and it will destroy everything on its path to get you coffee, perhaps figuring out in the process how to prevent every other human from turning it off. We would have to simultaneously be extremely talented engineers to build such an effective goal-oriented robot, and extremely stupid and care-less engineers to not put any obvious safeguards into its objective to ensure that it behaves properly".[22] This dismisses research which indicates that such AI drives do appear due to game theoretic and economic reasons [79].

An AI Is Not Pulled at Random from the Mind Design Space: Kruel has previously argued that "[a]n AI is the result of a research and development process. A new generation of AI's needs to be better than other products at *"Understand What Humans Mean"* and *"Do What Humans Mean"* in order to survive the research phase and subsequent market pressure" [80]. Of course, being better doesn't mean being perfect or even great, almost all existing software is evidence of very poor quality of the software research/develop-ment process.

AI Can't Generate Novel Plans: As originally stated by Ada Lovelace: "The Analytical Engine has no pretensions whatever to originate anything. It can do whatever we know how to order it to perform. It can follow analysis; but it has no power of anticipating any analytical relations or truths. Its prov-ince is to assist us to making available what we are already acquainted with" [81]. Of course, numerous counterexamples from modern AI [82] systems provide a counterargument by existence. This doesn't stop modern schol-ars from making similar claims, specifically arguing that only humans can have "curiosity, imagination, intuition, emotions, passion, desires, pleasure, aesthetics, joy, purpose, objectives, goals, telos, values, morality, experience, wisdom, judgment, and even humor" [38]. Regardless of ongoing work [83], most AI Safety researchers are not worried about deadly superintelligence not having a superior sense of humor.

13.3.3 AI Safety-Related Objections

AI Safety Can't Be Done Today: Some people may agree with concerns about superintelligence but argue that AI Safety work is not possible in the absence of a superintelligent AI on which to run experiments [37]. This view is contradicted by a significant number of publications produced by the AI Safety community in recent years, and the author of this book (and his co-authors) in particular [8, 19, 84–89].

AI Can't Be Safe: Another objection to doing AI Safety work is based on publications showing that fundamental aspects of the control problem [90], such as containment [91], verification [16], or morality [92], are simply impos-sible to solve and so such research is a wasted effort. Solvability of the control problem in itself is one of the most important open questions in AI Safety, but not trying is the first step toward failure.

Skepticism of Particular Risks: Even people troubled by some AI Risks may disagree about specific risks they are concerned about and may disagree on safety methods to implement, which ones are most likely to be beneficial and which ones are least likely to have undesirable side effects. This is some-thing only additional research can help resolve.

Skepticism of Particular Safety Methods: AI companies may be dismissive of effectiveness of risk mitigation technology developed by their competitors in the hopes of promoting and standardizing their own technology [55]. Such motivated skepticism should be dismissed.

Skepticism of Researching Impossibility Results: Doing work on theoretical impossibility results [93–95] in AI Safety may not translate to problems in practice, or to at least not be as severe as predicted. However, such research may cause reductions in funding for safety work or to cause new researchers to stay away from the field of AI Safety, but this is not an argument against importance of AI Risk research in general.

13.3.4 Ethical Objections

Superintelligence Is Benevolence: Scholars observed that as humans became more advanced culturally and intellectually they also became nicer, less violent, and more inclusive [47]. Some have attempted to extrapolate from that pattern to superintelligent advanced AIs that they will also be benevolent to us and our habitat [96] and will not develop their own goals which are not programmed into them explicitly. However, superintelligence doesn't imply benevolence [97], which is directly demonstrated by Bostrom's Orthogonality Thesis [74, 75].

Let the Smarter Beings Win: This type of skeptic doesn't deny that superintelligent system will present a lot of risk to humanity but argues that if humanity is replaced with more advanced sentient beings it will be an overall good thing. They give very little value to humanity and see people as mostly having a negative impact on the planet and cognition in the universe. Similarly, AI rights advocates argue that we should not foist our values on our mind children because it would be a type of forced assimilation. Majority of AI researchers don't realize that people with such views are real, but they are and some are also AI researchers. For example, de Garis [42] has argued that humanity should make room for superintelligent beings. Majority of humanity is not on board with such self-destructive outcomes, perhaps because of a strong inherent pro-human bias.

Let's Gamble: In the vast space of possible intelligence [98], some are benevolent, some are neutral, and others are malicious. It has been suggested that only a small subset of AIs are strictly malevolent, and so we may get lucky and produce a neutral or beneficial superintelligence by pure chance. Gambling with future of human civilization doesn't seem like a good proposition.

MAI Is Not Worse Than Malevolent Humans: The argument is that it doesn't matter who is behind malevolent action, human actors or AI, the impact is the same [33]. Of course, a more intelligent and so more capable AI can be much more harmful and is harder to defeat with human resources, which are frequently sufficient to counteract human adversaries. AI is also likely to be cognitively different from humans and so find surprising ways to cause harm.

13.3.5 Biased Objections

AI Safety Researchers Are Non-Coders: An argument is frequently made that since many top AI Safety researchers do not write code, they are unqualified to judge AI Risk or its correlates.[23] However, one doesn't need to write code in order to understand the inherent risk of AGI, just like someone doesn't have to work in a wet lab to understand dangers of pandemics from biological weapons.

Majority of AI Researchers Are Not Worried: To quote from Dubhashi and Lappin – "While it is difficult to compute a meaningful estimate of the probability of the singularity, the arguments here suggest to us that it is exceedingly small, at least within the foreseeable future, and this is the view of most researchers at the forefront of AI research" [99]. Not only does this misrepresent actual views of actual AI researchers [100, 101], but it is also irrelevant, even if 100% of mathematicians believed 2 + 2 = 5, it would still be wrong. Scientific facts are not determined by democratic process, and you don't get to vote on reality or truth.

Anti-Media Bias: Because of how the media sensationalizes coverage of AI Safety issues, it is also likely that many AI researchers have Terminator-aversion, subconsciously or explicitly equating all mentions of AI Risk with pseudoscientific ideas from Hollywood blockbusters. While literal "Terminators" are of little concern to the AI Safety community, AI weaponized for military purposes is a serious challenge to human safety.

Keep It Quiet: It has been suggested that bringing up concerns about AI Risk may jeopardize AI research funding and bring on government regulation. Proponents argue that it is better to avoid public discussions of AI Risk and capabilities, which advanced AI may bring, as it has potential of bringing on another AI "winter". There is also some general concern about the reputation of the field of AI [55].

Safety Work Just Creates an Overhead Slowing Down Research: Some developers are concerned that integrating AI Safety into research will create a significant overhead and make their projects less competitive. The worry is that groups which don't worry about AI Risk will get to human-level AI faster and cheaper. This is similar to cost-cutting measure in software development, where security concerns are sacrificed, to be the first to the market.

Heads in the Sand: An objection from Turing's classic paper [56] arguing that "The consequences of machines thinking would be too dreadful. Let us hope and believe that they cannot do so". And his succinct response "I do not think that this argument is sufficiently substantial to require refutation" [56]. In the same paper, Turing describes and appropriately dismisses a number of common objections to the possibility of machines achieving human-level performance in thinking: The Theological Objection, the Mathematical Objection, the Argument from Various Disabilities, Lady Lovelace's Objection, the Argument from Continuity of the Nervous System, the Argument from Informality of Behavior, and even the Argument from Extrasensory Perception [56].

13.3.6 Miscellaneous Objections

So Easy It Will Be Solved Automatically: Some scholars think that the AI Risk problem is trivial and will be implicitly solved as a byproduct of doing regular AI research [102]. Same flawed logic can be applied to other problems such as cybersecurity, but of course, they never get completely solved, even with significant effort.

AI Regulation Will Prevent Problems: The idea is that we don't need to worry about AI Safety because government regulation will intervene and prevent problems. Given how poorly legislation against hacking, computer viruses, or even spam has performed, it seems unreasonable to rely on such measures for prevention of AI Risk.

Other Arguments: There are many other arguments by AI Risk skeptics, which are so weak they are not worth describing, but the names of arguments hint at their quality, for example, the arguments from Wooly Definitions, Einstein's Cat, Emus, Slavic Pessimism, My Roommate, Gilligan's Island, Transhuman Woodoo, and Comic Books [37]. Luckily, others have taken the time to address them [103, 104] so we did not have to.

Russell provides examples of what he calls "Instantly regrettable remarks", statements from AI researchers which they are likely to retract after some retrospection [53]. He follows each one with a refutation, but that seems unnecessary given low quality of the original statements:

- "Electronic calculators are superhuman at arithmetic. Calculators didn't take over the world; therefore, there is no reason to worry about superhuman AI".

- "Horses have superhuman strength, and we don't worry about proving that horses are safe; so we needn't worry about proving that AI systems are safe".

- "Historically, there are zero examples of machines killing millions of humans, so, by induction, it cannot happen in the future".

- "No physical quantity in the universe can be infinite, and that includes intelligence, so concerns about superintelligence are overblown".

- "We don't worry about species-ending but highly unlikely possibilities such as black holes materializing in near-Earth orbit, so why worry about superintelligent AI?"

While aiming for good coverage of the topic of AI Risk skepticism, we have purposefully stopped short of analyzing every variant of the described main types of arguments as the number of such objections continues to grow exponentially and it is not feasible or even desirable to include everything into a survey. Readers who want to get deeper into the debate may enjoy the following articles [105–113]/videos [114, 115]. In our future work, we may provide additional analysis of the following objections:

- Bringing up concerns about AGI may actively contribute to the public misunderstanding of science and by doing so contribute to general science denialism.
- Strawman objections: "The thought that these systems would wake up and take over the world is ludicrous" [29].
- We will never willingly surrender control to machines.
- While AGI is likely, superintelligence is not.
- Risks from AI are minuscule in comparison to benefits (immortality, free labor, etc.) and so can be ignored.
- "Intelligence is not a single dimension, so 'smarter than humans' is a meaningless concept" [116].
- "Humans do not have general purpose minds, and neither will AIs" [116].
- "Emulation of human thinking in other media will be constrained by cost" [116].
- "Dimensions of intelligence are not infinite" [116].
- "Intelligences are only one factor in progress" [116].
- You can't control research or ban AI [53].
- Malevolent use of AI is a human problem, not a computer problem [46].
- "Speed alone does not bring increased intelligence" [117].
- Not even exponential growth of computational power can reach the level of superintelligence [118].
- AI Risk researchers are uneducated/conspiracy theorists/crazy/etc., so they are wrong.
- AI has been around for 65 years and didn't destroy humanity, it is unlikely to do so in the future.
- AI Risk is science fiction.
- Just box it; just give it laws to follow; just raise it as a human baby; just …
- AI is just a tool; it can't generate its own goals because it is not conscious.
- I don't want to make important AI researchers angry at me and retaliate against me.
- Narrow AI/robots can't even do some basic things, certainly they can't present danger to humanity.
- Real threat is AI being too dumb and making mistakes.
- Certainly, many smart people are already working on AI Safety, they will take care of it.

- Big companies like Google or Microsoft would never release a dangerous product or service which may damage their reputation or reduce profits.
- Smartest person in the world [multiple names are used by proponents] is not worried about it, so it must not be a real problem.

13.4 Countermeasures for AI Risk Skepticism

First, it is important to emphasize that just like with any other product or service, the burden of proof [119] is on the developers/manufacturers (frequently AI Risk skeptics) to show that their AI will be safe and secure regardless of its capability, customization, learning, domain of utilization, or duration of use. Proving that an intelligent agent in a novel environment will behave in a particular way is a very high standard to meet. The problem could be reduced to showing that a particular human or an animal, for example, a Pit bull, is safe to everyone, a task long known to be impractical. It seems to be even harder with much more capable agents, such as AGI. The best we can hope for is showing some non-zero probability of safe behavior.

A capable AI researcher not concerned with safety is very dangerous. It seems that the only solution to reduce prevalence of AI Risk denialism is education. It is difficult for a sharp mind to study the best AI Risk literature and to remain unconvinced of scientific merits behind it. The legitimacy of risk from uncontrolled AI is undeniable. This is not fearmongering, we don't have an adequate amount of fear in the AI researcher community, an amount which would be necessary to make sure that sufficient precautions are taken by everyone involved. Education is likewise suggested as a desirable path forward by the skeptics, so all sides agree on importance of education. Perhaps if we were to update and de-bias recommendations from the 2009 AAAI presidential panel on Long-Term AI Futures to look like this: "The group suggested outreach and communication to people and organizations about the ~~low~~ likelihood of the radical outcomes, sharing the rationale for the overall ~~comfort~~ [position] of scientists in this realm, and for the need to educate people outside the AI research community about ~~the promise of~~ AI" [44], we could make some progress on AI Risk denialism reduction.

The survival of humanity could depend on rejecting superintelligence misinformation [51]. Two main strategies could be identified: Those aimed at preventing spread of misinformation and those designed to correct peoples' understanding after exposure to misinformation. Baum reviews some ways to prevent superintelligence misinformation, which would also apply to reducing AI Risk skepticism [51]: Educate prominent voices, create reputation costs, mobilize against institutional misinformation, focus media attention on constructive debate, and establish legal requirements. For correcting superintelligence misinformation Baum suggests: Building expert consensus and the perception of thereof, address pre-existing motivations for believing misinformation, inoculate with advance warnings, avoid close association with polarizing ideas, explain misinformation and corrections [51].

Specifically for politicized superintelligence skepticism Baum suggests [55]: "With this in mind, one basic opportunity is to raise awareness about politicized skepticism within communities that discuss superintelligence. Superintelligence skeptics who are motivated by honest intellectual norms may not wish for their skepticism to be used politically. They can likewise be cautious about how to engage with potential political skeptics, such as by avoiding certain speaking opportunities in which their remarks would be used as a political tool instead of as a constructive intellectual contribution. Additionally, all people involved in superintelligence debates can insist on basic intellectual standards, above all by putting analysis before conclusions and not the other way around. These are the sorts of things that an awareness of politicized skepticism can help with". Baum also recommends [55] to: "redouble efforts to build scientific consensus on superintelligence, and then to draw attention to it", "engage with AI corporations to encourage them to avoid politicizing skepticism about superintelligence or other forms of AI", and "follow best practices in debunking misinformation in the event that superintelligence skepticism is politicized." "... Finally, the entire AI community should insist that policy be made based on an honest and balanced read of the current state of knowledge. Burden of proof requirements should not be abused for private gain. As with climate change and other global risks, the world cannot afford to prove that superintelligence would be catastrophic. By the time uncertainty is eliminated, it could be too late" [55].

AI Risk education research [120] indicates that most AI Risk communication strategies are effective [121] and are not counter-productive and the following "good practices" work well for introducing general audiences to AI Risk [120]:

1. "Allow the audience to engage in guided thinking on the subject ("What do you think the effects of human-level AI will be?"), but do not neglect to emphasize its technical nature.

2. Reference credible individuals who have spoken about AI Risk (such as Stephen Hawking, Stuart Russell, and Bill Gates).

3. Reference other cases of technological risk and revolution (such as nuclear energy and the Industrial Revolution).

4. Do not reference science-fiction stories, unless, in context, you expect an increase in the audience's level of engagement to outweigh a drop in their perceptions of the field's importance and its researchers' credibility.

5. Do not present overly vivid or grave disaster scenarios.

6. Do not limit the discussion to abstractions (such as "optimization", "social structures", and "human flourishing"), although they may be useful for creating impressions of credibility".

Recent research indicates that individual differences in the AI Risk perception may be personality [122] and/or attitude [123, 124] dependent but are subject to influence by experts [125] and choice of language [126].

Healthy skepticism is important to keep scientists, including AI researchers, honest. For example, during early days of AI research, it was predicted that human-level performance will be quickly achieved [127]. Luckily, a number of skeptics [128, 129] argued that perhaps the problem is not as simple as it seems, bringing some conservativism to the overly optimistic predictions of researchers and as a result improving quality of research actually being funded and conducted by AI researchers. For a general overview of threat inflation, Thierer's work on technopanics [130] is a good reference.

13.5 Conclusions

In this chapter, we didn't reiterate most of the overwhelming evidence for AI Risk concerns, as it was outside of our goal of analyzing AI Risk skepticism. Likewise, we did not go in-depth with rebuttals to every type of objections to AI Risk. It is precisely because of skeptical attitudes from the majority of mainstream AI researchers that the field of AI Safety was born outside of academia [131]. Regardless, AI Risk skeptics need to realize that the burden of proof is not on AI Safety researchers to show that technology may be dangerous but on AI developers to establish that their technology is safe at the time of deployment and throughout its lifetime of operation. Furthermore, while science operates as a democracy (via majority of peer-reviewers), the facts are not subject to a vote. Even if AI Safety researchers comprise only a small minority of the total number of AI researchers that says nothing about the true potential of intelligent systems for harmful actions. History is full of examples (continental drift [132], quantum mechanics [133]) in which a majority of scientists held a wrong view right before a paradigm shift in thinking took place. Since, just like AI skeptics, AI Safety researchers also have certain biases, to avoid pro or con prejudice in judgment it may be a good idea to rely on impartial juries of non-peers (scientists from outside the domain) whose only job would be to evaluate evidence for a particular claim.

It is obvious that designing a Safe AI is a much harder problem than designing an AI and so will take more time. The actual time to human-level

AI is irrelevant; it will always take longer to make such an AI human friendly. To move the Overton window on AI Risk, AI Safety researchers have to be non-compromising in their position. Perhaps a temporary moratorium on AGI (but not AI) research similar to the one in place for human cloning needs to be considered. It would boost our ability to engage in differential technological development [134–136] increasing our chances of making the AGI safe. AI Safety research definitely needs to get elevated priority and more resources including funding and human capital. Perhaps AI Safety researchers could generate funding via economic incentives from developing safer products. It may be possible to market "Safe AI Inside" government certification on selected progressively ever-smarter devices to boost consumer confidence and sales. This would probably require setting up "FDA for algorithms" [137, 138].

Scientific skepticism in general and skepticism about predicted future events is of course intellectually defensible and is frequently desirable to protect against flawed theories [130]. However, it is important to realize that 100% proof is unlikely to be obtained in some domains and so a precautionary principle (PP) [139] should be used to protect humanity against existential risks. Holm and Harris, in their skeptical paper, define PP as follows [140]: "When an activity raises threats of serious or irreversible harm to human health or the environment, precautionary measures that prevent the possibility of harm shall be taken even if the causal link between the activity and the possible harm has not been proven or the causal link is weak and the harm is unlikely to occur". To use a stock market metaphor, no matter how great a return on investment one is promised, one should not ignore the possibility of losing the principal.

Notes

1. https://en.wikipedia.org/wiki/Internet_of_things#Security
2. https://web.archive.org/web/20170612055339/http://www.agreelist.org/s/advanced-artificial-intelligenc-4mtqyes0jrqy
3. https://en.wikipedia.org/wiki/Open_Letter_on_Artificial_Intelligence
4. https://futureoflife.org/open-letter-autonomous-weapons/
5. https://futureoflife.org/ai-principles/
6. https://futureoflife.org/ai-open-letter/
7. https://www.partnershiponai.org
8. https://futureoflife.org/
9. https://humancompatible.ai/
10. https://www.fhi.ox.ac.uk/
11. https://www.cser.ac.uk/
12. https://deepmind.com/
13. https://openai.com/
14. https://intelligence.org/

15. Comment on article by Steven Pinker.
16. I first used the term "AI risk denier" in a 2015 paper https://arxiv.org/abs/1511.03246, and AGI risk skepticism in a 2014 (co-authored) paper: https://iopscience.iop.org/article/10.1088/0031-8949/90/1/018001/pdf
17. https://en.wikipedia.org/wiki/Climate_change_denial
18. https://web.archive.org/web/20120611073509/http://www.discoverynews.org/2011/02/artificial_intelligence_is_not044151.php
19. https://twitter.com/benhamner/status/892136662171504640
20. https://wiki.lesswrong.com/wiki/Tool_AI
21. http://lesswrong.com/lw/cze/reply_to_holden_on_tool_ai/
22. https://www.facebook.com/yann.lecun/posts/10154220941542143
23. http://reducing-suffering.org/predictions-agi-takeoff-speed-vs-years-worked-commercial-software

References

1. Kurzweil, R., *The Singularity Is Near: When Humans Transcend Biology*. 2005: Viking Press.
2. Yampolskiy, R.V., *Predicting future AI failures from historic examples*. Foresight, 2019. **21**(1): p. 138–152.
3. Caliskan, A., J.J. Bryson, and A. Narayanan, *Semantics derived automatically from language corpora contain human-like biases*. Science, 2017. **356**(6334): p. 183–186.
4. Bolukbasi, T., et al., *Man is to computer programmer as woman is to homemaker? debiasing word embeddings*, in *Advances in Neural Information Processing Systems*. 2016.
5. Arkin, R., *Governing Lethal Behavior in Autonomous Robots*. 2009: CRC Press.
6. Fast, E., and E. Horvitz, *Long-term trends in the public perception of artificial intelligence*. arXiv preprint arXiv:1609.04904, 2016.
7. Bostrom, N., *Superintelligence: Paths, Dangers, Strategies*. 2014: Oxford University Press.
8. Yampolskiy, R.V., *Artificial Superintelligence: A Futuristic Approach*. 2015: CRC Press.
9. Sotala, K., and R.V. Yampolskiy, *Responses to catastrophic AGI risk: A survey*. Physica Scripta, 2014. **90**(1): p. 018001.
10. Yampolskiy, R.V., *Taxonomy of pathways to dangerous artificial intelligence*, in *Workshops at the Thirtieth AAAI Conference on Artificial Intelligence*. 2016.
11. Pistono, F., and R.V. Yampolskiy, *Unethical research: How to create a malevolent artificial intelligence*, in *25th International Joint Conference on Artificial Intelligence (IJCAI-16). Ethics for Artificial Intelligence Workshop (AI-Ethics-2016)*. 2016.
12. Vanderelst, D., and A. Winfield, *The dark side of ethical robots*. arXiv preprint arXiv:1606.02583, 2016.
13. Charisi, V., et al., *Towards moral autonomous systems*. arXiv preprint arXiv:1703.04741, 2017.
14. Corabi, J., *Superintelligent AI and skepticism*. Journal of Evolution and Technology, 2017. **27**(1): p. 4.

15. Herley, C., *Unfalsifiability of security claims*. Proceedings of the National Academy of Sciences, 2016. **113**(23): p. 6415–6420.

16. Yampolskiy, R.V., *What are the ultimate limits to computational techniques: Verifier theory and unverifiability*. Physica Scripta, 2017. **92**(9): p. 093001.

17. Babcock, J., J. Kramar, and R. Yampolskiy, *The AGI containment problem*, in *The Ninth Conference on Artificial General Intelligence (AGI2015)*. July 16–19, 2016. NYC, USA.

18. Callaghan, V., et al., *Technological Singularity*. 2017: Springer.

19. Ramamoorthy, A., and R. Yampolskiy, *Beyond mad? The race for artificial general intelligence*. ITU J, 2018. **1**: p. 1–8.

20. Majot, A.M., and R.V. Yampolskiy, *AI safety engineering through introduction of self-reference into felicific calculus via artificial pain and pleasure*, in *2014 IEEE International Symposium on Ethics in Science, Technology and Engineering*. 2014. IEEE.

21. Yampolskiy, R.V., *What to do with the singularity paradox?*, in *Philosophy and Theory of Artificial Intelligence (PT-AI2011)*. October 3–4, 2011: Thessaloniki, Greece.

22. Tegmark, M., *Life 3.0: Being Human in the Age of Artificial Intelligence*. 2017: Knopf.

23. Everitt, T., G. Lea, and M. Hutter, *AGI safety literature review*. arXiv preprint arXiv:1805.01109, 2018.

24. Juric, M., A. Sandic, and M. Brcic, *AI safety: State of the field through quantitative lens*. arXiv preprint arXiv:2002.05671, 2020.

25. Anonymous, *Existential risk from artificial general intelligence – skepticism*, in *Wikipedia*. Retrieved September 16, 2002. https://en.wikipedia.org/wiki/Existential_risk_from_artificial_general_intelligence#Skepticism.

26. Elkus, A., *A Rebuttal to a Rebuttal on AI Values*. Retrieved April 27, 2016. https://web.archive.org/web/20160720131956/https://aelkus.github.io/blog/2016-04-27-rebuttal_values.html

27. Doctorow, C., *AI Alarmism: Why smart people believe dumb things about our future ai overlords*. Retrieved December 23, 2016. https://boingboing.net/2016/12/23/ai-alarmism-why-smart-people.html.

28. Radu, S., *Artificial intelligence alarmists win ITIF's Annual Luddite Award*, in *Information Technology & Innovation Foundation*. Retrieved January 19, 2016. https://itif.org/publications/2016/01/19/artificial-intelligence-alarmists-win-itif%E2%80%99s-annual-luddite-award.

29. Togelius, J., *How many AGIs can dance on the head of a pin?* Retrieved October 30, 2020. http://togelius.blogspot.com/2020/10/how-many-agis-can-dance-on-head-of-pin.html.

30. Atkinson, R.D., *'It's Going to Kill Us!' And other myths about the future of artificial intelligence*. Information Technology & Innovation Foundation, 2016.

31. Brown, J.S., and P. Duguid, *A response to Bill Joy and the doom-and-gloom technofuturists*, in *AAAS Science and Technology Policy Yearbook*. 2001. p. 77–83. Routledge

32. Johnson, D.G., and M. Verdicchio, *AI anxiety*. Journal of the Association for Information Science and Technology, 2017. **68**(9): p. 2267–2270.

33. Lanier, J., The myth of AI, in *Edge*. Retrieved November 14, 2014. https://edge.org/conversation/jaron_lanier-the-myth-of-ai.

34. Alfonseca, M., et al., *Superintelligence cannot be contained: Lessons from computability theory*. Journal of Artificial Intelligence Research, 2021. **70**: p. 65–76.

35. Voss, P., *AI Safety Research: A Road to Nowhere*. Retrieved October 19, 2016. https://medium.com/@petervoss/ai-safety-research-a-road-to-nowhere-f1c7c20e8875.

36. McCauley, L., *Countering the Frankenstein complex,* in *AAAI Spring Symposium: Multidisciplinary Collaboration for Socially Assistive Robotics.* 2007.

37. Ceglowski, M., Superintelligence: The idea that eats smart people, in *Web Camp Zagreb.* Retrieved October 29, 2016. https://idlewords.com/talks/superintelligence.htm.

38. Braga, A., and R.K. Logan, *The emperor of strong AI has no clothes: Limits to artificial intelligence.* Information, 2017. **8**(4): p. 156.

39. Etzioni, O., No, the experts don't think superintelligent AI is a threat to humanity, in *MIT Technology Review.* Retrieved September 20, 2016. https://www.technologyreview.com/2016/09/20/70131/no-the-experts-dont-think-superintelligent-ai-is-a-threat-to-humanity/.

40. Weld, D.S., and O. Etzioni, *The first law of robotics (a call to arms),* in *Twelfth National Conference on Artificial Intelligence (AAAI).* 1994. p. 1042–1047.

41. Dafoe, A., and S. Russell, *Yes,* we are worried about the existential risk of artificial intelligence, in *MIT Technology Review.* Retrieved November 2, 2016. https://www.technologyreview.com/2016/11/02/156285/yes-we-are-worried-about-the-existential-risk-of-artificial-intelligence/.

42. Garis, H., *The Artilect War.* 2005: ETC Publications.

43. Babcock, J., J. Kramár, and R.V. Yampolskiy, *Guidelines for artificial intelligence containment,* in *Next-Generation Ethics: Engineering a Better Society,* A.E. Abbas, Editor. 2019. p. 90–112. Cambridge University Press

44. Horvitz, E., and B. Selman, *Interim report from the AAAI Presidential panel on long-term AI futures.* Retrieved August 2009. https://www.erichorvitz.com/panel_chairs_ovw.pdf.

45. Yudkowsky, E., and R. Hanson, The Hanson-Yudkowsky AI-Foom debate, in *MIRI Technical Report.* 2008. http://intelligence.org/files/AIFoomDebate.pdf.

46. Shermer, M., *Why artificial intelligence is not an existential threat.* Skeptic (Altadena, CA), 2017. **22**(2): p. 29–36.

47. Pinker, S., *The Better Angels of Our Nature: Why Violence Has Declined.* 2012: Penguin Group USA.

48. Yampolskiy, R.V., *Artificial Intelligence Safety and Security.* 2018: Chapman and Hall/CRC Press.

49. Benthall, S., *Don't fear the reaper: Refuting Bostrom's superintelligence argument.* arXiv preprint arXiv:1702.08495, 2017.

50. Wiblin, R., and K. Harris, *DeepMind's plan to make AI systems robust & reliable, why it's a core issue in AI design, and how to succeed at AI research.* Retrieved June 3, 2019. https://80000hours.org/podcast/episodes/pushmeet-kohli-deepmind-safety-research/.

51. Baum, S.D., *Countering superintelligence misinformation.* Information, 2018. **9**(10): p. 244.

52. Russell, S., *Provably beneficial artificial intelligence,* in Exponential Life, The Next Step. 2017.

53. Russell, S., *Human Compatible: Artificial Intelligence and the Problem of Control.* 2019: Penguin.

54. Aronson, J., *Five types of skepticism.* BMJ, 2015. **350**: p. h1986.

55. Baum, S., *Superintelligence skepticism as a political tool.* Information, 2018. **9**(9): p. 209.

56. Turing, A., *Computing machinery and intelligence.* Mind, 1950. **59**(236): p. 433–460.

57. Alexander, S., *AI researchers on AI risk*. Retrieved May 22, 2015. https://slatestarcodex.com/2015/05/22/ai-researchers-on-ai-risk/.
58. Brown, T.B., et al., *Language models are few-shot learners*. arXiv preprint arXiv:2005.14165, 2020.
59. Kaplan, J., et al., *Scaling laws for neural language models*. arXiv preprint arXiv:2001.08361, 2020.
60. Henighan, T., et al., *Scaling laws for autoregressive generative modeling*. arXiv preprint arXiv:2010.14701, 2020.
61. Bundy, A., *Smart machines are not a threat to humanity*. Communications of the ACM, 2017. **60**(2): p. 40–42.
62. Bringsjord, S., A. Bringsjord, and P. Bello, *Belief in the singularity is fideistic*, in *Singularity Hypotheses*. 2012, Springer. p. 395–412.
63. Bringsjord, S., *Belief in the singularity is logically brittle*. Journal of Consciousness Studies, 2012. **19**(7): p. 14.
64. Modis, T., *Why the singularity cannot happen*, in *Singularity Hypotheses*. 2012, Springer. p. 311–346.
65. Yampolskiy, R.V., *On the limits of recursively self-improving AGI*, in *Artificial General Intelligence: Proceedings of 8th International Conference, AGI 2015, AGI 2015, Berlin, Germany, July 22–25, 2015*. 2015. 9205. p. 394.
66. Bostrom, N., *Taking intelligent machines seriously: Reply to critics*. Futures, 2003. **35**(8): p. 901–906.
67. Logan, R.K., *Can computers become conscious, an essential condition for the singularity?* Information, 2017. **8**(4): p. 161.
68. Chalmers, D.J., *The Conscious Mind: In Search of a Fundamental Theory*. 1996: Oxford University Press.
69. Yampolskiy, R.V., *Artificial consciousness: An illusionary solution to the hard problem*. Reti, Saperi, Linguaggi, 2018. (2): p. 287–318. https://www.rivisteweb.it/doi/10.12832/92302
70. Hawkins, J., *The Terminator Is Not Coming. The Future Will Thank Us*. Retrieved March 2, 2015. https://www.vox.com/2015/3/2/11559576/the-terminator-is-not-coming-the-future-will-thank-us.
71. Kelly, K., *Why I Don't Fear Super Intelligence (Comments Section)*, in *Edge*. Retrieved November 14, 2014. https://edge.org/conversation/jaron_lanier-the-myth-of-ai.
72. Yudkowsky, E., *Artificial intelligence as a positive and negative factor in global risk*, in *Global Catastrophic Risks*, N. Bostrom and M.M. Cirkovic, Editors. 2008, Oxford University Press. p. 308–345.
73. Loosemore, R.P., *The Maverick Nanny with a dopamine drip: Debunking fallacies in the theory of AI motivation*, in *2014 AAAI Spring Symposium Series*. 2014.
74. Armstrong, S., *General purpose intelligence: Arguing the orthogonality thesis*. Analysis and Metaphysics, 2013. (12): p. 68–84. https://www.ceeol.com/search/article-detail?id=137912
75. Miller, J.D., R. Yampolskiy, and O. Häggström, *An AGI modifying its utility function in violation of the orthogonality thesis*. arXiv preprint arXiv:2003.00812, 2020.
76. Goertzel, B., *Superintelligence: Fears, promises and potentials*. Journal of Evolution and Technology, 2015. **25**(2): p. 55–87.
77. Searle, J.R., *What your computer can't know*. The New York Review of Books. 2014. **9**.

78. Baum, S., A. Barrett, and R.V. Yampolskiy, *Modeling and interpreting expert disagreement about artificial superintelligence.* Informatica, 2017. **41**(7): p. 419–428.

79. Omohundro, S.M., *The basic AI drives*, in *Proceedings of the First AGI Conference, Volume 171, Frontiers in Artificial Intelligence and Applications*, P. Wang, B. Goertzel, and S. Franklin, Editors. February 2008. IOS Press.

80. Kruel, A., *Four Arguments Against AI Risk.* Retrieved July 11, 2013. http://kruel. co/2013/07/11/four-arguments-against-ai-risks/.

81. Toole, B.A., *Ada, the Enchantress of Numbers: Poetical Science.* 2010: Betty Alexandra Toole.

82. Ecoffet, A., et al., *First return, then explore.* Nature, 2021. **590**(7847): p. 580–586.

83. Binsted, K., et al., *Computational humor.* IEEE Intelligent Systems, 2006. **21**(2): p. 59–69.

84. Majot, A.M., and R.V. Yampolskiy, *AI safety engineering through introduction of self-reference into felicific calculus via artificial pain and pleasure*, in *2014 IEEE International Symposium on Ethics in Science, Technology and Engineering.* 2014. IEEE.

85. Brundage, M., et al., *The malicious use of artificial intelligence: Forecasting, prevention, and mitigation.* arXiv preprint arXiv:1802.07228, 2018.

86. Aliman, N.-M., L. Kester, and R. Yampolskiy, *Transdisciplinary AI observatory—retrospective analyses and future-oriented contradistinctions.* Philosophies, 2021. **6**(1): p. 6.

87. Ziesche, S., and R. Yampolskiy, *Introducing the concept of ikigai to the ethics of AI and of human enhancements*, in *2020 IEEE International Conference on Artificial Intelligence and Virtual Reality (AIVR).* 2020. IEEE.

88. Miller, J.D., R. Yampolskiy, and O. Häggström, *An AGI modifying its utility function in violation of the strong orthogonality thesis.* Philosophies, 2020. **5**(4): p. 40.

89. Williams, R.M., and R.V. Yampolskiy, *Understanding and avoiding AI failures: A practical guide.* Retrieved April 30, 2021. https://arxiv.org/abs/2104.12582.

90. Yampolskiy, R.V., *On controllability of AI.* arXiv preprint arXiv:2008.04071, 2020.

91. Yampolskiy, R.V., *Leakproofing singularity-artificial intelligence confinement problem.* Journal of Consciousness Studies JCS, 2012: **19**(1–2), 194–214.

92. Brundage, M., *Limitations and risks of machine ethics.* Journal of Experimental & Theoretical Artificial Intelligence, 2014. **26**(3): p. 355–372.

93. Yampolskiy, R.V., *Unexplainability and incomprehensibility of AI.* Journal of Artificial Intelligence and Consciousness, 2020. **7**(2): p. 277–291.

94. Yampolskiy, R.V., *Unpredictability of AI: On the impossibility of accurately predicting all actions of a smarter agent.* Journal of Artificial Intelligence and Consciousness, 2020. **7**(1): p. 109–118.

95. Howe, W.J., and R.V. Yampolskiy, *Impossibility of unambiguous communication as a source of failure in AI systems.* 2020. https://api.deepai.org/publication-download-pdf/impossibility-of-unambiguous-communication-as-a-source-of-failure-in-ai-systems.

96. Waser, M.R., *Wisdom does imply benevolence*, in *First International Conference of IACAP.* July 4–6, 2011. Aarhus University. p. 148–150.

97. Fox, J., and C. Shulman, *Superintelligence does not imply benevolence*, in *8th European Conference on Computing and Philosophy.* October 4–6, 2010. Munich, Germany.

98. Yampolskiy, R.V., *The space of possible mind designs*, in *Artificial General Intelligence.* 2015, Springer. p. 218–227.

99. Dubhashi, D., and S. Lappin, *AI dangers: Imagined and real*. Communications of the ACM, 2017. **60**(2): p. 43–45.

100. Grace, K., et al., *When will AI exceed human performance? Evidence from AI experts*. Journal of Artificial Intelligence Research, 2018. **62**: p. 729–754.

101. Müller, V.C., and N. Bostrom, *Future progress in artificial intelligence: A survey of expert opinion*, in *Fundamental Issues of Artificial Intelligence*. 2016, Springer. p. 555–572.

102. Khatchadourian, R., The Doomsday Invention, in *New Yorker*. Retrieved November 23, 2015. https://www.newyorker.com/magazine/2015/11/23/doomsday-invention-artificial-intelligence-nick-bostrom.

103. Cantor, L., *Superintelligence: The idea that smart people refuse to think about*. Retrieved December 24, 2016.

104. Graves, M., *Response to Cegłowski on superintelligence*. Retrieved January 13, 2017. https://intelligence.org/2017/01/13/response-to-ceglowski-on-superintelligence/.

105. Kruel, A., *Why I Am Skeptical of Risks from AI*. Retrieved July 21, 2011. http://kruel.co/2011/07/21/why-i-am-skeptical-of-risks-from-ai/.

106. Wilks, Y., *Will there be superintelligence and would it hate us?* AI Magazine, 2017. **38**(4): p. 65–70.

107. Kurzweil, R., *Don't fear artificial intelligence*. Time Magazine, 2014: p. 28.

108. Smith, M., *Address the consequences of AI in advance*. Communications of the ACM, 2017. **60**(3): p. 10–11.

109. Dietterich, T.G., and E.J. Horvitz, *Rise of concerns about AI: Reflections and directions*. Communications of the ACM, 2015. **58**(10): p. 38–40.

110. Agar, N., *Don't worry about superintelligence*. Journal of Evolution and Technology, 2016. **26**(1): p. 73–82.

111. Yampolskiy, R.V., *The singularity may be near*. Information, 2018. **9**(8): p. 190.

112. Sotala, K., and R. Yampolskiy, *Risks of the journey to the singularity*, in *The Technological Singularity*. 2017, Springer. p. 11–23.

113. Sotala, K., and R. Yampolskiy, *Responses to the journey to the singularity*. The Technological Singularity, 2017: p. 25–83. https://link.springer.com/chapter/10.1007/978-3-662-54033-6_3

114. Booch, G., *Don't fear superintelligent AI*, in *TED*. Retrieved November 2016. https://www.ted.com/talks/grady_booch_don_t_fear_superintelligent_ai.

115. Etzioni, O., *Artificial intelligence will empower us, not exterminate us*, in *TEDx*. Retrieved November 2016. https://tedxseattle.com/talks/artificial-intelligence-will-empower-us-not-exterminate-us/.

116. Kelly, K., *The myth of a superhuman AI*, in *Wired*. Retrieved April 15, 2017. https://www.wired.com/2017/04/the-myth-of-a-superhuman-ai/.

117. Walsh, T., *The singularity may never be near*. AI Magazine, 2017. **38**(3): p. 58–62.

118. Wiedermann, J., *A computability argument against superintelligence*. Cognitive Computation, 2012. **4**(3): p. 236–245.

119. Haggstrom, O., *Vulgopopperianism*. Retrieved February 20, 2017. http://haggstrom.blogspot.com/2017/02/vulgopopperianism.html.

120. Garfinkel, B., A. Dafoe, and O. Catton-Barratt, *A survey on AI risk communication strategies*. Retrieved August 8, 2016. https://futureoflife.org/ai-policy-resources/.

121. Alexander, S., AI persuasion experiment results, in *Slate Start Codex*. Retrieved October 24, 2016. https://slatestarcodex.com/2016/10/24/ai-persuasion-experiment-results/.

122. Wissing, B.G., and M.-A. Reinhard, *Individual differences in risk perception of artificial intelligence.* Swiss Journal of Psychology, 2018. **77**(4): p. 149.
123. Li, J., and J.-S. Huang, *Dimensions of artificial intelligence anxiety based on the integrated fear acquisition theory.* Technology in Society, 2020. **63**: p. 101410.
124. Chen, Y.-N.K., and C.-H.R. Wen, *Impacts of attitudes toward government and corporations on public trust in artificial intelligence.* Communication Studies, 2021. **72**(1): p. 115–131.
125. Neri, H., and F. Cozman, *The role of experts in the public perception of risk of artificial intelligence.* AI & Society, 2019. **35**: p. 1–11.
126. Sharkey, L., *An intervention to shape policy dialogue, communication, and AI research norms for AI safety.* Retrieved October 1, 2017. https://forum. effectivealtruism.org/posts/4kRPYuogoSKnHNBhY/an-intervention-to-shape-policy-dialogue-communication-and
127. Muehlhauser, L., *What should we learn from past AI forecasts?* Retrieved May 2016. https://www.openphilanthropy.org/focus/global-catastrophic-risks/potential-risks-advanced-artificial-intelligence/what-should-we-learn-past-ai-forecasts.
128. Dreyfus, H.L., *What Computers can't Do: A Critique of Artificial Reason.* 1972: Harper & Row.
129. Searle, J., *Minds, brains and programs.* Behavioral and Brain Sciences, 1980. **3**(3): p. 417–457.
130. Thierer, A., *Technopanics, threat inflation, and the danger of an information technology precautionary principle.* Minnesota Journal of Law, Science & Technology, 2013. **14**: p. 309.
131. Yudkowsky, E.S., *Creating friendly AI – the analysis and design of benevolent goal architectures.* 2001. https://intelligence.org/files/CFAI.pdf
132. Hurley, P.M., *The confirmation of continental drift.* Scientific American, 1968. **218**(4): p. 52–68.
133. Vardi, M.Y., *Quantum hype and quantum skepticism.* Communications of the ACM, 2019. **62**(5): p. 7.
134. Bostrom, N., *Existential risks: Analyzing human extinction scenarios and related hazards.* Journal of Evolution and Technology, 2002. **9**. https://ora.ox.ac.uk/objects/uuid:827452c3-fcba-41b8-86b0-407293e6617c
135. Ord, T., *The Precipice: Existential Risk and the Future of Humanity.* 2020: Hachette Books.
136. Tomasik, B., *Differential Intellectual Progress as a Positive-Sum Project.* 2013: Center on Long-Term Risk.
137. Tutt, A., *An FDA for algorithms.* Administrative Law Review, 2017. **69**: p. 83.
138. Ozlati, S., and R. Yampolskiy, *The formalization of AI risk management and safety standards,* in *Workshops at the Thirty-First AAAI Conference on Artificial Intelligence.* 2017.
139. O'Riordan, T., *Interpreting the Precautionary Principle.* 2013: Routledge.
140. Holm, S., and J. Harris, *Precautionary principle stifles discovery.* Nature, 1999. **400**(6743): p. 398–398.

Index

Note: - Page references with *italics* for figure, in **bold** for tables and with "n" for end-notes.